Armenians and the Iranian Constitutional Revolution of 1905–1911

D1714898

Armenians and the Iranian Constitutional Revolution of 1905–1911

"The Love for Freedom Has No Fatherland"

Houri Berberian

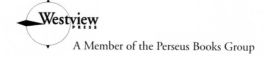

Westview
PRESS

A Member of the Perseus Books Group

Copyright © 2001 by Westview Press, A Member of the Perseus Books Group

Published in 2001 in the United States of America by Westview Press, 5500 Central Avenue, Boulder, Colorado 80301-2877, and in the United Kingdom by Westview Press, 12 Hid's Copse Road, Cumnor Hill, Oxford OX2 9JJ

Find us on the World Wide Web at www.westviewpress.com

Library of Congress Cataloging-in-Publication Data

ISBN 0-8133-3817-4

The paper used in this publication meets the requirements of the American National Standard for Permanence of Paper for Printed Library Materials Z39.48-1984.

PERSEUS
POD
ON DEMAND

  10   9   8   7   6   5   4   3   2   1

To my mother

Contents

Acknowledgments

There are many people who have in one way or another helped me to get to this point, but two in particular have been most influential in my intellectual development. Nikki R. Keddie and Richard G. Hovannisian have guided, inspired, and supported me at every step. My appreciation also extends to Janet Afary for her continued interest in my work and, most importantly, for her much-valued comments on my study. In addition, I thank Afshin Matin-Asgari for his critique of this study as well as his suggestions.

I owe a debt of gratitude to many institutions, programs, and individuals for their assistance in the research and writing of this study. The UCLA History Department and the Gustav E. Von Grunebaum Center for Near Eastern Studies have provided me with financial support and research opportunities. Support from the Kasper and Siroon Hovannisian Fellowship, National Resource Fellowship (Title VI), Armenian Relief Society, Armenian Professional Society, and Armenian General Benevolent Union have also facilitated the pursuit of this study. Graziella Stepanian and Saeed Damadi in Iran have been a great help in acquiring important research materials for my study. Tatoul Sonentz-Papazian at the Armenian Revolutionary Federation (Dashnaktsutiun) Archives in Watertown, Massachusetts, has been a tremendous help in allowing me unhindered access to the archives. David Hirsch, the Middle East bibliographer of the Young Research Library in UCLA, made many attempts to locate and acquire essential research materials. Several others have assisted by sharing knowledge and material at their disposal or by providing their valuable time. They are Hamo Vassilian, Aram Arkun, Rudolph Matthee, David Yaghoubian, and especially Jasamin Rostam-Kolayi. More recently, the College of Liberal Arts and the History Department of the California State University at Long Beach have provided me with the opportunity to continue research and writing. I thank Bob Freligh and Michael Capdeville at Audio Visual Services whose expertise brought forth the photographs and map, respectively, appearing in this book. My gratitude also extends to my colleagues and friends at the History Department for their support, as well as other colleagues and friends who throughout the years have inspired and challenged me.

Last but certainly not least, my heartfelt appreciation and gratitude go out to my family for their faith, encouragement, and support. I thank, particularly, my mother for her help in innumerable aspects, especially her undaunted strength, unquestioning faith, and unwavering support. I thank her also for making me laugh and raising my spirits. I dedicate this book to my mother, for she has been and will always be the most influential person in my life and the one I admire most. I regret that the book was not published before my maternal grandmother's passing. I know she would have indeed been proud, perhaps even more so because although she spoke several languages, she was not literate.

Preface

This book seeks to give a fuller picture of Armenian political and intellectual development and participation in the Iranian Constitutional Revolution of 1905–1911. The idea for the project originated from the attempt to combine two areas of interest, Iran and Armenians. It developed further, however, because of the significance and uniqueness of this case in history, that is, the commitment and collaboration of Caucasian and Iranian Armenians in a movement seemingly not their own. In reality, they identified with the movement, with revolutionary Iranians, and with constitutional change and its perceived consequences.

While this is the most comprehensive study attempted so far, it is only a step toward greater understanding of the Armenian commitment to the Iranian movement and does not claim to cover all aspects of the subject. For example, it focuses in greater detail on the Dashnaktsutiun party for two reasons: the significance of the role it played in the Iranian Constitutional Revolution, and a more pragmatic reason, the availability of sources.

This study seeks to make new contributions to this subject in several ways. It goes beyond the more common narrative of heroic exploits of individual Armenians. Instead, it provides an analytical study of how and why Armenians participated in the Iranian revolution and thus makes it a serious field of inquiry. The connection between the centuries-old existence of the Iranian Armenian community and Caucasian Armenian politicization had never before been explored as an important element of Armenian participation in the Iranian Constitutional Revolution. This book seeks to provide a brief history of that connection as a factor in Armenian collaboration with constitutionalist elements. The political and ideological motives of activists as well as the historical and circumstantial causes of engagement had never before been considered. This book strives to present a serious analysis of such motivations. The difficulties and issues Armenian activists faced regarding possible negative consequences of participation are explored in detail, for the first time, in order to demonstrate the decentralized nature of activities, the thought processes of participants, and the issues that most concerned them. Moreover, a close examination of collaboration and relations among Armenian revolutionaries and between Armenian and Iranian revolutionaries brings to the forefront the close and at times conflicting relationship between them. Ideological and personal rivalries often became an obstacle to cooperation, but more often were overcome, at the very least temporarily, for the sake of the revolutionary cause. The book ends with a discussion of the withdrawal of Armenians from participation in Iranian politics before the First World War when it became clear to them that the panacea of constitutionalism had, in fact, been a bitter disappointment. Of course, the world war brought with it many devastating changes to the Armenians and the entire region and forced Armenian communities to redirect their focus, at least temporarily, from Iran to the new Turkish and Russian states and then to the short-lived independent Armenian republic and the increasingly growing and diverse diaspora.

*   *   *

Note on Transliteration

Transliteration of Persian and Armenian is mostly based on the phonetic values of the two languages in order to provide a system that is more accessible to readers. In the case of Armenian, transliteration is for the most part based on modern Eastern Armenian, without diacritical marks, to provide consistency.

Iran

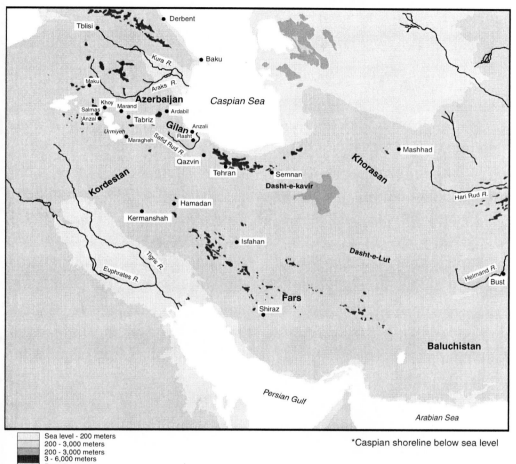

Sea level - 200 meters
200 - 3,000 meters
200 - 3,000 meters
3 - 6,000 meters
Desert

*Caspian shoreline below sea level

Special thanks to Rudi Matthee for making the original of this map available to me and allowing me to make modifications.

"Long live Armeno-Persian Iranian Brotherhood." A poster lauding the brother-hood of Iranians.

SOURCE: Amurian [Ter Ohanian], A[ndre]. *Hamasah-e Yeprem* [The epic of Yeprem]. Tehran: Javid Press, 1976.

Yeprem with Iranian comrades in arms.

SOURCE: *Hushamatian Hay Heghapokhakan Dashnaktsutian: Albom-Atlas* [Memory Book of the Armenian Revolutionary Federation: Album-Atlas], vol. 1: *Dutzaznamart, 1890–1914* [The Heroic Battle, 1890–1914]. Los Angeles: Hay Heghapokhakan Dashnaktsutian Arevmtian Amerikayi Kendronakan Komite, 1992.

Dashnakist activists in Azerbaijan. Yeprem is seated with the child of a friend on his lap. On his left is Nzhdeh and on his right are Murat, Balajan, and Marzpet. In the center, standing behind Yeprem and Murat is Samson.

SOURCE: Amurian [Ter Ohanian], A[ndre]. *Hamasah-e Yeprem* [The epic of Yeprem]. Tehran: Javid Press, 1976.

Armenian fedayi
SOURCE: Amurian [Ter Ohanian], A[ndre]. *Hamasah-e Yeprem* [The epic of Yeprem]. Tehran: Javid Press, 1976.

Petros Andreasian's group in 1909. All were hanged by the Russian military in Tabriz, 1912.
SOURCE: *Hushamatian Hay Heghapokhakan Dashnaktsutian: Albom-Atlas* [Memory Book of the Armenian Revolutionary Federation: Album-Atlas], vol. 1: *Dutzaznamart, 1890–1914* [The Heroic Battle, 1890–1914] (Los Angeles: Hay Heghapokhakan Dashnaktsutian Arevmtian Amerikayi Kendronakan Komite, 1992).

Yeprem's troops.

SOURCE *Hushamatian Hay Heghapokhakan Dashnaktsutian: Albom-Atlas* [Memory Book of the Armenian Revolutionary Federation: Album-Atlas], vol. 1: *Dutzaznamart, 1890–1914* [The Heroic Battle, 1890–1914]. Los Angeles: Hay Heghapokhakan Dashnaktsutian Arevmtian Amerikayi Kendronakan Komite, 1992.

Yeprem's wife Anahit surrounded by fedayi.

SOURCE: Amurian [Ter Ohanian], A[ndre]. *Hamasah-e Yeprem* [The epic of Yeprem]. Tehran: Javid Press, 1976.

Yeprem's wife Anahit surrounded by fedayi at the sight of Yeprem's death.

SOURCE: Amurian [Ter Ohanian], A[ndre]. *Hamasah-e Yeprem* [The epic of Yeprem]. Tehran: Javid Press, 1976.

Armenian girl

SOURCE: Ziya'pur, Jalil. *Zivarha-yi zanan-e Iran az dirbaz ta kanun* [The ornaments of the women of Iran from ancient times to the present]. Tehran: Jashn-e Farhang va Honar, 1969.

Introduction

The Iranian Constitutional Revolution of 1905–1911 was a movement for parliamentary representation, constitutional government, reform, and centralization. It was the consequence of a variety of Iranian developments in the nineteenth century: military defeats by Russia, commercial capitulations and concessions to Russia and Great Britain, European economic penetration, dislocation of local manufacturers, and subsequent social discontent. The revolution was also the result of the development of an intelligentsia that through contact with the West espoused constitutionalism, secularism, and nationalism, as well as the growing discontent among merchants, clerics ('*ulama*), and even court figures. In addition, the sale of Iranian women and girls by peasants to pay taxes or their abduction by Turkomans in northwestern Iran just prior to the revolution also served as one of the more immediate causes and foci of national grievance against the reigning government.[1] The organization of social discontent first led to the protest over a tobacco concession to a British subject (1891–1892)—a protest that has been referred to as a dress rehearsal for the Constitutional Revolution, as it brought together the traditional middle class, the modern intelligentsia, and the *ulama*. The first two groups began to form secret societies and move against the financially bankrupt and militarily and adminstratively ineffective Qajar government. The revolutionary movement was greatly influenced by the Russo-Japanese War of 1904–1905 and the Russian Revolution of 1905. The Russo-Japanese War ignited the revolution in Russia and both the war and the revolution kept Russia from military intervention in Iran until 1909, when the Iranian revolutionary movement was already well under way.[2] The devastating defeats suffered by the Russian military strengthened the perception that the Russian Empire had become incompetent and needed radical institutional reform.[3] Moreover, the Russian defeat reaffirmed the belief in the power of constitution by explicitly demonstrating the triumph of the only constitutional power in Asia over the only nonconstitutional power in Europe.[4] British scholar Edward Browne observed:

> It seems to me that a change must be coming over the East. The victory of Japan has, it would appear, had a remarkable influence all over the East. Even here in Persia it has not been without effect. . . . From the little study I have devoted to the question, it almost seems to me that the East is stirring in its sleep . . . In Persia, owing to its proximity to Russia, the awakening would appear to take the form of a movement towards democratic reform.[5]

The Russian Revolution of 1905, which challenged the autocratic tsarist regime with disturbances and uprisings by workers, peasants, students, intellectuals, and ethnic minorities, succeeded in establishing an elected legislature (duma) and undermining the tsar's rule. The revolution had great impact in the Caucasus, which had a significant Iranian migrant worker population, particularly when Russian laborers served in the Russo-Japanese War.[6] The Russian Revolution reached Iran through these workers who returned to the country with revolutionary ideas, printed propaganda, and arms. In addition, the influence of the Russian Revolution extended into Iran through the educational contacts of Iranian students in Russian universities, business contacts between Iranian and Russian merchants,[7] and the numerous Caucasian activists who fled persecution by the Russian government.[8]

The Iranian Constitutional Revolution began at the end of 1905 when a group of clerics and merchants took sanctuary (*bast*) in the royal mosque of Tehran. Among their demands was the creation of a representative House of Justice. Mozaffar al-Din Shah's (1896–1907) ineffectual promises to meet these claims fed the growing revolutionary sentiment. Revolutionary societies or councils (*anjomans*) began to grow at a rapid rate. In July 1906, another *bast*, this time in the British Legation of Tehran, attracted thousands of protestors and forced the convening of the first national assembly (*majles-e melli*). The move from the demand for a House of Justice to a representative assembly was in large part because of the increased influence of modern educated students, faculty, and secular reformers among the protestors. The 1906 Iranian constitution, written by a committee of the Majles, based largely on the Belgian constitution, guaranteed unprecedented freedom of the press and assembly, which made possible the flourishing of journals and *anjomans*. During the reign of Mohammad Ali Shah (1907–1909), the son of Mozaffar al-Din Shah, Britain and Russia signed the Anglo-Russian agreement (31 August, 1907), dividing Iran into spheres of influence, without the acquiescence of the Iranian government. The entente between Russia and Britain helped the anti-constitutionalist Mohammad Ali Shah by galvanizing support around him. In June 1908, the Shah carried out a successful coup d'état, bombarded and closed the Majles, and arrested many leaders of the constitutionalist movement. In July, a civil war broke out in the northwestern province of Azerbaijan, where the capital city of Tabriz, the residence of the crown prince, became the center of resistance. Tabriz benefited from its contact with intellectual and political trends in the Caucasus as well as the participation of Caucasian revolutionaries with expertise in the Russian Revolution of 1905. In July 1909, the revolutionaries from the north, with the help of the Bakhtiari tribe from the south, retook Tehran and deposed the Shah and a new, more moderate regency was established with Ahmad Shah, the twelve-year-old son of Mohammad Ali. The second constitutional period (1909–1911) was marked by a disintegration in relations among constitutionalists. A conflict arose in the Majles between the liberal Democrats and the more conservative Moderates, resulting in the assassination of the moderate leader Sayyid 'Abdollah Behbahani, the departure from Iran of democrat leader and Tabriz delegate Sayyid Hasan Taqizadeh, and the disarming of pro-Moderate revolutionaries like Sattar Khan and Baqer Khan. External Russian pressures worsened the situation when in November 1911, Russian troops occupying northern Iran delivered an ultimatum to the Iranian government, threatening to seize Tehran. Among the Russian demands was the dismissal of the Majles-supported American treasurer-general Morgan Shuster, whose policies imperiled the Russian sphere of influence in the north. Although the Majles stood firm in opposition to the ultimatum, the Regent and the ruling cabinet of the underage Ahmad Shah dismissed Shuster in December and dissolved the Majles. The Iranian Constitutional Revolution had for all practical purposes come to an end. The Majles did not convene again until 1914; under Russian occupation many revolutionaries and constitutionalists in Azerbaijan were murdered or deported, *anjomans* were dissolved, and the government was restored to a conservative cabinet under British and Russian control.

One of the most interesting aspects of the Iranian Constitutional Revolution was the participation of Caucasians in the Iranian struggle. Georgians, Russians, and to an even greater degree, Armenians and Muslim Caucasians (later called Azeris) played a significant role in the constitutional movement, especially in the decisive battles in northwestern Iran against royalist forces. Armenians made further intellectual contributions to constitutionalism and the formation of Iranian democratic parties.

Until recently, Armenian participation in the Iranian Constitutional Revolution has been largely neglected by the historiography of the period. With the exception of the prominent intellectual and historian Ahmad Kasravi and, to a lesser extent, Mehdi Malekzadeh, Iranian historians have given very little, if any, attention to the military and ideological role

of the Armenians in service of constitutional government and democracy.[9]
Even Kasravi's treatment is limited compared with the significance of
their contribution. While one may attribute this omission to nefarious intentions, it is more likely that the role of the Armenians was minimized or
ignored for the same reasons that the role of Caucasians, Azali Babis, and
women was overlooked—reasons that still need investigation and are beyond the scope of this study, though one may note that most nationalist
writers wished to stress national unity rather than divisions.

More recently, Mansureh Ettehadieh Nazam Mafi, Isma'il Ra'in, and
especially Cosroe Chaqueri and Janet Afary have given considerable attention to the extent of Armenian contribution.[10] Armenian scholarship
on the subject, too, has been minimal and suffers from both a lack of ade-
quate analysis and an excess of veneration and aggrandizement regarding the Armenian role. The contribution of one Armenian scholar, Andre
Amurian, to the study of Armenians in the Iranian Constitutional Revolution differs from the rest in form and value. His compilations of relevant documents and those of Chaqueri and Iraj Afshar are noteworthy.[11]
Not surprisingly, party rivalries among Armenians have also affected the
writing of history, as Dashnakist and Hnchakist authors have each
played down or misrepresented the role of the other in order to exagger-
ate their own contribution.[12] Even non-Armenians like the Georgian Social Democrat Tria (Vlass Mgzeladze), an active participant in the Russian Revolution of 1905 and in the defense of Tabriz as a lieutenant under
Sattar Khan, took part in this rivalry. Tria asserted that the Dashnaktsutiun, a so-called socialist party, abstained from active participation in the
revolution because it did not have faith in victory. "It wasn't until after
the capture of Tabriz, when all the city and the arsenal also were in the
hands of the revolutionaries and that the SD [Social Democrat] Organization represented by many militants, could deploy its flag, that the Dash-
naktsakan [sic] decided to take part in the Persian revolution."[13] Tria also
concluded that the Dashnaktsutiun dreaded participation, because in
case of failure the Armenian bourgeoisie would suffer.[14]

There has not been to this date a comprehensive study of the Armenian
role in the Iranian Constitutional Revolution. There has been some work
done on the major Armenian figure of the revolution, Yeprem Khan
(1862–1912), and on one of the principal proponents of constitutionalism,
Malkom Khan (1833–1908), who was in Europe during the first period of
the revolution. The emphasis on one or two individuals is a problem, because it takes away from the larger dynamics and does not provide a
clear and accurate picture of the complexities of the Armenian role, the
political and ideological causes for participation, the internal and external conflicts, and the involvement of not just individuals such as Yeprem
Khan but also Armenian political parties, which represented Armenian

communities in Iran, the Caucasus, Ottoman Armenian provinces, Europe, and the United States.

Armenian participation in this revolution is significant, because it brings to the fore unique and unusual aspects of both Iranian and Armenian history and of both the Constitutional Revolution and the Armenian role in it. Three factors explain this unique phenomenon: (1) the revolutionary and intellectual milieu of the Caucasus and its influence on the centuries-old Iranian Armenian community; (2) the communal violence between Caucasian Armenians and Muslims and the desire of the political left to counter this by encouraging collaboration of the two peoples in the Iranian movement; and (3) the fluidity of identities that made participation in a revolutionary movement outside the Ottoman and Russian Empires possible.

The Caucasus and Iran

Armenians had lived in Iran for centuries before the Iranian Constitutional Revolution, yet most of those who played major roles in the revolution came from the Caucasus. By the beginning of the nineteenth century, Armenians in the Caucasus were more educated, more urbanized, and more aware of European intellectual trends than most Armenians in the Ottoman Empire or Iran. They studied in Moscow, St. Petersburg, Leipzig, and Berlin; took in European culture through contacts with Russian intellectuals; and were subject to the same intellectual influences as their Russian colleagues. In addition, Armenians formed an important segment of the Caucasian working class in Tiflis (Tbilisi), Baku, and Batum. At the turn of the century, Armenians made up 25 to 29 percent of the working class in Baku, the largest ethnic contingent.[15] By the early twentieth century, Armenian workers were influenced by the new revolutionary intellectuals who adopted socialism and nationalism.

Armenians in the Caucasus in the early twentieth century had become by far the most revolutionary of the three Armenian communities in Iran, the Ottoman Empire, and the rest of the Russian Empire. Three major events between the years 1903 and 1906 helped mobilize Caucasian Armenians. The first was the confiscation of Armenian Church properties in 1903 by Tsar Nicholas II on the advice of the governor-general of the Caucasus, Prince Grigorii Golitsyn (1896–1904). The second event was the participation of Armenians in the peasant uprisings and worker and student strikes of the Russian Revolution of 1905. And the third was the violent conflict from 1905 to 1907 between Caucasian Muslims and Armenians.

In 1908, however, the Russian government cracked down on all revolutionary activity. The severe repression of Caucasian revolutionaries and activists carried out by the president of the Russian Council of Ministers,

P. A. Stolypin, resulted in arrests and executions. Many revolutionaries were forced to stop or decrease their activities; others were arrested, killed, exiled, or had to flee to Iran. Armenian revolutionaries were among those who sought refuge in Iran and free expression and activity in the Iranian Constitutional Revolution.

The role played by the Caucasian Armenians in Iran was only possible because of an already-existing community and political activity in Iran, especially in the heart of the revolution, the Azerbaijan province. While the Armenian community in Iran dates back to as early as fourth century B.C.E., by the end of the nineteenth century, the total Armenian population of Iran stood at 63,000 to 70,000. The greatest concentration of Armenians was in Isfahan and Azerbaijan.[16] By the turn of the century, Tabriz had become a major Armenian educational and political center, largely because of its strategic proximity to the Caucasus and the two-way traffic of teachers, political activists, and militants,[17] much as Baku intellectuals, activists, and workers had a great influence on the intellectual and political development of Muslims in Iranian Azerbaijan.[18]

Armenian political parties began activities in Iran in the 1890s. The Hnchakian party and the Dashnaktsutiun (as well as the Armenakan party, which did not take part in the Iranian Constitutional Revolution) sent members from the Caucasus to Iran to establish party branches and disseminate party ideology. In the late nineteenth and early twentieth centuries, both Hnchakists and Dashnakists organized small military groups that would train in centers such as Tabriz, Salmas, and Khoy and then cross over into the Ottoman Empire in order to arm and defend Armenian communities against Kurdish and Turkish aggression.

Therefore, the revolutionary and intellectual milieu of turn-of-the-century Caucasus, the strong educational and cultural foundations of the Armenian community in Iran, and the revolutionary activity of the Armenian political parties in the strategically located Azerbaijan province partially explain the strong Caucasian Armenian role in the Iranian Constitutional Revolution.

Caucasian Communal Violence

Armenian collaboration with Iranian and Caucasian Muslims in the Iranian Constitutional Revolution came less than two years after the violent clashes between the Armenians and Muslims in the Caucasus, sometimes referred to as the Armeno-Tatar wars or the Armeno-Azeri clashes. This background leads to the interesting question of how Armenian political parties who took part in the conflict were able to join in common cause with Caucasian Muslims against whom they were engaged in bloody fighting. How and why did they put aside the recent past to cooperate for the future of Iran? The violent clashes that took place from February 1905 to the spring of 1906 between the Armenians and the Muslims of the Caucasus, according to one eyewitness source, took the lives of more than 2,000 people and left 14,760 people injured and 286 villages plundered.[19] The Dashnaktsutiun and to a much lesser extent the Hnchakian party took a leading role in the arming of Armenian workers and peasants and in the actual fighting.

By the end of the clashes, the Hnchakian party, affected by the ethnic and religious violence among the peoples of the Caucasus, reasserted its commitment to the Social Democratic principle of international class struggle. At the same time, the Dashnaktsutiun, in response to the criticism of the Social Democrats and to the internal ideological tensions in its party, reassessed its policy and actions. In June 1905, the Dashnaktsutiun declared its "Caucasian Project," in which it defined itself as the party of the working masses, and recognized class struggle as a priority and the need for a socialist revolution.[20] This stance was further expanded in the Dashnaktsutiun's 1907 Program adopted at the Fourth General Congress (Vienna, February–May 1907). The party revised its principles in an attempt to embrace more firmly socialist ideals and, as a logical consequence, called for collaboration with progressive forces as a major component in its struggle.[21] At the same time, it retained its nationalist aim of Armenian liberation. Moreover, the program made special mention of the Armeno-Azeri clashes and the necessity of establishing solidarity with "Turkish elements."[22]

Thus, by the end of the communal clashes, both the Dashnaktsutiun and Hnchakian parties had reexamined their policies and their actions in part because of the terrible violence between the two ethnically and religiously different peoples and in part because of the internationalist message and active role they played in the strikes and insurrections of the Russian Revolution of the same year. This reevaluation made it possible for Armenian revolutionaries to take active part in the Iranian Constitutional Revolution.

In addition, the Stolypin crackdown of 1908 made it impossible in a practical sense to work in the Caucasus. Therefore, those Caucasians, specifically the Armenians, who had become to some degree "professional" activists and militants were forced to carry on their revolutionary activity elsewhere—in Iran. Moreover, the Young Turk coup and the restoration of the Ottoman constitution of 1876 in June 1908 made feasible revolutionary activity outside of the Ottoman Empire as both parties revised their strategy toward the new Ottoman government and opted against armed struggle.[23]

Armenian revolutionaries committed themselves to the Iranian Constitutional Revolution with the strong conviction that they had overcome and learned from the brutality they had suffered and inflicted in their violent conflict with Muslims throughout the Caucasus. Referring to the collaboration of Armenians, Iranians, and others, they declared: "The love of freedom makes brothers of those two religiously different elements, that for centuries have learned to hate each other under subjugation."[24] The Russian Social Democrat Tria, commenting in 1911 on the Iranian Constitutional Revolution, wrote: "The Persian revolution was a miracle; nations that had been warring for centuries united in the name of liberty against the common enemy. Persians, Armenians, Georgians and Jews gathered under the same banner of revolt."[25]

Blurred Identities

These statements shed light on the special case of identity in the turn-of-the-century Near East and Caucasus. How can one explain the participation of Armenians in a revolution outside Armenian communities in the Ottoman and Russian Empires? Also, how could a Christian Armenian from the Caucasus feel enough affinity with his neighboring Iranian and Caucasian Muslims to join in common cause for constitution and democracy?

Just as sociologists Nathan Glazer and Daniel Moynihan have remarked about the term "ethnicity": "one senses a term still on the move," so too ethnicity or ethnic identity is "on the move," fluid and even blurred, shaped by circumstances and social processes, and not static.[26] In the early twentieth-century Near East, ethnic identity was not fixed; it was more malleable, or as anthropologist A. L. Epstein would remark, "negotiable."[27]

One might say that Armenians were experiencing a kind of "double consciousness."[28] There are a few parallel developments taking place within the Iranian Armenian community in the late nineteenth and early twentieth centuries that help clarify the somewhat complex process and condition of double consciousness or multiple identity. Because of developments in the Iranian Constitutional Revolution and because of the special circumstances of Iranian Armenians, specifically their centuries-old existence within Iran, two parallel identities existed, a more particularist Christian Armenian and a wider Iranian. This was made even more complex by a smaller segment of highly politicized intellectual Armenians in Iran who sought to go beyond the boundaries of nationalism in favor of internationalism and socialism. They also seemed torn between multiple identities and loyalties and perhaps desired to transcend narrower visions of identity and perception in order to escape the inconsistencies or multiplicity within them.

In a "polyethnic" region and situation such as Iran and the Constitutional Revolution, ethnic identity is only one among many other forms of social identity. "For the individual, therefore, whether and to what extent, he acquires a sense of ethnic identity always involves some element of choice."[29] Armenians from the Caucasus and Iran, participating in the Iranian Constitutional Revolution, could have multiple identities and thus a variety of loyalties. They participated in the revolution not necessarily and not exclusively as Armenians but also as political activists and revolutionaries, as agents of change, seeing the revolution as a struggle for democracy and freedom everywhere. Shifting ethnic allegiances, or more appropriately for this case, unifying ethnic allegiances allowed Caucasian and Iranian Armenians to pursue their political and ideological goals. As Patricia Higgins aptly states, "Individual decisions depend on the perception of economic, political, social, or even psychological interests."[30] Thus, the interest of those Armenians who took part in the Iranian Constitutional Revolution lay in adopting, consciously or not, a less rigid and more multifaceted identity in order to explain or justify to themselves and others the commitment to constitutional struggle and collaboration with Iranian and Caucasian Muslims. This occurred at the same time as the Iranian constitutionalists were redefining what it meant to be Iranian. For instance, the journal *Iran-e No*, in its editorial, stated: "Iranians are of one *millat*, a *millat* that speaks in different dialects and worships God in various ways."[31] This was clearly a change from the older meaning of *millat* as religious community.

Ethnic or religious differentiation was much less relevant in the Iranian Constitutional Revolution than it was in the violent clashes between the Armenians and Muslims of the Caucasus and even less so than it became years later. This is not to say that ethnic differentiation completely disappeared in the Constitutional Revolution, but ethnic loyalties and interests overlapped, blurring a clear separation between Armenian and Iranian, between Christian and Muslim, and so on. This occurred despite the continued identification of Armenians primarily with their religion and their national church. This religious identification was institutionalized in both the Ottoman and Russian Empires and recognized in Iran. The rise of a new national consciousness in the late nineteenth century that emphasized ethnicity over religion began to challenge identification as a religious community, although "Armenian" overwhelmingly referred to a church and even included people with different native languages.[32] As Craig Calhoun points out:

> every collective identity is open to both internal subdivision and calls for incorporation into some larger category of primary identity. Tension between identity—putatively singular, unitary and integral—and identities—plural, cross-cutting, divided—is inescapable both at individual and collective lev-

els. As lived, identity is always a project, not a settled accomplishment . . .
Identities can and to some extent do always change. There are always internal tensions and inconsistencies among various identities and group mem-
berships of individuals.[33]

The willingness of Caucasian and Iranian Armenians to struggle actively for political and social transformation in Iran may be explained in
such terms. This fluidity and multiplicity of ethnic identity—Iranian
Armenian, Armenian Iranian, Armenian Russian, Russian Armenian,
Caucasian Armenian, Armenian Caucasian—or multiplicity of individual identity—Armenian nationalist, Armenian nationalist/socialist, Armenian internationalist/socialist, Armenian revolutionary or just revolutionary, and so forth—is a major part of the motivation for commitment
to the "Iranian" cause and a major part of why Armenians fought side by
side in Iran with Caucasian Muslims in common cause only a year or two
after they violently clashed in the Caucasus.

Overview

This study addresses the issue of Armenian politicization and participation in the Iranian Constitutional Revolution. In order to comprehend the
reasons behind Armenian commitment to the Iranian movement and the
activities of Armenians in the struggle, it is imperative to be aware of the
process of Armenian politicization in the late nineteenth century in both
the Ottoman and Russian Empires. The first chapter explains the political, economic, and social situation of Armenians in the nineteenth century, with a special emphasis on the Armenian provinces of the Ottoman
Empire and the Russian-ruled Caucasus. The Ottoman Armenian
provinces became the focus of the Armenian revolutionary movement in
the late nineteenth century while the Russian-ruled Caucasus became the
source of this nationalist and socialist revolutionary movement. The
chapter ends with a discussion of the Armenian revolutionary movement
of the late nineteenth century and of the ideology and program of the
major Armenian political parties, the Hnchakian and the Dashnaktsutiun
parties. Discussion of Armenian communities in the Ottoman and Russian Empires points to a rising political consciousness and activism of a
number of Armenians as well as to the growing education level of a
larger proportion of the population, especially in the Caucasus, which
contributed greatly to the intellectual, cultural, and political development of Iranian Armenian communities, and without which there would
not have been an increasingly active political and intellectual stratum.
The second chapter provides a detailed account of the Armenian community in Iran, beginning with its early history but with a concentration on

the nineteenth century. In addition, this chapter deals with the establishment of political party branches in the Iranian Armenian community, especially in the northwestern province of Azerbaijan, explaining why they were there and what their goals and activities were, and demonstrates the importance of Caucasian Armenians in these activities. This section also underscores the importance of an already-existing, centuries-old Armenian community in Iran that, because of its political transformation and advances in popular education in which Iranian Armenian women played a significant role, possessed the potential to provide a foundation for political activism in the Iranian Constitutional Revolution. The third chapter illustrates the ideological and political motivations of the Armenians who participated, with a greater concentration on the Dashnaktsutiun, the Armenian party that contributed most to the Iranian Constitutional Revolution. The fourth chapter explores the collaboration of Armenian and Iranian constitutionalists, drawing special attention to negotiations between the two and the ideological and military contribution of Armenians as well as the internal and external conflicts among Armenian activists and between Armenian and Iranian constitutionalist elements. The fifth chapter concludes with a discussion of the causes and consequences of the retreat of Armenians from the contemporary Iranian political scene.

Notes

1. For a study of this incident, its significance, and its absence from the historiography of the Iranian Constitutional Revolution, see Afsaneh Najmabadi, *The Story of the Daughters of Quchan: Gender and National Memory in Iranian History* (New York: Syracuse University Press, 1998).

2. According to Edward G. Browne, "Until the recent Russo-Japanese war Persia was beset by the fear of inevitable subjection to Russia." See Edward G. Browne, *The Persian Revolution, 1905–1909* (1910; new edition edited by Abbas Amanat and with essays by Abbas Amanat and Mansour Bonakdarian, Mage Edition, 1995), 429.

3. For a discussion of the consequences of the Russo-Japanese War on Russian society, see Abraham Ascher, *The Revolution of 1905: Russia in Disarray* (Stanford: Stanford University Press, 1988), 1: 43–53.

4. See Nikki R. Keddie, "Religion and Irreligion in Early Iranian Nationalism," in *Iran: Religion, Politics and Society*, ed. Nikki R. Keddie (London: Frank Cass, 1980), 13–14; Nikki R. Keddie, "Iranian Revolutions in Comparative Perspective," *American Historical Review* 88, 3 (June 1983): 586.

5. Browne, *Persian Revolution*, 122.

6. According to one source, in 1905 there were 62,000 Iranian migrant workers in Russia. See Ivar Spector, *The First Russian Revolution: Its Impact on Asia* (Engle-

wood Cliffs, NJ: Prentice Hall, 1962), 39. Another source cites 11,132 Iranians for 1903. See Audrey L. Altstadt, *The Azerbaijani Turks: Power and Identity Under Russian Rule* (Stanford: Hoover Institution Press, 1992), 32.

7. Spector, *First Russian Revolution*, 38–40.

8. In reference to the Tabriz delegates to parliament, arriving in Tehran in 1907, who had been met by enthusiastic crowds, Browne suggests: "These Tabriz deputies, who were regarded as being sincere patriots almost to a man, represented the more extreme or radical party, and seem to have been influenced by the ideas of the Russian reformers." See Browne, *Persian Revolution*, 146.

9. Ahmad Kasravi, *Tarikh-e mashruteh-ye Iran* [History of the constitution of Iran] (1951; reprint, Tehran: Amir Kabir, 1984); Ahmad Kasravi, *Tarikh-e hijdah saleh-ye Azerbaijan* [The eighteen-year history of Azerbaijan], 2 vols. (Tehran: Amir Kabir, 1978).

10. See, for example, Janet Afary, *The Iranian Constitutional Revolution, 1906–1911: Grassroots Democracy, Social Democracy, and the Origins of Feminism* (New York: Columbia University Press, 1996); Cosroe Chaqueri, "The Role and Impact of Armenian Intellectuals in Iranian Politics 1905–1911," *Armenian Review* 41, 2 (Summer 1988): 1–51; Mansureh Ettehadieh Nezam Mafi, *Paidayesh va tahavvol-e ahzab-e siyasi-ye mashrutiyat: dowreh-ye avval va dovvom-e majles-e showra-ye melli* [Appearance and evolution of political parties of constitutionalism: the first and second period of the National Consultative Assembly] (Tehran: Gostardeh Press, 1982); Mansureh Ettehadieh Nezam Mafi, ed., *Majmu'eh-ye motun va asnad-e tarikhi* [Collection of texts and historical documents], vol. 4 (Tehran: Nashr-e tarikh-e Iran, 1982); Ra'in Isma'il, *Yeprem Khan-e Sardar* [Commander Yeprem Khan] (Tehran: Zarin, 1971).

11. See A[ndre] Amurian, *Dashnaktsutiun, Yeprem, parskakan sahmanadrutiun, H. H. D. kendronakan arkhiv* [A. R. Federation, Yeprem, Persian constitution, A. R. F. central archives], 2 vols. (Tehran: Alik, 1976–1979); A[ndre] Amurian, *H. H. Dashnaktsutiune Parskastanum, 1890–1918* [The A. R. Federation in Persia, 1890–1918] (Tehran: Alik, 1950); Cosroe Chaqueri, ed., *La Social-démocratie en Iran: articles et documents* (Florence: Mazdak, 1979). See also A[ndre] Amurian, ed., *Heghapokhakan Yepremi Vodisakane* [Revolutionary Yeprem's odyssey] (Tehran: Alik, 1972); A[ndre] Amurian, *Hamasah-e Yeprem* [The epic of Yeprem] (Tehran: Javid Press, 1976). In this regard, Iraj Afshar's collected material on Hasan Taqizadeh also sheds light on the Armenian role. See his edited work, *Awraq-e tazehyab-e mashrutiyat va naqsh-e Taqizadeh* [Newly found constitutional papers and the role of Taqizadeh] (Tehran: Bahman Press, 1980).

12. "The Hnchakists not only did not participate in the Iranian revolution, but were also opposed to it . . ." See Amurian, *Arkhiv*, 1: 216 n. 1. Regarding the Federation of Anzali of Social Democratic Party Hnchakist, the Dashnaktsutiun told the International Socialist Bureau that the Hnchakist group "is composed of young men without a single intellectual or moral authority and having no single relation with socialism . . . On the contrary . . . they were steeped in the reactionary current." See "Socio-démocrates persans à Anzali," in Cosroe Chaqueri, ed., *Social-démocratie*, 229. Regarding Dashnakists, see, for example, Arsen Kitur, *Patmutiun S. D. Hnchakian Kusaktsutian* [History of the S. D. Hnchakian party] (Beirut: Shirak Press, 1962), 1: 401.

13. Tria, "La Caucase et la révolution persane," trans. from the Russian by M. Pavlovitch, *Revue du monde musulman*, 13, 2 (February 1911): 327–28.

14. Tria, "La Caucase et la révolution persane," 330.

15. Other groups in Baku: 17–20 percent Russian workers, 12–13 percent Caucasian Muslims, 19–21 percent Iranian workers. See Anaide Ter Minassian, *Nationalism and Socialism in the Armenian Revolutionary Movement (1887–1912)*, trans. from the French by A. M. Berrett (Cambridge, MA: The Zoryan Institute, 1984), 25. For the French original see Anahide Ter Minassian, "Nationalisme et socialisme dans le mouvement révolutionnaire arménien," *La Question arménienne* (Roquevaire: Editions Parenthèses, 1983), 73–111. In 1903, out of a population of about 155,876 in Baku, 26,151 (almost 17 percent) were Armenians; 44,257 (almost 28.5 percent) were Caucasian Muslims; 11,132 (more than 7 percent) were Iranian citizens; and 56,955 (about 36.5 percent) were Russians. See Altstadt, *Azerbaijani Turks*, 32 table 3.2.

16. See chapter 2, note 24.

17. A. G. Abrahamian, *Hamarot urvagits hay gaghtavaireri patmutian* [Brief outline of the history of Armenian colonies] (Yerevan: Hayastan, 1967), 2: 237–40.

18. See Seyyed Hassan Taqizadeh, "Document: The Background of the Constitutional Movement in Azerbaijan," trans. from the Persian by Nikki R. Keddie, *The Middle East Journal* 14, 4 (Autumn 1960): 456–65.

19. E. Aknuni [Khachatur Malumian], *Boghoki dzayn: kovkasahay kaghakakan bantarkialnere (tsarakan halatsanki mi ej* [The voice of protest: Caucasian Armenian political prisoners (a page from tsarist persecution)] (Beirut: Ghukas Karapetian, 1978), 59–60, n. 1. For the English version, see E. Aknouni, *Political Persecution: Armenian Prisoners of the Caucasus (A Page of the Tzar's Persecution*, trans. A. M. and H. W. (New York: n.p., 1911), 30 n. 6. According to Aknuni, the number of Muslims killed was greater than the number of Armenians, which add up to 1,173. He does not provide any numbers stating that the Muslims "according to some strange custom conceal everything pertaining to the number killed and other such information." Another source places the total number killed at more than 10,000. See Filip Makharadze, *Ocherki revoliutsionnovo dvizheniia v Zakavkaz'e* [Studies of the revolutionary movement in Transcaucasia] (Tiflis, 1927), 300, 307, cited in Richard G. Hovannisian, *Armenia on the Road to Independence, 1918* (Berkeley and Los Angeles: University of California Press), 264 n. 64.

20. "Kovkasian nakhagitse" [The Caucasian project], *Niuter H. H. Dashnaktsutian patmutian hamar* [Materials for the history of the A. R. Federation], ed. and comp. Hratch Dashnabedian [Hrach Tasnapetian] (Beirut: Hamazagayin, 1973), 2: 231–36.

21. For text of 1907 program, see Dasnabedian, *Niuter*, 3: 315–28; *Droshak*, no. 5, May 1907.

22. Ibid.

23. Ter Minassian, *Nationalism*, 54; S. Sabah-Giulian [Stepan Ter Stepanian], "Trkakan reformistakan sharzhume" [The Turkish reform movement], *Hnchak*, no. 7, June–July 1908; "Declaration to the Social Democratic Hnchakian Party Ranks," 13–26 November 1910, in Kitur, *Patmutiun*, 1: 328.

24. "Parskastan: sahmanadrutiune verahastatvats" [Persia: the constitution reestablished], *Droshak*, no. 5, May 1909.

25. Tria, "La Caucase et la révolution persane," 332.

26. Nathan Glazer and Daniel A. Moynihan, eds., *Ethnicity: Theory and Experience* (Cambridge: Harvard University Press, 1975), 33.

27. A. L. Epstein, *Ethos and Identity: Three Studies in Ethnicity* (London: Tavistock, 1978), 59–60.

28. The concept of "double consciousness" was first created and applied by W. E. B. Du Bois in describing the "American Negro." Du Bois wrote:

> One ever feels his two-ness, — an American, a Negro; two souls, two thoughts, two unreconciled strivings; two warring ideals in one dark body, whose dogged strength alone keeps it from being torn asunder.
>
> The history of the American Negro is the history of this strife, — this longing to attain self-conscious manhood, to merge his double self into a better and truer self. In this merging he wishes neither of the older selves to be lost.

Du Bois directly referred to the struggle of American blacks after Emancipation to forge an identity that would allow them to be both black and American, to evade the contempt of whites, and to have the "doors of Opportunity" open to them. In *The Black Atlantic Modernity and Double Consciousness*, Paul Gilroy takes Du Bois's concept of double consciousness further by stating that Du Bois intended "not just to express the distinctive standpoint of black Americans but also to illuminate the experience of post-slave populations in general." Gilroy explains that double consciousness "emerges from the unhappy symbiosis between three modes of thinking, being, and seeing": racially particularist, nationalist, and diasporic or hemispheric or at times global and universalist. While acknowledging that Du Bois was specifically speaking of the post-slavery experience and struggle of American blacks, the concept of double consciousness may be applied, with some modifications, to the case of Iranian Armenians who were, of course, by no means a post-slave population. While the circumstances of turn-of-the-century Iranian Armenian and American black communities are very different, the situation of multiple identity for both populations contains within it similar elements. See, W. E. B. Du Bois, *The Souls of Black Folk* (New York, 1990), 8–9; Paul Gilroy, *The Black Atlantic: Modernity and Double Consciousness* (London, New York, 1993), 126–27.

29. Epstein, xiv.

30. Patricia J. Higgins, "Minority-State Relations in Contemporary Iran," in *The State, Religion, and Ethnic Politics: Afghanistan, Iran, and Pakistan*, ed. Ali Banuazizi and Myron Weiner (Syracuse: Syracuse University Press, 1986), 170.

31. *Iran-e No*, 16 February 1910, cited in Mohammad Tavakoli-Targhi, "Refashioning Iran: Language and Culture During the Constitutional Revolution," *Iranian Studies* 23, 1–4 (1990): 98–99.

32. Ronald Grigor Suny, "Introduction,"in *Looking Toward Ararat: Armenia in Modern History*, ed. Ronald Grigor Suny (Bloomington and Indianapolis: Indiana University Press, 1993), 9.

33. Craig Calhoun, "Social Theory and the Politics of Identity," in *Social Theory and the Politics of Identity*, ed. Craig Calhoun (Cambridge, MA: Blackwell, 1994), 27.

1

Armenians in the Nineteenth Century

In order to understand the political, intellectual, and military role of Armenians in the Iranian Constitutional Revolution it is necessary to have some knowledge of the nineteenth-century development and politicization of Armenians that took place in the Ottoman and Russian Empires. It is this process that laid the foundation for and made possible their participation in the Iranian revolution.

At the turn of the nineteenth century, Armenians constituted a minority in three empires, the Ottoman, Russian, and Persian, and were dispersed in much smaller communities all over the world. The largest communities of Armenians existed in the six Ottoman *vilayets* (provinces) of Van, Bitlis, Erzerum, Diarbekir, Sivas, and Kharput (Mamuret al-Aziz) in eastern Anatolia. Those Armenians who prospered both commercially and educationally, however, lived outside Ottoman Armenian provinces in the urban centers of Istanbul (Constantinople) and Izmir (Smyrna) and had very little contact with the majority of Armenian peasants. The Armenians, like the Greek Orthodox and Jewish communities, were organized into the *millet* system, whereby they were accorded autonomy over internal affairs within their community. As *dhimmi*, non-Muslim peoples protected under Islamic law, the Armenians, like other Christian and Jewish communities, were allowed a certain amount of autonomy in communal affairs and freedom to worship while subject to a special tax as well as certain limitations such as not being allowed to carry arms or wear certain colors, thus distinguishing them from Muslims. The Armenian *millet* was headed by the Patriarch of Constantinople who was recognized by the Ottoman sultanate as leader of all Armenians of the empire until the nineteenth century, when Armenian Catholics and Protestants fell under the authority of the newly recognized Catholic and Protestant *millets*. The Armenian Patriarch was allowed sole control over

his community in exchange for keeping his co-religionist Ottoman subjects in check and making certain that the necessary taxes were collected
for the Ottoman government.[1]

Population statistics for the Ottoman Armenians in eastern Anatolia
and Cilicia in southern Anatolia where the last Armenian king ruled until
1375 come from the Armenian Patriarchate, European traveler accounts,
and Ottoman censuses. Sources do not agree and some figures are open
to question and have their own biases and political motivations. Given
the lack of unbiased and exact statistics, scholars must make do with
what is available. For the year 1882, the Armenian Patriarchate placed the
number of Armenians at about 2,500,000, while Vahe Sarafian's study of
the Ottoman Armenian population indicates that there were more likely
2,130,000 Armenians, with the largest number in the province of Van,
near the border with Russia and Iran.[2] There was also a substantial number of Armenians in Istanbul, somewhere between 180,000 and 250,000.[3]
Sarafian estimates that at a minimum 1 percent yearly increase, the Ottoman Armenian population stood at about 2,998,000 in 1908.[4] Levon
Marashlian, based on a study of the accounts of the Armenian Patriarchate, European travelers, Ottoman censuses, and Ottoman revisionist
historians, estimates that by 1912 there were about 2,000,000 Armenians
in the Ottoman Empire. The Ottoman census for 1844 accounts for
2,400,000 Armenians, but after the internationalization of the Armenian
Question at the Berlin Congress (1878), the Ottoman census of 1881/82
cites a much reduced number of 1,000,000 Armenians.[5]

A much smaller Armenian community existed in the Araxes valley and
Ararat plain, designated as the Armianskaia oblast (Armenian district)
by the Russian Empire after the Torkmanchai Treaty (1828). The oblast
was abolished in 1840 but nine years later was included in the Yerevan
guberniia (province), which became the fifth province of the Russian-
ruled Caucasus. However, barely one-third of Armenians of the Caucasus lived in the Yerevan province. In 1896 Armenians in Yerevan formed
a majority at 53 percent. The estimated population for the Caucasus for
1886 stood at about 4,700,000, of which only 20 percent (about 940,000)
were Armenian.[6] The Russian Imperial Census for 1897 lists the number
of Armenians at 1,200,000 while the 1896 census estimates an Armenian
population of 1,400,000 out of a total Caucasian population of 6,000,000.
According to this census, Armenians formed 50 percent of the population
of the Yerevan province, 35 percent of the Elisavetpol province, about 24
percent of the Tiflis (Tbilisi) province, and about 8 percent of the Baku
province.[7]

The Armenian community of Iran, unlike the Armenians in the Ottoman and Russian Empires, constituted a very small minority of the
Iranian population. Most of the more highly populated areas of the

northeastern section of the Armenian Plateau and the khanates (provinces) of Yerevan and Nakhijevan had been lost to the Russian Empire in the Treaties of Golestan (1813) and Torkmanchai (1828). Furthermore, many Armenians, as part of the provisions of the Torkmanchai Treaty, were allowed to resettle from northern Iran to north of the Araxes River.[8] At the end of the nineteenth century, the total Armenian population of Iran stood at about 63,000 to 70,000, concentrated in the provinces of Azerbaijan and Isfahan.[9]

Nineteenth-century Armenians living in eastern Anatolia, the Caucasus, and Iran were divided not only by geography, but also by the disparity in social, economic, intellectual, and political development. In general, Ottoman Armenians were poorer, less educated, less urbanized, and less in touch with the world beyond the borders than their Russian Armenian counterparts. In addition, they lived in a less secure environment, often threatened by their Turkish and Kurdish neighbors. Although the majority of Armenians on both sides of the border were peasants, small urban commercial elites existed in Istanbul and Izmir in the Ottoman Empire and in Baku, Batum, and Tiflis in the Russian Caucasus, all cities outside the Ottoman Armenian and Russian Armenian provinces. These elites were among the most Europeanized elements of the empires, which made the division between the urban elite and the peasant majority in both regions even more acute as physical and social contact between the two was almost nonexistent. In addition, Armenians had no single leadership recognized by all, although the national church came closest to such a position.[10]

The Ottoman Armenian Community

For Ottoman Armenians, the nineteenth century, especially the second half, was at the same time a period of great promise and great disappointment. Armenian students began to travel abroad and learned about European, especially French, intellectual and political trends and came in contact with intellectuals. Nineteenth-century Ottoman Armenians also experienced a political and national awakening that resulted in conflict between the classes, the creation of an Armenian National Constitution, the proliferation of journals, a literary renaissance, and the formation of secret revolutionary societies. The Ottoman Armenian community was also very much influenced by the Tanzimat reforms begun by Sultan Abdulmejid (1839–1861) and the internationalization of the Armenian Question in the last quarter of the nineteenth century.

The first generation of students to study in Europe came mainly from the urban commercial elite of Istanbul and studied in Italy in the 1830s and 1840s. Later generations studied most often in Paris and were greatly inspired by the ideas of the French Revolution. Some even witnessed the revolutions of 1830 and 1848 and returned home motivated by the ideas of liberty, fraternity, and equality—ideas that conflicted with those of the older generation of Armenian and Ottoman leaders.[11] The struggle was waged by the younger intelligentsia and *esnaf* class of guild members to free the affairs of the community from the control of the *amira* class and this time the Patriarch as well. The decades-long contest resulted in the Armenian National Constitution, adopted by the Supreme Assembly in May 1860, later revised, and then accepted by the sultan in March 1863.[12] It is important to note that although its authors and later Armenian sources named this set of community regulations a constitution, the word used by official Ottoman sources was a less controversial term, *nizamnameh*, meaning "statute." One of the authors of the Armenian constitution, Krikor Odian, who was also an advisor to Midhat Paşa, chairman of the Ottoman constitutional commission, participated in the framing of the Ottoman constitution of 1876.[13]

Although the National Constitution did little to settle community affairs, it had a positive effect, laying the foundation for a system of public education and changing the character of journals and literary works, which became more concerned with the situation of Ottoman Armenians and the bulk of which centered on nationalist aspirations and sentiments.[14] For the first time, the Armenian intelligentsia began to see its role as service to the people rather than to the church and although these intellectuals emerged out of the middle class, they formed "a social bridge," because of their identification with the lower classes.[15] The number of both schools and journals increased at the same time as the clergy's dominant role in both decreased. In the decades before the 1860s, the Armenian Church and clergy were the main source of education, the press, and literature.[16] This changed radically as another conflict arose—this time regarding the use of vernacular (*ashkharabar*) versus classical (*grabar*) Armenian as the form of literary expression.[17] The majority of Armenians were illiterate and understood nothing of the classical language. Those who favored the vernacular were the same European-educated or European-influenced intellectuals who had brought forth the National Constitution and had taken the lead in attempting to establish modern education for Ottoman Armenians.

The cultural and political revival of the Armenian community paralleled the administrative, financial, and military breakdown of the Ottoman Empire and with it the mistreatment and at times persecution of its Armenian subjects. The Ottoman reform movement was in large part a sincere attempt to revitalize and solve the problems within the empire. The Tanzimat reforms and the internationalization of the Armenian Question dramatically influenced the politicization of Ottoman Armenians. The Tanzimat reforms began under the leadership of reformers like Minister of Foreign Affairs Mustafa Reşid Paşa. In 1839, the promulgation of the *Hatt-i Şerif* of *Gülhane* (Noble Rescript of the Rose Chamber) radically broke with Islamic tradition in proclaiming equality before the law of all Ottoman subjects regardless of religion. The implication that non-Muslims were no longer inferior and separate greatly disturbed those who had a vested interest in the status quo, especially the Muslim clerics (*'ulama*), provincial governors, and even the Greek clergy.[18]

The *Hatt-i Şerif* was promulgated under some degree of pressure from Europe, particularly Great Britain, whose rulers believed reforms would save the Ottoman Empire from dissolution. The subsequent *Hatt-i Hümayun* (Imperial Rescript) of 1856 was a direct consequence of the preliminaries to the Treaty of Paris following the Crimean War and a condition to the acceptance of the Ottoman Empire as a participant in the Concert of Europe.[19] The *Hatt-i Hümayun* reasserted the equality of all subjects and laid down in greater detail equality in military service, administration, justice, taxation, and so forth. In addition, the rescript banned the use of disparaging expressions "tending to make any class whatever of the subjects of my [sultan's] empire inferior to another class on account of religion, language or race."[20] This rescript, too, like its predecessor, aroused mostly opposition among the Muslim subjects who considered it a foreign concession that gave away too much to the non-Muslim subjects.[21]

While both rescripts promised a great deal, neither was applied in a degree that would cause substantive changes in the treatment of non-Muslim subjects. The Tanzimat period culminated in the promulgation of a constitution and creation of a parliament in 1876 that was dissolved by Sultan Abdul-Hamid II in 1878.[22] The decrees promising equality and their scarce implementation actually worsened the situation of Armenians in the empire, who became, even more than in the past, the target of violence.[23] Perhaps because of the failure of these Tanzimat reforms and the political and cultural (re)awakening of the Armenian *millet*, the leaders of the community sought the aid of the Russian Empire after its victory in the Russo-Turkish War (1877–1878), asking Russia to include implementation of Armenian reforms as a stipulation in its treaty with the Ottoman Empire. Article 16 of the Treaty of San Stefano, signed in March 1878, determined that Russian troops would withdraw from Armenian-inhabited provinces of the Ottoman Empire only after the implementation of reforms there.

The treaty was disliked by the European powers, especially Britain, who felt threatened by the Russian Empire's influence in the region. Threats by these powers forced Russia to participate in the Congress of Berlin to revise the agreement signed only a few months earlier. An Armenian delegation went to Berlin with a reform program at hand, which requested local self-government, civil courts of law, mixed Christian and Muslim militias, voting privileges for adult males, and the allocation of a large portion of local taxes for local improvement projects. Article 61 of the Berlin Congress, in a symbolic reversal of Article 16 of the San Stefano Treaty, demanded immediate Russian withdrawal and required the Ottoman sultan to promise implementation of reforms and report progress to the European powers.[24] This was a great blow to the Armenian *millet*, since it meant that although the Armenian Question had now reached international status, reforms would not be implemented. Furthermore, Armenian communities, especially those from which Russian troops withdrew, became victim to attacks by Kurdish irregular forces encouraged and armed by the Ottoman government.[25]

In a short time, Armenian disillusion with legal and ineffectual pleas for reform encouraged extralegal means, as some Armenian youth began to look to the Bulgarians and Greeks, who had succeeded in revolts against the Ottoman Empire, as models to emulate. Moreover, Ottoman Armenian students began to feel and see the impact of Western concepts of nationality and nationhood, and their self-perception as a religious community began to shift to that of a nationality. In the 1870s and especially in the 1880s, Ottoman Armenians began to form local self-defense groups. Two such groups were the Black Cross Organization (Sev Khach Kazmakerputiun) formed in Van in 1878 and the Protectors of the Fatherland (Pashtpan Hayreniats) formed in Erzerum in 1881, both of which sought to protect unarmed Armenians from extortion and violence by some Turks and Kurds.[26]

The first revolutionary party whose goal went beyond self-defense was founded by students of Mkrtich Portugalian (1848–1921). Portugalian, the son of a banker, was born in the Armenian quarter of Kum Kapu in Istanbul. Portugalian served as teacher, publisher, and was active in founding schools and promoting adult education until 1885, when the Ottoman government closed one of these schools in Van and banned him from the province. He then traveled to France and never returned to the Ottoman Armenian provinces. In Marseilles, Portugalian began publishing the newspaper *Armenia* as a means to draw attention to the plight of Ottoman Armenians and to procure the support of diaspora Armenians. His students rallied around the paper and were successful in forming the Armenakan party, whose name derived from *Armenia*. The program stated that the purpose of the party was to achieve self-determination for Ottoman Armenians. Its methods included the preparation of the Armenian people for revolution through oral and written dissemination of "revolutionary ideas" and the arming and training of Armenians. The Armenakan party's activities centered in the Ottoman Empire, with branches also in the Caucasus and Iran. Its centers in Salmas and Tabriz in northwestern Iran were the second-most important bases next to Van as the Armenakans bought arms and munitions there and then smuggled them into Ottoman territory to arm Armenian peasants against Kurdish aggression.[27]

The Russian Armenian Community

While the journalistic and literary renaissance and the revolutionary movement had strong resonance among the Ottoman Armenians, they reached their peak and were more fully developed by Russian Armenian intellectuals and revolutionaries. The majority of Armenian journals, including the most influential of them, like *Mshak* (Cultivator, 1872–1920), were printed in the Caucasus.[28] The first novel in the vernacular Armenian was written by Khachatur Abovian, a Russian Armenian. The first Armenian journal in vernacular, *Ararat,* was published in Tiflis in 1849.[29] Raffi (Hakob Melik-Hakobian, 1835–1888), one of the most popular writers whose nationalist novels inspired generations, although born in Salmas, received his education in Tiflis.

While Ottoman Armenians studied mostly in France, Russian Armenians pursued their education in Moscow, St. Petersburg, Dorpat, Leipzig, and Berlin; took in European culture through contacts with Russian intellectuals; and were subject to the same intellectual influences as their Russian colleagues. In addition, Armenians formed an important segment of the Caucasian working class in Tiflis, Baku, and Batum.[30] Armenian peasants had easier access to urban life, as these cities became the destination for those fleeing rural overpopulation and seeking work in factories. In this way, there was greater social mobility and contact with Western movements for Russian Armenians than for Ottoman Armenians. Also, changes taking shape in Europe, like the growth of cities, market economies, and industrialization, deeply affected the Caucasus. The expansion of market economy, railroads, the telegraph, and improvement of roads brought distant places and peoples closer, linking them with Caucasian and Russian administrative, commercial, and industrial centers. Even the rural sections of the Caucasus were transformed by these developments.[31] Most of all, however, the rise of the economy and urbanization caused the growth of the Armenian bourgeoisie in the Caucasian cities of Tiflis, Baku, and Batum. For example, in 1876, out of a total merchant population of 6,851 in the Caucasus, Armenians numbered 4,249. From 1890 to 1900, Armenians controlled 62.5 to 74.6 percent of commercial industrial enterprises and four out of six banks, and almost half of the real estate. In Baku, Armenians controlled more than half of the city's oil wells (155 out of 195), 25 percent of the commercial enterprises, and most of the shares of the Caucasian banks. These numbers are even more significant, considering that in 1873, only 5 percent of the Baku population was Armenian and, in 1900, 23 percent. The situation in Batum was similar.[32] The Armenian bourgeoisie made up only about 7 percent of the total Armenian population of the Caucasus, the majority of whom, 70 percent, were lower- to middle-class peasants and the rest workers, about 16 percent, and artisans and craftsmen, almost 6 percent.[33]

The disparity between population size and dominant economic position tended to be a cause of tension between the Armenian bourgeoisie and the larger population of Georgians and Muslims, and this situation was readily exploited by the Russian government to its benefit. For example, in the case of Tiflis, Armenians controlled trade and the craft industry through guilds and monopolies. By the mid-nineteenth century, most government contracts and businesses were handled by the Armenian bourgeoisie despite competition from Russian rivals.[34] After 1860, relations between Armenians and Georgians in Tiflis took a turn for the worse, as the Georgian nobility began to feel threatened by the financial establishment of the Armenian bourgeoisie. Although Armenian merchants had settled in Georgian towns as early as the eleventh century with the encouragement of Georgian monarchs, David "The Rebuilder" (1089–1125) and Queen Tamar (1184–1212), and although Armenians to a great extent controlled the commercial capital of Tiflis, the Georgian and Armenian elements came in physical proximity only in the second half of the nineteenth century with the change from agrarian to market economy and its consequences.[35] As Ronald Suny demonstrates, "Social distinctions between classes were reinforced by cultural and linguistic differences."[36] As Georgians began to migrate to Tiflis, Armenians no longer formed a majority in the city. For example, while in 1801, at the time of Russian annexation of Georgia, Armenians constituted three quarters of the city's population, in 1886 they constituted only 20 percent of the inhabitants, but continued to maintain control over the economy and city politics.[37] The dominance of Armenians, despite the demographic shift in the city, caused great resentment among the Georgians, who by the latter half of the nineteenth century were also experiencing an increase in nationalist sentiment that found expression in an anti-Armenian campaign by the threatened Georgian nobility and Georgian nationalist writers.[38]

Growing Georgian nationalism paralleled the rise of Russian nationalism in the government, with the Armenians perceived as a threat to Russian hegemony over the Caucasus.[39] In addition to administrative transformations and changes in land and peasant policies, all carried out, according to one scholar of the region, "to check regional and ethnic separatist movements or tendencies and at the same time to prevent any nationality from becoming a preponderant majority in any major province,"[40] Russia began to restrict Armenian cultural, philanthropic, and political institutions in the latter half of the nineteenth century. The policy of Russification that had begun in 1885 in the Baltic region and Finland, reached the Caucasus and the Armenians when the governor of the Caucasus, A. M. Dondukov-Korsakov, ordered the closing of all 500 Armenian parish schools with 20,000 students and 900 teachers. In response to the closings, secret schools were set up. By 1886, although schools were reopened, the staff had been replaced and strict Russian control established.[41] A year later, the Russian government ordered that religion in Armenian schools must be taught in Russian. These measures came as a surprise to most Armenians who had, generally, a positive view of Russian rule, especially compared to their opinion of the Ottoman government. In 1896, the Viceroy of the Caucasus, Prince Grigorii Golitsyn (1896–1903), shut down Armenian schools, and in 1898 he closed down all philanthropic societies and libraries. Moreover, printing of the words "Armenian people" or "Armenian nation" was prohibited.[42] A few years later, in 1900, major Armenian publishing associations were also shut down.[43] The great blow came in 1903, however, when the Russian government seized all properties of the Armenian Church. This was a radical change from the *Polozhenie* (Decree) of 1836, which recognized the religious freedom of all Armenians and institutionalized the traditional role of the Armenian church as leader of the Armenian community. The decree had also allowed the opening of Armenian schools under the control of the church. Therefore, the attack on the church in 1903 was also aimed at Armenian schools, which, under the influence of the Russian- and European-educated Armenian elite, were modernized and secularized and served to politicize Armenian students throughout the nineteenth century. They contributed greatly to the development of national consciousness.[44] Schools such as the Nersisian Academy (founded in Tiflis, 1823/1824), the Gevorgian Academy (founded in Ejmiatsin, 1874), and the Lazarian Academy (founded in Moscow, 1814/1815) contributed immensely to producing Armenian intellectual literati as well as activists and revolutionaries. Some graduates from these schools continued their education in the universities of Germany and Russia and returned to the Caucasus influenced by German and Russian intellectual trends.[45] This new generation of Russian Armenian elites took the lead in the secularization and modernization of schools, in the establishment of the vernacular as the literary language (which had been achieved by 1890 in Russian Armenia), and in the revolutionary movement.

The Russification policy was to some extent driven by the changes taking place within the Armenian community in the Caucasus. Despite the growing secularization of the Armenians and despite the literary and cultural revival among them, Armenians did not desire to be a separate entity. Many had become Russified under the rule of Alexander II (1855–1881); they had adopted Russian names and saw Russian interests as their own. Suny argues that both Russian and Ottoman policies of the last quarter of the nineteenth century pushed Armenians, who in general were willing to assimilate in both regions, to recognize themselves as a separate group.[46] In the Russian Empire, the closing of schools, libraries, and benevolent societies and the confiscation of church properties under Tsars Alexander III (1881–1894) and Nicholas II (1894–1917) paralleled the rise of persecution culminating in the massacres of Armenians (1894–1896) under Sultan Abdul-Hamid II.

The Armenian revolutionary movement, simultaneously nationalist and socialist, originated and developed partly in the above context, as a reaction or response to increasing repression in the Russian and Ottoman Empires in the last quarter of the nineteenth century. It was also influenced by Western secular nationalism, industrialization, urbanization, the spread of literacy and popular education, and to a great degree, the failure of a viable resolution of the Armenian Question. In the Caucasus, Armenians were also affected by their contact with Russian intellectuals and exposure to Russian revolutionary populism. As Suny has suggested, the ideologies of the Armenian political parties formed by Russian Armenian intellectuals mirrored many of the debates, disputes, and complexities of the Russian revolutionary movement.[47] Although very few Armenians were involved in the Russian populist movement (*narodnichestvo*), which relied on the peasantry rather than an urban proletariat for social revolution, and very few adopted the aims of the populists, namely a form of peasant socialism based on the village commune, most young Armenian intellectuals emulated the populist call to serve the "people." The populist *khozhdenie v narod* (going to the people) became transformed, for the Armenians, into the more nationalist *depi yerkir* (toward the homeland). For the Russian Armenian revolutionaries, the homeland meant Ottoman Armenian provinces. For instance, a small group, inspired by the terrorist wing of the Russian populists, formed in 1880 with the goal of liberating Armenians from Ottoman rule.[48]

The political parties of the Russian Armenians were characterized by two major factors: by the concentration on the situation of Ottoman Armenians and by a perpetual debate over the relevancy of socialism to the cause of Armenian "liberation." A more detailed discussion of the two major parties, the Hnchakian Revolutionary Party (subsequently the Social-Democrat Hnchakian Party) and the Armenian Revolutionary Federation (Hay Heghapokhakan Dashnaktsutiun), will illustrate this point. While some of the founders of both parties were members of the militant populist group Narodnaya Volya (People's Will),[49] others agreed with the former populist Georgi Plekhanov, who argued against peasant socialism and adopted Marxist socialism and its reliance on the urban proletariat as the main instrument of revolution.[50] The founders of the Hnchakian party were in the latter group and were well acquainted with Plekhanov and Vera Zasulich, both well-known Russian Social Democrats.[51]

The Hnchakian party was founded in Geneva in 1887 by six Russian Armenian intellectuals: Avetis Nazarbekian (Nazarbek, Lerents), Mariam (Maro) Vardanian, Gevorg Gharajanian (S. T. Arkomed), Ruben Khanazatian (Khan-Azat), Kristapor Ohanian, and Gabriel Kafian (Shmavon). Nazarbekian's education was financed by his uncle, who was one of the wealthiest capitalists of Tiflis, and although Nazarbekian was born in Tabriz, he had spent his childhood and received his education in Russia.[52] His fiancée, Maro Vardanian, had studied in St. Petersburg, was a member of a Russian revolutionary group, and met Nazarbekian in Paris where she had fled because of "political difficulties."[53] The rest of the group were all students: Gharajanian and Ohanian from Montpelier and Khanazatian and Kafian from Geneva. According to one of the first members of the party, Vardanian was the "ruling intellect of the group."[54] The Hnchakian party had no official name until 1890 at which time it took its name from its organ, *Hnchak* (Bell), named after *Kolokol*, the paper founded by the Russian populist and socialist intellectual Alexander Herzen.

The immediate objective of the Hnchakian party, as expressed in its program, was the political and national liberation of the Ottoman Armenians who lived without security of life and property, who were persecuted for their religion, and who had "reached physical and political destruction and economic poverty." Only after achieving that goal would it be possible to continue the struggle to liberate all Armenians, Russian and Iranian, and to establish a socialist world, which was the party's future objective. Revolutionary activity in Ottoman Armenia, including violence against the Ottoman government, became the means by which the immediate goal would be met. Tactics included: (1) "propaganda" to educate the Armenian people about the revolution's main ideas of national freedom, democracy, and socialism and to prepare them for revolution; (2) "agitation" to revitalize the people's morale, to incite them against the persecution of the government and "other enemies," and to demand reforms, refuse to pay taxes, and carry out demonstrations; (3) "terror" in order to protect the people, to develop a revolutionary spirit among them, and to intimidate the government, decrease its power, and lower its prestige; and (4) "organization" of workers and peasants into revolutionary groups. The program also made note of the necessity of gaining the sympathy and cooperation of non-Armenians like Kurds and Assyrians in the Armenian revolutionary struggle against a common oppressor.[55]

Therefore, the Hchakist program included within it aspects of nationalism, socialism, and populism. The immediate goal was nationalist, the future goal was socialist, and the means to achieve both was populist. This contradiction or dichotomy of nationalism and socialism brings to light the complexity of the Armenian situation and the Armenian revolutionary movement. The debate over the appropriateness of a socialist agenda for the Ottoman Armenian provinces took into consideration the degree of economic development of the region and the position of the majority Armenian peasantry. For many Armenian intellectuals, the absence of industrial capitalism and a vital urban proletariat precluded a socialist revolution and socialist economic structure. They instead envisioned a liberal political revolution modeled after western European revolutions. For others who had been more active in the Russian revolutionary movement and were greatly motivated by Marxists in Western Europe and Russia, a socialist program assumed priority. They too, however, had to take into account the economic development of Ottoman Armenian provinces, and in doing so, socialism took a backseat in the Hnchakist, and especially Dashnakist, program.

Despite its secondary importance to nationalist aims, socialism remained very appealing for Russian Armenian intellectuals for several reasons. At the same time as Russian Marxist and Georgian Menshevik influence increased in the Caucasus especially in the 1890s, Armenians faced growing Russian and Georgian anti-Armenian sentiment and prejudice that may have forced them to reevaluate their place in Caucasian society and espouse a future socialist society that suggested, at the very least, harmonious coexistence. The appeal of socialism to Armenian nationalists may have been further reinforced by the decline of European interest in the Armenian Question after the 1880s and the subsequent disenchantment to some degree with European moderate liberal nationalism and the realization for the need for a more radical socialist ideology. Moreover, the popularity of socialism was, in large part, due to the perceived political, cultural, and economic freedom that its Armenian adherents envisioned.[56] To them a socialist society promised deliverance from foreign rule and oppression, first Ottoman, then Russian. No matter how strong the appeal, socialism continued to serve, as Suny asserts, as a "rhetorical cover behind which the national struggle was fought."[57]

This was especially applicable for the Dashnaktsutiun (Federation), which came to the fore in an attempt to bring together the different elements in the Armenian community—Armenian revolutionaries, including members of the Hnchakian party, Narodnaya Volya, and liberal nationalists—under the authority of one political party. The majority of those present at the meetings in Tiflis advocated liberal nationalism and a minority espoused socialism, and thus the national question took precedence over the social one. In the spirit of compromise, the representative of the Hnchakian party, Khanazatian, accepted the outcome with the explicit promise from his Tiflis comrades that the umbrella party would be socialist in principle, if not in name.[58] Hay Heghapokhakanneri Dashnaktsutiun (Federation of Armenian Revolutionaries) was founded in 1890 in Tiflis by three Russian Armenians: Kristapor Mikayelian (1859–1905), Rostom (Stepan Zorian, 1867–1919), and Simon Zavarian (1866–1913). All had received their secondary education in Tiflis, had been students at the Moscow Institute of Agronomy, and had been in Russian socialist circles. Mikayelian had even been a member of Narodnaya Volya.

The union did not last long, as the Hnchakian party split from the *Hay Heghapokhakanneri Dashnaktsutiun* in 1891 and this party was renamed the *Hay Heghapokhakan Dashnaktsutiun* (Armenian Revolutionary Federation). The Dashnaktsutiun did not have a program until 1892, although a Manifesto published after the conclusion of the Tiflis meetings called for the undefined notion of "political and economic freedom of Ottoman Armenia."[59] The program was the result of the First General Congress of the party held in Tiflis in 1892 on the behest of Dashnakists in Iran, specifically the Tabriz branch of the party, which saw the need for clarification of party goals and strategy.[60] It began with a discussion of the pattern of history as the political and economic domination and exploitation of one class over another and more specifically the situation of Armenians as an exploited class under Ottoman rule. It also recognized the complicity of the Armenian bourgeoisie in the exploitation of the majority of the Armenians as well as the inclusion of non-Armenians among the exploited. In addition, it foresaw the overthrow of the bourgeoisie by the proletariat. While the writers of the program refrained from using the word "socialist," the language used and the principles espoused were clearly socialist.

The program, like the Manifesto, called for the "political and economic freedom of Armenia" but, unlike the Manifesto, provided specific demands and tactics that help one to understand this rather vague notion. The demands incorporated a variety of political and social reforms, including a popular democratic government, elections, and freedoms of speech, press, and assembly. The party did not advance the independence or separation of Ottoman Armenian provinces from the Ottoman Empire, unlike the Hnchakian party.[61] The reforms would be achieved through revolution against the Ottoman government. To that end, the party would (1) propagandize the party's principles and the idea of revolution, (2) organize fighting groups, (3) arm and protect the people, and (4) terrorize government officials and establishments, traitors, and "all kinds of exploiters." Furthermore, the Dashnaktsutiun, like the Hnchakian party, also advocated collaboration with non-Armenian subjects of the Ottoman Empire, specifically Kurds, Assyrians, Yezdis, and Turks, and like the Hnchakian party failed to act on it in any effective or lasting way.[62]

The platforms and tactics of both parties went through some minor and major changes in the early twentieth century as the debate over socialism continued. A new issue also arose as Armenian revolutionaries and intellectuals debated over the inclusion of the Caucasus as a locus for revolutionary struggle. Both these issues caused internal opposition and splits within both Hnchakists and Dashnakists. From the inception of the two parties, members had concentrated on the immediate goal of physical security, freedom of culture, education, and religion for Ottoman Armenians. In a sense, most Armenian nationalists and socialists sought the reforms promised in the Berlin Congress and some form of autonomy for the Ottoman Armenian community. In general, most felt unprepared for independence and must have taken into account the dispersion of the Armenian community even within eastern Anatolia, where they did not make up a majority. Only the Hnchakian party called for separation from the Ottoman Empire, but even it could not fully agree on tactics. At no time did either party achieve complete theoretical or ideological agreement with each other or within its own membership.

In 1896, the Hnchakists split over the issue of political struggle in the Caucasus. The Reformed (Verakazmial) faction retained the nationalist program, opposed socialism, and drew its membership mainly from the Ottoman Empire and the United States. The Hnchakist Center, which included mostly Caucasian intellectuals, preserved its socialist aims. Although the party was officially reunified in 1902, it continued to have two programs, one stressing a class struggle exclusively in the Russian Empire and the other choosing to fight battles both in the Caucasus and the Ottoman Empire. In 1905, the party reaffirmed its goal to carry on a class struggle in the Caucasus with other social democratic groups without abandoning the Ottoman Armenian cause.[63] In 1906, the Dashnaktsutiun split over a similar disagreement regarding involvement in the Caucasus and the appropriateness of socialism, but the conflict was resolved in 1907 when the party congress accepted the inclusion of both socialism and a struggle in the Caucasus.

It is important to note that the movement itself did not have the support of the bourgeoisie, which as the "exploiter" class profited from its position in the cosmopolitan cities of the Ottoman and Russian Empires.[64] Perhaps because of the Armenian bourgeoisie's refusal to participate in or to contribute to the effort, the Armenian revolutionary movement claimed to express the aspirations of the lower classes and became more radical and more socialist as it developed primarily under the influence of Russian socialist intellectuals.[65] Furthermore, the adoption of both nationalist and socialist ideals by the Dashnaktsutiun and Hnchakian parties made apparent two very strong currents among Armenian intellectuals and activists. These ideologies continued to exist side by side even within the same programs, despite the contradiction between nationalism and socialist internationalism.

Notes

1. For a discussion of the Patriarchate, see Kevork B. Bardakjian, "The Rise of the Armenian Patriarchate of Constantinople," in *Christian and Jews in the Ottoman Empire: The Functioning of a Plural Society*, vol. 1: *The Central Lands*, ed. Benjamin Braude and Bernard Lewis (New York: Holmes & Meier Publishers, Inc., 1982), 89–100.

2. Vahe A. Sarafian, "Turkish Armenia and Expatriate Population Statistics," *Armenian Review* 9, 3 (Autumn 1956): 119. See also Sarkis Atamian, *The Armenian Community: The Historical Development of Social and Ideological Conflict* (New York: Philosophical Library, 1955), 43–44; Patriarchat Arménien de Constantinople, *Population arménienne de la Turquie avant la guerre* (Paris: Imprimerie H. Turabian, 1920); Malachia Ormanian [Patriarch of Constantinople, 1896–1908], *L'Église arménienne: son histoire, sa doctrine, son régime, sa discipline, sa liturgie, sa littérature, son présent* (Paris: Ernest Leroux, 1910), 181–89. Ormanian's manuscript was first published in French, then translated into Armenian in 1911, and then into English in 1955. See also H. F. B. Lynch, *Armenia: Travel and Studies*, vol. 2, *The Turkish Provinces* (1901; reprint, New York: Armenian Prelacy, 1990), 427–28. Lynch estimates a more conservative number of 1.5 million Ottoman Armenian subjects.

3. Lynch, *Armenia*, 2: 427. Ernest Chantre, *Recherches anthropologiques dans l'Asie occidentale. Mission scientifique en Transcaucasie, Asie Mineure, et Syrie* (Lyon, 1895), 11–12. See also Sarafian, "Expatriate Population Statistics," 119.

4. Sarafian, "Expatriate Population Statistics," 120.

5. For figures as well as the debate surrounding Ottoman Armenian population statistics, see Levon Marashlian, *Politics and Demography: Armenians, Turks, and Kurds in the Ottoman Empire* (Cambridge, MA: The Zoryan Institute, 1991), 36–37, 58. See also Kemal H. Karpat, *Ottoman Population, 1830–1914: Demographic and Social Characteristics* (Madison: University of Wisconsin Press, 1985), 16, 148; Justin McCarthy, *Muslims and Minorities: The Population of Ottoman Anatolia and the End of the Empire* (New York: New York University Press, 1983), 31, 112; Stephan Astourian, review of *Ottoman Population, 1830–1914: Demographic and Social Characteristics* by Kemal H. Karpat (Madison: University of Wisconsin Press, 1985), *Jusūr* 2 (1986): 123–26.

6. Georgians made up 25 percent and Muslims 45 percent of the total population. See Richard G. Hovannisian, *Armenia on the Road to Independence, 1918* (Berkeley and Los Angeles: University of California Press, 1967), 13. See also Vartan Gregorian, "The Impact of Russia on the Armenians and Armenia," in *Russia and Asia: Essays on the Influence of Russia and the Asian Peoples*, ed. Wayne S. Vucinich (Stanford: Hoover Institution Press, 1972), 190; Lynch, although using the same census of 1886, asserts that the Armenians made up nearly one quarter

of the Caucasian population, numbering 962,426 out of 4,186,000. Lynch, *Armenia*, 1: 447–48.

7. Vahe A. Sarafian, "The Problem of Caucasian Population Statistics Under Tsarist and Soviet Rule," *Armenian Review* 23 (September 1953): 111–12.

8. Hovannisian, *Road to Independence*, 8.

9. See chapter 2, note 24.

10. Ronald Grigor Suny, "Armenia and Its Rulers," in *Looking Toward Ararat: Armenia in Modern History*, ed. Ronald Grigor Suny (Bloomington and Indianapolis: Indiana University Press, 1993), 20.

11. For a more detailed discussion, see Kevork A. Sarafian, *History of Education in Armenia* (La Verne, CA: 1930); Archag Tchobanian, *Victor Hugo, Chateaubriand, et Lamartine dans la littérature arménienne* (Paris: Librairie Ernest Leroux, 1953); and, James Etmekjian, *The French Influence on the Western Armenian Renaissance, 1843–1915* (New York: Twayne, 1964).

12. For a discussion of the *amiras*, see Hagop Barsoumian, "The Dual Role of the Armenian *Amira* Class Within the Ottoman Government and the Armenian *Millet* (1750–1850)," Braude and Lewis, eds., *Christian and Jews*, 1: 171–84; Sarukhan, *Haykakan khndiren yev azgayin sahmanadrutiune Turkiayum, 1860–1910* [The Armenian Question and the National Constitution in Turkey, 1860–1910] (Tiflis, 1912), 5–10. For a discussion of the economic role of the *amira* class, see Hagop Barsoumian, "Economic Role of the Armenian Amira Class in the Ottoman Empire," *Armenian Review* 31, 3 (March 1979): 310–16. For a discussion of the constitution, see M. Herardian, *Azgayin sahmanadrutiun* [National Constitution] (Antilias, Lebanon: Tparan Katoghikosutian Hayots Metsi Tann Kilikioy, 1959); Vartan Artinian, "A Study of the Historical Development of the Armenian Constitutional System in the Ottoman Empire," Ph.D. dissertation (Brandeis University, 1970). For an English translation of the Armenian National Constitution, see Lynch, *Armenia*, 2: 445–67.

13. See V[ardan] A[ram] Parsamyan, *Hay zhoghovrdi patmutiun (1801–1917)* [History of the Armenian people (1890–1917)] (Yerevan: Luys, 1967), 3: 236. See also Anahide Ter Minassian, "The Role of the Armenian Community in the Foundation and Development of the Socialist Movement in the Ottoman Empire and Turkey: 1876–1923," in *Socialism and Nationalism in the Ottoman Empire, 1876–1923*, ed. Mete Tunçay and Erik Jan Zürcher (London: British Academic Press, 1994), 116–17; Enver Ziya Karal, "Non-Muslim Representatives in the First Constitutional Assembly, 1876–1877," in Braude and Lewis, eds., *Christian and Jews*, 1: 391.

14. Louise Nalbandian, *The Armenian Revolutionary Movement: The Development of Armenian Political Parties Through the Nineteenth Century* (Berkeley and Los Angeles: University of California Press, 1963), 48.

15. Suny, "Armenia and Its Rulers," 22.

16. During the period from 1885 to 1917, there were more than 500 periodicals. See Garegin Levonyan, comp., *Hayots parberakan mamule: liakatar tsutsak hay Iragrutyanskzbits minjev mer orere (1794–1934)* [The Armenian periodical press: complete list from the beginning of Armenian journalism to our days (1794–1934)] (Yerevan: Hratarakutyun Melkonyan Fondi, 1934).

17. For a study of the history of the Armenian vernacular, see S. A. Galstyan, *Aknarkner ashkharhabari patmutyan (1850–1860-akan tvakanner)* [Glances at the his-

tory of the vernacular (1850–1860s)] (Yerevan: Haykakan SSR Gitutiunneri Akademia, 1963).

18. Bernard Lewis, *The Emergence of Modern Turkey* (1961; 2d ed., Oxford: Oxford University Press, 1968), 107; Roderic H. Davison, *Reform in the Ottoman Empire, 1856–1876* (Princeton: Princeton University Press, 1963), 40–43.

19. Lewis, *Emergence of Modern Turkey*, 116.

20. Thomas Xavier Bianchi, *Khaththy Humaïoun, ou charter impériale ottomane du 18 février 1856, en français et en turc* (Paris, 1856), 12 n. 1, cited in Davison, *Reform*, 55–56.

21. Ibid., 57–58.

22. Lewis, *Emergence of Modern Turkey*, 164–69.

23. Richard G. Hovannisian, "The Historical Dimensions of the Armenian Question, 1878–1923," in *The Armenian Genocide in Perspective*, edited by Richard G. Hovannisian (New Brunswick and London: Transaction Publishers, 1986), 22.

24. Leo [A. Babakhanian], *Hayots hartsi vaveragrere* [Documents of the Armenian Question] (Tiflis, 1915), 56–58, 113–33; Gabriel Lazian, *Hayastan yev hay date (vaveragrer)* [Armenia and the Armenian question (documents)] (Cairo: Husaber, 1946), 86–88; and A. O. Sarkissian, *History of the Armenian Question to 1885* (Urbana: University of Illinois Press, 1938), 89–90.

25. Hovannisian, "Historical Dimensions," 24.

26. Nalbandian, *Armenian Revolutionary Movement*, 84–85.

27. For the program of the Armenakan party, see Artak Darbinian, *Hay azatagrakan sharzhman oreren (husher 1890 en 1940)* [From the days of the Armenian liberation movement (memoirs 1890 to 1940)] (Paris: Araks Topalian Brothers, 1947), 125–28. For a more detailed discussion of the Armenakan party, see Nalbandian, *Armenian Revolutionary Movement*, 90–103.

28. Nalbandian, *Armenian Revolutionary Movement*, 56–57.

29. Ronald Grigor Suny, "The Armenian Patriotic Intelligentsia in Russia," in Suny, *Armenia in Modern History*, 58–59.

30. According to one source Armenians in Baku made up 25–29 percent of the working class, Russians 18–20 percent, Caucasian Muslims 12–13 percent, Iranians 19–21 percent. See Anaide Ter Minassian, *Nationalism and Socialism in the Armenian Revolutionary Movement (1887–1912)*, trans. from the French by A. M. Berrett (Cambridge, MA: The Zoryan Institute, 1984), 25. For the French original, see Anahide Ter Minassian, "Nationalisme et socialisme dans le mouvement révolutionnaire Arménien," *La Question arménienne* (Roquevaire: Editions Parenthèses, 1983). Ter Minassian's source is Peter I. Lyaschenko, *History of the National Economy of Russia to the 1917 Revolution*, trans. L. M. Herman (New York: Macmillan, 1949), 631. According to Audrey Altstadt, in 1903, out of a population of about 155,876 in Baku, 26,151 (almost 17 percent) were Armenians; 44,257 (almost 28.5 percent) were Caucasian Muslims; 11,132 (more than 7 percent) were Iranian citizens; and 56,955 (about 36.5 percent) were Russians. See Audrey L. Altstadt, *The Azerbaijani Turks: Power and Identity Under Russian Rule* (Stanford: Hoover Institution Press, 1992), 32 table 3.2. Altstadt's source is *Perepis' naseleniia gor. Baku, 1903* [Population census of the city of Baku] (Baku: Kaspii, 1905). It must be noted that these figures are not meant to express exact numbers but are approximate figures.

31. Suny, "Armenia and Its Rulers," 18–21.

32. Gregorian, "Impact of Russia," 186–88. For Tiflis, see also Ronald G. Suny, *The Making of the Georgian Nation* (1988; 2d ed., Bloomington and Indianapolis: Indiana University Press, 1994), 118.

33. Gregorian, "Impact of Russia," 189.

34. Suny, *Georgian Nation*, 92–94.

35. Ibid., 87–88.

36. Ibid., 115.

37. Ibid., 116, 118. See also Gregorian, "Impact of Russia," 190.

38. Suny, *Georgian Nation*, 143.

39. Ronald Suny points out that while the services of the Armenian bourgeoisie was valued by the Russian government, they were still treated with distrust and disdain. He compares Russian images of Armenians to those of Jews. See his "Images of Armenians in the Russian Empire," in Suny, *Armenian in Modern History*, 31–51.

40. Gregorian, "Impact of Russia," 180.

41. Suny, "Images of the Armenians," 46.

42. Ibid., 47.

43. Gregorian, "Impact of Russia," 197.

44. Ibid., 195–96.

45. Suny, "The Emergence of the Armenian Patriotic Intelligentsia in Russia," in Suny, *Armenia in Modern History*, 58. According to Gregorian, the founding of the Nersisian Academy is 1825. See Gregorian, "Impact of Russia," 198–99.

46. Suny, "Armenia and Its Rulers," 22–23.

47. Ronald Grigor Suny, "Populism, Nationalism, and Marxism among Russia's Armenians," in Suny, *Armenia in Modern History*, 64.

48. Ibid., 67–68. For a discussion of socialism and the workings of Armenian political parties in the Ottoman Empire, see Ter Minassian, "Role of the Armenian Community."

49. Suny, "Populism, Nationalism, and Marxism," 69. See also Ronald Grigor Suny, *Armenia in the Twentieth Century* (Chico, CA: Scholars Press, 1983), 5, 10–12; Ter Minassian, *Nationalism and Socialism*, 15. For an account of a cofounder of the Dashnaktsutiun regarding his activities with the populists, see K[ristapor] Mikayelian, "Bekorner im husherits," *Hayrenik Amsagir* 2, 10 (August 1924): 54–62. He mentions the formation of a Tiflis Narodnaya Volya group, in the 1880s, composed of three Armenians and three Georgians, of whom one was a Georgian woman and the other an Armenian woman.

50. Suny, "Populism, Nationalism, and Marxism," 73.

51. Much of the information about the Hnchakian party comes from a series of articles by one of its founders, Ruben Khan-Azat, "Hay heghapokhakani husherits" [Memoirs of an Armenian revolutionary], *Hayrenik Amsagir* 5, 8 (June 1927) to 7, 7 (May 1929), and especially 5, 9 (July 1927): 55. For secondary sources on the party, see, for example, Leo [A. Babakhanian], *Tiurkahay heghapokhutian gaghaparabanutiune* [The ideology of the Turkish Armenian revolution], vol. 1 (Paris: Pahri, 1934); Hrand Gangruni, *Hay heghapokhutiune osmanian brnatirutian dem (1890–1910)* [The Armenian revolution against Ottoman oppression (1890–1910)] (Beirut: n.p., 1973); Arsen Kitur, *Patmutiun S. D. Hnchakian Kusaktsutian*

(1887–1962) [History of the S. D. Hnchakian Party (1887–1962)], 2 vols. (Beirut: Shirak, 1962).

52. Nalbandian, *Armenian Revolutionary Movement*, 208 n. 14.

53. Ibid., 105.

54. From Nalbandian's interview with Mushegh Seropian. Ibid., 113.

55. The program was first published in *Hnchak*, 11–12 (October–November 1888). For the text of the program, see also Kitur, *Patmutiun*, 1: 32–37.

56. See, for example, the introductory pages to the Dashnaktsutiun Program of 1892, S[imon] Vratsian, ed., *Divan H. H. Dashnaktsutian* [Records of the A. R. Federation], (Boston: H. H. D. Amerikian Komite, 1934), 1: 96–100.

57. Ronald Grigor Suny, "Labor and Socialism Among Armenians in Transcaucasia," in Suny, *Armenia in Modern History*, 93.

58. Khan-Azat, "Hay heghapokhakani husherits," 6, 2 (December 1927): 121–23.

59. "H. H. Dashnaktsutian manifeste" [The Manifesto of the A. R. Federation], in Vratsian, *Divan*, 88–89.

60. "Hraver arajin endhanur zhoghovi hay heghapokannerin" [Invitation to the First General Congress of Armenian revolutionaries], in Vratsian, *Divan*, 95.

61. This view is further elaborated by articles that appeared in the Dashnakist organ, written by the founders of the party. See "Ayb u Ben" [A and B], *Droshak*, no. 5, November 1893; no. 6, January 1894; no. 7, March 1894; no. 8, May 1894.

62. See 1892 program in Vratsian, *Divan*, 95–102.

63. Kitur, 1: 292–93. For a more detailed discussion of the division see Nalbandian, *Armenian Revolutionary Movement*, 128–31. See also documents 1, 9, 12, 15, 20, 22, *Nork* 2 (January–March 1923): 281–84, 292–94, 297–99, 301–5, 309–10, 310–14.

64. See, for example, Ter Minassian, *Nationalism and Socialism*, 20–21; Suny, *Armenia in the Twentieth Century*, 7.

65. The Armenian bourgeoisie were often the target of revolutionaries who used terrorism to extract money for the movement—a form of forced tax collection.

2

The Iranian
Armenian Community

A study of the Iranian Armenian community of the late nineteenth century demonstrates a period of transformation, especially in the areas of education and political activity, for a significant segment of the population. The rising educational level and political consciousness of this centuries-old community, which was influenced by Caucasian developments and contact, helped provide the basis for its participation in the Iranian Constitutional Revolution.

The presence of Armenians in Iran dates back as far as the Achaemenid period (559–330 B.C.E.), but little information exists regarding an ancient Armenian community. One cannot speak of an Iranian Armenian community with extensive knowledge or evidence until the early seventeenth century when Safavi ruler Shah 'Abbas I (1587–1629) forced tens of thousands of Armenians to migrate from Ottoman and Russian Armenian regions like Yerevan, Kars, and Nakhijevan to the Iranian provinces, especially but not exclusively to the capital, Isfahan. Armenian chroniclers writing about the period before this forced migration, specifically the twelfth to fifteenth centuries, concentrate mostly on the previous forced migrations of Armenians during the Seljuk and Mongol advances (eleventh to thirteenth centuries) into Iran and rarely deal with the settled communities.[1] European traveller accounts for the period provide some valuable information, pointing to settled Armenian communities in the Azerbaijan province in northwestern Iran.[2] A greater body of literature has been written on the Iranian Armenians of the sixteenth to nineteenth centuries, especially the New Julfa community of Isfahan.[3] Primary and secondary sources on the nineteenth-century Iranian Armenian community cover a variety of subject matters, including the social and economic situation of Iranian Armenians in the different provinces, their population numbers, the development of secular education for boys and girls, the press, theater, women's charitable organizations, and the establishment and activity of Armenian political party branches on Iranian soil, all of which will be discussed in this chapter in order to help explain the foundations on which participation by Armenians in the Iranian Constitutional Revolution was based.[4] Although Caucasian Armenians played a leading role among Armenian participants, their activism was made possible only by the existence of an Armenian community within Iran, with schools, churches, reading rooms/libraries, press, and social and political organizations. Moreover, Caucasian Armenians greatly influenced the development of the Armenian community in the nineteenth century through personal contact as teachers and political activists. Therefore, by the late nineteenth century an educated and politicized segment of Iranian Armenians began to form, especially in Azerbaijan because of its close proximity to the Caucasus, which facilitated and supported political activity in collaboration with Iranian constitutionalists and revolutionaries.

Armenians in Iran Before the Nineteenth Century

Armenians voluntarily and forcibly migrated to Iran centuries before the Safavis came to power. They settled most often in Azerbaijan. The reasons for migration varied. While some fled war and its consequences, others were relocated for military and strategic considerations. Others, like merchants, sought economic opportunities in Iran and left freely while many more were resettled to help build or revive local economies. In the fourth century C.E., Sasanian King Shahpur II forced thousands of Armenians into Iran. It is very likely that most, if not all, assimilated throughout the years. Centuries later, Seljuk leaders like Tughril Bey and Alp Arslan settled an unspecified number of Armenians in large part in Azerbaijan and Isfahan in the second half of the eleventh century.[5] Armenian colonies grew in size and number during the Mongol period, when Armenians settled in Iran voluntarily as well as forcibly, creating new colonies and adding to existing ones. Many Armenian merchants were drawn to the trade routes that crossed Tabriz.[6] Therefore, it is not surprising that Marco Polo, traveling in the 1270s, came across Armenians in Tabriz.[7] Regions like Maku, Khoy, Salmas, Urumieh, and Qarahdagh and their Armenian populations came under the control of Timur Leng (Tamerlane, 1370–1405), who had conquered Iran and Anatolia by the fifteenth century.[8] From the eleventh to the fourteenth centuries, Armenian settlements existed in Tabriz, Maragha, Rasht, and Sultaniyeh. In the mid-sixteenth century, because of the harsh conditions and famine created by the Jalali revolt in the Ottoman Empire, many Armenians migrated and settled in Tabriz.[9]

The battles between the Safavis and the Ottomans during most of the sixteenth century subjected the border populations, including the Armenians, to constant plunder and devastation. According to seventeenth-century historian Arakel Davrizhetsi, these conditions and heavy taxation brought whole villages of Armenians, both notable and peasant, to Iran. They sought protection from Shah 'Abbas and asked to settle in Isfahan.[10] While the first wave of immigration to Isfahan was voluntary, those that followed were forced deportations by Shah 'Abbas of masses of Armenians from the Ararat plain. Shah 'Abbas's aim was twofold. The immediate goal was to depopulate the area before the advance of the Ottoman armies. Shah 'Abbas also had a more far-reaching plan: by resettling the Armenian population in and around his capital, he hoped to advance the country's economy, especially through the internationally connected merchant class of Julfa, the commercial center on the bank of the Araxes River. According to Vartan Gregorian, Shah 'Abbas sought to change the trade routes so that they no longer passed through the Ottoman Empire and went exclusively through Iran, thus transforming Isfahan into a significant trade center. In addition, Shah 'Abbas sought to control the silk industry through the Armenian merchants under his protection and control who, as his subjects, would compete against European merchants.[11]

The forced migrations began in 1603 and lasted until the 1620s. Shah 'Abbas ordered the deportation of tens of thousands of Armenians from areas he had captured in war against the Ottomans, like Yerevan, Kars, Nakhijevan, and Julfa. The Safavi armies under Shah 'Abbas's orders took special care of the Julfa Armenians, who were to play a major economic role once they reached Isfahan. Shah 'Abbas, while easing their travel, also destroyed the city of Julfa in order to underscore the permanence of the move.[12] While Julfa Armenians received the special assistance of Safavi forces, the rest of the deportees had to survive on their own. Many drowned while crossing the Araxes River. Those who made it across the river were forced to spend the harsh winter in the Azerbaijan countryside and more died from exposure and starvation.[13] Most of the Julfa Armenians, who had spent the winter in Tabriz, settled in Isfahan where they established the town of New Julfa. Many remained in Tabriz and surrounding areas or settled in Qazvin, Hamadan, Gilan, and other regions while tens of thousands were sent to Mazandaran.[14] The Armenians of New Julfa received special privileges from Shah 'Abbas in exchange for the services they would render the Safavi state and economy. They possessed complete religious freedom, including the right to hold public processions and ring church bells, rights that no other Christian community in Iran held. In addition, they had their own courts, judges, the right to buy and sell property, and no restrictions on clothing, again unlike other non-Muslim communities in Iran.[15] The total number of Armenians moved from Ottoman Armenian communities is unclear. Davrizhetsi estimated that 60,000 families, meaning 300,000 people, were forced to move. The French traveler Jean-Baptiste Tavernier placed the number of Armenians brought from these areas at 20,000 families (about 100,000).[16]

The New Julfa Armenian community played a significant role in the domestic and international commerce of Iran, taking advantage of its contacts within and outside the country, with ties to Europe and Russia. Furthermore, the Armenian merchants dominated the silk trade and held almost complete control over the silk and cloth market.[17] Tabriz, with its strategic position near the border of Iran and the Russian Empire, also gained a certain amount of prosperity by maintaining commercial ties between the two regions. In the seventeenth century, New Julfa became a cultural, intellectual, and religious center for Iranian Armenians, closely followed by Tabriz. The New Julfa community produced and attracted some of the finest Armenian miniature and fresco painters, like Minas Tsaghkogh, Hovhannes Mrkuz, Hakob Jughayetsi, and Bogdan Saltanov.[18] In 1633, the first school was opened; in 1636 the first press was founded by Archbishop Khachatur Kesaratsi; and in 1638, the first book, *Saghmos* (Psalms), was printed, all in New Julfa.[19]

The situation for the New Julfa community declined beginning in the last quarter of the seventeenth century under the Safavi shahs, Safi II (subsequently Soleiman, 1666–1694) and Sultan Hosein (1694–1722). Armenians encountered persecution, forced conversion, and heavy taxes in addition to a new situation whereby Armenian merchants were no longer protected against European competition.[20] The new insecurity of life and property continued into the eighteenth century as caravan routes became unsafe and merchants were more often subject to theft.[21] A combination of forces, including increased taxes, rigid enforcement of Shi'ism, weakening of the center, incompetence of later Safavi rulers, and ensuing rebellions, led to the collapse of the Safavi dynasty. Afghan invaders dealt the last blow by overtaking and destroying the capital, Isfahan, in 1722. New Julfa became the target of destruction and pillage, causing many Armenians to flee Iran.[22]

Iranian Armenian Communities in the Nineteenth and Early Twentieth Centuries

The nineteenth century, especially the last quarter, and the early twentieth century are a period of increasing secular education for a greater number of boys and the beginning of such education for girls, of rising Caucasian intellectual and revolutionary influence through the influx of Caucasian Armenian teachers and political activists who were often one and the same, and of growing politicization of a certain stratum of Armenians. Politicization came through Caucasian influence as well as through political developments in Ottoman Armenian communities, especially the pogroms of Ottoman Armenians by Sultan Abdul-Hamid II in the mid-1890s, causing many refugees to flee to Salmas and Urumieh in northwestern Iran.

In the nineteenth and early twentieth centuries Armenians were concentrated in Azerbaijan and Isfahan and under the religious jurisdiction of the Catholicos of Ejmiatsin, represented by two prelates, one heading the community in northern Iran, the other heading the communities in the central and southern regions of the country.[23] Sources indicate that the number of Armenians decreased after the Treaty of Torkmanchai that ended the war of 1826–1828 between Russia and Iran. This treaty ceded the khanates of Yerevan and Nakhijevan to Russia and permitted the emigration of Armenians from northern Iran. Sources estimate that 35,000 to 45,000 Armenians left Iran, mostly from towns in Azerbaijan and Isfahan, while peasants stayed behind, resulting in a population of more than 70,000 Armenians. If these figures are accurate, the number of Armenians in Iran before 1828 reached more than 100,000.[24]

Estimates for the number of Iranian Armenians come from the two dioceses of Azerbaijan and Isfahan, European travel accounts, and contemporary surveyors or chroniclers. Exact numbers are difficult to obtain because of the lack of an official census as well as differences in accounting. While some sources list the numbers of both households and people, others do only one or the other. In cases where only the households are taken into account, it is assumed that there were five to six persons per household. At the turn of the century, there were somewhere between 63,000 and more than 70,000 Armenians in all of Iran. About 25,000 to 34,000 Armenians lived in Azerbaijan, concentrated in the regions of Tabriz (6,000), Salmas (10,000), Urumieh (5,000 to 6,000), and Qarahdagh (4,000 to 7,000). A more or less equal number of Armenians, about 30,000, resided in central and southern Iran, mainly in the regions of Fereydan (8,000 to 10,000), Chaharmahal (2,000 to 4,000), Burvar (1,500 to 3,500), and New Julfa (3,000 to 3,800). Some demographic studies distinguish the number of women in the total population, but those numbers are always conspicuously less than those for men, since male heads of families often did not report female family members.[25]

The majority of the Iranian Armenian population were landless peasants well into the twentieth century. Generally, men and boys as young as six or seven worked in the fields while women and girls took care of the household and the animals. Women spent their evenings doing needlework. Older women spun wool and prepared threads to weave rugs in the winter.[26] In the towns, most Armenians were involved in trade with a great number of artisans working as goldsmiths, blacksmiths, gunsmiths, carpenters, and a significant number of wine makers and sellers. Armenian commercial firms in Azerbaijan and Isfahan as well as other towns played an important role in the trade between Iran, Europe, and Russia.[27] Ernest Gellner, in a discussion on diaspora nationalism, indicates that it has often been the case that minority groups have had a virtual monopoly of such "mysteries" as the forging of metals and finance, because they are "easily culturally identifiable" and "excluded from office, from the ultimate control of the tools of coercion, and from honour," and for that reason they are in a sense trusted or, at the very least, lack the power to act in opposition to state interest.[28] Iranian Armenians, as metalworkers, merchants, and bankers under Qajar rule in the nineteenth century and previously under Safavi rule correspond to Gellner's interpretation of a diaspora community. Moreover, Armenians were prohibited from working as butchers, bakers, even leather smiths, because of the proscription against Christians.[29] Interestingly, the wine trade was in the hands of women, because alcohol could not be sold openly and was therefore sold out of the home.[30] It seems, though, that not only did Armenians supply alcohol but they also consumed large amounts of it, prompting one observer to assert that alcoholism was far too common, alleging, for instance, that "the Khoy Armenian is generally a real alcoholic."[31] The predominance of women was also an aspect of the wine trade that was considered harmful by some. Connecting women's honor with national well-being, the popular novelist and nationalist Raffi (Hakob Melik-Hakobian), in his accounts of the Iranian Armenian community, declared: "The Armenian by the wine trade sells also his pride, especially because the trade is in the hands of women."[32] Women also were the chief carpet weavers in villages like Chaharmahal in Isfahan.[33]

There is little primary and secondary information on the situation of the majority of lower-class Iranian Armenian peasant women. More material is available regarding the role of urban upper middle-class and upper-class women in community service, providing for the poor, and in the case of a handful of women, taking part in revolutionary political activity.

The available information on the peasant Iranian Armenian women focuses on those in the Isfahan province, mainly the quarters of Chaharmahal and Fereydan (Peria in Armenian).[34] Iranian Armenian women as members of a religious and ethnic minority had retained their cultural distinctiveness far more than Iranian Armenian men who were much more likely to come into contact with the dominant group of Muslim Iranians. For instance, women retained their distinctive dress and head-cover well into the 1930s while men had given way and adopted the Iranian hat, *qaba* (tunic/cloak), and *shalvar* (loose pants).[35] Women's dress generally consisted of several layers of undergarments, shirts, long skirts, aprons, ornamental belts, *rial* coins in place of buttons, necklaces and other ornaments of beads and silver coins, headcovers decorated with *rials* hanging from the forehead, and mouth covers, usually in white.[36] Not surprisingly, the costumes of Iranian Armenian women resembled to a great extent those of Caucasian Armenian women in the region of Zangezur and those of Ottoman women in Van and Ardahan. In some cases, they were also very much like those of the tribal women of Lorestan and Kordestan, with some variations. In addition, the dress of Isfahan's Armenian women seemed to be much more ornamental and studded with more jewels and coins than that in Azerbaijan and the Caucasus, signifying perhaps the greater prosperity of that community.[37]

There were several categories of women's dress depending on age and marital status. For example, younger girls wore a distinct headcover; unmarried older girls did not have a nose or mouth cover while new brides covered both with a white cloth. Middle-aged women dressed more simply, in darker colors, sometimes mixed with white, and wore no ornaments, while elderly women dressed even more simply and wore a white headcover and often did not cover their nose or mouth.[38] Girls and boys were expected to marry at fifteen or sixteen in order to add to the number who could assist in the fields. Sometimes boys of eleven or twelve were married to much older girls, which resulted in "undesirable circumstances or witty and amusing anecdotes," none of which the author specifies.[39] Neither would see the other until the wedding ceremony. The new bride, whose mouth was covered, could not speak or eat in the presence of her husband's family. She could speak only through younger boys and girls who would relay messages for her. If, however, no children were present, the bride would speak with her hands or facing a wall. According to Levon Minasian, curator of New Julfa's All Saviour's Monastery museum, women's dress and behavior, including segregation during mealtime and church services, remained basically unchanged in the rural Iranian Armenian communities until the mid-twentieth century.[40] Women, therefore, did not merely physically reproduce their children, but as mothers who were the major influence in their lives, they were also the socializers of children, reproducing the culture through dress, behavior, and use of language as well as culinary and other customs.[41]

Many sources refer to the poverty of most peasants, evidenced by the short-term migration of young men to the Caucasus and to ports on the Caspian Sea in order to find work, leaving many families with very few or no males in the household.[42] While poverty was a large factor, Hassan Hakimian demonstrates that the concentration of short-term labor migrants from Azerbaijan, the Iranian province nearest the Caucasus, indicated that "the powerful drive of economic transformation in Russia" was what attracted a few hundred thousand Iranian workers, some of whom were Armenians.[43] Unlike the case with Iranian migrant workers, there are no clear estimates of the number of Armenian migrant workers; however, like the Iranian migrant workers, one may assume that their Armenian counterparts, too, returned to their communities influenced or affected by labor trends and the more politicized Caucasian Armenian community.[44] It is less difficult to get a clear picture of life in the Iranian Armenian communities, especially in the latter part of the nineteenth century and in the early twentieth century. A petition submitted in 1855 by the prelate of the Azerbaijan diocese to Naser al-Din Shah (1848–1896) sheds some light on the concerns of at least northern Iranian Armenians. The petition named fourteen grievances and called for improvements on all. Several important issues were raised in this appeal regarding missionary activity; the exploitation of peasants by landowners; the treatment of Armenians, especially girls; the state of boys' education; and the status of the Armenian Church. The diocese appealed to the shah to prohibit converts to Islam from demanding the property of their relatives, to forbid conversions of Armenians to Islam, and to ban American missionaries from preaching in Iran.[45] A plea also went out to prevent landowners from making extra demands on Armenian peasants, to free the Armenians of Tabriz and Tehran from taxation, to prevent and punish the abduction of girls, to donate 250 *tomans* to the boys' school in Tabriz, to gather the dispersed Iranian Armenians in one region, to allow the sounding of Armenian church bells, and to legalize Armenian Church properties. Although one source asserts that Naser al-Din Shah accepted all but the sounding of church bells, evidence indicates that most of the issues raised remained unresolved throughout the nineteenth century.[46]

This is especially true in the case of missionaries, whose continued presence and activity both infuriated Armenian Church and lay leaders and impelled them to act. Catholic missionaries, had begun work in Iran as early as the fourteenth century. Both the Catholic missionaries in the sixteenth century and the American Protestant missionaries in the second quarter of the nineteenth century began to work actively among Iranian Christian minorities, since Christian missionaries had almost no success among the Muslim population and were forbidden by law in most cases to work among them.[47] American Protestants first established themselves and opened a school in Urumieh in 1834 because of large Nestorian and Armenian communities. Later in the 1870s, they expanded to Tabriz, Tehran, Rasht, and Hamadan.[48] The missionary schools attracted Armenian families, in large part because they offered free Western-style education for boys and girls, the first to do so in the country, as well as instruction in the Armenian language.[49] In Urumieh, for example, the first girls' school, the Fiske Seminary, was opened in 1838.[50] By the 1890s, American

Protestant missionaries ran 147 schools with 2,666 students, the majority of whom were Armenians and Nestorians.[51] Although the Western-style Dar al-Fonun first opened its doors through the efforts of Amir Kabir (Mirza Taqi Khan) in 1851, it trained civil servants and military personnel. The traditional elementary schools, *maktabs*, dominated until the 1890s when secular Western-style elementary education began to take shape with the initiative and financial support of individuals rather than the government. The constitutional laws of 1906 and 1907 addressed free public education and gave the Ministry of Arts, subsequently the Ministry of Education, the responsibility of establishing new schools.[52]

Education

The opening of Armenian secular Western-style schools was in part a way to offset the influence of missionary schools, which attracted a large number of Armenian students and resulted in the conversion of many students to the missionaries' brand of Christianity. The author Raffi, who was also a teacher at an Armenian school from 1875 to 1877, referring to the conversion of Armenians, remarked that the work done by missionaries was a serious threat to the Armenian community.[53] Although somewhat anticlerical like many Armenian nationalists of the period, Raffi recognized the essential role of the Armenian National Church in maintaining Armenian cultural and national distinctiveness, asserting that "the Armenian, by leaving the Armenian Church, ceases to be called an Armenian," adding sarcastically, "this is the benefit given to us by the missionaries."[54] He pointed to poverty as the first cause of conversion, especially during the famine of 1871, followed closely by the apathy of local churches.[55] Yervand Frangian, also a teacher and Dashnakist activist, summed it up this way: "The existence of those schools [missionary] . . . is not only unnecessary but also harmful. It is imperative to expand the national schools and to try to neutralize the missionaries."[56]

The influence of missionaries through education and conversion was not the only reason for opening Armenian schools and expanding the education first of boys and later of girls. Another concern was the assimilation or acculturation, to a certain degree, of a segment of the Iranian Armenian community, particularly in regions like Maku, Khoy, and Urumieh where many Armenians did not form a majority and lived in "mixed" neighborhoods with Muslim Iranians, Turks, or Kurds.[57] In southern Urumieh, for example, many Armenians communicated with each other in Turkish or Kurdish rather than Armenian, although they were still recognized by their neighbors and identified themselves as Armenians because of their ties to the Armenian National Church, which in some Iranian Armenian communities delivered mass in Kurdish or Turkish.[58] The concern for these Iranian Armenian communities often came from teachers and leaders outside those districts and not necessarily from a leadership within. For instance, a group of Armenian women from Tabriz exerted great efforts in opening schools for Turkish-speaking Armenian communities in southern Urumieh.[59] Therefore, schools were opened, in some cases decades after elementary secular education made an appearance in major Armenian communities like New Julfa and Tabriz.

Clearly, schools existed in Iranian Armenian communities before the nineteenth century. Evidence indicates that the first school may have opened as early as the 1630s, and there were many schools that opened thereafter. These early schools, however, differed from those emerging in the mid-nineteenth century, because they were geared toward educating the children of priests, the wealthy, or those pursuing the priesthood, thus providing a predominantly religious education.[60] The incentive or rather the ability to raise funds and establish schools continued to come from leaders of the Armenian Church.[61] New Julfa was the first to open schools starting in 1833. As in many of the Armenian schools throughout Iran, classes were generally held in churchyards for the first few years until a building was donated by a wealthy Armenian patron.[62] Donations often came from Caucasian Armenians.

Tabriz closely followed New Julfa by establishing a boys' school in 1852. It first bore the name "Nersisian," but was renamed "Aramian" after 1875. In its first year, the Aramian school taught 60 students and by the 1890s that number had increased tenfold to 600 students in seven grades and 24 teachers, some of whom were women. The school curriculum, which differed from year to year depending on the school's finances and the availability of teachers, included Armenian, Persian, French, Russian, Armenian history, religion, geography, mathematics, and other subjects.[63] The school received the praise of Qajar monarchs Naser al-Din Shah (1848–1896), who made an annual donation of 250 *tomans* for a number of years, and Mozaffar al-Din Shah (1896–1907).[64] The school also attracted the attention of other Iranian and European dignitaries, among them Mirza Javad Khan, the head of the Tabriz royal school, and a Tabriz *mojtahed*.[65] Most teachers came from the Caucasus, especially Tiflis, but also from Ottoman Armenian provinces.[66] They included, among others, writers like Raffi, scholars like linguist Hrachia Acharian and educator and Dashnakist theoretician Nikol Aghbalian (subsequently minister of education of the Armenian Republic), also known by the pseudonym N. Hanguyts, and revolutionary activists and leaders like Dashnakist Rostom (Stepan Zorian) and Hnchakist Rafael Movsisian. Other teachers like Yervand Frangian and Hayrapet Panirian wrote about the Iranian Armenian community of which they were a part, and in doing so have left behind a wealth of information regarding the late nineteenth- and early twentieth-century community.[67] Beginning in the 1870s, dozens of schools appeared not only in the urban areas of Azerbaijan and Isfahan, but also in Tehran (1870), which had a small Armenian community in this period, and in the rural areas of Salmas, Qarahdagh, Urumieh, Hamadan, and others.[68] For the most part, schools taught only at the primary/elementary level until the late nineteenth and early twentieth centuries; a few also taught at the secondary level in New Julfa and Tabriz.[69] In addition, kindergartens began to appear in the late 1890s in large part through the efforts of Armenian women. It is difficult to approximate how many students attended the large number of schools in the different provinces of Iran, although sources do provide some figures for certain schools and academic years. Frangian has made an attempt to calculate the number of students in Azerbaijan. He estimated that at the time he was writing, circa 1904–1905, of the 700 households in Tabriz there were 800 students, thus calculating more than one student per household. In the Azerbaijan province alone, 5,000 to 6,000 boys and girls attended school.[70]

Women's Activism

Before the advent of girls' schools, only the daughters of affluent parents learned to read and write. They received their education, which consisted of Armenian and perhaps French and/or Russian in addition to needlework, sewing, and/or a musical instrument, at home. Iskuhi Hakovbiants (Hakobian), in her brief memoirs, explained her own situation as one of six daughters of Simeon Tumanian, one of the wealthiest Armenians in the Middle East and Caucasus, whose family owned several commercial houses in the region. She, along with her cousin, was taught to read by her mother. When her brother left for Lazarian College in Moscow, she began to read textbooks he had left behind. She remembered being very envious of the boys at the Aramian school, wanting very much to attend also.[71]

New Julfa had its first school for girls in 1858, soon after the first school for boys.[72] Tabriz was farther behind. Although something of a school for girls existed as early as 1868 in the form of a group of girls being taught how to read, write, and do needlework, it closed within two years.[73] The first public call for the education of Armenian girls in Tabriz appeared in 1877 in the pages of the newspaper *Mshak* (Cultivator), published in Tiflis. The champion of girls' education was Raffi, who had begun teaching in the Aramian school in 1875. In *Mshak*, Raffi criticized opposition to girls' education and attacked those who resisted attempts to establish such education.[74] He recounted a chance meeting and conversation (perhaps fictional) with a peasant Armenian girl near a spring. He asked her whether she knew how to read, to which the young girl replied: "I'm not a cleric that I should know how to read." After their parting and some deliberation, Raffi denounced such an idea:

> "I am not a priest to know how to read," she said. No, I will take this aberration out of your innocent head, poor girl, you need to read more than the cleric and the priest; you have to educate the new generation, you have to level the path to our brilliant future. You have to learn to read, then you will no longer be poor and wretched, and your children will pass their days happy and in comfort.[75]

The response given by the young girl was not uncommon as most of Iranian Armenian society, men and women alike, could not fathom the necessity of educating girls. After all, what would they do with an education?[76]

The ideas expressed by Raffi regarding the education of girls and the reasons behind his support of opening schools for girls are not unique to the Armenian case, but correspond to nationalist thought and the role of women in the nationalist process in general. Women were seen by nationalist proponents of education as symbols of national progress, and their education was encouraged and praised, because as mothers they were the reproducers and socializers of children. Transforming the Iranian Armenian community and Armenian society in general meant educating and thus transforming women to serve the Armenian people or nation better.[77] The Iranian Armenian community in Tabriz, at least, was unprepared to accept girls' education and resented Raffi's attacks, so much so that a few weeks after publication of his article, a group of about 30 men barged into a class in progress and, threatening Raffi with violence, demanded that he leave the school.[78] He left Tabriz soon after, but his stance on girls' education drew more supporters and the debate continued. In 1879, with the donation of the Tumanian family, the first girls' school opened in Tabriz with 45 students, varying in ability and age. A few years later, the Tumanians donated a new building for the Annayian school, which only a few years earlier had been Raffi's residence. The Annayian school drew the interest of then crown prince, Mozaffar al-Din, who visited the school a few years after its formation.[79] The courses throughout its years of existence included Armenian, Persian, religion, mathematics, Armenian history, geography, natural science, needlework, and others. French and Russian in general were not offered until the girls' schools joined with those of the boys.[80] The girls did not always complete school. For example, in 1881, 22 students had not returned, because they had either gotten engaged or married. But there were always new students to take their place.[81] More girls' schools opened in the late nineteenth and early twentieth centuries in both urban and rural Iranian Armenian communities, some of which joined with a boys' school and became coeducational, usually for financial reasons and not necessarily out of higher, more enlightened motives, although such aspirations also existed.[82]

A major force behind the expansion of boys' and girls' education was the Armenian women of Azerbaijan, who, like the supporters of schools for Armenian boys, felt threatened by the free missionary schools that attracted Armenian girls. Armenian women, organized into charitable organizations, went a step farther by not only helping to establish new schools but also by providing students with tuition, clothing, and school supplies. Tabriz had two women's groups in the predominantly and at times exclusively Armenian towns of Ghala and Lilava. The Lilava Women's Society (subsequently the Armenian Women's Benevolent Society), established in 1890–1891, proposed "to provide for the clothes and educational needs of the poor female students of the Lilava district's Armenian Girls' School."[83] According to the society's records, the founders were members of the wealthy strata of the Tabriz Armenian community: Shushanik Makintsian (president), Iskuhi Hakobian (Hakovbiants, treasurer), the daughter of the wealthy patron Simeon Tumanian, and Mariam Melik Sargisian (secretary), whose husband often cared for the society's expenses.[84] In its first year, the society had 32 members, including male members, whose dues, in addition to fund-raisers and individual donations, provided the society with its budget.[85] The society visited Armenian homes in Lilava in order to convince families to send their children to the Armenian schools rather than the Protestant missionary schools.[86] Through its charitable care, the society provided hundreds of girls with the opportunity to receive an education, opened several schools, including the first kindergarten in Iran (1896), and started sewing and carpet weaving schools and workshops, run by the Dashnakist activist Satenik Matinian (Tsaghik/Flower) and Srbuhi Amatuni (known simply as *mayrik*, mother).[87]

Similar organizations were founded in New Julfa in 1892, called the Armenian Women's Benevolent Society, and in the Ghala district of Tabriz in 1895, named the Azerbaijan Armenian Women's Benevolent Union. The New Julfa organization was established by senior students of the Katarinian girls' school and a male teacher to provide students with school clothes and supplies. In 1901, the organization changed its name to the New Julfa Armenian Women's Benevolent Society and adopted a broader program to spread enlightenment among New Julfa Armenians. They worked to maintain coeducational schools, help the poor with the cost of education, set up reading rooms, assist the suffering during famines, epidemics, and so forth.[88]

The more limited goal of the Azerbaijan Armenian Women's Benevolent Union was "to help in the effort for national education of poor female children and in general to spread certain necessary trades among Armenian women and girls."[89] The Lilava and Ghala organizations united in 1901 after several months of talks and named the union the Tabriz Armenian Women's United Benevolent Society.[90] Together they could boast of two kindergartens, eight schools, and three workshops. By 1904, they supported four schools and between 400 and 500 students.[91] Both societies also got involved in the relief of Armenian refugees fleeing the massacres by Sultan Abdul-Hamid. Starting in 1896, the women's organizations collected money, clothing, and wheat and at times personally saw to the distribution of the latter two.[92] Referring to the work done by Armenian women in this and other spheres, one observer wrote, "She with her good, caring, meticulous activity alleviated the pain of the wretched, softened the situation of the destitute, wiped away the tear of the unfortunate . . . and her hand went wherever her neighbors suffered."[93]

The flight of Armenian refugees to Azerbaijan, especially Salmas, in some sense opened the eyes of the Iranian Armenian community, specifically the women who took an active role in collecting and giving money and clothes, to the plight of neighboring Ottoman Armenians. At the same time, the increasing number of new Armenian schools in Iran brought teachers who were often political activists, Caucasian and Ottoman Armenians, women and men, in order to fill the demand that the Iranian Armenian community could not yet satisfy. Under the direct and indirect influence of these teachers, a new more politicized and conscious generation of Iranian Armenians began to develop. The mid- to later 1890s, therefore, became a time of intellectual, cultural, and political transformation for many in the Iranian Armenian community. This period saw, among other things, the publication of the first Armenian journals, such as *Shavigh* (Path, Tehran, 1894), whose editor was Hovhannes Khan Masehian (translator and later Majles delegate);[94] the first Armenian women allowed to have roles in a public performance;[95] and the flourishing of schools, reading rooms, and plays.

Reading rooms or libraries began to appear in the 1870s in Iranian Armenian communities, although one observer wrote that they were not utilized by many in New Julfa since most of the population still remained in "deep ignorance."[96] Frangian, referring to Salmas Armenians, expressed similar sentiments, stating that reading was a low priority.[97] Frangian also indicated that no records were kept of the number of users or the socioeconomic background of reading room visitors; however, he surmised that on the whole they were teachers and students of the Armenian schools. Although the number of frequenters is uncertain, both the reading rooms in Tabriz (Ghala and Lilava) were used 303 times in 1901. This of course does not indicate 303 visitors. The Tabriz reading rooms possessed 1,800 books by 1902, of which 500 were in a language other than Armenian. The reading rooms also received Armenian, French, and Russian journals.[98] The late nineteenth and early twentieth centuries witnessed the appearance of many reading rooms in Azerbaijan and Isfahan.[99] The Tabriz Women's Benevolent Society had its own reading room, because according to the society, "regional customs and understandings" hindered women from taking full advantage of existing reading rooms.[100]

While on the one hand many changes took place, on the other hand many things for much of the Iranian Armenian community remained the same. For example, Armenian women, in general, stayed inside the home and did not open doors to strange men in the absence of husbands, both for practical reasons and so as not to bring dishonor to the family. One observer remarked, "The woman is the honor of the house."[101] The work of women activists was made more difficult by this atmosphere, yet it became easier with the increasing education and politicization of the communities.

Primary and secondary sources, including memoirs, on the late nineteenth- and early twentieth- century Armenian community in Iran rarely mention the presence of Armenian women. Some information is available regarding the public presence or activity of women in the late nineteenth century and early twentieth century. Authors in this period often point to the progress of Armenian women in terms of education and charitable work in direct contrast to their Muslim neighbors. Women were seen by these authors as symbols of national progress and their education and public activity was encouraged and praised, because as participants in charitable organizations they were carrying out their duty to the Armenian people. This is especially true for women who actively participated in political parties.

Prerevolutionary Political Activities

Armenian political parties began activities in Iran in the late nineteenth century. "Persian soil became a mecca for revolutionaries," many of whom were Armenians from the Caucasus.[102] Many sources, some of whose authors were revolutionaries or political activists, themselves testify to the significance and number of Armenians who came down to Iran from Tiflis, Baku, and other cities and towns in the Caucasus in the late nineteenth century.[103] Since the latter half of the nineteenth century, these Armenians had been identified by the populace and referred to themselves as *fedayis*—a term borrowed from Islam meaning "those who sacrifice themselves." *Fedayis* crossed over to northwestern Iran from the Caucasus; trained in centers such as Tabriz, Salmas, and Khoy; and planned expeditions into Ottoman Armenian provinces. The three major Armenian political parties—the Armenakan party, followed by the Hnchakian party and the Dashnaktsutiun—used Iran as a launching ground for operations in Ottoman Armenian provinces. There they secretly organized small military groups, established party branches, and disseminated party ideology, all with the purpose of liberating, to one degree or another, Ottoman Armenians. They also transported arms from regions in the Russian Empire to be sent across the border to the Ottoman Empire. Arms, revolutionary literature, and *fedayis* were also transferred from Iran to Baku, especially during the Russian Revolution of 1905, and during the clashes between the Caucasian Armenians and Muslims, which began in Baku in February 1905, spreading to other areas of the Caucasus, and lasted until the spring of 1906.[104] Although the Russian Empire may have had some part in provoking the violence between the two peoples to distract them from involvement in the Russian Revolution, economic and ethno-religious rivalry caused thousands of casualties as well as considerable property loss.

Although the organs of the Dashnaktsutiun and the Hnchakian party and other journals published in Europe and the Caucasus were brought into Iran, both parties ran their own newspapers within Iran as well. For example, the Hnchakists published *Zang* (Ring, 1910–1922?, Aleksandr Ter Vardanian, editor)[105] and the Dashnakists published *Aravot* (Morning, 1909–1912, Hayrapet Panirian, editor) and *Ayg* (Dawn, 1912–1922, G. Hakobian, editor).[106]

The Dashnaktsutiun even had an arms factory in 1891 in Tabriz that was used mostly as an assembly plant. According to Dashnakist historian Mikayel Varandian, the Khariskh Zinagortsaran (Central Arms Factory) was founded by one of the first Dashnakist organizers in Tabriz, Tigran Stepanian.[107] A second source on the history of the party names Aristakes Zorian (Karo), Galust Aloyan (Toros), and Katanian (possibly a pseudonym) as the ones who established the plant while the report prepared by the Azerbaijan Vrezh (Vengeance) Central Committee and presented to the Fourth General Congress of the Dashnaktsutiun (Vienna, 1907), stated that the arms factory was set up just by Katanian(ts) and the proposal to prepare arms for transfer was made by Constantine Khatisian.[108] The report added that between 1891 and 1906, the arms factory had 36 workers. Its workers came from the Tula arms factory in Russia. Military equipment like guns and munitions was transported to Tabriz after being bought from Russian armory workers in Tula and Tiflis and stored in different Caucasian cities. After they were assembled in Tabriz, they were delivered to various points near the Ottoman border and later across that border into Ottoman territory.[109] The Dashnaktsutiun kept arms stored also in New Julfa for transfer to Ottoman Armenian provinces or to be given to *fedayis* passing through New Julfa.[110] The Monastery of Derik in Salmas served as an important refuge near the border. Especially in the 1890s, the monastery, which had been in decay for centuries, was restored by the Armenakan and Dashnaktsutiun parties and used both as sanctuary and arsenal.[111] The Menavor monastery (also known as Gaghtashen or St. Thadeus) in Maku also functioned as a bridge between Iran and the Ottoman and Russian Empires. The Dashnaktsutiun rebuilt the monastery in 1899 and operated it as a post through which arms were transferred. For example, in 1904 and 1905, 66 firearms passed through the monastery across the Ottoman border, usually through the Salmas-Bashkal-Sham route or in some cases through the Khoy-Qotur line.[112] Many of the *fedayis*, like Zulumat (Pasetsi Hovhannes), who later took part in the Iranian revolution were stationed at the monastery. Zulumat was a native of Istanbul who arrived in Iran in 1905, fought in the Tabriz resistance in 1908 as well as in later battles, and was killed near Khoy in 1911.

In addition to firearms, Dashnakists transported newspapers, pamphlets, and other literature. For example, in 1905, 7,000 copies of *Droshak* were carried into Ottoman Armenian provinces and the Caucasus.[113] Although activities in the monastery continued fairly smoothly for the years 1899–1905, the Azerbaijan Dashnakist body pointed to seven to eight searches of the monastery "by request of the Turkish and Russian consuls," all carried out without incident or without serious consequence.[114] In addition to the arms factory and the monasteries, the Dashnaktsutiun kept four "houses" to accommodate the movement of *fedayis*.[115] These houses were usually occupied by several Dashnakists at a time as a place of refuge and rest for *fedayis* traveling through Iran as well as a place to store arms.[116] The Hnchakists also had such a house in Payajuk in northwestern Iran.[117]

Dashnakist and Hnchakist movement of arms and men was virtually free of any impingement from the Iranian government. However, after the Khanasor expedition, which left Salmas in July 1897, the Iranian government began to crack down on Armenian revolutionaries in Salmas and Tabriz. The Khanasor expedition consisted of a few hundred Armenian *fedayis* whose goal was to cross the Iranian-Ottoman border and avenge the killing of comrades by a Kurdish tribe led by Sharaf Bey. The expedition ended in failure, causing the death of many of the *fedayis*, although it is positively remembered in nationalist literature and Armenian collective memory for its courage and daring. According to the five-year report of the Azerbaijan Central Committee, the Ottoman

TABLE 2.1 Male and Female Membership of the Azerbaijan Central Committee by Region

Region	Male Members	Female Members	Total
Anzali	48	15	63
Ardabil	15	20	35
Khoy	104	16	120
Maku	–	–	40–50
New Julfa	–	–	80
Qarahdagh	–	–	560
Qazvin	37	12	49
Rasht	95	36	131
Salmas	38 groups	2 groups	536
Tabriz	159	42	201
Tehran	–	–	128
Urumieh	–	–	200
Others	–	–	39

SOURCES: Report of Activity in Vrezhstan, in Dasnabedian, *Niuter*, 4: 228–37; Regional Congress of Azerbaijan, Sessions 2–7, 2–8 February 1906 and session 17, 20 February 1906, in Dasnabedian, *Niuter*, 4: 240–58; Report of Minaret [Salmas] Region, 1904–1905, in Dasnabedian, *Niuter*, 4: 266–70; Report of Avarayr [Khoy] Region, 1 February 1906, in Dasnabedian, *Niuter*, 4: 270–75; Report of Shahsevan [Ardabil] and Andar [Astara] Regions, 1 February 1906, in Dasnabedian, *Niuter*, 4: 295–98.

government demanded the removal of the Salmas revolutionaries. In response, the Iranian government began the search for *fedayis* and arms in Salmas and surrounding areas. The Central Committee successfully distanced the *fedayis* from Salmas, but some were arrested in Tabriz. The pursuit of the Armenians by Iranian forces strained relations between the *fedayis* and the peasants in whose villages they sought sanctuary. Tension between the two reached its peak when the *fedayis* were asked to leave Mahlam. Dashnakist bodies resumed their activities in the winter of 1899 when calm prevailed.[118]

The Azerbaijan Central Committee of the Dashnaktsutiun boasted more than 2,000 members organized into 242 groups under its auspices in all of Iran. These groups included women members who formed about 30 percent of the total Dashnakist membership in all of Iran. Women members of each region formed on average about 24 percent of the total membership of that region: for example, 21 percent for Tabriz, 27.5 percent for Rasht, 24 percent for Anzali, and 25 percent for Qazvin. The exceptions are Khoy and Ardabil. While Khoy's female membership stands at about 13.5 percent of the total membership of that region, Ardabil's is much higher than the mean at 57 percent.[119] The table indicates that not

all regions specify the number of women and men members, and therefore no accurate estimate for other regions can be given.

There is no clear indication that the Dashnakist women members were
fedayis who took part in actual fighting; a few, however, were involved in
propaganda and the transfer of arms. In Tabriz, the Dashnaktsutiun used
the houses of two of its women members, Mariam Makarian (Maro) and
Atoyan, both of whom propagated party ideas among Armenian women.
Satenik Matinian is also frequently mentioned as one of the more active
members of the party in Tabriz and Salmas who had the respect of both
the men and women among whom she propagated.[120] Javahir Melik
Hakobian, Raffi's sister, also participated in the transfer of arms by the
Hnchakists.[121] Satenik Matinian, like most of her male counterparts, arrived from the Caucasus in the early 1890s as a teacher. Her family home
in Tiflis served as a revolutionary and intellectual center, attracting Armenian and Russian activists.[122] Matinian lived and worked in Tabriz
and Salmas both as a teacher and a revolutionary. In Tabriz, she was a
member of the principal Dashnakist body.[123] She worked among Iranian
Armenian women, propagating the ideas of the party, informing them of
the plight of Ottoman Armenians, and exhorting them to organize and
assist their fellow sisters. According to Samson, the Dashnakist leader in
Salmas, she was the driving force behind the organization of the
women's benevolent society in Tabriz.[124] Her great unfulfilled desire,
however, remained crossing the border to Ottoman Armenian provinces
along with her Dashnakist comrades. Although she made a few attempts,
both illegal and legal, she failed. Matinian remained behind the scenes,
although less than other Armenian women, always making the preparations for the expeditions of Dashnakist *fedayis* but never taking part in
them. The Tabriz and Salmas women's organizations, for instance, took
the responsibility of mending and providing the *fedayis* with clothes as
well as preparing travel essentials.[125] During a stay in the Derik
monastery in the mid-1890s, the monastery was attacked by a group of
Kurds. While the *fedayis* fought off the assault, Matinian went from one
post to the next, passing out bullets.[126] Mariam Makarian, like Matinian,
came to Iran as a teacher from Tiflis, and like her she was an active member of the Dashnakist bodies in Azerbaijan.[127] There were many more
whose names and deeds have not been recorded, who hence shall always
remain anonymous.

It is difficult to establish an estimate of the number of Hnchakists in
Iran. Their political and revolutionary activity began in the early 1890s in
Tabriz and Salmas and spread to Qazvin, Anzali, Rasht, and other areas in
northwestern Iran with the help of Tiflis, members sent by the party to es-
tablish branches in those regions.[128] In general, information regarding the
Hnchakist branches in Iran is not as extensive as the Dashnaktsutiun for a

number of reasons. While the Dashnaktsutiun has published and made public some of the records regarding the party's activities in Iran, the Hnchakian party has not. Most sources on the Hnchakian party, therefore, are limited in material and scope. Furthermore, although the Hnchakists established groups in Azerbaijan beginning in 1891, a few years earlier than the founding of the Dashnaktsutiun, their position was greatly weakened by the factional split in 1896, about the same time as the Dashnaktsutiun began forming branches in the region. Thus, although Hnchakists made a significant contribution to the Iranian Constitutional Revolution, especially in their contribution to Iranian social democracy, their efforts were nevertheless overshadowed by the leading role played by Dashnakists and perhaps because the leading Armenian figure in the Iranian Constitutional Revolution, Yeprem Khan, was a Dashnakist.

By the time the Dashnaktsutiun became involved in the Iranian Constitutional Revolution, it had gained tremendous popularity and strength, both of which had influenced its presence and activity in Iran. A number of events led to the heightening of the party's authority, specifically its activities in the years following the Russian confiscation of Armenian Church properties in June 1903. Swayed by the arguments of the governor-general of the Caucasus, Prince Grigorii Golitsyn (1896–1904), Tsar Nicholas II transferred all property of the Church of Armenia "not essential to the performance of religious services" to Russian ministries and took over jurisdiction of Armenian schools. The Dashnaktsutiun, along with other Armenian socialist organizations, including the Hnchakian party, who were known for their opposition to the church, organized mass demonstrations and targeted Russian bureaucrats with violence.[129] After the Russian government rescinded the decree in August 1905, the influence and authority of the Dashnaktsutiun increased.

The role the party played in the clashes between Caucasian Armenians and Muslims (1905–1906) had a similar effect on its prestige as the Dashnaktsutiun and to a much lesser extent the Hnchakian party took a leading role in the arming of Armenian workers and peasants and in the actual fighting.[130]

From 1903 to 1907, while the Hnchakists were facing internal disputes and splits, the Dashnakists became a hegemonic party that could claim 55 out of 60 delegates in the Congress of Armenians held in Ejmiatsin in 1906. Also, in 1907 upon joining the Second International (the European federation of socialist organizations), the Dashnaktsutiun prepared a report to the Bureau of the Socialist International in which it professed to have 165,000 militants and to have organized 20,000 workers and 67,000 peasants.[131]

From 1908 to 1912, the center for all revolutionary activity, Dashnakist and other, changed from the Caucasus to Ottoman Turkey and Iran. The severe repression of Caucasian revolutionaries and activists carried out by the president of the Russian Council of Ministers, P. A. Stolypin, resulted in many arrests and executions. Many of those revolutionaries, specifically Armenians, who were exiled or fled the Caucasus ended up in Iran, where they were able to continue their political and militant activity with relative freedom, thus adding and building on the already existing activity of Armenian political parties.[132] Some of the Dashnakists, like Keri (Arshak Gavafian, 1863–1916), who arrived during this time were instrumental in leading Armenian volunteers in the battles of the Iranian Constitutional Revolution.[133] The Muslim Iranian Social Democratic group, like the Armenian political parties, had also become very much involved in the smuggling of arms from Baku to Anzali.[134] The Tiflis committee of the Russian Social Democratic Workers Party (RSDWP) sent 135 Georgians headed by Hnchakist Sedrak Banvorian (Mirzoyan) to Iran.[135] The Georgians, like the Armenians, set up laboratories to produce explosives.[136] As Caucasian revolutionaries and Iranian workers returning from Baku spread news of Dashnakist military exploits and ties to the Second International, the prestige of the Dashnaksutiun transferred over into Azerbaijan.[137]

Another significant factor facilitated Dashnakist and Hnchakist operations in Iran. In general, relations between the two parties had always been tense since the inception of the Dashnaktsutiun, and this was no different in Iran, where strained relations sometimes became very hostile, ending in killings on both sides. An example is the wounding of the Dashnakist gunsmith Petros by Hnchakists and the subsequent vengeful killing in April 1906 of the Hnchakist Mher Manukian, Golitsyn's attacker, by the Dashnakist Zulumat, a future participant in the Iranian Constitutional Revolution.[138] In November 1906, however, the two parties held three meetings to discuss their deteriorating relationship. The main goals of the negotiations were to prevent the recurrence of "sad and painful events which have reached the degree of fratricide" and to establish harmonious relations and collaboration between the parties. After considerable and heated debate, representatives from both parties reached agreement on several issues, including the creation of a bipartisan court whose decisions would be binding.[139]

Conclusion

It is apparent that factors existed within Iran to serve as foundation for Armenian participation in the Iranian Constitutional Revolution. The Iranian Armenian community had, at the least, a history of a few hundred years. Beginning in the seventeenth century the towns of New Julfa and Tabriz became cultural and intellectual centers for the Iranian Armenian community. But more importantly, beginning in the mid-nineteenth century, the Iranian Armenian communities throughout Azerbaijan and Isfahan went through a major transition in terms of education and politicization. The creation of secular schools for boys and girls, partly in response to missionary activity, allowed for the learning of a greater number of Armenians. These students were very much influenced by their teachers, who arrived in large part from the Caucasus. These Caucasian Armenian teachers not only taught courses in the school curriculum but, as intellectuals and political activists, imparted a sense of political consciousness to their students. With the aid of newly formed women's organizations in the late nineteenth century, a greater number of students from the lower socioeconomic class, especially girls, began to attend these schools, so that by the early twentieth century a segment of the Iranian Armenian community had been exposed to Caucasian intellectual and political influences. These influences also came from the influx of Caucasian members of the Armenian political parties, especially the Dashnaktsutiun and the Hnchakian parties, which began operations in Iran in the 1890s.

The popularity of these parties, especially the Dashnaktsutiun because of its Caucasian activities in the early twentieth century, spread to segments of the Iranian Armenian community. The revolutionary workings of Armenian political parties within Iran, in a sense, set the stage and prepared them for future participation in the Iranian Constitutional Revolution. Therefore, a combination of factors, mainly the existence of an Iranian Armenian community in intellectual and political transformation and the inflow of Caucasian intellectuals, political activists, and revolutionaries, laid the foundation for future action. These factors, however, were not enough in and of themselves to warrant or explain the commitment made by the Armenian parties to the Iranian Constitutional Revolution. Political, ideological, and even practical concerns were very much involved in the decision to participate, and the continually transforming Iranian Armenian community provided the necessary launching ground.

Notes

1. For information regarding the origins of Armenian colonies in Iran, see, for example, Matteos Urhayetsi [Matthew of Edessa], *Zhamanakagrutiun* [Chronology] (1898; Yerevan: Petakan Hamalsaran, 1991); Aristakes Lastiverttsi, *Patmutiun Aristakes Lastiverttsvo* [History by Aristakes Lastiverttsi] (Venice, 1901); Kirakos Gandzaketsi, *Patmutiun Hayots* [History of the Armenians] (Yerevan: Haykakan SS HA Hrat., 1961); Tovma Metsobetsi, *Patmutiun Lank-Temuray yev hajordats iurots* [History of Timur Leng and his successors] (Paris: Gortsatan I K. V. Shahnazarian, 1860).

2. For the thirteenth century see, for example, Willem van Ruysbroeck, *The Mission of Friar William of Rubruck: His Journey to the Court of the Great Khan Moengke, 1253–55* (1900; London: Hakluyt Society, 1990); Marco Polo, *The Travels*, trans. Ronald Latham (New York: Penguin Books, 1958). For the fifteenth and sixteenth centuries, see, for example, Caterino Zeno, *A Narrative of Italian Travels in Persia in the Fifteenth and Sixteenth Centuries*, trans. Charles Grey (London: Hakluyt Society, 1873). See also A. G. Abrahamyan, *Hamarot urvagits hay gaghtavaireri patmutian* [Brief outline of the history of the Armenian colonies], vol. 1 (Yerevan: Hayastan Publishing, 1967); Hovhannes Hakobyan, *Aghbyurner Hayastani yev Andrkovkasi patmutyan: ughegrutiunner* [Sources for the history of Armenia and the Caucasus: travel writings] (Yerevan: Melkonyan, 1932).

3. Arakel Davrizhetsi, *Hayots patmutiun* (Vagharshapat, 1896). Davrizhetsi was an eyewitness to some of the events that he described and wrote about between 1651 and 1662. The study was first published in 1669 when he was still living. Khachatur Jughayetsi, *Patmutiun Parsits* [History of the Persians] (Vagharshapat: Tparan Mayr Atoroy Srpoy Ejmiatsni, 1905). Jughayetsi wrote his study in the last quarter of the eighteenth century. For the Nadr Shah period, see Abraham III Kretatsi [Catholicos of Armenia], *Patmutiun hamarhot harhaji zhamanakn Nadr Shahin* [Brief history of Nadr Shah's first period] (Yerevan, 1973). Regarding New Julfa, see Harutiun Ter Hovhaniants, *Patmutiun Nor Jughayu vor Haspahan* [History of New Julfa and Isfahan],. 2 vols. (New Julfa, 1880). For a more general study of Armenian migration, see Arshak Alpoyachian, *Patmutiun hay gaghtakanutian: Hayeru tsrvume ashkharhi zanazan masere* [History of Armenian migration: the dispersion of Armenians to various parts of the world], vols. 2 and 3, pt. 1 (Cairo: Nor Astgh, 1955–1961). For a brief discussion of primary sources regarding the Armenian origins in Iran, see Abrahamyan, *Hamarot urvagits*, 1: 234–37.

4. For a discussion of Iranian Armenian women compared to other Middle Eastern religious and ethnic minority women, see Houri Berberian, "Armenian Women in Turn-of-the-Century Iran: Education and Activism," in *Iran and Beyond: Essays in Middle Eastern History in Honor of Nikki R. Keddie*, ed. Rudi Matthee and Beth Baron (Costa Mesa, CA: Mazda, 2000), 70–98.

5. See Urhayetsi, *Zhamanakagrutiun*; Lastiverttsi, *Patmutiun*.

6. Abrahamyan, *Hamarot urvagits*, 1: 239–44. See also Gandzaketsi, *Patmutiun Hayots*.

7. Marco Polo, *Travels*, 57.

8. For this period, see Metsobetsi, *Patmutiun Lank Temuray*.

9. Nazar H. Goroyiants, *Parskastani Hayere: patmakan, teghagrakan yev vijakagrakan hamarot teghekutiunner Parskastani Hayeri masin amenahin zhamanaknere minjev 1898 t.* [Persia's Armenians: brief historical, demographic, and statistical information about Persia's Armenians from the most ancient times to the year 1898] (Tehran: Modern, 1968), 51, 59; H. G. Injikyan, ed., *Merdzavor yev Mijin Arevelki yerkrner yev zhoghovurdner* [Countries and Peoples of the Near and Middle East], vol. 8, *Iran* (Yerevan: Haykakan SSH Gitutyunneri Akademia, 1975), 193–94.

10. Davrizhetsi, *Hayots patmutiun*, 16–17.

11. Vartan Gregorian, "Minorities of Isfahan: The Armenian Community of Isfahan, 1587–1722," *Armenian Studies* 7, 3–4 (Summer–Autumn 1974): 663.

12. Davrizhetsi, *Hayots patmutiun*, 40–41; Ter Hovhaniants, *Patmutiun Nor Jughayu*, 24–25. See also Alpoyachian, *Patmutiun hay gaghtakanutian*, 3, 1: 141–42.

13. Alpoyachian, *Patmutiun hay gaghtakanutian*, 3, 1: 143–44; George Bournou-tian, "The Armenian Community of Isfahan in the Seventeenth Century," *Arme-nian Review* 24, 4 (Winter 1971): 32. See also N. Falsafi, *Zandegani-ye Shah 'Abbas Avval* [The life of Shah 'Abbas the First] (Tehran, 1955), 3: 203; Edmund Herzig, "The Deportation of the Armenians in 1604–1605 and Europe's Myth of Shāh 'Abbās I," in *Persian and Islamic Studies in Honour of P. W. Avery*, ed. Charles Melville (Cambridge: University of Cambridge Centre of Middle East Studies, 1990), 59–71.

14. Ter Hovhaniants, *Patmutiun Nor Jughayu*, 30. According to Goroyiants, sources estimate 7,000–18,000 Armenians were sent to Mazandaran. See Goroyiants, *Parskastani Hayere*, 306; Bournoutian and Alpoyachian cite 30,000. See Bournoutian, "Armenian Community of Isfahan," 32; Alpoyachian, *Patmutiun hay gaghtakanutian*, 3, 1: 162. Some of the supplanted Armenian women became prostitutes. See Rudi Matthee, "Prostitutes, Courtesans, and Dancing Girls: Women Entertainers in Safavid Iran," in *Iran and Beyond: Essays in Middle Eastern History in Honor of Nikki R. Keddie*, ed. Rudi Matthee and Beth Baron (Costa Mesa, CA: Mazda, 2000), 129, 130, 132.

15. See Ter Hovhaniants, *Patmutiun Nor Jughayu*, 1: 35–48. See also J. B. Tav-ernier, *Les Six voyages de Turquie et de Perse* (1679; Paris: Librairie François Maspero, 1981), 2: 152; Gregorian, "Minorities of Isfahan," 665. According to Vazken Ghougassian's calculations, which rely heavily on Davrizhetsi, the num-ber of Armenians may have reached as high as 400,000. See Vazken Ghougassian, *The Emergence of the Armenian Diocese of New Julfa in the Seventeenth Century* (At-lanta: Scholars Press, 1998), 31.

16. Davrizhetsi, *Hayots patmutiun*, 40, 52–53; Tavernier, *Les Six voyages de Turquie et de Perse*, 2: 91. See also Alpoyachian, *Patmutiun hay gaghtakanutian*, 3, 1: 156, 159.

17. For further information on the New Julfa Armenian merchants, see Edmund Herzig, "The Armenian Merchants of New Julfa, Isfahan: A Study in Pre-Modern Asian Trade," Ph.D. dissertation, University of Manchester, 1991; Ina Baghdiantz McCabe, *The Shah's Silk for Europe's Silver: The Eurasian Trade of the Julfa Armenians in Safavid Iran and India (1530–1750)* (Atlanta: Scholars Press, 1999); Ina Baghdiantz McCabe, "Armenian Merchants of New Julfa: Some Aspects of Their International Trade in the Seventeenth Century," Ph.D. dissertation (Columbia University, 1993). See also Rudolph P. Matthee, *The Politics of Trade in Safavid Iran: Silk for Silver 1600–1730* (Cambridge: Cambridge University Press, 1999); R. Savory, *Iran Under the Safavids* (Cambridge: Cambridge University Press, 1980).

18. See Abrahamyan, *Hamarot urvagits*, 1: 262; H. L. Pahlevanyan, *Iranahay hamaynke (1941–1979)* [The Iranian Armenian Community] (Yerevan: Haykakan KhAH Gitutiunneri Akademia, 1989), 246–47.

19. For information regarding the first printing press in Iran, see W. M. Floor, "The First Printing-Press in Iran," *Zeitschrift der Deutschen Morgenländischen Gesellschaft*, 130, 2 (1980): 369–71.

20. Laurence Lockhart, *The Fall of the Safavi Dynasty and the Afghan Occupation of Persia* (Cambridge: Cambridge University Press, 1958), 32. Persecution of Jews

and Zoroastrians in this period intensified too and, unlike the Armenians, the Iranian Jews were often targets of horrible persecution and forcible conversions. See P. Raphael du Mans, *Estat de la Perse en 1660* (Paris, 1890), 49, 193–94, 274; Robin E. Waterfield, *Christians in Persia* (London, 1973), 72. See also Vera B. Moreen, "The State of Religious Minorities in Safavid Iran, 1617–61," *Journal of Near Eastern Studies* 40, 2 (April 1981): 125–27.

21. Abrahamyan, *Hamarot urvagits*, 1: 259; Gregorian, "Minorities of Isfahan," 671.

22. Abrahamyan, *Hamarot urvagits*, 1: 260; Alpoyachian, *Patmutiun hay gaghtakanutian*, 3, 1: 207; Lockhart, *Fall of the Safavi Dynasty*, 151–53.

23. A third district, Tehran, was added in the 1940s and soon after jurisdiction changed from the Catholicos of Ejmiatsin to the Catholicos of Cilicia, residing in Lebanon. See Injikyan, *Merdzavor yev Mijin Arevelki yerkrner yev zhoghovurdner*, 8: 225; A[ndre] Amurian and M. Kasheff, "Armenians of Modern Iran," *Encyclopaedia Iranica*, ed. Ehsan Yarshater (London & New York: Routledge & Kegan Paul, 1987), 478. For the establishment of the Armenian diocese in New Julfa, see Ghoughassian, *Emergence of the Armenian Diocese*.

24. Goroyiants, writing in 1898, cites Russian official figures to indicate that approximately 35,000 Armenians from Azerbaijan and Isfahan resettled in the newly acquired territories of Yerevan and Nakhijevan. See Goroyiants, *Parskastani Hayere*, 88. See also Abrahamyan, *Hamarot urvagits*, 2: 221, 224; Alpoyachian, *Patmutiun hay gaghtakanutian*, 3, 1: 220. See also articles 3 and 5 of the Torkmanchai Treaty, in G[abriel] Lazian, *Hayastan yev hay date est dashnagreru* [Armenia and the Armenian cause according to treaties] (Cairo: Husaber, 1942), 8.

25. The information has been obtained from the following sources: Abrahamyan, *Hamarot urvagits*, 2: 228–30; Ter Hovhaniants, *Patmutiun Nor Jughayu*, 1: 312–14; George N. Curzon, *Persia and the Persian Question* (1892; London: Frank Cass and Co., 1966), 1: 548. E. [Yervand] Frangian, *Atrpatakan* [Azerbaijan] (Tiflis: Hermes, 1905), 175; Goroyiants, *Parskastani Hayere*, 147–219, 304–38; Sir John Malcolm, *The History of Persia from the Most Early Period to the Present Time* (London: John Murray, 1829), 2: 374; L[evon] G. Minasian, *Patmutiun Periayi Hayeri (1606–1956)* [History of Fereydan's Armenians, 1606–1956] (Antilias, Lebanon: Tparan Katoghikosutian Hayots Metsi Tann Kilikio, 1971), 449–50, 453–55; Pahlevanyan, *Iranahay hamaynke*, 31–34; Raffi, *Parskakan patkerner* [Persian images] (Vienna: Mkhitarian, 1913), 529–30; Norayr Mamian, "Atrpatakani Hayots Teme" [Azerbaijan's Armenian Diocese], in *Raffi taregirk* [Raffi yearbook] (Tehran: Modern, 1969), 349, 410; Z. G. Hananian, "Tehrani arajin haykakan tparane yev Iranahay andranik parberakane" [Tehran's first Armenian printing press and first Iranian-Armenian periodical], in *Raffi taregirk* [Raffi yearbook] (Tehran: Modern, 1970), 278; Av[etis] Kah[ana] V. Yedgarian, *Irani Chharmahal gavare* [Iran's Chaharmahal province] (Tehran: Ani, 1963), 16; Aram Yeremian, *Spahani Peria gavare* [Isfahan's Fereydan province] (New Julfa: S. Amenaprkchian Vank, 1919), 95; Aram Yeremian, *Nor Jugha* [New Julfa] (New Julfa: S. Amenaprkchian Vank, 1919), 8; Galust, "Chanaparhordutian Parskastanum (Tavrizits depi Urmia)" [Travel in Persia (from Tabriz to Urumieh)], *Murch* [Hammer] 18, 11–12 (November–December 1906): 39. Another source places the total number of Armenians in Iran at a very improbable half million. See Abd al-Hosein Khan Sepehr, *Mer'at al-vaqaye '-e Mozaffari va yaddashtha-ye Malek al-*

Movarrekhin [Mirror of events of the Mozaffar period and memoirs of Malek al-Movarrekhin], ed. 'Abd al-Hosein Nava'i (Tehran: Zarin, 1989), 97.

26. This information is taken from Iskuhi Hakovbiants (Hakobian), who as a child spent most of her summers in Muzhambar (Mujumbar), as cited in Norayr Mamian, "Muzhambar," in *Raffi taregirk* (1969), 186.

27. Goroyiants, *Parskastani Hayere*, 130–34; Frangian, *Atrpatakan*, 185–89. See also Ter Hovhaniants, *Patmutiun Nor Jughayu*, 1: 288.

28. Ernest Gellner, *Nations and Nationalism* (Ithaca: Cornell University Press, 1983), 102–3.

29. Pahlevanyan, *Iranahay hamaynke*, 61–63; Abrahamyan, *Hamarot urvagits*, 3, 1: 233; Goroyiants, *Parskastani Hayere*, 107; Raffi, *Parskakan patkerner*, 396–97, 536, 547–49. Raffi, whose accounts of the Iranian Armenian community first appeared in the Tiflis (Tbilisi) journals *Mshak* [Cultivator] and *Pordz* [Trial] in the early and mid-1870s, points out that many of the gunsmiths often hired themselves out to the Kurds and Talish. See Raffi, *Parskakan patkerner*, 547–48; Yedkarian, *Irani Chharmahal gavare*, 46; Yeremian, *Nor Jugha*, 97–99.

30. Frangian, *Atrpatakan*, 56; Raffi, *Parskakan patkerner*, 549.

31. Frangian, *Atrpatakan*, 56.

32. Raffi, *Parskakan patkerner*, 536.

33. Yedgarian, *Irani Chharmahal gavare*, 46.

34. See, for example, Minasian, *Patmutiun Periayi Hayeri*; Yeremian, *Spahani Peria gavare*; Yedgarian, *Irani Chharmahal gavare*.

35. Minasian, *Patmutiun Periayi Hayeri*, 376; Yedgarian, *Irani Chharmahal gavare*, 158–62; Yeremian, *Spahani Peria gavare*, 122–23.

36. Minasian, *Patmutiun Periayi Hayeri*, 376–78; Yedgarian, *Irani Chharmahal gavare*, 162–67; Yeremian, *Spahani Peria gavare*, 123–26. See also Gregory Lima, *Hayuhin yev ir taraznere* [The Armenian woman and her costumes] (Tehran: International Communicators, 1974[?]), figs. 12, 14, 15, 16. Armenian and English text.

37. For pictures of the dress of Caucasian Armenian women, see Yves Ternon and J.-C. Kebabdjian, *Armenie 1900* (Paris: Editions Astrid, 1980), 73–75, 82–83; Srbui Lisitsian, *Starinnye pliaski i teatral'nye predstavleniia Armianskovo naroda* [The ancient dances and theatrical presentations of the Armenian people] (Yerevan: Izdatelstvo Akademii Nauk Armianskoi SSR, 1972), 2: figs. 78, 85, 86, 91. Lisitsian states that Iranian dress was influenced by Caucasian dress, especially from Tiflis, Georgia. See 100. For Ardahan, see, fig. 100. For Vaspurakan and Zangezur, see fig. 92; Lima, *Hayuhin yev ir taraznere*, figs. 23, 30. See also Nazik Avagyan, *Haykakan zhoghovrdakan taraze (XIV d.–XX d. skizb)* [Armenian popular dress (from the 14th century to the beginning of the 20th century)] (Yerevan: Haykakan SSH Gitutyunneri Akademia, 1983); Arakel Patrik, *Haykakan taraz: hnaguyn zhamanaknerits minjev mer orere* [Armenian costume: from ancient times to our days] (Yerevan: Sovetakan Grogh, 1983). For pictures of Iranian Armenian dress, see figs. 110, 111; Jalil Ziya'pur, *Zivarha-yi zanan-e Iran az dirbaz ta kanun* [The ornaments of the women of Iran from ancient times to the present] (Tehran: Jashn-e Farhang va Honar, 1969), 413, 414, 448, 455.

38. Minasian, *Patmutiun Periayi Hayeri*, 378–79.

39. Ibid., 383.

40. Ibid., 384–85; Yeremian, *Spahani Peria gavare*, 98–99.

41. Deniz Kandiyoti provides the example of Turkey's Kurds. See Deniz Kandiyoti, "Identity and Its Discontents: Women and the Nation," in *Colonial Discourse and Post-Colonial Theory: A Reader*, ed. Patrick Williams and Laura Chrisman (New York: Columbia University Press, 1994), 382–83.

42. Raffi, *Parskakan patkerner*, 424. Frangian contends that about 70 percent of the male population of the Salmas district were migrant workers while very few of Urumieh's male population left Iran. See Frangian, *Atrpatakan*, 74, 90, 106. This corresponds to the words in *Siyahatnameh-ye Ibrahim Bik* cited by Hakimian: "It seems as if one has entered a city of women!" See Zein al-'Abidin Maragheh'i, *Siyahatnameh-ye Ibrahim Bik* [The travel account of Ibrahim Bik] (Tehran: Sipideh, 1974), 28, as cited in Hasan Hakimian, "Wage Labor and Migration: Persian Workers in Southern Russia, 1880–1914," *International Journal of Middle Eastern Studies* 17 (1985): 457.

43. Hakimian, "Wage Labor and Migration," 444, 454.

44. See, for example, Audrey Altstadt, *The Azerbaijani Turks: Power and Identity Under Russian Rule* (Stanford: Hoover Institution Press, 1992), 32, 37; Hakimian, "Wage Labor and Migration," 445–47, 449. See also Bagratuni, "Namak Bagvits" [Letter from Baku], 16 July 1908, *Hnchak*, no. 6–7, June–July 1908.

45. There is no indication that the petition referred to forcible conversion. If that were the case, it would have most likely specified so.

46. Abrahamyan, *Hamarot urvagits*, 2: 226–27. It seems that the abduction of girls was a serious problem in many villages, as Yeremian writes that, unlike others, the villages of the Fereydan district did not practice that "custom." Here he is referring specifically to abduction of girls in a discussion on marriage. It is not clear from his discussion whether these are abductions in name only, since in some cases marriages outside the Armenian Church or family obligations, including evasion of the dowry, occurred and were frowned upon by the church or some families and therefore labeled abductions, or whether the abductions that took place were really done against the will of the girls themselves. It is also unclear whether these were abductions by Armenian Christian or Muslim males. See Yeremian, *Spahani Peria gavare*, 110.

47. Tavernier, *Les Six voyages*, 153 n. 10; Ghougassian, *Emergence of the Armenian Diocese*, 18, 127–28.

48. Reza A. Arasteh, *Education and Social Awakening in Iran, 1850–1968* (1962; 2d rev. ed., Leiden: E. J. Brill, 1969), 158–59. See also Mansour Soleimani, "The Educational Impact of American Church Missionaries on the Educational Programs of Iran (1834–1925 C.E.)." Ed.D. dissertation (University of the Pacific, 1980), 32.

49. See Goroyiants, *Parskastani Hayere*, 128.

50. Arasteh, *Education*, 159.

51. Arasteh, *Education*, 159, 164. See also Goroyiants, *Parskastani Hayere*, 128; Mamian, "Atrpatakani Hayots Teme," 371.

52. Arasteh, *Education*, 69, 73, 182. For English text of education sections of constitution, see 222–31.

53. Raffi, *Parskakan patkerner*, 501, 535.

54. Ibid., 533.

55. Ibid., 535.

56. Frangian, *Atrpatakan*, 117. For further discussion of the influence of missionary schools among Armenians, see 53–54, 95. See also Pahlevanyan, *Iranahay hamaynke*, 192–93.

57. Frangian writes that there was also a considerable amount of conversions to Islam in Khoy. See Frangian, *Atrpatakan*, 25, 52, 93.

58. Frangian, *Atrpatakan*, 93–94. See also Malkhas [Artashes Hovsepian], *Aprumner* [Life experiences] (Boston: Hayrenik, 1931), 247.

59. Pahlevanyan, *Iranahay hamaynke*, 203.

60. Minasian, *Patmutiun Periayi Hayeri*, 337–38; Pahlevanyan, *Iranahay hamaynke*, 199–200. Goroyiants, *Parskastani Hayere*, 108; Abrahamyan, *Hamarot urvagits*, 2: 239. For the seventeenth- and eighteenth-century seminary whose graduate was the seventeenth-century historian Arakel Davrizhetsi, see Mamian, "Atrpatakani Hayots Teme," 359.

61. Frangian, *Atrpatakan*, 106.

62. Yeremian, *Nor Jugha*, 51–51; Goroyiants, *Parskastani hayere*, 283–84.

63. A[leksan] Ter Vardanian, comp. *Hamarot patmutiun Tavrizi Aramian dprotsi vatsunamiaki goyutian* [Brief history of the sixty-year existence of the Tabriz Aramian school] (Tabriz: Paros, 1913), 15, 18; Hayk Achemian, *Patmutiun Aramian azgayin dprotsi: hariuramia hobeliani artiv, 1835–1935* [History of the Aramian national school: on the 100th anniversary jubilee, 1835–1935] (Tabriz: Atrpatakani Hayots Temakan Tparan, 1936), 33, 41–42, 57, 63–64; Goroyiants, *Parskastani Hayere*, 111, 116; Pahlevanyan, *Iranahay hamaynke*, 200. For Armenian schools in Tabriz, see also Hosein Omid, *Tarikh-e farhang-e Azerbaijan* [History of the culture of Azerbaijan] (Tabriz: Farhang, 1953), 1: 93–96.

64. For Naser al-Din Shah, see Achemian, *Patmutiun Aramian azgayin dprotsi*, 57; Ter Vardanian, *Hamarot patmutiun Tavrizi Aramian dprotsi*, 11; Omid, *Tarikh-e farhang-e Azerbaijan*, 93–94. For an Armenian translation of Mozaffar al-Din Shah's *fermans*, see Frangian, *Atrpatakan*, 108–9.

65. See Raffi, *Parskakan patkerner*, 512–14.

66. See Injikyan, *Merdzavor yev Mijin Arevelki yerkrner yev zhoghovurdner*, 8: 244.

67. Mamian, "Atrpatakani Hayots Teme," 361, 364, 367, 368. See Frangian, *Atrpatakan*; H[ayrapet] Panirian, *Heghapokhakan sharzhumnere Parskastanum* [Revolutionary movements in Persia] (Tabriz: Paros, 1917). See also Panirian's memoirs written in 1923 but published decades later as a series, H[ayrapet] Panirian, "Hayrapet Paniriani Husherits" [From the memoirs of Hayrapet Panirian], *Hayranik Amsagir* 30, 6 (June 1952)–31, 7 (July 1953).

68. Frangian, *Atrpatakan*, 112–14; Goroyiants, *Parskastani Hayere*, 296–97; Minasian, *Patmutiun Periayi Hayeri*, 338, 342; Pahlevanyan, *Iranahay hamaynke*, 192, 200–202.

69. Pahlevanyan, *Iranahay hamaynke*, 201, 206; Mamian, "Atrpatakani Hayots Teme," 364, 366.

70. Frangian, *Atrpatakan*, 117, 118, 122. See also Injikyan, *Merdzavor yev Mijin Arevelki yerkrner yev zhoghovurdner*, 244.

71. Iskuhi Hakovbiants, "Tavrizi hay gaghuti antsialits" [From the past of the Tabriz Armenian community], *Hayrenik Amsagir* 35, 11 (November, 1957): 91, 98; Iskuhi Hakovbiants, "Yeghbayrk Tumaniantsnere" [Tumanian brothers], *Hayrenik Amsagir* 43, 9 (September 1965): 2–3.

72. Frangian, *Atrpatakan*, 110. It joined with a boys' school in 1892 and became coed. See, Pahlevanyan, *Iranahay hamaynke*, 206.

73. Goroyiants, *Parskastani Hayere*, 117.

74. Achemian, *Patmutiun Aramian azgayin dprotsi*, 66; Pahlevanyan, *Iranahay hamaynke*, 200; Mamian, "Atrpatakani Hayots Teme," 361.

75. Raffi, *Parskakan patkerner*, 454–56.

76. Hakovbiants, "Tavrizi hay gaghuti antsialits," 92.

77. For similar discussions of women and the nationalist process, see, for example, Floya Anthias and Nira Yuval-Davis, eds., *Woman, Nation, State* (London: MacMillan, 1989); Beth Baron, "Mothers, Morality, and Nationalism in Pre-1919 Egypt," in *The Origins of Arab Nationalism*, ed. Rashid Khalidi et al. (Chicago: University of Chicago Press, 1991); Deniz Kandiyoti, "Islam, Nationalism, and Women in Turkey," in *Women, Islam, and the State*, ed. Deniz Kandiyoti (Philadelphia: Temple University Press, 1991); Deniz Kandiyoti, "Identity and Its Discontents: Women and the Nation," in *Colonial Discourse and Postcolonial Theory: A Reader*, ed. Patrick Willimas and Laura Chrisman (New York: Columbia University Press, 1994); Afsaneh Najmabadi, "Zanha-ye Millet: Women or Wives of the Nation," *Iranian Studies* 26, 1–2 (Spring 1994): 51–72; Parvin Paidar, *Women and the Political Process in Twentieth-Century Iran* (New York: Cambridge University Press, 1995); Julie Peteet, *Gender in Crisis: Women and the Palestine Resistance Movement* (New York: Columbia University Press, 1991).

78. Achemian, *Patmutiun Aramian azgayin dprotsi*, 66–69. Raffi visited the Tumanian family often and took part in heated discussions regarding a girls' school with Simeon Tumanian, a patron of the school whose six daughters attended the school once it was opened. See the memoirs of Tumanian's daughter, Hakovbiants, "Tavrizi hay gaghuti antsialits," 90, 92.

79. Hakovbiants, "Tavrizi hay gaghuti antsialits," 98.

80. Frangian, *Atrpatakan*, 196; Hakovbiants, "Tavrizi hay gaghuti antsialits," 93–94, 97. See also Goroyiants, *Parskastani Hayere*, 118.

81. Hokovbiants, "Tavrizi hay gaghuti antsialits," 95.

82. Pahlevanyan, *Iranahay hamaynke*, 200–201; Mamian, "Atrpatakani Hayots Teme," 361–62; Goroyiants, *Parskastani Hayere*, 124–25; Abrahamyan, *Hamarot urvagits*, 2: 241.

83. This society, like the Armenian schools, was praised by Mozaffar al-Din Shah and allowed to use the royal seal of the lion and sun on official correspondence and records. See Emile Hakobian, "Tavrizi hayots kanants miutiunnere," in *Divan Atrpatakani Hayots patmutian* [Records of the history of the Azerbaijan Armenians], ed. Vardan Demirchian (Tabriz: Nurbashkh, 1966), 1: 8. For the shah's *fermans*, see 1: 81–82. See also Frangian, *Atrpatakan*, 130–31; Mamian, "Atrpatakani Hayots Teme," 377.

84. From the regulations of the society, signed on 1 August 1891, compiled by Khachatur Grigorian in Tabriz, 1936, in Demirchian, *Divan*, 1: 85–86. It seems Hakovbiants began her charitable work as a young schoolgirl, when she asked her mother to increase the amount of hot food that was brought for her and her sisters so that it could be shared with those who could not bring hot meals. See Hakovbiants, "Tavrizi hay gaghuti antsialits," 96.

85. Frangian, *Atrpatakan*, 127, 130.

86. Session 6, 8 September 1891, in Demirchian, *Divan*, 1: 87. See also Samson, "Atrpatakani hay kanants gortsuneutiune" [The activity of the Armenian women of Azerbaijan], *Hayrenik Amsagir* 18, 1(205) (November 1939): 88.

87. See sessions 6–17 in Demirchian, *Divan*, 87–94. See also Frangian, *Atrpatakan*, 127, 129; Goroyiants, *Parskastani Hayere*, 126.

88. Yeremian, *Nor Jugha*, 60–62. The first women's charitable organization in Tehran, the Benevolent Society of Armenian Women, was organized in 1907. See Pahlevanyan, *Iranahay hamaynke*, 139. Another source suggests that such an organization existed as early as 1871. See Amurian, *H. H. Dashnaktsutiune Parskastanum*, 127.

89. Hakobian, "Tavrizi hayots kanants miutiunnere," 83.

90. For the full citation of the agreement signed between the two societies, see Frangian, *Atrpatakan*, 137.

91. Ibid., 141.

92. Sessions 15, 18–23, 2 October 1896, in Demirchian, *Divan*, 1: 93, 95–97.

93. Samson, "Atrpatakani hay kanants gortsuneutiune," *Hayrenik Amsagir* 18, 1 (November 1939): 103.

94. Garegin Levonyan, comp., *Hayots parberakan mamule: liakatar tsutsak hay Iragrutyan skzbits minjev mer orere (1794–1934)* [The Armenian periodical press: complete list from the beginning of Armenian journalism to our days (1794–1934)] (Yerevan: Hratarakutyun Melkonyan Fondi, 1934).

95. Frangian, *Atrpatakan*, 162.

96. Yeremian, *Nor Jugha*, 75.

97. Frangian, *Atrpatakan*, 170–71.

98. Ibid., 168–69.

99. See, for example, Frangian, *Atrpatakan*, 170–72; Yeremian, *Nor Jugha*, 75–77.

100. Frangian disagrees with the society, adding that he did not see the necessity of separate reading rooms. See Frangian, *Atrpatakan*, 170.

101. Samson, "Atrpatakani hay kanants gortsuneutiune": 86.

102. Louise Nalbandian, *The Armenian Revolutionary Movement: The Development of Armenian Political Parties Through the Nineteenth Century* (Berkeley and Los Angeles: University of California Press, 1963), 173.

103. See, for example, Malkhas, *Aprumner*. Malkhas, a member of the Dashnaktsutiun, participated in the traffic of arms and men through Iran. See also Arsen Kitur, *Patmutiun S. D. Hnchakian Kusaktsutian* [History of the S. D. Hnchakian Party] (Beirut: Shirak Press, 1962), 1: 203, 208, 209.

104. An abundance of information and detail regarding transportation of arms and literature and the traffic of *fedayis* may be found in the correspondence, reports, and minutes of Dashnakist bodies and members in the Dashnaktsutiun Archives. See also Andre Amurian, *H. H. Dashnaktsutiune Parskastanum, 1890–1918* [The A. R. Federation in Persia, 1890–1918] (Tehran: Alik, 1950), 12–13.

105. Levonyan, *Mamul*, 62.

106. S[imon] Vratsian, ed., *Hushapatum H. H. Dashnaktsutian, 1890–1950* [Memorial to the A. R. Federation] (Boston: Hayrenik, 1950), 568; Levonyan, *Mamul*, 57, 71. According to Yeprem Khan's biographer and participant in the Iranian Constitutional Revolution, Hovsep Hovhannisian (Elmar, 1881–1975), the idea behind the paper was his. The first editorial board was made up of him,

Iskuhi Aghajanian, who later became his wife, Baghdasar Melik Baghdasarian (Baghdik), Simeon Mirzayan (Bazen), and Avag Melik Vardanian. After the sixth issue, the Azerbaijan Central Committee of the Dashnaktsutiun decided to bring in to the board a few Dashnakist Lilava teachers, K. Pionian, S. Araratian, and G. Hakobian, and named Hayrapet Panirian, an Ottoman subject, as editor in order to protect the paper against possible Russian persecution. Hovhannisian states that although he did not object, he felt it would have been fairer to name him as editor. See Hovsep Hovhannisian, *Husher* [Memoirs] (Yerevan: Abolon, 1995), 213–14. Panirian gives a different picture, stating that he was one of the founders of the paper, and also asserts that non-Dashnakist social revolutionaries worked on the paper as well. See Panirian, "Hayrapet Panirian Husherits," *Hayrenik Amsagir* 30, 11 (November 1952): 50–51. Hovhannisian, who questioned Panirian's memory as well as his integrity, refuted many points in Panirian's series in an article that was published a month after the last of Panirian's series appeared in *Hayrenik Amsagir*. See H. Elmar [Hovsep Hovhannisian], "H. Paniriani Husheri Masin" [About H. Panirian's memoirs], *Hayrenik Amsagir* 31, 8 (August 1953): 77–87.

107. Mikayel Varandian, *H. H. Dashnaktsutian Patmutiun* [History of the A. R. Federation] (Cairo: Husaber Publishers, 1950), 1: 123–125.

108. Hratch Dasnabedian [Hrach Tasnapetian], *H. H. Dashnaktsutiune ir kazmutenen minjev Zh endhanur zhoghov (1890–1924)* [The A. R. Federation from its formation to the Tenth General Congress (1890–1924)] (Athens: Droshak, 1988), 199; for the English version, see Hratch Dasnabedian, *The History of the Armenian Revolutionary Federation Dashnaktsutiun (1890–1924)* (Milan: Grafiche Editoriali Ambrosiane, 1990), 186; Report on central arms factory of Vrezh [Tabriz] presented to Fourth General Congress. This piece is undated, unsigned, and unsealed, but was most probably prepared in 1906 by the Azerbaijan Central Committee as it was found among the committee's papers. It is a brief history of the factory from 1891 to 1906, and includes a list of gunsmiths, their apprentices, and the years they worked. It also mentions that by 1896, the factory had produced 600 firearms. See Dasnabedian, *Niuter*, 4: 284–87.

109. For the arms "factory," see Malkhas, *Aprumner*, 141, 331.

110. Amurian, *Dashnaktsutiune Parskastanum*, 65.

111. Varandian, *Dashnaktsutian patmutiun*, 1: 123–25. Varandian's account of the Monastery of Derik is confirmed by the memoirs of participants in and eyewitness to activities there, such as Samson (Stepan Tadeosian), Nikol Duman (Nikoghayos Ter Hovhannisian), and others. See N. Hanguyts [Nikol Aghbalian], comp., "Samsoni hushere" [Samson's memoirs], *Hayrenik Amsagir* 1, 10 (August 1923): 78–97; Hovak Stepanian, "Nikol Duman (mahvan 15-amiaki artiv)" [Nikol Duman (on the occasion of the 15th anniversary of his death)], *Hayrenik Amsagir* 8, 4 (February 1930): 79–91; Artak Darbinian, *Hay azatagrakan sharzhman oreren (husher 1890 en 1940)* [From the days of the Armenian liberation movement (memoirs 1890 to 1940)] (Paris: Araks Topalian Brothers, 1947), 391–92. Regarding Tula, see Malkhas, *Aprumner*, 162.

112. Report of Activity in Vrezhstan [Azerbaijan], 1904–1906 to the Fourth General Congress, Vienna, 1907, in Dasnabedian, *Niuter*, 4: 228–37.

113. Minutes of Azerbaijan Regional Congress, Session 3, 3 February 1906, in Dasnabedian, *Niuter*, 4: 240–58.
114. Ibid., Session 4, 4 February 1906. See also Malkhas, *Aprumner*, 146, 288–95.
115. Report of Activity in Vrezhstan, 1904–1906, in Dasnabedian, *Niuter*, 4: 228–37.
116. See, for example, Malkhas, *Aprumner*, 137, 141, 144.
117. Kitur, *Patmutiun*, 1: 208
118. Report of Five-year Activity of the Azerbaijan Central Committee, 1898–1903, in Dasnabedian, *Niuter*, 2: 137–47.
119. The information is drawn from several sources: Report of Activity in Vrezhstan, in Dasnabedian, *Niuter*, 4: 228–37; Regional Congress of Azerbaijan, Sessions 2–7, 2–8 February 1906, and session 17, 20 February 1906, in Dasnabedian, *Niuter*, 4: 240–58; Report of Minaret [Salmas] Region, 1904–1905, in Dasnabedian, *Niuter*, 4: 266–70; Report of Avarayr [Khoy] Region, 1 February 1906, in Dasnabedian, *Niuter*, 4: 270–75; Report of Shahsevan [Ardabil] and Andar [Astara] Regions, 1 February 1906, in Dasnabedian, *Niuter*, 4: 295–98.
120. See Hanguyts, "Samsoni hushere," 86. Hanguyts also relates the story of Matinian's leading role in the escape of her husband from prison. See 4 (February 1924): 138. For a further discussion of the work done by Armenian women in Azerbaijan, see Samson, "Atrpatakani hay kanants gortsuneutiune."
121. Kitur, *Patmutiun*, 1: 209.
122. Malkhas, *Aprumner*, 340.
123. Amurian, *Dashnaktsutiune Parskastanum*, 30–31.
124. Samson, "Atrpatakani hay kanants gortsuneutiune," 90.
125. Amurian, *Dashnaktsutiune Parskastanum*, 25.
126. Malkhas, *Aprumner*, 341–42; A[braham] Giulkhandanian, *Heghapokhakan Hayhuyiner* [Revolutionary Armenian women] (Paris: Araks, 1939), 56–57; Gabriel Lazian, *Hayhuyin yev hay heghapokhutiune* [The Armenian woman and the Armenian revolution] (Cairo: Husaber, 1959), 19–20; Sona Zeytlian, *Hay knoj dere hay heghapokhakan sharzhman mej* [The role of the Armenian woman in the Armenian revolutionary movement] (Antilias: Tparan Katoghikosutian Hayots, 1968), 35–41.
127. Makarian committed suicide in 1896, a few months before her fiancé, Aristakes Zorian (Karo), died after crossing the border to the Ottoman Empire. Dashnakist sources believe that Makarian's motive for killing herself was to free Zorian to pursue the revolutionary struggle. He was part of the Khanasor expedition to avenge the killings of Armenians by a Kurdish tribe. Matinian married Hovsep Arghutian (Ishkhan, Yervand), a survivor of the expedition who during the brief interlude of the Armenian Republic became envoy to Iran. See Giulkhandanian, *Heghapokhakan Hayhuyiner*, 59–60; Lazian, *Hayhuyin*, 17; Zeytlian, *Hay knoj dere*, 45–47.
128. Kitur, *Patmutiun*, 1: 200–204, 396.
129. Hnchakists wounded Golitsyn in October 1903. See Richard G. Hovannisian, *Armenia on the Road to Independence* (Berkeley, Los Angeles: University of California Press, 1967), 18–20. The Hnchakist believed to be responsible for that

attempt on Golitsyn's life, Mher Manukian, resided in Azerbaijan after the attempt until his death by a Dashnakist in April 1906. See Kitur, *Patmutiun*, 1: 397.

130. For a more detailed discussion, see chapter 3.

131. Anahide Ter Minassian, "The Revolution of 1905 in Transcaucasia," *Armenian Review*, 42, 2 (Summer 1989): 16–17, admits that these figures might be inflated but even so, Dashnakist popularity and power at the time cannot be denied. The party was, however, accused by Armenian, Russian, and Georgian Social Democrats, in 1905/1906, of stirring up racial and religious antagonisms and destroying the unity of the revolutionary movement and class consciousness. Partly as a result of this, it revised its program by increasing its socialist orientation. See 11–12. See also the party's program of 1907, in Dasnabedian, *Niuter*, 3: 315–28, also in *Droshak*, no. 5, May 1907.

132. See, for example, the testimony of Malkhas, an active Dashnakist involved in such activity. Malkhas, *Aprumner*, 137.

133. For a list of names, see Amurian, *Dashnaktsutiune Parskastanum*, 57.

134. See Mangol Bayat, *Iran's First Revolution: Shi'ism and the Constitutional Revolution of 1905–1909* (Oxford and New York: Oxford University Press, 1991), 156; Ter Minassian, "Revolution," 19.

135. Kitur, *Patmutiun*, 1: 399. For the French translation, see Cosroe Chaqueri, ed., *La Social-démocratie en Iran: articles et documents* (Florence: Mazdak, 1979), 237.

136. Ahmad Kasravi, *Tarikh-e mashruteh-ye Iran* [History of the constitution of Iran], (1951; Tehran: Amir Kabir, 1984), 2: 727. One such laboratory was located in Tabriz and was under the supervision of a Dashnakist named Gevorg Kirakosian who died while making a bomb in March 1910. The supervision of the laboratory was taken over by one of the founders of the Dashnaktsutiun, Rostom (Stepan Zorian). See Hovhannisian, *Husher*, 203–5; H. Elmar [Hovsep Hovhannisian], *Yeprem* (Tehran: Modern, 1964), 143–44; also in Hratch Dasnabedian [Hrach Tasnapetian], ed., *Rostom: mahvan vatsunamiakin artiv* [Rostom: on the occasion of the sixtieth anniversary of his death] (Beirut: Hamazgayin Vahe Setian, 1979), 268–69.

137. Anaide Ter Minassian, *Nationalism and Socialism in the Armenian Revolutionary Movement (1887–1912)*, trans. from the French by A. M. Berrett (Cambridge, MA: The Zoryan Institute, 1984), 25. For the French original, see Anahide Ter Minassian, "Nationalisme et socialisme dans le mouvement révolutionnaire Arménien," *La Question Grménienne* (Roquevaire: Editions Parenthèses, 1983), 54.

138. For two different viewpoints, see Malkhas, *Aprumner*, 494–96; Kitur, *Patmutiun*, 1: 397.

139. Negotiations were held from 14 to 16 November 1906 in Tabriz. See Minutes and Decisions of the Interparty Congress, in Dasnabedian, *Niuter*, 4: 329–32.

3

Ideological, Political, and
Pragmatic Motivations

Prior to the Constitutional Revolution, Armenian political parties such as the Hnchakian and Dashnaktsutiun used Iranian soil as a base for operations in Ottoman Armenian provinces and did not involve themselves with Iranian politics. There were several reasons why both parties, especially the Dashnaktsutiun, joined the Iranian Constitutional Revolution in 1907 and continued participation and support of the movement through its various stages. It is important to note that these reasons acted together in prompting one or both parties to arrive at such a decision. Therefore, to some extent the causes for participation were mutually dependent and each reason contained within it aspects shared by one or more of the others.[1]

Among the most important reasons Armenians participated in the Iranian Constitutional Revolution were the following:

- Ottoman aggression toward Iran and the movement of Ottoman troops beginning at the end of 1905 into northwestern Iran, which negatively affected both Armenian and Iranian populations at the Ottoman-Iranian border and the progress of the constitutional movement, thus troubling Dashnakists and Hnchakists;

- the coup of the Committee of Union and Progress and the restoration of the 1876 constitution in 1908, which prompted Hnchakists and especially Dashnakists to cease terrorist activity against the Ottoman government and to redirect to some degree their focus away from operations in Ottoman Armenian provinces to Iran;

- the perception by both Armenian parties of the revolution as a struggle against domination and exploitation by Russia, which

sought to stop the constitutional movement—a perception fueled by Russian persecution of Armenians inside Russia;

- Russian policy in the Caucasus, which forced both parties to reexamine their tactics and policy, driving them toward solidarity
with Russian opposition forces and widening their field of activity to the Caucasus;

- the reevaluation of policy, which was further influenced by the
role of Dashnakists and Hnchakists in the communal violence
between Caucasian Armenians and Muslims from 1905 to 1906,
moved both parties to question their overt nationalism and
opened the way to greater attempts at solidarity and the internationalist ideals of socialism;

- the perception and depiction of the Iranian Constitutional Revolution as a stage in the socialist struggle, which necessitated collaboration with progressive forces, namely with Caucasian and
Iranian Socialists only a year or two after horrific violence between Caucasian Armenians and Muslims;

- the banning of the Dashnakist organ *Droshak* (Banner) in July
1906 by the preconstitutional Iranian government, which caused
the Dashnaktsutiun to question its stance regarding the Iranian
government and to safeguard against the impact of government
actions on the party's operations in Iran;

- the period between December 1906 and December 1907 in Iran
highlighted by the debate over constitutional laws and the revo-
lutionization of Tabriz, which demonstrated a new Iranian political reality and new insecurity of life, causing the parties to re-
think neutrality;

- the Stolypin crackdown beginning in 1908, which forced many
political activists to flee from Russia and the Caucasus to Iran
where they embraced a new cause—the Iranian Constitutional
Revolution.

The Ottoman Empire: Peril and Hope

Ottoman Aggression

The stance and policy of the Dashnaktsutiun and Hnchakian parties toward the Ottoman Empire and the Ottoman Empire's territorial aggression toward Iran combined to form the first motivating factor for the parties to take constructive action in the Iranian Constitutional Revolution.

No greater foe existed for the Dashnaktsutiun and the Hnchakian parties than Sultan Abdul-Hamid's regime. A year after the start of the revolution, in an article that best summarizes its opposition to the Ottoman

government, the Dashnaktsutiun warned that the Ottoman Empire not only desired territory "as if to show, contrary to international principle, that Turkey, indeed, is able to expand," but also desired the failure of the establishment of a liberal government in Iran. The article stated: "We would like to hope that the Persian people, with a praiseworthy patriotism and selfless persistence, will cut through and pass this historically stormy cape, will be able to become forceful and expel the bloodthirsty Sultan's irregular troops, hired thieves, [and] will know to protect against foreign encroachment and intrigues."[2]

Ottoman aggression toward Iran had begun at the end of 1905 when Ottoman troops moved into Vezneh (southwest of Lake Urumieh) and Lahijan (southeast of Rasht, near the Caspian Sea), at the same time that antigovernment protests and sanctuary-seeking (*bast*) were taking place in Tehran.[3] Negotiations having failed between the governments of the shah and the sultan, Ottoman troops from Mosul moved toward the Iranian border in June 1906. According to scholar V. A. Bayburdyan, "From all signs, it looked as if the Ottoman armed forces had in mind to move toward strategically and economically significant Urumieh."[4] A year later, in July 1907, Ottoman troops from Van entered western Urumieh destroying villages and *anjomans* (councils) that resisted.[5] In the fall, they occupied the northwestern towns of Dashtebil and Oshnu. In the summer, they strengthened the Targavar, Dasht, and Margavar regions in Urumieh with the help of a Kurdish tribe. The Ottoman occupation caused thousands of people, especially Armenians and Assyrians, to flee toward the north and east.[6]

The Dashnaktsutiun felt threatened by Ottoman aggression into a highly Armenian-populated region, which was also the hub of Dashnakist activity and expeditions into Ottoman Armenian provinces.[7] Moreover, Dashnakists believed that Iran did not have the money, force, or diplomatic influence to stop Abdul-Hamid's forces.[8] In a session of the Azerbaijan Central Committee in Tabriz, the body considered fighting on the side of the Iranians against Ottoman forces at the border. "All the comrades agreed that as the children of the same country" faced with the same danger to the "interests of the fatherland, we are obligated to come out and fight the Turkish forces."[9] The Dashnakists even had an agreement with Assyrians to send fighters to the Iranian-Ottoman border.[10] The Hnchakists too recognized the danger of Ottoman troop maneuvers toward Iran, pointing to the prohibition of the movement of people and goods across the border. They warned against merely being observers in the goings-on at the border, for the events taking place would have impact on the Armenians and their aspirations.[11]

For the Armenian parties and communities, Ottoman troop movement into northern Iran represented an assault on two fronts—ideological and physical. On the physical plane, they confronted a real danger to life, property, and activities, while on the ideological plane, they faced a threat to aspirations and ideals espousing liberation and constitutionalism.

Young Turk Promise

The coup by the Committee of Union and Progress (İttihad ve Terakki), commonly referred to as the Young Turks, and the restoration of the Ottoman constitution of 1876 somewhat altered the deeply entrenched hostility of the Dashnakists and Hnchakists to the Ottoman regime, promising a new era of government. It also changed the focus of political and revolutionary opposition away from the new Ottoman regime.

After the Young Turk coup and the restoration of the Ottoman constitution of 1876 on 24 July 1908, warnings against the Ottoman danger in Iran no longer appeared in the Dashnakist organ *Droshak*.[12] For the Hnchakists, the danger still existed as late as 1910 as stated by Grigor Yeghikian, a Hnchakist theoretician in Gilan and subsequently an ally of Kuchek Khan, leader of the Jangali movement (1914–1921).[13] Yeghikian believed that the Ottoman government still desired expansion into Iran; however, this aspiration was tempered by pan-Islamic ideals. "The young Ottoman [government] is also planning war against this land [Iran]; that is to say, that is what it wishes and hopes for, however, because of its ideas on Islamic unity, it can never attain such a goal. . . . The young Ottoman [government] has adopted the way of Abdul-Hamid."[14]

The Dashnaktsutiun stopped outright attacks against the government largely because of the support given by the Dashnakists to the Young Turks. The new and promising political situation in the Ottoman Empire made it possible for both the Dashnaktsutiun and the Hnchakian parties to concentrate their efforts outside of the Ottoman Empire. The Dashnaktsutiun had attended both congresses of Ottoman liberals in Paris (1902 and 1907). The 1907 congress agreed to overthrow Sultan Abdul-Hamid by any means, including armed resistance, and demanded the establishment of a representative government. In a declaration signed by the Committee of Union and Progress (Young Turks), the Dashnaktsutiun, Ottoman Jewish organizations, and others, the congress announced that the parties would unite fraternally, respecting each other's autonomy and promising not to put down their weapons until they brought out a new dawn for the empire.[15] The agreement reached between the Young Turks and the Dashnakists transcended words as they jointly planned terrorist activity.[16] The Dashnaktsutiun also made clear that the party "has not had nor does it have any separatist aspiration in Turkey" but only seeks autonomy.[17] The Hnchakian party, on the other hand, had refused to take part in the congresses, although it did hold separate and unsuccessful talks at the request of Young Turk representatives such as Ahmet Rıza Bey and Nazım Bey.[18]

Although the Dashnaktsutiun had not taken part in the actual coup carried out by Young Turk officers and soldiers, it was pleased and optimistic about the prospect of constitutionalist rule, and when it first brought up the subject in the pages of *Droshak*, the party oscillated between uncensored elation and guarded caution. While excited about the promise of representative rule for all Ottoman subjects, especially Armenians, the editorial reminded its readers that Abdul-Hamid remained sultan and caliph and suggested they be "neither extremely pessimistic nor extremely optimistic."[19] Even with that kind of prudence, the Dashnaktsutiun continued to sing the praises of the coup, which represented and promised, according to the party, the French revolutionary ideals of "liberty, equality, fraternity."[20] The party also congratulated itself for being the only Armenian political party to collaborate with the Young Turks in meetings in Paris in face of "persecution" and "insult" from its opponents, namely the Hnchakists, adding that the present circumstances only "prove that neither our blood, nor our effort, nor our dedication was expended in vain."[21] Even when the Dashnaktsutiun expressed some concern regarding the discrepancy between the Young Turk government's ideals and its actions, the party was quick to add that it still believed that the "current unruly chaos" was temporary and that the period of oppression had ended not only in the Ottoman capital but also in Asia Minor.[22]

The Hnchakian party, although welcoming constitutionalism in the Ottoman Empire and recognizing the significance and merit of the Young Turks' general principles, remained very cautious of the party and the new regime.[23] According to the Hnchakists, the Young Turks lacked the organizational structure of a "real" party and the popular support from the empire's various elements. Moreover, they lacked a clear plan of legislative action once in power, and the mere promise of the reestablishment of the constitution did not necessarily signify positive change for the different peoples and the working class. Also, the party objected to the Young Turks' precondition to solidarity and collaboration, namely recognition of Ottoman independence and union, because it believed that that would somehow nullify the rights achieved by the peoples of the empire. In addition, the party rejected the Young Turks' view that all peoples of the empire had suffered equally under the sultan's oppressive regime. Most importantly, according to the Hnchakists, the "first and essential aspiration of the 'Young Turks' is to suppress the Armenian cause as other causes." The party, however, did not completely rule out solidarity and demanded, as its prerequisites for possible collaboration, the recognition of the concept of an autonomous Armenia. It further distinguished between the Young Turks as a party and the Turkish people with whom solidarity and collaboration were always possible.[24]

Even the Hnchakian party, which questioned Young Turk policy and the appropriateness of the Dashnaktsutiun's ties to the new regime, however, reevaluated its strategy within the Ottoman Empire and decided, in its Sixth Congress (July–October 1909), to pursue legal political activity. The fact that the congress was held in Istanbul is significant in itself for it demonstrates that the party had come out in the open and felt secure enough to meet in the capital of the Young Turks. It stated in a declaration to its ranks that "by saluting the constitutional situation that came about in Turkey and Persia, the Congress [of the Hnchakian party] put aside terrorist activity in those areas and decided to give strength by every means to the preservation and advancement of the constitutional ranks."[25] The Hnchakian party also sought solidarity with social democratic groups within the Ottoman Empire, especially with Turkish social democratic organizations.[26]

The Dashnaktsutiun continued its support of and loyalty to the regime even after the Young Turks (and supporters of the sultan) were implicated in the massacre of thousands of Armenians in Adana and other parts of Cilicia in 1909. The party directly attributed the killings to the continued indifference of the government to Armenian demands for reforms and warnings against elements of the "old regime."[27] Moreover, the Young Turk government's "explaining away" of events by dividing the blame between Armenians and Turks alike worried the Dashnaktsutiun, which lamented: "We had thought and hoped that, from the old regime, only Sultan Abdul-Hamid's kiss would have remained on the forehead of the [Ottoman] Assembly's president, but with a relentless evil the events come to retort that there are still more and many surprises reserved."[28] In the same issue of *Droshak*, however, the party reaffirmed its "small faith in the victory of justice" and its cautious hope that the new constitutional regime would find and appropriately punish the guilty.[29] By September 1909, the Dashnaktsutiun went a step further by signing an accord with the ruling Ottoman party, the Committee of Union and Progress, to ensure the freedom and territorial and political integrity of the "fatherland," the Ottoman Empire, and to fortify mutual relations. In recognition of the Adana "tragedy," both agreed, among other things, to work together to implement the constitution and to lay to rest rumors of Armenian separatism.[30] The solidarity and at times cordial relations between the Young Turks and the Dashnaktsutiun, which had been firmly established in 1907, continued until 1912 when the Young Turks dissolved parliament and successfully put down the liberal opposition.[31]

Another reason for reevaluation of the Dashnaktsutiun's outlook regarding Ottoman territorial intentions in Iran was the policy taken by the

Young Turk government, which seemed on the surface to be in complete opposition to the aggressive policy of Sultan Abdul-Hamid. Just a month after the coup, the Young Turk government announced that it would withdraw its troops from the disputed line and begin negotiations with the Iranian government.[32] Once evacuation began in September, however, it became clear that the Young Turk government was not fully committed to the idea as it retained its forces in Anzal (not to be confused with Anzali), Somay, Baranduz, and other regions in northwestern Iran.[33] Dashnakist bodies in Iran were very much concerned with Ottoman troop movements at the border and considered their options, including sending fighters to the border area.[34]

In the beginning of 1909, the Young Turk government declared its intentions to actively assist the Iranian revolutionary movement and sent delegates from Salonika to Azerbaijan to work toward that aim while continuing to pursue expansionist aspirations in Azerbaijan.[35] The Dashnaktsutiun, publicly at least, remained supportive of or silent toward the Young Turk government despite even outright aggression in Iran, such as in Maku when in 1910, Ottoman troops entered the town and with the help of anti-constitutionalist forces destroyed Iranian *fedayi* organizations and devastated the populace.[36]

The Young Turk coup and the restoration of the constitution that promised liberalization, representation, and equality changed to some extent the Dashnaktsutiun and Hnchakian parties' view of the Ottoman government and, for the Dashnaktsutiun, led to cooperation and collaboration with Young Turks. The decision by both parties to cease military operations against the Ottoman government made it possible for the Armenian revolutionaries of both parties to concentrate their efforts outside of the Ottoman Empire, specifically Iran.

The Russian Empire: Imperilment and Inspiration

Tsarist Russia Outside Its Borders

An important factor prompting Dashnakist and Hnchakist participation in the Iranian Constitutional Revolution was the role played by tsarist Russia both outside its borders in its relations with Japan and Iran and inside its borders in its policy toward its Armenian subjects. As was the case with the Ottoman Empire, the Russian Empire's treatment of its own subjects greatly influenced Dashnakist and Hnchakist perception of Russia in relation to the Iranian Constitutional Revolution and to the necessity of involvement.

The Dashnakists and the Hnchakists perceived the Iranian Constitutional Revolution as a struggle against foreign domination, especially

Russian, of Iran. Although Britain was also criticized for its exploitation of Iran and the Anglo-Russian Agreement of 1907 that divided Iran into spheres of influence, Russia took center stage as the enemy of constitution and freedom.[37] *Droshak* labeled the two governments thieves and lamented the accord as it would only impede Iran's constitutional advances.[38]

During the Russo-Japanese War of 1904–1905, and especially after Russia's defeat, Russia began to be seen as a decaying nonconstitutional Western empire that had lost to the only constitutional power in Asia. Various groups in Asia came to look upon constitutions as the "secret of strength."[39] The Dashnaktsutiun ascribed Japanese military success to Japan's "free political organization," which was more "civilized."[40] An editorial in *Droshak* explained that while many reasons could be found for Japan's recent victories in battle with Russia, only one overshadowed the others—"Russia's tyrannical regime."[41]

At the first signs of Russian losses, the Hnchakists compared the Russian Empire to a "'giant ancient tree whose inside, rotten and empty, bows in face of a storm or collapses with the powerful blow of an axe."[42] Russia was clearly perceived to be the aggressor who had forced Japan into war.[43] The "'giant' eastern bear," as an article in *Hnchak* called Russia, had fallen when faced with the smaller Japan, further comparing the war to the battle between David and Goliath.[44]

The Dashnaktsutiun, like the Hnchakian party, placed great hopes in the influence that Japan's victory would have on the rest of Asia: "Asia is resurrected. Asia for the Asians. . . . The source for the new movements in Asia must be sought in the Japanese victories."[45] The same concept was stated by the Tabriz Committee of the Social Democratic Party of Iran in its declaration: "Now, thanks to our unity any undertaking is possible, just as Japan, thanks to her alertness and iron determination defeated an enemy like Russia."[46] The Dashnakists and Hnchakists, like the Russian Socialists, hoped that with Russian defeat would come the end of tsarist tyranny and the deliverance not only of the peoples of the empire but of all civilization and humanity.[47] They believed that Russia's defeat had to some degree brought about a constitutional, albeit imperfect, Russia.[48] The direct impact on the Dashnakist bodies of the Russo-Japanese War and Japan's ultimate victory is evidenced by the namesake of an Armenian *fedayi* group in Iran—Japan.[49]

According to the Dashnaktsutiun, the Iranian Constitutional Revolution was not just a movement for constitution but also one for independence from Russian oppression and exploitation and from "Russia's blind or seeing tool," the shah.[50] The shah was perceived to be the worst of all traitors, willing to sacrifice his own people and the country in order to stay in power and stop the constitutional drive.[51] *Droshak* proclaimed: "One could not have searched and found a greater enemy to Persia than [Mohammad] Ali Shah," who had succeeded the constitution-granting Mozaffar al-Din Shah in 1907.[52] Iranian Constitutionalist newspapers such as *Ruh al-Qodos* (The Holy Spirit) and *Mosavat* (Equality) expressed similar sentiments regarding the new shah. For example, the former called the shah an enemy of the constitution who conspired with foreign powers while the latter accused the shah of neglecting border security and conspiring to overthrow the Majles.[53] In addition, the Dashnaktsutiun believed that the Russian government sought to put a stop to the constitutional movement in Iran.[54] Referring to the coup by the shah, utilizing the Cossack Brigade, and the bombardment of the Majles in June 1908, *Droshak* blamed Russia, stating: "Again tsarism . . . It interfered moreover in Persia's bloody sorrow, with its usual cynical barbarity and extinguished the emancipatory blaze." The editorial specifically targeted Colonel Vladimir Liakhov, head of the Cossack Brigade, and Tsar Nicholas II who, according to the organ, had reached Sultan Abdul-Hamid's infamous status.[55] In addition, *Droshak* articles warned Iran against Russian intentions to annex northern Iran.[56] These warnings and assaults on Russia intensified after Tabriz revolutionaries held out against the shah's coup d'état and as Russian troops moved into Tabriz in April 1909 and disarmed the revolutionaries.[57] The Dashnaktsutiun's view of Russia was not unique to the party or to Armenians. For example, Lenin expressed similar views about Russian intentions concerning Iran: "That Russia, with the knowledge of the powers, is fighting the Persian revolution with every means at her command, from intrigue to the sending of troops, is a fact. That her policy is to occupy Azerbaijan, is likewise beyond doubt."[58]

Armenian parties questioned both Russian and Ottoman intentions toward Iran, accusing them both of attempting to block the constitutional movement and to acquire Iranian territory. In this sense, the two regimes were likened to each other and placed at the same level of condemnation for their aggressive policies toward Iran. Their actions clearly served as motivating factors in the Dashnakist and Hnchakist decisions to involve themselves in the Iranian Constitutional Revolution.

Tsarist Russia Inside Its Borders

The view of tsarist Russia as the enemy of Iran's constitutional movement and as the ally of the autocratic shah was amplified further by Russification policies at home, which for the first time mobilized Caucasian Armenian communities against the Russian government.

Russian confiscation of Armenian Church properties in 1903 and the Stolypin crackdown in 1908 directly influenced the Dashnaktsutiun's view of Russia as one of Armenia's foremost enemies, not the champion of its rights. The anti-Armenian policies of Tsar Nicholas II (1894–1917) and governor-general of the Caucasus, Prince Grigorii Golitsyn (1896–1905), began with the closing down of Armenian schools, libraries, and charities in 1896 and the prohibition, two years later, of the publication of words referring to Armenians as a people or a nation. These policies reached culmination on 12 June 1903 when the Russian government ordered the confiscation of Armenian Church properties. By this decree, church properties and income, including donations, were placed under the authority of the Department of State Properties and the Ministries of Education and Agriculture. Furthermore, the measure affected both the status of church schools, which were placed under Russian government control, and the position of the Armenian clergy who, by this measure, became government employees.[59] The Catholicos Mkrtich Khrimian, who still holds a special place in Armenian collective, memory and historiography as Khrimian Hayrik (Father Khrimian), requested a postponement of the implementation of the order, but when he was rejected by Interior Minister V. K. Plehve (1902–1904),[60] he refused to give up any church estates.[61] He was supported and encouraged not only by the Dashnakists and Hnchakists, but by the Armenian populace, who for the first time openly resisted the tsarist government. Peaceful and spontaneous marches in support of the Catholicos's resistance to the tsarist order began in July and lasted until September. A few thousand to several thousand Armenians of all classes took part in the demonstrations in Alexandropol, Yerevan, Ejmiatsin, Kars, Ganje (Gandzak, Elisavetpol), Baku, Tiflis, and Shusha. In Alexandropol, for example, the Catholicos was greeted by 5,000 marchers who appealed to him to continue his defiance of the Russian government. In Ejmiatsin, the seat of the Catholicos, 400 to 500 women of some 3,000 demonstrators were reported to have begun their own protest separate from the larger crowd, shouting slogans like, "Long live the Armenian church and its inalienable rights!" and "Death to oppression!" In Kars, too, women made their presence known. When told by their male counterparts they could disperse and that their signatures on a petition were unnecessary, the women did not budge, insisting that they too would sign. Even those who were illiterate asked others to sign in their place. The demonstrations, however, soon turned violent as Russian soldiers fired upon several thousand protestors in Ganje made up of men and women as well as young boys and girls, killing 30, including a 13-year-old girl, and wounding 50. Funeral processions and memorials in Ganje, Tiflis, and villages and towns in many parts of the Caucasus, as

well as attempts by the Russian government to confiscate church posses-
sions, turned into violent confrontations with Russian soldiers who, like
the Russian government, were unprepared for such resistance from the
Armenian populace. Towns such as Yerevan and Alexandropol further indicated their support of the Catholicos's stance by closing their stores. In
addition to the wounded and dead, a few hundred Armenians, including
clergy, were arrested and exiled.[62] Coincidentally, the demonstrations occurred at the same time as the general strikes in Baku and Rostov-on-Don
in which Armenian workers participated.[63]

The Dashnaktsutiun and the Hnchakian parties were pleasantly surprised by the new activism of the Armenian populace, and the Dashnaktsutiun quickly moved to organize the resistance by creating the Self-
Defense Central Committee whose goal it was to direct the newly
aroused enthusiasm of the Caucasian Armenians.[64] Both the Hnchakists
and the Dashnakists commended the Armenian Church for heeding the
call of the people and continuing resistance to the tsar.[65] In an attempt to
politicize further the reasons for the popular show of resistance, the
Dashnakists added that the popular protest was not so much against the
confiscation of church properties as "against the systematic persecution
that sought to strangle Armenian individual [and] national rights."[66]
Both parties, encouraged and impressed by the new unyielding disposition of the Caucasian Armenians, attacked the Russian government's
confiscation policy. The Hnchakist organ attempted to expose the Russian government as a brigand who pretended to be acting in the interest
of the Armenian community but instead was robbing the Armenian
Church of property and income.[67] Both *Hnchak* and *Droshak* attacked Tsar
Nicholas personally, comparing him to Sultan Abdul-Hamid. While *Hnchak* in a matter-of-fact way called the tsar "Sultan Nikolai," *Droshak* declared: "The Armenian people . . . already sees today how similar Hamid
and Nikolai are."[68] *Droshak* further commented that Russia, with its policies, had successfully competed with the Ottoman Empire and had
demonstrated that its policies were stamped with "deep hatred . . . toward all that is Armenian."[69] According to a circular signed by Dashnakist bodies, both aspired to destroy the Armenian people by different
means but with similar zeal. Because of this, the party began to place the
struggle against the Ottoman and Russian empires on equal footing, stating, "The battle, therefore, against the Turkish yoke is simultaneously a
battle against tsarist policy."[70]

As Russian and Ottoman governments were previously equated because of their actions against Iran, so too were Iranians and Armenians as
victims of the same oppressors and therefore potential allies in the struggle against despotism and exploitation.

New Caucasian Policy and Reevaluation of Tactics

The new struggle on two fronts, Ottoman and Russian, induced to some degree by the Russian confiscation of church properties and the ensuing resistance of the Armenian populace, became a point of contention within the party but was nevertheless formalized by 1905. The so-called Caucasian Project, by directing the Dashnaktsutiun's struggle against tsarist Russia in addition to the Ottoman Empire, formally declared tsarism the enemy of the Armenian people and opened the way for collaboration with Russian parties opposed to tsarism, reevaluation of socialism, and participation in the Iranian Constitutional Revolution.

Russia's elevation to the status of serious enemy made its officials and its collaborators targets of both parties. Governor-General Golitsyn, the architect of the confiscation policy, was wounded in an assassination attempt by three Hnchakists in October 1903 and soon after left the Caucasus.[71] Both parties supported, encouraged, and carried out terrorism against those considered to be collaborators of the tsarist anti-Armenian policy, including Russians and Armenians, laymen and clergy.[72] Golitsyn was even accused of preparing Armenian pogroms and trying to turn neighboring Caucasian peoples against each other. A *Droshak* article, appearing almost a year before the start of violent clashes between Armenians and Caucasian Muslims, asked Caucasian Armenians to remain loyal to the principle of harmony and not to heed Golitsyn's attempts to create a schism between Caucasians. It also warned Armenians to be prepared to defend against attacks by "Turks" or other Caucasian peoples instigated by Golitsyn.[73]

The Russian government's policies and schemes were perceived to be a major threat by both Hnchakists and Dashnakists, causing them to reconnoiter and revise tactics and policy. Collaboration with Russian anti-tsarist socialist parties, especially Russian social revolutionaries, whose views and strategy corresponded most closely to those of the Dashnakists, became one such strategy for the Dashnaktsutiun. The Third Congress of the party, meeting in Sofia, Bulgaria, from February to March 1904, decided that the Dashnaktsutiun could no longer neglect the worsening conditions and suppression of the rights of Caucasian Armenians and would adopt as part of its goal the defense of those rights. The congress accepted the use of oral and written propaganda, terror, popular demonstrations, and armed resistance, as well as the participation of Armenian workers in general strikes.[74]

In an attempt to strengthen opposition to the tsarist government, a multiparty conference took place in November 1904 in Paris and was attended by several socialist parties, Russian, Polish, Finnish, and Georgian, as well as the Dashnaktsutiun. Although an invitation went out to

Social Democrats, they declined.[75] The non-Marxist parties present affirmed their willingness to collaborate together but indicated also the desire to preserve their own programs and tactics. They agreed on the following principles regarding Russia: (1) the eradication of oppression; (2) the replacement of tyranny with a democratic regime based on general elections; (3) the right of national self-determination and the removal of all oppressive measures placed upon individual nationalities.[76]

The Caucasian Regional Congress of the Dashnaktsutiun, meeting in December, after considerable discussion agreed to accept the decisions of the interparty conference.[77] A second meeting took place between the same parties with the addition of the Belorus and Latvian Socialists in April 1905 in Geneva, the same month that the Caucasian Project was verified.[78] The Caucasian Project reasserted commitment to opposition to the tsar and solidarity with Russian socialist parties in the overthrow of tsarism and the establishment of federalism, which was believed to be the only form of political organization that would guarantee the free and unimpeded progress of the numerous Caucasian nationalities and religions.[79] The Caucasian plan reasoned that the Caucasian revolutionary movements had gained momentum, that Russian tyranny had weakened because of external enemies (referring to the loss to Japan) and internal revolutionary opposition, and that the immediacy of the situation would not allow waiting for the next General Congress for decisions on this historic moment in the Caucasus. Having taken those points into consideration, the Dashnaktsutiun Council, made up of representatives of the highest Dashnakist bodies, resolved that the party would "advance from the period of self-defense to real revolutionary activity" in the Caucasus. The preoccupation of Caucasian youth with the plight of Ottoman Armenians had kept them from possible action in the Caucasus, but "the confiscation of Armenian church properties came as a strong, jolting incentive to displace that hindrance. The spirit of rebellion, condensed during decades . . . was expressed in the form of popular armed and unarmed movements in the fall of 1903."[80] In addition to the renewed plan of revolutionary struggle on both the Ottoman and Caucasian fronts, the party indicated a renewed commitment to socialism by stressing the significance of eliminating economic disparity and exploitation of the working class as well as the eradication of political oppression within the Caucasian plan.[81]

A few months afer the approval of the Caucasian Project, Golitsyn's replacement as governor of the Caucasus, Count I. I. Vorontsov-Dashkov (1905–1915) convinced Tsar Nicholas to rescind the confiscation edict in August 1905. Vorontsov-Dashkov was able to assure the tsar that such a move would only quell the revolutionary tide and the anti-tsarist disposition of the Caucasian Armenians and thus regain their loyalty. This did not have the great effect Vorontsov-Dashkov expected, as the Dashnakt-sutiun's popularity rose and the party considered the repeal of the measure a personal victory, as did some segments of the Armenian populace who displayed their trust in the party by joining its ranks.[82] The party's reputation also affected membership in Iran.[83] Despite the repeal of the decree and the establishment of a representative assembly (duma) in Russia, anti-Russian views continued to persist among Hnchakists and Dashnakists.[84]

The adoption of the Caucasian project and the issue of socialism magnified the tension, in spring 1906, that had always existed within the party between the "Ottomanists" (Mihranakans) whose only desired field of battle was the Ottoman Empire and the "Caucasianists" (Young Dashnaks) who wanted to concentrate most efforts in the Caucasus in joint cooperation with Russian socialist parties. While the Caucasianists ultimately left the party, the debate continued into the Fourth Congress in early 1907 where it was officially resolved, and the party was able to regain its strength and unity.[85] Therefore, the Caucasian plan, along with the violent confrontation between Caucasian Armenians and Muslims in 1905–1906, set the stage for further reevaluation of party policy in 1907.

For the Hnchakian party, the debate over the inclusion of the Caucasus as part of the greater goal of the party began a few years earlier but took shape only after the Russian edict of confiscation of Armenian Church properties and was influenced to a great extent by the internal divisions that caused the party to split in 1896. The main issue of contention was whether "socialism is superfluous and harmful to the Armenian cause."[86] This view was most strongly expressed by Ottoman Armenian Hnchakists, who criticized the party center of Caucasian Armenians led by one of the party founders, Avetis Nazarbekian, for pursuing the cause of Caucasian Armenian workers against tsarism and economic exploitation and thus taking away from the struggle on the Ottoman front.[87] The anti-socialist faction split off to form the Verakazmial (Reformed) Hnchakian party with a strong following in Egypt, the Ottoman Empire, and the United States. The division in the party extended beyond ideological debates and took on a violent turn as killings occurred in Europe, the Caucasus, and the United States.[88] At the Third Congress of Delegates meeting in London from October 1901 to March 1902, the party was formally reunified, despite the continued disagreements regarding the issue of socialism and the Caucasian front.[89] The alliance between the Caucasian Socialists and the mainly Ottoman liberal nationalists was the consequence of a new common enemy, the Nazarbekian faction, which had previously supported the Caucasian elements of the party. These Hnchakists now went a step further in their commitment to the Caucasus by proposing to dissolve the Caucasian branch of the party in order to join the Russian Social

Democratic Workers Party (RSDWP) with which they would carry on the class struggle.[90] In reality, therefore, the union of forces was to some extent in name only as each side retained its own program.

The congress of September 1905, meeting in Paris, reasserted the unity of the party, rejecting the concept of dissolution into the RSDWP, because the Hnchakian party could not and would not give up the struggle in Ottoman Armenian provinces. The Congress resolved, "The cause of the emancipation of Western [Ottoman] Armenia equally interests both the bourgeois and working class of the Caucasus. The class struggle that exists between them cannot cause them to forget the freedom of the oppressed Turkish Armenian classes."[91] At the same time, it could not overlook the new situation for Armenians as well as the growing proletarian movement in the Caucasus and for that reason the party tried to strengthen its social democratic views and work more closely with the RSDWP, especially in the worker strikes and uprisings of the Russian Revolution of 1905.[92] Therefore, the 1905 congress resolved "To struggle and obtain political democracy based on Marxist principles" in Ottoman Armenian provinces and "proletarian revolutionary activity in the Caucasus."[93] Those Caucasian Hnchakists who preferred to concentrate their activities in the Caucasus and on the class rather than nationalist struggle renounced the new program and seceded from the party to join the RSDWP.[94] Some, like Vram Pilosian and Sedrak Banvorian, who seceded from the party, later contributed intellectually to the Iranian Constitutional Revolution by helping to found the Tabriz Social Democratic party in 1905 and the Democrat party in 1909 of which Sayyid Hasan Taqizadeh, the well-known Tabriz delegate to the Majles, was also a founding member.[95]

A third attempt at union between the Hnchakian Center and the Reformed faction indicated that in fact true solidarity had not been reached in the previous attempts. In December 1907, another pact of solidarity was signed by the two sides "regarding all significant and essential points that concern Turkish Armenian revolutionary activity."[96] The party carefully set out the meaning of solidarity, indicating that it did not mean the assimilation of parties into one, but rather moral, financial, and physical collaboration on points of agreement.[97]

Therefore, the Hnchakian party reevaluated its policy in the Caucasus, thus widening its options and field of activity as did the Dashnaktsutiun. Unlike the Dashnaktsutiun, however, the Hnchakian party was greatly weakened by its internal divisions, the consequences of which—secession—had a deleterious impact on the party's activities in the Caucasus, thus explaining to some degree the increased ascendancy of the Dashnaktsutiun in the region. The new predominance of the Dashnaktsutiun in the Caucasus was to some extent also both the result and cause of its role in the violent confrontations between Caucasian Armenians and Muslims. Moreover, the actions of both parties, especially the Dashnakt-sutiun, in the communal violence as well as the Russian Revolution of 1905 further promoted reevaluation of party policies on the Caucasian front, which in turn, along with political circumstances, shaped policies outside the Ottoman and Russian fronts—those in Iran.

Caucasian Communal Violence and Reevaluation of Policy

More than any other factor, the communal violence between Caucasian Armenians and Muslims became at the same time the most disturbing and the most inspiring for those involved. The extent and nature of the violence were, of course, what made it most disturbing to the partici-pants. The reevaluation of attitudes and policy of the Dashnakists and Hnchakists that encouraged solidarity and led to actual collaborative ef-forts with Iranians and Caucasian Muslims in the Iranian Constitutional Revolution only a year or two after the hostilities was directly inspired by the conflict and the resulting self-questioning.

The violent attacks and reprisals of Caucasian Armenians and Muslims began in February 1905 and lasted until spring 1906. The conflict affected most communities in the Caucasus that had both an Armenian and a Muslim population, and according to an eyewitness source, took the lives of more than 2,000 people and left 14,760 people injured and 286 vil-lages plundered.[98] The Dashnaktsutiun and to some extent the Hn-chakian party took a leading role in the arming of Armenian workers and peasants and in the actual fighting. They were assisted by a few women whose responsibility was to transfer arms and provide safe passage for Armenian fighters.[99]

Most sources on the subject agree that the conflict took place between Caucasian Muslims and Armenians. However, both the Hnchakists and Dashnakists reported the participation of Iranians in the conflict. These Iranians were almost surely migrant workers in the Caucasus. *Droshak* re-ported that a large part of the arms was acquired by Caucasian Muslims through "co-religionists" in Iran and Turkey.[100] Both *Hnchak* and *Droshak* discussed the role of Iranians in the attacks against the Armenians in the Caucasus.[101] News of the violence in Baku and its spread to other areas in the Caucasus reached Iran almost immediately. Iranian Armenian popu-lations in the northwest feared that violence would also take hold there, especially since some Iranian immigrant workers from Baku had begun to return to Azerbaijan.[102] The correspondence of Dashnakists in Azerbai-jan indicated both a cautionary change in attitude among the Iranian population and the belief that some Baku Iranians as well as Caucasian Muslims who had crossed the border to Iran wanted to instigate violence against the Armenians. Furthermore, they pointed to the involvement of Russian government agents, like a Russian bank director named Ekzempliarov, in these schemes.[103] Hnchakist Grigor Yeghikian also stated that Calcutta's pan-Islamic paper *Habl al-Matin* (The Firm Cord) was advising Iranians to act against Armenians.[104] Others, while recognizing the role of the Russian government, maintained that Iranians were fully aware of Russian attempts at instigation and therefore would not be affected by them.[105] One such letter even alluded to Russia's tarnished image among Iranians due to its losses against Japan.[106]

In an effort to avoid any possible conflict, Dashnakist bodies placed guards in mixed Armenian Muslim communities. Every village was appointed a commander who would do everything possible to steer away from potentially dangerous situations or opportunities.[107] Although individual acts of violence occurred against Armenians by Caucasian Muslims crossing the border to Ardabil and by Azerbaijani Iranians, the mass violence did not reach northwestern Iran.[108] In large part, the Dashnaktsutiun attributed the lack of serious conflict to the efforts of the Iranian government and clergy, both of whom in collaboration at times with the party successfully thwarted violence. For example, meetings took place between Dashnakists, Armenian clergy, Iranian clergy, and judges in Khoy and Salmas as well as joint public calls for peace in mosques.[109]

By the time the violence had subsided, almost everyone involved was blaming the Russian government and particularly Russian officials like Baku Governor-General Prince Nakashidze, whom the Dashnakists assassinated in May 1905, for inciting both sides against each other.[110] *Hnchak* placed blame on the Russian regime, accusing it of inciting the Muslims against the Armenians and doing nothing to stop the violence.[111] An editorial stated, "The facts, documents and real course of events prove irrefutably and conclusively that those terrible clashes are thus the crimes of tsarism."[112] In *Droshak*, the Dashnaktsutiun took the same route and found Russia completely culpable, as did foreign observers like Luigi Villari who referred to the "old principle of *divide et impera* [divide and conquer]."[113] The Caucasian Muslim intellectual Ahmet Ağaev (Ağaoğlu) told crowds gathered at a mosque in Ganje that Muslims and Armenians had lived together in peace for centuries before the arrival of the Russians in the region.[114] At the same time, he was creating the Difâî (Defense), a secret political association, which carried out terrorism against officials hostile to Caucasian Muslims or favorable to Armenians. The secret society, which was active until the Stolypin crackdown in 1908, believed that the goal of the Dashnaktsutiun was the creation of a "national [*milli*] independent administration" for Armenians by crushing Caucasian Muslims and occupying their lands. The Difâî stated in its program that the "party's goal is to create sincere brotherhood and unity

among the separate Caucasian peoples" and if the program of the Dashnaktsutiun "does not include points that would violate the freedom and
independence of the separate Caucasian nations [*millitler*], then we will
always be ready to extend our own united hand to them." The organization warned, however, that if the Dashnaktsutiun "continues deceitfully
and cruelly in its attacks on the Muslims, as it has before, it will get a suit-
able answer from us, and the Caucasus will become the scene of endless,
unremitting bloodshed."[115] The Dashnaktsutiun's formal response came
in November 1906 when it reprinted the Difâî's program and refuted the
organization's claims by referring to sections of its own manifesto. By doing so, the party stated, the Difâî could examine the Dashnaktsutiun's
goals and extend the "hand of solidarity . . . clean, pure hands . . . we
await you."[116]

Difâî's call for peace accompanied by the threat of violence paralleled
the stance of the Dashnaktsutiun, which also pleaded for peace at the
same time as it promised combat.[117] Moreover, although both the Dashnakists and Hnchakists blamed Russia for the conflict, they also faulted
the majority of Caucasian Muslims for being manipulated by the Russian
government and not being sophisticated enough to realize they were being duped into attacking the Armenians.[118] As for Muslim intellectual,
political, and financial leaders like Ahmet Ağaev (editor, *Hayat*), Ali Mardan Topçibaşi (Topchibashev; editor, *Kaspii*), millionaire Haji Zeynal
Abidin Tağiyev (owner, *Kaspii*), literary figure Yusuf Vezirov, and others,
the Dashnaktsutiun found them all guilty of leading or abetting the communal violence.[119]

Representatives of the Dashnaktsutiun as well as other Caucasian Armenians and Muslims made some attempts beginning in the earliest
phase of the fighting in February to find peace between the two peoples
and successfully brokered temporary cease-fires.[120] After the first such
halt in violence, which came only a month after the Russian Revolution
was under way (January 1905), the Baku Central Committee of the Dashnaktsutiun declared its commitment to the end of fratricidal killings, informing its members that "arms painted with the blood of neighbors"
have been put down and that they were only raised to defend Armenian
lives and dignity.[121] After the agreement to cease fire, meetings continued
to take place in Baku. The gatherings had two goals: to investigate the
conflict and to expose the Russian government and Baku administration
for their roles as provocateurs.[122] According to a Dashnakist participant,
4,000 Armenians, Muslims, Russians, and others attended the first meeting, held on 11 February 1905. Among those speaking were Ahmet Ağaev
and Hovhannes Kachaznuni (subsequently the Armenian Republic's first
premier). The resolution resulting from the meeting stated that no ethnic
or religious enmity existed between the Caucasian Armenians and Mus-

lims, that both peoples had lived and worked together in peace for centuries, and that Russian officials had instigated the violence and had not
acted to stop it. On the same day, another meeting of 1,000 Armenian,
Muslim, and Russian workers took place in Baku's oil region and came to
an almost identical conclusion, adding that it was the duty of all the Caucasian peoples to put aside differences and come together to bring down
tsarist tyranny.[123] Similar meetings attracting thousands took place for the
next two weeks, all proclaiming the brotherhood of Caucasians and con-
demning Russia.[124] On 12 February 1905, a circular signed by the Dashnakists and Hnchakists, as well as the Russian social revolutionaries, Social Democrats, and Social Federalists, appeared in Tiflis, addressed to all
Caucasian peoples, and reasserted Russian blame.[125] Although sincere attempts seem to have been made on both sides, the fighting continued until spring 1906, indicating that in addition to Russian instigation, ethnic,
religious, and economic rivalries fueled the violent conflict.[126]

In the meantime, Russian, Georgian, and Armenian Social Democrats
condemned the armed actions of the Dashnaktsutiun, accusing it of "being manipulated by the Russian bureaucracy, inflaming racial and religious hatreds, stifling class consciousness under nationalism and racism,
[and] breaking the unity of the Caucasian revolutionary movement."[127]
The Russian Social Revolutionaries, however, according to a contemporary Dashnakist observer and participant, assisted the Dashnaktsutiun in
the buying, storing, and transferring of arms in the beginning of the conflict.[128] Interestingly, even the Hnchakists who had themselves taken part
in the violence criticized the extreme nationalism that had inflamed the
conflict. The Hnchakian party's role in the conflict was, in reality, minimal, since it had been greatly weakened by the ideological split in the
party. In addition, according to letters of Hnchakist members from Baku,
the Hnchakists had trouble acquiring arms and ammunition during the
conflict.[129] *Hnchak* spoke of the "fleeting mirage of nationalism" that had
"poisoned the ravished hearts of the youth," creating obstacles in the
path to harmony and solidarity. It declared that the nationalist "par ex-
cellence" was the Caucasian bourgeoisie of any ethnicity, who by sepa-
rating the workers of each ethnic group from the other and by making
enemies out of them, used its own working class to destroy the other. The
editorial then quoted directly from the RSDWP organ, *Sotsialist*, which
stated that the conflict between the Armenians and Muslims only
strengthened the power of the Russian government and weakened social
democracy. Only social democracy would bring the two peoples together, and it must do so by "fighting unceasingly against nationalism
and annihilating it by its roots!"[130] In an attempt to justify its actions, the
Hnchakian party explained that it had not raised arms against the Muslims because of nationalist vengeance but had acted only because the

Muslim element was the tool of the Russian government. Therefore, by defeating the Muslims, the party intended to strike a blow against Russian oppression. Furthermore, its actions were merely defensive as it found "the enemy in front of our door . . . gun in hand, ready to overrun us."[131] The Dashnaktsutiun, too, tried to defend itself against charges of nationalism, by pointing to its attempts at solidarity with Caucasian Muslims and Young Turks as well as Russian, Georgian, Finnish, and Polish Socialists and its new Caucasian Project, which called for solidarity with anti-tsarist forces and accepted the basic principles of the Socialist International. Moreover, it asserted that one could be socialist and still defend national rights and liberation.[132]

The horror of the violent conflict, the mobilization of the Caucasian Armenian communities and political parties, the potential threat to Iranian Armenian communities, the attempts at reconciliation, and last the criticism and self-examination resulted in a reevaluation of strategy and policy, thus opening the way to greater internationalization through socialism and solidarity.

Socialism and Solidarity

The Iranian Constitutional Revolution was depicted by various Socialists as the first stage in the struggle ultimately ending in socialism. Lenin, who was in exile in western Europe at the time, had even set hopes on the Tabriz resistance for the "rise of the East." He praised Iranian revolutionary leaders like Sattar Khan who were fighting for national liberation against colonialism.[133] Armenian Social Democrats in Tabriz, who had close links with the RSDWP, sought the advice of Marxist theorists like German social democratic leader Karl Kautsky regarding the role of Social Democrats in the Iranian Constitutional Revolution.[134]

The Social Democratic Group of Tabriz was headed by Armenian Social Democrats Arshavir Chilinkirian, Vram Pilosian, Vasso Khachaturian, and two individuals identified only as Sedrak I and Sedrak II.[135] The group was formed before the start of the Iranian Constitutional Revolution in 1905 as indicated by a letter, dated 15 September 1905, from Joseph Karakhanian to Georgi Plekhanov, a founder of the Russian Marxist paper *Iskra* (Spark).[136] Having read Plekhanov's article, "Patriotism and Socialism," Karakhanian wanted to pursue the issue of nation and nationalities with the author. He asked Plekhanov whether civilization would eventually lead to "assimilation of all peoples and all cultures," adding that he believed that such a thing as a "nation with determined and invariable spiritual traits does not exist: the Swiss are not what they were in the Middle Ages, we Armenians, we differ actually a lot from our ancestors.[137] After Mohammad Ali's coup of June 1908 and the rise of the

Tabriz resistance, the ranks of the Tabriz Social Democrats were reinforced by Social Democrats arriving from the Caucasus.[138] Khachaturian
himself was part of a Baku group of the RSDWP who arrived in Tabriz in
August 1908 to join the struggle.[139] The major concern of the Iranian Armenian Social Democrats became what role Social Democrats should
play in the revolution. According to Chilinkirian, until that time the
group had been occupied with the propagation of Marxism but political
developments in the country had led them to plan a conference for September 1908 to discuss their role in the constitutional struggle. The Social
Democrats differed in opinion and sought the advice of the two leaders
of the Socialist International, Karl Kautsky and Georgi Plekhanov. The
question revolved around two points. First, what was the character of the
Iranian Constitutional Revolution—was it progressive or regressive? If
democratic and progressive, what kind of participation could the Social
Democrats have in such a movement? Second, if regressive, what role
should they play, if any? The second point concerned Iran's stage of capitalist production.[140]

Kautsky advised participation in the democratic bourgeois revolution:
"But I believe that one can say in all conscience that the socialists are obligated to take part in a democratic movement. The socialists participate in
combat like simple democrats among bourgeois democrats and petit-
bourgeois; but for them the struggle is for democracy, it is the struggle of
classes."[141] Kautsky added that reactionary tendencies had and would always exist even in democratic movements, but that this would not necessarily give them their character and therefore did not preclude participation. Iran met the first condition of industrial development, foreign
capitalism and exploitation, and the victory of democracy in this revolution would open the way for the final class struggle and thus social democracy. Khachaturian and Chilinkirian also wrote to Georgi Plekhanov.
Chilinkirian informed him of the success of the Tabriz Social Democrats
whose rally in December 1908 had attracted 10,000 people, including Sattar Khan, and Khachaturian told him of the group's plans to organize
trade unions.[142] Moreover, Khachaturian asked Plekhanov's advice on
several issues. Referring to Kautsky's statement that if the country had
no modern proletariat, then Social Democrats must take part in the revolution as Democrats, Khachaturian inquired whether Plekhanov agreed.
Would it be right, he continued, to refrain from organizing workers and
struggling for increases in salary "in order to force capitalists to intro-
duce a sophisticated system of production?" Khachaturian must have
been urgently waiting for a response, as he indicated that this issue had
been the topic of heated debate and caused many to leave the group. He
also sought answers to questions regarding the role of Social Democrats
in the struggle against foreign capital and in favor of free trade. Last, he

asked Plekhanov whether as Social Democrats they could organize a
militia. In principle, he added, Tabriz Social Democrats were against popular militias, which would ultimately be transformed into a permanent
army by the bourgeoisie; therefore, he did not know whether to accept or
refuse the responsibility of a militia that had been placed on his shoul-
ders.[143] It is not known whether Plekhanov responded to Khachaturian
and Chilinkirian as no record of his correspondence to them has yet been
found.

The proposal presented by Khachaturian and Chilinkirian at a meeting
of 30 Tabriz Social Democrats on 17 October 1908 was a modified version
of Kautsky's response.[144] The proposal, which was accepted by the majority, stated that because Iran had entered the stage of manufacturing
and industrial production and had developed a small class of workers
alongside a larger class of small artisans, a foundation for socialist agitation already existed. Furthermore, while they agreed with Kautsky on
the issue of participation in a democratic bourgeois revolution, which
they considered the Iranian Constitutional Revolution to be, they differed in adding that their role in the revolution also involved fighting for
the social and economic interests of the landless masses. Therefore they
could not struggle merely as Democrats and "collaborate with the bourgeoisie during the revolution," as Kautsky had suggested, but as Social
Democrats whose worldview significantly departed from that of mere
Democrats. Their role at all times was to mobilize and agitate among
workers and intellectuals and arouse a "class consciousness for the socialist struggle." The minority view presented by Sedrak II and Pilosian
maintained that Iran had not entered the stage of industrial production
and had no modern proletariat and therefore no basis for social democratic agitation. They asserted that for the success of the bourgeois revolution, which after all would usher in the next stage of socialist revolution, it was "rational and appropriate" for Social Democrats "to leave
aside momentarily purely social democratic work, to enter the ranks of
democracy, to cleanse reactionary tendencies," and to struggle as the
"most radical elements" within the revolution.[145]

Historian Janet Afary points out that although both wings of the Tabriz
Social Democrats were cognizant of peasant movements, the issue of organizing peasants, whose rebellions in Azerbaijan and the Caspian Sea
region were well-known in this period, was "never taken up in a systematic way," a factor the Iranian Armenian Communist Sultanzadeh (Avetis
Mikayelian) considered to be one of the reasons for the failure of the
Iranian revolution. Moreover, she asserts that by calling for a social-
democratic struggle in the midst of Iran's Constitutional Revolution, they
had gone against the two leading Social Democrats of the time, Kautsky
and Plekhanov, and seemed closer to Rosa Luxemburg.[146]

In looking back at the history of the nascent social democratic movement in Tabriz, it is remarkable to see that this small group, which was deprived of the direct theoretical influence of thinkers such as Luxemburg, nevertheless went so far as to directly challenge the dominant thought of European social democracy. Moreover, such a view was shared by the majority in the conference [Fifth Congress of the RSDWP]. The extent to which these young revolutionaries were aware of the theoretical debates within the Second International cannot be ascertained from the existing documents. Nevertheless, the discussion of the majority wing in Tabriz says much about their independence of mind as well as their political confidence, which was a product of the revolutionary movement in which they were involved.[147]

Therefore, the Armenian Social Democrats in Tabriz perceived the Iranian Constitutional Revolution as one that would dramatically alter the course of Iran's social, political, and economic conditions; bring forth democracy and perhaps socialism within the country; and affect the rest of the region. As Kautsky pointed out, "The peoples of the Orient, who seek to overthrow capitalism there, do not only fight for socialism in their country, but for socialism here in Europe. . . . Persia and Turkey by struggling for their liberation, struggle for the liberation of world proletariat."[148]

The Dashnakists, as well, considered the revolution an international revolution having wide ramifications in the Near East. Their ideas were not always couched in socialist terms, although they could be and at times must be interpreted as such. In general, the revolution was for national liberation and democracy; the struggle was humanitarian and not necessarily national or religious. In speaking about the Armenians in Sattar Khan's army, *Droshak* exclaimed, "The love for freedom has no fatherland; whosoever is brave and has a heart, the world is open to him; to him a gun and a bullet is all that's necessary. If Armenians have gone to help Sattar Khan, as other nationalities, that is the consequence of the same universal historical outlook; there, nationalities have no place."[149]

Furthermore, the success of a constitutional movement in Iran would influence neighboring autocracies such as the Russian and Ottoman Empires and that could only improve conditions for Ottoman and Russian Armenians. As the Dashnakists observed, the situation of Armenians was directly dependent upon the situation of their neighbors and their governments:

The Armenians, with whose existence is tied any political and popular transformation in those areas, could not, naturally, remain indifferent to such a struggle that simultaneously spoke to the mind and the heart. They, as with all liberal and humanitarian movements, threw themselves into the bloody field, wherein was waiting for them the crown of martyrdom . . . From the Caspian Sea to the Urumieh, it is the shadow of the Armenian revolutionaries that accompanies the Persian groups. The religion of freedom makes brothers of those two religiously different elements, that for centuries have learned to hate each other under subjugation.[150]

In 1907, therefore, when the Dashnaktsutiun decided to involve itself in the revolution, it referred to a "popular awakening" that would overtake the East.[151]

A significant factor leading to this view and opening the way for the Dashnaktsutiun's involvement in the revolution was the new program adopted at the party's Fourth General Congress (Vienna, February–May 1907) wherein the party reformulated its general precepts to come closer to the ideals of socialism and, among other points, called for solidarity with progressive forces as a major component in its struggle.[152] The Dashnaktsutiun's socialism, however, still provided a special place for national problems by stressing the complexity of the class struggle in countries where the dominant nation and the oppressed minorities existed side by side. The program stated, "The class struggle becomes complicated especially in those countries where the representatives of the dominant people, by taking control of all federal and public institutions, oppress the minorities." It asserted that such situations were an obstacle to the development of class antagonism among the oppressed peoples, as well as an obstacle to the solidarity of the working classes of both oppressor and oppressed peoples, and thus hampered the struggle toward socialism. Moreover, while the workers of the dominated culture opposed their own bourgeoisie, they were at the same time "ardent about their distinct national culture which has created a unique popular psychology."[153]

The party recognized and even upheld the ideas that "the socialist movement is by essence internationalist," and that the workers of the world, "as victims of the same economic system," would unite in universal brotherhood and "cognizant of their great mission, confident of their victory," would struggle toward socialism. It further supported the goal of socialism to eliminate all borders and distinctions between nations, seeking to establish "one harmonious, integral humanity" in place of a divided world. It did not, however, consider this an immediate aim but one that would come in the unspecified future. "The realization of socialism does not demand *at present* the final dissolution of distinct [nations]," because by their "historically inherited, copious, distinctive qualities [they] will only enrich the future socialist humanity" (emphasis added).[154]

The more common interpretation of the Dashnaktsutiun's stance on socialism is that the party did not consider the doctrine the goal toward which it aspired, that socialism was the selected weapon used to battle national oppression rather than or more than the inevitable stage in economic development.[155] While this might have been the case in different periods of the Dashnaktsutiun's history, there was a concerted effort and desire in 1907 to reconcile the present of national subjugation and the future of socialism. Although the immediate purpose at all times and without question was the liberation of the Armenian people, the distant aim was socialism. This duality made the Dashnaktsutiun the target of many critics further on the left (e.g., Hnchakists and other Social Democrats) who reproached the Dashnaktsutiun for its diluted version of socialism. Some even refused to recognize it as a socialist party.[156] Despite the opposition of such critics, the Dashnaktsutiun was allowed to join the Second Socialist International in 1907 at Stuttgart, Germany.[157] In its report to the International, the party spoke of its socialist program; its activities on behalf of the Armenian people in the Ottoman and Russian Empires; its efforts at solidarity and collaboration before, during, and after the Caucasian communal violence; and its work among workers and peasants.[158] The decision to petition for membership came in the Fourth General Congress when the Dashnaktsutiun declared itself the party of the Armenian working class, whose goal it was "to protect the general interests [i.e., economic-class, human-political and national-cultural] of Armenian working masses" and "put the reins of government in the hands of the people."[159] The party applied the same class theory to peasants as to workers—the struggle of peasant against landlord was the same as that of worker against bourgeoisie. In this sense, the Dashnaktsutiun more closely resembled the peasant socialism of the Social Revolutionaries than the orthodox Marxism of the Social Democrats.[160]

Although the Hnchakian party was one of the critics of Dashnakist socialism, it too became the target of critics farther to the left who questioned the party's brand of socialism and insisted that it was essentially nationalist or who accused the party of contradiction and dualism, pointing to a nationalist agenda in the Ottoman Empire and a socialist one in the Russian Empire. In response to such criticism, the Hnchakian party began in 1906 to address its critics in the pages of *Hnchak*. The party reaffirmed its socialist program and especially its social democratic viewpoint. It pointed out that it was no more nationalist than French or German Social Democrats and rejected any notion of duality or contradiction.[161] "We have not been nationalists . . . We have been socialists" in both the Ottoman and Russian spheres of activity.[162]

The first component of the Dashnakist 1907 program resolved in the Vienna General Congress, the reformulation of socialism, was linked directly with the second component of the program, collaboration with progressive forces. While the first provided the party with an international character, the second initiated involvement in international activity.

On 16 April 1907, the debate in the Vienna Congress concerned itself with who was considered "progressive," with whom should the Dash-nakists work, and perhaps more importantly, with whom could they work? The Balkan Central Committee representative, Aram Ashot (Mi-nasian), first read a statement stressing that the idea of collaboration and solidarity with other revolutionary forces had always existed within the party but had not been firmly established. He then addressed the issue of working with Ottoman parties who were opposed to Sultan Abdul-Hamid and had a political program with a federative character. Minasian also added that cooperation must first be established among Armenian parties. The discussion then revolved around the issue of collaboration with Social Revolutionaries. Hamo Mherian, which was the alias of Hamazasp Ohanjanian, later prime minister and foreign minister of the Armenian Republic (1918–1920), dismissed any cooperation with Rus-sian Social Democrats, because "they differ from us in their historical/philosophical world view, and moreover they perceive the rural issue in a completely different way and defend a different political system." As for the Georgian Social Democrats, "they cannot cooperate with us, because they are imbued against us with racial hatred; they call themselves internationalists, but they are the most stringent chauvin-ists."[163] He preferred rather the Russian Social Revolutionaries (although he found them "slack") and called for a union under a federation with them and others while at the same time maintaining "complete party in-dependence." Dr. Hovhannes (Ivan) Zavrian of the Yerevan Central Committee informed the session that the Social Revolutionaries related their desire in December 1906 to form a Social Revolutionary federation including all Russian Social Revolutionaries and the Dashnaktsutiun, if "we cultivate a program which corresponds to the S[ocial] R[evolution-ary] spirit."[164]

The Congress decided to pursue collaboration with socialist parties: "Considering the union of revolutionary elements against the oppressive ranks essential, especially at the present political period, the Congress recommends that its Caucasian bodies work to bring about collaboration among those socialist and revolutionary parties and organizations which, with their profession of faith and their actions, are close to those of the A. R. Federation [i.e., the Dashnaktsutiun]."[165] Included among those elements close to the Dashnaktsutiun were those who accepted the inclusion of the peasantry in the class/labor theory and those who wished to solve the national issue with a broad form of federation.[166] This new policy then excluded, in principle, the Social Democrats but in-cluded the Social Revolutionaries. In reality, however, Dashnakists worked very closely with Iranian and Caucasian Social Democrats in the Iranian Constitutional Revolution, despite ideological differences. The congress reasserted the notion of solidarity and cooperation by asking that the Dashnakist branches work in their communities to propagate this policy: "To spare no effort to place in communication the Armenian communities with local labor circles and socialist organizations as a desirable method toward strengthening solidarity."[167] The communal violence between the Caucasian Armenians and Muslims played an important and decisive role in the stance taken by the Dashnakists regarding both socialism and collaboration. The party, "filled with deep anguish," considered three factors before coming to a decision: that the enmity between the two peoples was harmful to the general revolutionary movement, that the tsarist regime had not abandoned its divisive policy, and that the ignorance and anti-Armenian sentiments of the Muslims continued to be exploited. The congress then resolved to carry out a strong campaign of solidarity among both Armenians and Muslims, to put great effort into creating revolutionary organizations with or without the help of Muslim intellectuals, to strike at those Armenian elements who incite hatred and enmity, to assist those Muslim organizations that work toward solidarity, and to establish ties between Armenian and Muslim workers.[168] Although these points referred directly to relations between Armenians and Muslims in the Caucasus, they had a direct impact on the party's relationship with Caucasian and non-Caucasian Muslims in Iran.

This move toward greater solidarity between socialist organizations influenced by wider-reaching socialist goals, which were in turn influenced by the Caucasian political reality from 1903–1906, extended to attempts at cooperation between Armenian parties as well. The Hnchakist proposal to hold a congress of Armenian revolutionary parties was considered "premature" and thus rejected by the Dashnaktsutiun.[169] The parties did, however, reach some sort of rapprochement in the Caucasus by calling on their members to cease immediately all enmity and begin to work together.[170] Meetings had already taken place in Iran in November 1906 to discuss the deteriorating relationship that had led to killings between the Hnchakists and the Dashnakists.[171] These negotiations led to the creation of a bipartisan court whose decisions would be binding.[172] Most importantly, therefore, the parties had achieved some semblance of peace and solidarity in Iran, which could only facilitate participation in the Iranian Constitutional Revolution.

Therefore, a combination of factors contributed to the perception of the Iranian Constitutional Revolution as an international struggle, requiring alliances beyond borders and beyond partisanship. There was, after all, some positive image to be gained by the Hnchakist and Dashnakist insistence on defining themselves as Socialists among the Russian, Caucasian, and Iranian opposition, even when the Armenian parties did not fully follow socialism, prioritizing the nationalist agenda of Armenian liberation over internationalism, or even if some members were ignorant of or had little knowledge of socialism. But even beyond that, the acceptance of socialism to whatever degree implied recognition of its internationalist character, which helped explain and set the ideological basis for participation in the Iranian Constitutional Revolution.

Iran: New Realities and New Possibilities

The ideological and political causes did not alone provide sufficient incentive for the Dashnakists and Hnchakists to join the Iranian Constitutional Revolution. That became possible only because of the changes taking place within the Iranian constitutional movement and communities.

Droshak *Banned*

For the Dashnaktsutiun, a factor in the decision to participate was the Iranian government's banning of its organ, *Droshak*, which was regularly sent from Geneva for distribution among party members and subscribers as well as for use as an instrument to propagate party ideas. In its reports on the workings of the Dashnakist branches in Azerbaijan for the years 1904–1906, the Vrezh (Vengeance) Central Committee wrote that the Iranian government had always been aware of the Dashnaktsutiun's activities, mainly the transporting of arms and the traffic of *fedayis* to Ottoman Armenia, because of the Iranian government's "good spy network." It had never, however, in those years disturbed or interfered in such activities. Sometimes materials had been seized but were always released once a bribe was offered and accepted.[173] In fact, a few skirmishes between Iranian troops and *fedayis* did occur, causing some concern for the party, which was afraid other problems would arise with more serious consequences.[174]

The Dashnaktsutiun was disappointed when on 3 July 1906, the Iranian Postal and Customs Ministry prohibited the import of its organ, *Droshak*, along with "other revolutionary brochures" and ordered the immediate confiscation and destruction of the journal and revolutionary pamphlets.[175] It is very probable that Dashnakists were also quite surprised at this new development, considering many of Iran's customs officers were Armenians. Both the Azerbaijan Central Committee report and an article appearing in *Droshak* blamed Russia for exerting pressure on the Iranian government. The party found prohibition "unjust" as the organ had "free entrance for 16 years and has never occupied itself with that country [Iran] and its government." The article conceded that prohibition in the Ottoman and Russian Empires was understandable but that the party would not accept such measures in Iran, adding that it had information from credible sources that the move came in response to requests made by Russia in 1905 when the party published critical articles in *Droshak* against the tsarist regime.[176]

In a letter dated one day after the ban, Stepan Stepanian (Tseruni, Vrezhuni, Balajan), of the Azerbaijan Central Committee, wrote to the Dashnaktsutiun's Eastern Bureau, stating: "We had foreseen this [*Droshak* burning] and had written to the Tehran Dashnakist body to find a way by which to convince the Iranian government that *Droshak* does not present a threat to Iran." Stepanian added: "Today we received . . . 3000 copies of *Droshak*, no. 6. Customs-house supervisor M. Laverse . . . ordered *Droshak* burned." He attributed this decision to the intrigues of the Hnchakists, Ahmet Ağaev (Ağaoğlu), and the Ottoman government. He found it rather suspicious that Hnchakist papers were not subject to confiscation and surmised that "they have begun to work against us in government circles and have succeeded."[177] He believed the Hnchakists to be the "satellites" in Iran of Ahmet Ağaev, an editor of Baku's first and most important daily, *Hayat Gazetesi* (Life Newspaper—in Azerbaijani Turkish).[178] While this seems improbable, it sheds light on the hostile and sometimes violent relations between the two parties. In addition, he asserted that persons close to the Iranian government believed that Sultan Abdul-Hamid II somehow had a part in convincing the Iranian monarchy to ban the organ. Stepanian concluded the letter by asking that the new situation facing Iranian Armenians be addressed at the next General Congress of Delegates.[179]

In July 1906, 2,500 copies of the organ were destroyed in Tabriz and 1,170 destroyed in Anzali.[180] In the same month, the Dashnaktsutiun protested the actions of the Iranian government in the form of a letter to the foreign affairs minister in Tehran, reiterating that "our struggle is directed against the Ottoman and Russian governments" and asking that the minister intervene on its behalf with the shah.[181] Protest telegrams were also sent to the Iranian embassies in Berlin and Paris.[182] Moreover, Dashnakist branches in Azerbaijan and Tehran attempted to have the order rescinded and in the meantime to find ways to elude it. For example, in Anzali, a Dashnakist who was on good terms with the assistant to the local postal director received advice on how to continue to import *Droshak* undetected and conveyed that information to the paper's staff in Geneva. Thus, while the organ no longer reached certain areas, by December 1906 Anzali was again receiving *Droshak*.[183]

The Dashnaktsutiun considered the banning and burning of *Droshak* in mid-1906 a "heavy blow," indicating to its leading bodies that there was a change in the policy of the Iranian government regarding the party's operations within Iran.[184] The threat to the party's organ and its rather unchecked activities served as a warning to the Dashnaktsutiun and thus contributed to initiating a change in or modifying party policy regarding political movements in Iran.

Further Changes and Pragmatism

The period from Mozaffar al-Din Shah's signing of the constitution on 30 December 1906 to the attempted coup of Mohammad Ali Shah in December 1907 was a decisive one for Iranian Armenian communities and political parties for several reasons, all of which revealed a new Iranian reality and urged them to act constructively in such a reality.

A report by the Azerbaijan Central Committee to the Fourth General Congress regarding activities for the years 1904–1906 shows that until that date Dashnakists had rejected participation for "very understandable reasons." They had heard from "dependable sources" that Crown Prince Mohammad Ali Mirza, who resided in Tabriz, and his supporters wanted to create an Armenian-Turkish clash in order to force the British consulate to distance itself from the movement's leaders. They planned to convince the British that the Iranian movement was not a political movement but merely a consequence of the Armenian and Muslim conflicts in the Caucasus. "A small opportunity would have been sufficient for bloodletting and we could have been the victims of that provocation." The report further stated that the Iranian "masses" perceived the Dashnaktsutiun to be an "enemy of Islam" thanks to papers such as those of Ahmet Ağaev's Baku-based *Hayat Gazetesi* (Life Newspaper) and the Calcutta-based *Habl al-Matin* (The Firm Cord).[185] Another report of the Vrezh Central Committee of Azerbaijan, unsigned but dated 25 November 1906, made further reference to the "religious and purely nationalist aspirations" of the revolutionaries and added that the committee had remained neutral, because no organization existed among the Iranians and the movement's demands were "extremely insufficient" for the Armenians.[186]

As events proceeded, however, neutrality was no longer an option as Armenian populations in Iran, along with Jewish, Zoroastrian, Azali Babi, and Baha'i communities, were increasingly feeling the pressure of anti-revolutionary forces as well as conservative *'ulama*.[187] The Fourth General Congress of the Dashnaktsutiun had already made self-defense a priority, but attention to self-defense became particularly significant for the Azerbaijan Central Committee because of events taking place in the region.[188] By 1907, Azerbaijan was actively involved in the revolution. In mid-1907, the debate over Article Eight of the Supplementary Constitutional Laws became heated in Tabriz. The article stated, "The People of the Persian Empire are to enjoy equal rights before the law."[189] From outside the Majles, Sheikh Fazlollah Nuri led conservative *'ulama* and the pro-clerical party in the Majles to oppose the article on grounds that it contradicted *shari'a*, religious law.[190] The Azerbaijani delegates to the Majles and the Tabriz Anjoman (Tabriz Provincial Council) opposed Nuri's attempts to revise the proposed laws. Tabriz revolutionaries expelled the leading clerics of the city as other regions, including Rasht, Anzali, Isfahan, and Shiraz, joined to resist attempts by conservative elements to increase or retain the authority of the *'ulama* and the shah.[191] The debate took on a violent turn when the Shahsevan tribe led by Rahim Khan's son, who had the strong support of the shah, plundered villages and killed many near Tabriz.[192]

The debate over constitutional laws directly affected all non-Muslim minorities, including Armenians. The Electoral Laws of 1906 made no mention of the right of non-Muslims to elect their own representatives, but by 1909, a new law was written that stated, "Finally the Armenians, 'Chaldeans' (i.e. Nestorian Christians), Zoroastrians and Jews have each one Representative."[193] According to Nazem al-Islam Kermani, founding member of the Secret Anjoman (Anjoman-e makhfi) formed in early 1905 and author of a history of the Iranian Constitutional Revolution's early years, the issue of non-Muslim electoral rights became a topic of debate in mid-1906. Kermani explained that merchants and intellectuals taking sanctuary in July 1906 in the British legation in Tehran challenged the shah's granting of a *majles-e islami* (Islamic assembly). Instead, they demanded and received a decree for a *majles-e melli* (national assembly). They reasoned that the wording "Islamic assembly" could be problematic. For example, Kermani elaborated, a delegate to the Majles might be expelled for being non-Muslim, an "infidel," and that someone like the conservative cleric Fazlollah Nuri might denounce the whole of the Majles as heretical in an effort to incite Muslims against it. In addition, "the Jews and Armenians and Zoroastrians must also send their deputies to the assembly and the word . . . melli [national] is appropriate," while the word *islami* (Islamic) would not be applicable.[194] However, when the electoral laws were drawn up in August 1906, no mention of non-Muslim minorities was made although non-Muslims had insisted on electing their own representatives. According to Kermani, the Secret Anjoman had informed the Armenians, Jews, and Zoroastrians that "this request would cause the objection of the 'ulama of Najaf and Isfahan" as well as disturbances and resentment. The members of the Anjoman were able to "change the minds" of the Armenians and Jews after considerable turmoil. Kermani added that the Armenians "with the highest decency and sensibility transferred their right in the first elections to his excellency [Sayyid Mohammad] Tabataba'i" and that Sayyid Abdollah Behbahani represented the Jews, thus giving up any claims to a representative of their own.[195] On the insistence of the Zoroastrians, whose pre-Islamic history in Iran provided them with an advantage, they were allowed a representative. Moreover, the Supplementary Laws ratified on 7 October 1907 further indicated that Iran's government was not moving toward a secular concept of nation, which many of the constitutionalists had envisioned and that Iranian Armenians understandably preferred, but rather toward a more religious one. This is evidenced most strikingly by the first article of the Supplementary Constitutional Laws, which were eventually ratified—"The official religion of Iran is Islam, according to the rightful Twelver Ja'fari [doctrine], the faith the Shah of Iran must hold and promote."[196] The second and fifty-eighth articles, which asserted that no law enacted by the Majles could contradict the *shari'a* and that only a Muslim could become minister, respectively, further indicated the inferior position of non-Muslims in Iran.[197] Religious and political leaders of the Armenian community objected to the constitutional laws that limited the rights of non-Muslims and requested via telegrams equal rights for Iranian Armenians.[198]

A second major development in Tabriz took place in April 1907 when a dispute broke out between the villagers of Qarachaman (located on the road between Tabriz and Tehran) and the landowners. As the peasants refused to pay their share of the crop, the landlord appealed to the governor and the leading *mojtahed*, Mirza Hasan. The governor sent in troops, who burned, pillaged, and killed. The Qarachaman peasants later brought their case to the Tabriz Anjoman. After considerable debate, Mirza Hasan and other clerics were expelled. The membership of the Anjoman also changed as conservative individuals were replaced by more liberal ones.[199]

Life in Azerbaijan had become unsafe and harder in 1907, evidenced by food riots in Tabriz and as events in the region affected the lives of all its residents.[200] The difficult political situation also affected Salmas where, according to an observer, roads had been closed all of June 1907, making Dashnakist activity, mainly transportation of arms, impossible.[201] *Droshak* stated: "Persia at this moment is passing through a crisis full of unexpected happenings," adding that the current situation was chaotic and formidable.[202] In addition, Tabriz was becoming more revolutionary, but also more liberal, a factor that clearly appealed to the Armenian parties.[203]

Thus, in 1907, the Dashnaktsutiun considered involvement in the Iranian revolutionary movement progressive, while only a year earlier it had considered it reactionary. While the two ranking clerics, Sayyid Abdollah Behbahani and Sayyid Mohammad Tabataba'i, had emerged as leaders of the Constitutional Revolution in its early stages, the constitutional movement moved farther to the left, especially in Azerbaijan, as Social Democrats, specifically from Tabriz, became more involved and kept the goals of the revolution as well as the revolution itself alive. The Dashnaktsutiun then realized that the movement was changing from what it believed in 1906 to be a movement with a "nationalist/religious nature" to one with a more internationalist character.[204] Although much less information exists regarding the Hnchakian party, it would be safe to assume that its decision to participate in the Iranian Constitutional Revolution was also affected by the new Iranian political reality, highlighted by the debate over new electoral and supplement laws affecting the status of non-Muslim minorities and the new insecurity experienced by the Armenian communities.

Pragmatism and the Flight of Revolutionaries

The ideological and political motivations to join the Iranian Constitutional Revolution were closely followed by more practical considerations, such as the new insecurity of life in northwestern Iran and the flight of "professional" activists from the Caucasus into Iran. An era of political persecution succeeded the Russian Revolution. It was led by P. A. Stolypin, chairman of the Russian Council of Ministers, whose reactionary policy led to the arrest, exile, and execution of thousands of antitsarist activists, including Armenians. In the Yerevan province alone, 5,351 arrests were made in 1908.[205] Despite attempts by Viceroy Vorontsov-Dashkov, the Dashnaktsutiun became a major target of Stolypin's actions.[206] The party felt its existence endangered.[207] *Droshak* condemned tsarist policy, accusing Russia of persecuting Armenians within and outside its borders, referring to Armenians as "death toys" in the hands of the Russians, and lamented: "Still with a historical blindness we naively believe that Russia is the 'traditional' protector of the Armenians."[208] The party planned to carry out a census of the "victims of [Russian] oppression" and asked its members to send in the number of comrades imprisoned and/or exiled in the years 1907 and 1908, the number still imprisoned and/or exiled, and the time they remained so.[209] Those Armenians who escaped persecution most often fled to Iran and were absorbed by the already existing political party branches there. Therefore, in addition to the ideological motivations for joining the constitutional movement, there were practical considerations as the focus of the Armenian political parties, especially the Dashnaktsutiun, shifted from the Caucasus, where political activity was harshly suppressed, to Iran, where freer political conditions and the influx of Caucasian revolutionaries contributed to Armenian political activity in northwestern Iran.

Conclusion

Participation in the Iranian Constitutional Revolution and joint ventures with Iranian constitutionalists and more significantly with Caucasian Muslim revolutionaries in Iran became possible for the Dashnaktsutiun and the Hnchakian parties only in 1907 because of the reevaluation of policy and tactics, stressing socialism and solidarity, in the face of Russian persecution, communal violence in the Caucasus, Ottoman aggression in Iran, and the Young Turk coup. Moreover, a new political situation wherein the parties found their operations in Iran threatened, a new insecurity of life and property in Iranian Armenian communities, and the greater influence of Socialists in the revolution further propelled them into serious deliberation regarding the nature and extent of participation.

Notes

1. For a shorter version of a discussion on Dashnakist motivations, see Houri Berberian, "The Dashnaktsutiun and the Iranian Constitutional Revolution, 1905–1911," *Iranian Studies* 29, 1–2 (Winter/Spring 1996): 7–33.

2. "Kaghakakan tesutiun: tiurk-parskakan" [Political perception: Turko-Persian], *Droshak*, no. 10, October 1907. See also "Kaghakakan tesutiun" [Political perception], no. 11–12, November–December 1907; "Kaghakakan tesutiun," no. 4, April 1908; "Kaghakakan tesutiun," no. 5, May 1908.

3. V. A. Bayburdyan, *Turk-Iranakan haraberutiunnere, 1900–1914* [Turko-Iranian relations, 1900–1914] (Yerevan: Haykakan SSH Gitutiunneri Akademia, 1974), 73–74. See also Aso, "Namak parska-trkakan sahmanglkhits" [Letter from the Perso-Turkish border], 14 May 1906, *Hnchak*, no. 5, May 1906.

4. Bayburdyan, *Turk-Iranakan haraberutiunnere*, 82.

5. Ibid., 90. See also "Kaghakakan tesutiun," *Droshak*, no. 4, April 1908; no. 5, May 1908; Marzpet to Eastern Bureau, Tiflis, 25 September 1907, Archives of the Armenian Revolutionary Federation [Dashnaktsutiun], Watertown, Massachusetts, file 473, document 124a.

6. Bayburdyan, *Turk-Iranakan haraberutiunnere*, 93–94.

7. See, for example, Paylak [Ruben Derdzakian] to Comrades, 7 January 1905, 468/5; Samson and Marzpetuni to Western Bureau, 25 April 1906, 470/28; Samson to Torgom, 27 April 1906, 470/29; Minutes of the Azerbaijan Central Committee, Session 58, 8 August 1907, and Session 33, 28 July 1908, 540/b.

8. See, for example, "Kaghakakan tesutiun: turk-parskakan," *Droshak*, no. 10, September 1907; "Kaghakakan tesutiun," *Droshak*, no. 4, April 1908; no. 5, May 1908; Samson and Marzpetuni to Western Bureau, 25 April 1906, 470/28; Vardan to Koms, 13 October 1906, 471/133; Minutes of the Azerbaijan Central Committee, Session 61, 4 September 1907, 540/b. Vrezhstan Third Regional Congress, 19 December 1907–13 January 1908, Session 8, n.d., 473/156.

9. Minutes of the Azerbaijan Central Committee, Session 54, 31 July 1907, 540/b.

10. Mohammad Mukhlis to Samson, 16 November 1324/1906, 565/1; Mohammad Mukhlis to Samson, 14 November 1324/1906, 565/2.

11. Aso, "Namak trko-parskakan sahmanaglkhits," *Hnchak*, no. 9–10, September–October 1906.

12. Note that the last such article appeared in *Droshak*, no. 5, May 1908.

13. For a study of Armenians and the Jangalis, see Aram Arkun, "Armenians and the Jangalis," *Iranian Studies* 30, 1–2 (Winter/Spring 1997): 25–52.

14. "Nashriyat-e ferqah-ye sosyal demokrasi-e Iran" [Publication of the Social Democratic Group of Iran], in Khosrow Shakeri [Cosroe Chaqueri], comp. and ed., *Asnad-e tarikhi-ye jonbesh-e kargari/sosyal demokrasi va komunisti-ye Iran* [Documents of the history of the labor/social democratic and communist movement in Iran] (Tehran: Padzahr Press, 1983), 6: 5, 9. French translation in Cosroe Chaqueri, ed., *La Social-démocratie en Iran: articles et documents* (Florence: Mazdak, 1979), 142, 146.

15. "Haytararagir: Osmanian kaysrutian endimatir tarreru congrein, gumarvats Yevropayi mej" [Declaration: to the congress of the Ottoman Empire's oppositional elements, convened in Europe], *Droshak*, no. 1, January 1908.

16. For a jointly planned assassination, see "Gortsi propagande" [Propaganda of deed], *Droshak*, no. 10, October 1907.

17. "Chorrort Endhanur Zhoghovi voroshumner: hamerashkhutiun Tiurkioy aylatarr tsegheru het (13)" [Decisions of the Fourth General Congress: solidarity with Turkey's dissimilar races] in Dasnabedian, *Niuter*, 3: 304–5. See also same in *Droshak*, no. 5, May 1907.

18. Arsen Kitur, *Patmutiun S. D. Hnchakian Kusaktsutian* [History of the S. D. Hnchakian Party] (Beirut: Shirak Press, 1962), 1: 313–14.

19. "Tiurkioy heghapokhutiune" [Turkey's revolution], *Droshak*, no. 7, July 1908. See also "Heghapokhakan sharzhum" [Revolutionary movement] in the same issue.

20. "Heghapokhakan sharzhum," *Droshak*, no. 7, July 1908; "Osmanian kaysrutiune yev Hayere" [The Ottoman Empire and the Armenians], *Droshak*, no. 8, August 1908.

21. "Shrjaberakan: II" [Circular: II], 2 August 1908; *Droshak*, no. 8, August 1908.

22. "Teghatvutiun" [Ebb], *Droshak*, no. 9–10, September–October 1908. See also "Turkia" [Turkey], *Droshak*, no. 2–3, February–March 1909.

23. "Tiurkiayum" [In Turkey], *Hnchak*, no. 8–12, August–December 1908; "Trkakan reformistakan sharzhume" [Turkish reform movement], *Hnchak*, no. 6–7, June–July 1908; "Noraguyn Tiurkian" [New Turkey], *Hnchak*, no. 8–12, August–December 1908. For earlier arguments against collaboration with the Young Turks, see "Menk yev mer knnadatnere" [We and our critics], *Hnchak*, no. 9–10, September–October 1906; "Hratap khndire" [Urgent problem], *Hnchak*, no. 11, November 1906.

24. "Turk brnapetutiune yev Yeritasard Turkere" [Turkish despotism and the Young Turks], *Hnchak*, no. 1, January 1908. See also "Mer khorhurde" [Our advice], *Hnchak*, no. 2, February 1907; *Hnchak*, no. 6–7, June–July 1908.

25. "Haytararutiun Sots[ial] Dem[okrat] Hnchakian Kusaktsutian sharkerun" [Declaration to the Social Democratic Hnchakian Party ranks], 26 November 1910, *Hnchak*, no. 1–2, August–September 1910.

26. "Kaghvatskner Sots[ial] Dem[okrat] Hnchakian Kusaktsutian Tachk[akan] Patg[amovarakan] A[rajin] Zhoghovi voroshumneren" [Extracts from the decisions of the Social Democratic Hnchakian Party's First Turkish Congress of Delegates], *Hnchak*, no. 3–4–5, March-April-May 1910. See also Hrand Gangruni, *Hay heghapokhutiune Osmanian brnatirutian dem, 1890–1910* [The Armenian revolution against Ottoman despotism, 1890–1910] (Beirut: n.p., 1973), 379–83.

27. "Yerkrord heghapokhutiun" [Second revolution], *Droshak*, no. 4, April 1909.

28. "Kilikian ariunaver" [Bloody Cilicia], *Droshak*, no. 4, April 1909. See also "Pashpanvenk" [Let us defend ourselves], *Droshak*, no. 5, May 1909.

29. "Yerkrord heghapokhutiun," *Droshak*, no. 4, April 1909.

30. The agreement, signed by both parties, appeared in the Istanbul-based *Azatamart* [Battle for Freedom], 24 August/6 September 1909, and may be found in Gabriel Lazian, comp., *Hayastan yev hay date est dashnagreru* [Armenia and the Armenian cause according to treaties] (Cairo: Husaber, 1942), 71–72. See also Feroz Ahmad, "Unionist Relations with the Greek, Armenian, and Jewish Communities of the Ottoman Empire, 1908–1914," in *Christians and Jews in the Ottoman Empire: The Functioning of a Plural Society*, vol. 1, *The Central Lands*, ed. Benjamin Braude and Bernard Lewis (New York: Holmes & Meier, 1982), 420–21.

31. *Droshak* published a series of articles entitled "Nor Tiurkian" [New Turkey] from 1909 to 1911, exploring the Ottoman constitution, the new regime, and issues like electoral rights, representation, women's rights, democracy, justice, and religious/national problems.

32. Bayburdyan, *Turk-Iranakan haraberutiunnere*, 146–47.

33. Ibid., 148. See also Marzpet to Eastern Bureau, Tiflis, 2 October 1907, 473/127; Samson et al. to Avarayr [?] (Khoy), 12 November 1907, 473/137.

34. See, for example, Samson to Western Bureau, Geneva, 25 September 1907, 473/124a; Marzpet to Eastern Bureau, Tiflis, 2 October 1907, 473/127; Samson et al. to Avarayr [?] (Khoy), 12 November 1907, 473/137; Azerbaijan Central Committee to Western Bureau, Geneva, 20 November 1907, 473/141.

35. Bayburdyan, *Turk-Iranakan haraberutiunnere*, 163–64.

36. Ibid., 171.

37. "Kaghakakan tesutiune: tiurk-parskakan," *Droshak*, no. 10, September 1907; "Vtangali herankar" [Dangerous prospect], *Droshak*, no. 11–12, November–December 1907; "Kaghakakan tesutiun: Parskastan" [Political perception: Persia], *Droshak*, no. 11–12, November–December 1907.

38. "Kaghakakan tesutiun: Parskastan," *Droshak*, no. 11–12, November-December 1907.

39. Nikki R. Keddie, "Iranian Revolutions in Comparative Perspective," *American Historical Review* 88, 3 (June 1983): 586; Nikki R. Keddie, "Religion and Irreligion in Early Iranian Nationalism," in *Iran: Religion, Politics and Society*, ed. Nikki R. Keddie (London: Frank Cass, 1980), 13–14. For a study of Japan as a topic in the political debate of twentieth-century Iran, see Roxane Haag-Higuchi, "A Topos and Its Dissolution: Japan in Some 20th-Century Iranian Texts," *Iranian Studies* 29, 1–2 (Winter/Spring 1996): 71–83.

40. "Kovkasum spasvogh pahesti zorakochi artiv" [On the occasion of the awaited reserve conscription in the Caucasus], *Droshak*, no. 11, November 1904. For a similar statement, see "Paterazmi aritov" [On the occasion of war], *Hnchak*, no. 7, July 1904.

41. "Tsarizmi tem" [Against tsarism], *Droshak*, no. 10, October 1904.

42. Letter by Dzasum, 23 February 1904, *Hnchak*, no. 3, March 1904.

43. See "Tsarizm" [Tsarism], *Hnchak*, no. 4–5, April–May 1904; "Kovkasum" [In the Caucasus], *Droshak*, no. 2, February 1904.

44. "Paterazmi aritov," *Hnchak*, no. 7, July 1904.

45. "Parskastan: brnakalutian ankume" [Persia: the collapse of despotism], *Droshak*, no. 7, July 1909. See also "Khaghaghutian dashinke" [The peace treaty], *Droshak*, no. 10, October 1905. For similar sentiments, see "Motik Arevelkum" [In the Near East], *Hnchak*, no. 1, January 1908.

46. See "Declaration of the Social-Democrats of Iran," signed by the Tabriz Committee of the Social-Democratic Party of Iran, 1906, in Chaqueri, *Social-démocratie en Iran*, 139.

47. "Paterazme yev Sotsialistnere" [The war and the socialists], *Droshak*, no. 3, March 1904; "Kovkasum spasvogh pahesti zorakochi artive," *Droshak*, no. 11, November 1904; "Tsarizm," *Hnchak*, no. 4–5, April–May 1904; "Paterazmi aritov," *Hnchak*, no. 7, July 1904.

48. "1905–1906," *Droshak*, no. 1, January 1906.

49. Malkhas [A. Hovsepian], *Aprumner* [Life experiences] (Boston: Hayrenik, 1931), 256–57.

50. "Parskastan: brnakalutian ankume," *Droshak*, no. 7, July 1909.

51. "Parskastan: sahmanadrutiun verahastatvats," [Persia: reestablished constitution], *Droshak*, no. 5, May 1909.

52. "Parskastan: ariunrusht hetadimutiune" [Persia: bloodthirsty regression], *Droshak*, no. 11–12, November–December 1908.

53. Mehdi Malekzadeh, *Tarikh-e enqelab-e mashrutiyat-e Iran* [History of the constitutional revolution of Iran] (Tehran: Soqrat, 1949–1953), 3: 596–98. See also Janet Afary, *The Iranian Constitutional Revolution, 1906–1911: Grassroots Democracy, Social Democracy, and the Origins of Feminism* (New York: Columbia University Press, 1996), 136–37. *Ruh al-Qodos*, edited by Sultan al- 'Ulama Khorasani, was well known for its personal attacks on Mohammad Ali Shah. *Mosavat* (1907–1908), edited by Mohammad Reza Shirazi and Abd al-Rahim Khalkhali, was a great supporter of civil rights. See 118; Edward G. Browne, *The Press and Poetry of Modern Persia* (1914; reprint, Los Angeles: Kalimát Press, 1983), 87–88, 138–39.

54. "Kaghakakan tesutiun: tiurk-parskakan," *Droshak*, no. 10, September 1907.

55. "Tiezerakan reaktsan yev sotsializme" [Universal reaction and socialism], *Droshak*, no. 6, June 1908. See also "Kaghakakan tesutiun," in the same issue; "Parskastan: heghapokhutiune anenkcheli" [Persia: the invincible revolution], *Droshak*, no. 9–10, September–October 1908; "Parskastan: ariunrusht hetadimutiun," *Droshak*, no. 11–12, November–December 1908.

56. "Kaghakakan tesutiun," *Droshak*, no. 4, April 1908; "Kaghakakan tesutiun," no. 5, May 1908; no. 7, July 1909.

57. "Parskastan: sahmanadrutiune verahastatvats," *Droshak*, no. 5, May 1909. Regarding Russian intervention, see Afary, *Iranian Constitutional Revolution*, 224–27.

58. V. I. Lenin, "Events in the Balkans and Persia," *Proletary* [Proletariat], no. 37, 16 (29) October 1908, cited in *V. I. Lenin: Collected Works*, vol. 15,: *March 1908-August 1908*, ed. and trans. Andrew Rothstein and Bernard Isaacs (Moscow: Progress Publishers, 1973), 230.

59. For a text of the decree in Armenian, see Lazian, *Hayastan yev hay date est dashnagreru*, 121–23. See also "Yerkrord harvatse" [The second assault], *Droshak*,

no. 6, July 1903; "Rusahayastanum avazakayin hramane" [The thieving order in Russian Armenia], *Hnchak*, no. 9–10, September–October 1903.

60. Plehve was assassinated in July 1904 by Russian Social Revolutionaries.

61. For actual correspondence between the Catholicos and the Interior minister, see, for example, *Droshak*, no. 7, August 1903, and no. 9, November 1903.

62. For more details of the demonstrations, see "Haykakan tsuytser Kovkasum" [Armenian demonstrations in the Caucasus], *Droshak*, no. 7, August 1903; no. 8, September 1903; no. 9, November 1903; "Achkakaputiune" [Blindfolding], *Hnchak*, no. 9–10, September–October 1903; Letter by Dzasum, 23 February 1904, no. 3, *Hnchak*, March 1904.

63. Anaide Ter Minassian, *Nationalism and Socialism in the Armenian Revolutionary Movement (1887–1912)*, trans. A. M. Berrett (Cambridge: The Zoryan Institute, 1984), 32. For the French original, see Anahide Ter Minassian, "Nationalisme et socialisme dans le mouvement révolutionnaire arménien," *La Question arménienne* (Roquevaire: Editions Parenthèses, 1983).

64. "Kovkasahayi tagnape" [The Caucasian Armenian's predicament], *Droshak*, no. 7, August 1903; "Rusahayastanum avazakayin hramane," *Hnchak*, no. 9–10, September–October 1903. For the Self-Defense Committee, see the Dashnaktsutiun's Regional Congress of the Caucasus (April–May? 1904) in Dasnabedian, *Niuter*, 2: 201; Circular by the Western Bureau of the Dashnaktsutiun, 30 November 1904, in *Niuter*, 2: 202–3.

65. E. Aknuni, "Kovkasian khabrikner" [Caucasian news], *Droshak*, no. 2, February 1904; "Rusahayastanum avazakayin hramane," *Hnchak*, no. 9–10, September–October 1903.

66. "Yerevani tsuytsi taredartzin" [On the anniversary of the Yerevan demonstration], signed by the A. R. Federation [Dashnaktsutiun] Self-Defense Central Committee, *Droshak*, no. 8, September 1904.

67. "Achkakaputiune," *Hnchak*, no. 9–10, September–October 1903. For similar sentiments, see an announcement by the Dashnaktsutiun Western Bureau to Non-Russian Armenians, 18/5 January 1904, in Dasnabedian, *Niuter*, 2: 101–3.

68. "Rusahayastanum avazakayin hramane," *Hnchak*, no. 9–10, September–October 1903; "Yerkrord harvatse," *Droshak*, no. 6, July 1903.

69. "Yerkrord harvatse," *Droshak*, no. 6, July 1903; E. Aknuni, "Kovkasian khaprikner," *Droshak*, no. 3, March 1904. For similar perceptions, see "Karmir sultan–karmir tsar" [Red sultan–red tsar], *Droshak*, no. 2, February 1905.

70. "Koch Kovkasahayerin" [Call to Caucasian Armenians], 3 August 1903, signed by the Independent Committee of Caucasian Dashnakists, in Dasnabedian, *Niuter*, 2: 99–101.

71. A list of tsarist officials on whom assassination attempts were made may be found in D. Ananun, *Rusahayeri hasarakakan zarkatsume* [The social development of Russian Armenians] (Venice, 1926), 3: 45–48.

72. See, for example, "Haykakan tsuytser Kovkasum," *Droshak*, no. 8, September 1903; no. 9, November 1903; "Drutiune Kovkasum" [The situation in the Caucasus], no. 10, December 1903; "Terore Rusastanum" [The terror in Russia], *Droshak*, no. 8, August 1904; "Zhoghovrdi kamke" [The people's will], *Hnchak*, no.

7, July 1904; "Hishatakeli tvakan (1904–1905)" [Memorable date (1904–1905)], *Droshak*, no. 1, June 1905.

73. "Patrast yeghek" [Be prepared], *Droshak*, no. 3, March 1904. Another article reported on such preparations as the distribution of arms by Russian officials to Caucasian Muslims during the confiscation period. See "Kovkasian khabrikner," *Droshak*, no. 1, January 1905.

74. "Miutiun kam hamerashkhutiun hay heghapokhakani yev otar tarreru het" [Unity or solidarity with Armenian revolutionary and foreign elements], Third General Congress (February–March 1904, Sofia), in Dasnabedian, *Niuter*, 2: 118–19. See also Circular by the Western Bureau of the Dashnaktsutiun, 30 November 1904, in Dasnabedian, *Niuter*, 2: 202–3.

75. For a discussion of some of the reasons for the objection of Social Democrats, including the "national issue," see V. I. Lenin, "Speech on an Agreement with the Socialists-Revolutionaries, April 23 (May 6)," made at the Third Congress of the Russian Social Democratic Labor Party (1905), in *V. I. Lenin: Collected Works*, vol. 8, *January–July 1905*, ed. V. J. Jerome and trans. Bernard Isaacs and Isidor Lasker (Moscow: Progress Publishers, 1962), 416–21.

76. For a text of the decisions, see, for example, "Heghapokhakan dashn tsarizmi dem" [Revolutionary pact against tsarism], *Droshak*, no. 12, December 1904; *Heghapokhakan dashn: mijkusaktsakan khorhrdazhoghovneri voroshumnere* [Revolutionary pact: decisions of the interparty conferences] (Geneva: Droshak Tparan, 1905). See also a circular sent out by the Dashnaktsutiun's Western Bureau, 10 January 1905, in Dasnabedian, *Niuter*, 2: 225–26.

77. Fourth Regional Congress of Caucasus, 1904, Session 2, in Dasnabedian, *Niuter*, 2: 213.

78. "Heghapokhakan kusaktsutiunneri dashn tsarizmi dem" [Pact of revolutionary parties against tsarism], *Droshak*, no. 5, May 1905.

79. "Nakhagits kovkasian gortsuneutian" [Plan for Caucasian activity], June 1905, in Dasnabedian, *Niuter*, 2: 232.

80. Ibid. See also the council's resolution, April 1905, in Dasnabedian, *Niuter*, 2: 229–30.

81. "Nakhagits kovkasian gortsuneutian," 232–34.

82. "Chorrort Shrjanayin Zhoghovi voroshumneri ardzanagrutiune" [Registration of the decisions of the Fourth Regional Congress], in Dasnabedian, *Niuter*, 2: 206–8; "Khonarhvogh tage" [The yielding crown], *Droshak*, no. 9, September 1905; "Boghoki ardiunke" [The result of protest], signed by the Dashnaktsutiun's Central Committee in the Caucasus, *Droshak*, no. 10, October 1905. The party also congratulated the Armenian people for their victory. See "Zhoghovrdakan arajin haghtutiune (tghtaktsutiun)" [The first popular victory (correspondence)], 6 August 1905, *Droshak*, no. 10, October 1905.

83. For details, see, for example the correspondence of the Shahstan [Tehran] Central Committee, 579/1/25/32/44/62.

84. See, for example, "Sahmanadrutiun" [Constitution], *Hnchak*, no. 8, August 1905; "Drutiune Rusastanum," *Hnchak*, no. 8, August 1905; "Drutiune Rusastanum," *Hnchak*, no. 9–10, September–October 1905.

85. See Ter Minassian, *Nationalism and Socialism*, 45. See also M[ikayel] Varandian, "Che kay anjatum" [There is no separation], *Droshak*, no. 5, May 1907; "Anjatman khndire" [The question of separation], *Droshak*, no. 5, May 1907.

86. For an extract of the actual decision reached by the assembly of those opposed to the party center, see Kitur, *Patmutiun*, 1: 269.

87. Kitur, *Patmutiun*, 1: 267.

88. Ibid., 288.

89. Ibid., 277–78. See also the declaration of the party in *Hnchak*, no. 4, April 1902.

90. Kitur, *Patmutiun*, 1: 281–83.

91. Ibid., 292.

92. See "XVIII Tari" [18th Year], *Hnchak*, no. 1, January 1905; "Bagui gortsadule" [The Baku strike], *Hnchak*, no. 1, January 1905; "Heghapokhutiun Rusastanum" [Revolution in Russia], *Hnchak*, no. 2, February 1905; "Kazmakerpvats kriv" [Organized battle], *Hnchak*, no. 3, 20 February 1905. For Armenian worker and peasant participation in the Russian Revolution, see, for example, Ts. P. Aghayan, *Revolyutsion sharzhumnere Hayastanum, 1905–1907 t.t.* [Revolutionary movements in Armenia, 1905–1907] (Yerevan: Haykakan SAR Gitutiunneri Akademia, 1955); V[artan] A[ram] Parsamyan, *Revolyutsion sharzhumnere Hayastanum, 1905–1907 t.t.* [Revolutionary movements in Armenia, 1905–1907] (Yerevan: Petakan Hamalsaran, 1955).

93. Kitur, *Patmutiun*, 1: 293. For similar perceptions, see also "Hnchakian Kusaktsutiune" [The Hnchakian Party], *Hnchak*, no. 1–2, January–February 1906.

94. For further elaboration, see "Mi kani akamay khosker" [A few obligatory words], *Hnchak*, no. 3, March 1906.

95. Kitur lists the names of those who seceded from the Hnchakian party and settled in Tabriz. See Kitur, *Patmutiun*, 1: 294.

96. "Hamerashkhutian dashink Hnchakian Kusaktsutian yev Verakazmial Kusaktsutian mijev" [Solidarity treaty between the Hnchakian Party and the Reformed Party], 20 December 1907, *Hnchak* (Supplement), no. 11, 1907.

97. S. Sapah-Giulian [Stepan Ter Stepanian], "Hamerashkhutian kaghabari shurje" [Around the idea of solidarity], *Hnchak*, no. 12, December 1907.

98. E. Aknouni [Aknuni/Khachatur Malumian], *Political Persecution: Armenian Prisoners of the Caucasus (A Page of the Tzar's Persecution*, trans. A.M. and H.W. (New York: n.p., 1911), 30 n. 6. According to Aknuni, the number of Muslims killed was greater than the number of Armenians, which add up to 1,173, although he does not specify the numbers of Muslims killed. For the Armenian version, see E. Aknuni, *Boghoki dzayn: kovkasahay kaghakakan bantarkialnere (tsarakan halatsanki mi ej)* [Voice of protest: Caucasian Armenian political prisoners (a page from tsarist persecution)] (Beirut: Ghukas Karapetian, 1978), 59 n. 1. Another source places the total number killed at more than 10,000. See Filip Makharadze, *Ocherki revoliutsionnovo dvizheniia v Zakavkaz'e* [Studies of the revolutionary movement in Transcaucasia] (Tiflis, 1927), 300, 307, cited in Richard G. Hovannisian, *Armenia: On the Road to Independence, 1918* (Berkeley and Los Angeles: University of California Press, 1967), 264 n. 64. See also Anahide Ter Minassian, "The Revolution of 1905 in Transcaucasia," *Armenian Review* 42 (Summer 1989): 10–11; Tadeusz Swietochowski, *Russian Azerbaijan, 1905–1920: The Shaping of National*

Identity in a Muslim Community (Cambridge: Cambridge University Press, 1985). For eyewitness accounts, see, for example, A. Giulkhandanian, *Hay-Tatarakan endharumnere* [The Armeno-Tatar clashes], vol. 1, *Bakui arajin endharumnere* [Baku's first clashes] (Paris: Typographie Franco-Caucasienne, 1933); Luigi Villari, *Fire and Sword in the Caucasus* (London: T. Fisher Unwin, 1906).

99. See Giulkhandanian, *Hay-Tatarakan endharumnere*, 1: 100–3.

100. "Inch das tvets irakanutiune?" [What lesson did reality give?], August 30 (Yerevan), *Droshak*, no. 11, November 1905.

101. See, for example, also "Natsionalisme Kovkasum" [Nationalism in the Caucasus], *Hnchak*, no. 7, July 1905; "Drutiune Rusastanum," *Hnchak*, no. 8, August 1905; "Andrkovkasi ariunahegh endharumnere" [Transcaucasia's bloody clashes], 2 June (Tiflis) and 9 June (Yerevan), *Droshak*, no. 8, August 1905; "Zangezuri shrjanum" [In the Zangezur region], 26 February, *Droshak*, no. 4, April 1906. See also Sebouh, Mrgastan [Yerevan] Central Committee to Azerbaijan Central Committee, 11 December 1905, 293/21.

102. Azerbaijan Central Committee to Western Bureau, 21 February 1905, 468/40; Urvakan to Comrades, 21 February 1905, 468/41; Samson to Western Bureau, 18 July 1905, 468/183; Azerbaijan Central Committee to Paylak [Ruben Derdzakian], 2 March 1905, 468/48; Senikh to Paylak [Ruben Derdzakian], 2 March 1905, 468/50; Garegin to Azerbaijan Central Committee, 10 March 1905, 468/54; Paylak [Ruben Derdzakian] to Malkhas, 3 June 1905, 468/154.

103. See, for example, Urvakan to Comrades, 21 February 1905, 468/41; Azerbaijan Central Committee to Western Bureau, 17 March 1905, 468/47; Report of Gilan Committee, 15 December 1905, 580/28; Pakhot to Western Bureau, 3 October 1905, 580/24; Samson to Western Bureau, 18 July 1905, 468/183; Azerbaijan Central Committee to Paylak [Ruben Derdzakian], 2 March 1905, 468/48; Senikh to Paylak [Ruben Derdzakian], 2 March 1905, 468/50; Garegin to Azerbaijan Central Committee, 10 March 1905, 468/54; Samson to Western Bureau, 24 May 1905, 468/143; Azerbaijan Central Committee to Western Bureau, 12 June 1905, 468/164; Bagratuni to Western Bureau, 5 October 1905, 468/25; Garegin to Vaspurakan (Van) Central Committee, 29 July 1906, 470/101; "Tsarizmi davere Parskastanum" [Tsarist plots in Persia], 24 September 1905, *Droshak*, no. 11, November 1905.

104. See G. Astghuni [Grigor Yeghikian], "Chshmartutiunner Parskastani heghapokhakan sharzhumneri masin (akanatesi hishoghutiunnerits)" [Truths about the Persian revolutionary movements (from the memoirs of an eyewitness)], *Yeritasard Hayastan*, no. 36, 13 June 1913. There were two Persian-language papers with the name *Habl al-Matin*, a pan-Islamic–oriented paper published in Calcutta and a liberal one in Tehran. The editor of the Tehran paper, Sayyid Hasan Kashan, was the brother of the Calcutta-based *Habl al-Matin*'s editor. The Tehran paper began publication in 1907, ceased publication after the coup of 1908, but was later published in Rasht in the winter of 1909 and then Tehran after July 1909. See Afary, *Iranian Constitutional Revolution*, 118. See also Browne, *Press and Poetry*, 73–75.

105. Samson to Western Bureau, 26 March 1905, 468/69; Garegin to Azerbaijan Central Committee, 26 March 1905, 468/70.

106. Samson to Western Bureau, 26 March 1905, 468/69.

107. Azerbaijan Central Committee to Western Bureau, 17 March 1905, 468/47; Minaret [Salmas] Report, undated but found in 1905 correspondence file, 469/19; N. Hanguyts [Nikol Aghbalian], comp., "Samsoni hushere" [Samson's memoirs], *Hayrenik Amsagir* 2, 9 (July 1924): 138; Andre Amurian, *H. H. Dashnaktsutiune Parskastanum, 1890–1918* [The A. R. Federation in Persia, 1890–1918] (Tehran: Alik, 1950), 105–6. See also Report on the Activity in Vrezhstan, 1904–1906, in Dasnabedian, *Niuter*, 4: 228–37.

108. Azerbaijan Central Committee to Western Bureau, 12 June 1905, 468/164; Entsayr [Gevorg Vardapet] to Comrades, 16 June 1905, 468/169; P. Sahakian to *Droshak* (Geneva), 3 September 1905, 580/22; Amurian, *Dashnaktsutiune Parskastanum*, 105–6. See also Report of Activity in Vrezhstan, 1904–1906, in Dasnabedian, *Niuter*, 4: 228–37; Aso, "Namak parska-trkakan sahmanglkhits," 14 May 1906, *Hnchak*, no. 5, May 1906.

109. Samson to Western Bureau, 26 March 1905, 468/69; Yeghishe Khy. Mkrtchian to Petros, 7 June 1905, 468/160. See also Azerbaijan Central Committee to Western Bureau, 17 March 1905, 468/47; Vrezh Central Committee to Western Bureau, 12 June 1905, 468/164; Garegin to Sako, 14 June 1905, 468/167; Pakhot to Western Bureau, 3 October 1905, 580/24; Bagratuni to Western Bureau, 5 October 1905, 580/25; Shavarsh to Western Bureau, 8 March 1906, 581/7.

110. See, for example, "Bagvi depkere (namakov)" [Baku events (by letter)], 14 February 1905 and 23 February 1905 [from Tiflis], *Droshak*, no. 3, March 1905. For assassination, see first-page announcement, *Droshak*, no. 6, June 1905; "Bagvi terore (namak Bagvits)" [Baku's terror (letter from Baku)], *Droshak*, no. 7, July 1905.

111. See, for example, M. Manilian, "Tghtaktsutiunner" [Correspondence], 15 April 1905, *Hnchak*, no. 4–5, April–May 1905; "Drutiune Rusastanum," *Hnchak*, no. 8, August 1905; "Namak Tiflizits" [Letter from Tiflis], 10 June 1906, *Hnchak*, no. 6, June 1906.

112. "Kotoratsner yev tsarizm" [Slaughters and tsarism], *Hnchak*, no. 6, June 1905.

113. See, for example, "Bagvi depkere (namakov)," *Droshak*, no. 3, March 1905; "Nakhamtatsvats tsragire (tghtaktsutiun)" [The aforethought plan (correspondence)], *Droshak*, no. 8, August 1905; Villari, *Fire and Sword*, 169–70, 192–97. See also Caucasian Regional Congress, November 1905, Tiflis, in Dasnabedian, *Niuter*, 2: 238.

114. Tadeusz Swietochowski, "National Consciousness and Political Orientations in Azerbaijan, 1905–1920," in *Transcaucasia, Nationalism, and Social Change: Essays in the History of Armenia, Azerbaijan, and Georgia*, ed. Ronald Grigor Suny (1983; Ann Arbor: University of Michigan Press, 1996), 215–16.

115. Shissler, "Ahmet Ağaoğlu (Aghaev), Turkish Identity between Two Empires 1869–1919," Ph.D. dissertation (University of California, Los Angeles), 1995, 192–94. For the origins of the Difâî, see also Audrey L. Altstadt, *The Azerbaijani Turks: Power and Identity Under Russian Rule* (Stanford: Hoover Institution Press, 1992), 67.

116. "Hamerashkhutian 'dzerke'" [The "hand" of solidarity], *Droshak*, no. 11, November 1906.

117. "Yerb ardeok ke khratvenk" [When perhaps will we heed advice], *Droshak*, no. 3, March 1905; "Kazmakerpakan azder" [Organizational notices], Circulars

dated 23 November (signed Tiflis Central Committee), 24 November (signed Tiflis Central Committee and Self-Defense Committee), and 28 November (signed Dashnaktsutiun), *Droshak*, no. 1, January 1906.

118. "Kovkasi bolor azgutiunnerin" [To all Caucasian nationalities], *Droshak*, no. 3, March 1905; Grigor, "Namak Tiflizits," 13 February 1906, *Hnchak*, no. 1–2, January–February 1906. For similar perceptions, see also "Mishd patrast" [Always prepared], *Hnchak*, no. 3, March 1906; "Namak Tiflizits," 10 June 1906, *Hnchak*, no. 6, June 1906.

119. "Kovkasian khabrikner," *Droshak*, no. 10, October 1905; "Andrkovkasi ariunahegh endharumnere" [Transcaucasia's bloody clashes], *Droshak*, no. 11, November 1905.

120. Giulkhandanian, *Hay-Tatarakan endharumnere*, 1: 50. For the decision of the Dashnakist Congress of Eastern Bodies regarding solidarity, see Minutes of the Regional Congress of Caucasus, Session 4, 30 March 1906, in Dasnabedian, *Niuter*, 2: 267.

121. "Bagvi Turkerin" [To the Turks of Baku], *Droshak*, no. 3, March 1905.

122. Giulkhandanian, *Hay-Tatarakan endharumnere*, 1: 117.

123. Extracts from both meetings in Giulkhandanian, *Hay-Tatarakan endharumnere*, 1: 121–23. For the latter meeting, see also "Bagvi depkere (namakov)," *Droshak*, no. 3, 1905.

124. For extracts of meetings, see Giulkhandanian, *Hay-Tatarakan endharumnere*, 1: 124–26.

125. "Kovkasi bolor azgutiunnerin," *Droshak*, no. 3, March 1905.

126. According to a Dashnakist source, Caucasian Muslims proposed the creation of a binational committee made up of ten Armenians and ten Muslims from the "bourgeois class" to assist in the process of reaching peace, but because of differences of opinion nothing constructive was achieved and the committee was later dissolved. See "Depkits hetoy" [After the event], *Droshak*, no. 5, May 1905; "Bagvi terore (namak Bagvits)," *Droshak*, no. 7, July 1905.

127. Anaide Ter Minassian, *Nationalism and Socialism*, 43. See also Giulkhandanian, *Hay-Tatarakan endharumnere*, 1: 113. Altstadt also writes about Russian press coverage of the communal violence. See Altstadt, *Azerbaijani Turks*, 41. For the Dashnaktsutiun's response to the attacks, see "Andrkovkasi arunahegh endharumnere," *Droshak*, no. 12, December 1905.

128. Giulkhandanian, *Hay-Tatarakan endharumnere*, 1: 110–11.

129. Documents 18 and 19, 3 June 1905 and 15 June 1905, *Nork* 2 (January–March 1923): 307–9. See also Letter by M. M., 29 May 1905, *Hnchak*, no. 6, June 1905; "Lusantskum" [On the margin], *Hnchak*, no. 8, August 1906. A Hnchakist writing from Yerevan states that the Hnchakists there had a sufficient supply as arms were being brought to them by comrades but that they needed money. See Letter by M. Chenatsi, 26 May 1905, *Hnchak*, no. 6, June 1905.

130. "Natsionalizme Kovkasum," *Hnchak*, no. 7, July 1905.

131. Grigor, "Namak Tiflizits," 13 February 1906, *Hnchak*, no. 1–2, January–February 1906. For similar perceptions, see also "Mishd patrast," *Hnchak*, no. 3, March 1906.

132. "Andrkovkasi ariunahegh endharumnere," *Droshak*, no. 13, December 1905.

133. Mangol Bayat, *Iran's First Revolution: Shi'ism and the Constitutional Revolution of 1905–1909* (Oxford: Oxford University Press, 1991), 241–42.

134. For a more detailed discussion of the role of Armenian Social Democrats, see Janet Afary, *Iranian Constitutional Revolution*; Afary, "Social Democracy and the Iranian Constitutional Revolution of 1906–1911," in *A Century of Revolution: Social Movements in Iran*, ed. John Foran (Minneapolis: University of Minnesota, 1994); Cosroe Chaqueri, "The Role and Impact of Armenian Intellectuals in Iranian Politics 1905–1911," *Armenian Review* 41, 2 (Summer 1988): 1–51.

135. Chilinkirian's name has appeared in various forms, including Chilinkarian, Chalankarian, and Tchilinkirian. Pilosian was one of those Hnchakists who left the party in 1905 to join the RSDWP, but later returned, according to Kitur, *Patmutiun*, 1: 396. Sedrak I and Sedrak II are most probably Sedrak Banvorian, who had also left the party in 1905 to join the RSDWP, and Sedrak Avakian, an editor of the Hnchakist organ *Zang* (Bell), which began publication in Iran in 1910. See Kitur, *Patmutiun*, 1: 294, 403–4. For a French translation, see Chaqueri, *Social-démocratie en Iran*, 237–38, 243. Afary reaches the same conclusion. See Afary, *Iranian Constitutional Revolution*, 383 n. 68. For articles by Chilinkirian translated from the German from *Neue Zeit* (1908–1911), see Chaqueri, *Asnad*, 19: 48–75. One of Chilinkirian's articles, entitled "Sahmanadrakan Parskastane yev ir kariknere" [Constitutional Persia and its needs], also appeared in a series in the Tiflis-based *Mshak* (Cultivator) from 21 January to 23 January 1910, nos. 13–15. See also an English translation of another article by Chilinkirian in Cosroe Chaqueri, ed., *The Armenians of Iran, The Paradoxical Role of a Minority in a Dominant Culture: Essays and Documents* (Cambridge: Center for Middle Eastern Studies of Harvard University, 1998), 193–239, which also appeared in the original Armenian in *Mshak* in 1909. According to Panirian, the editor of the Dashnakist organ *Aravot*, Chilinkirian ran the Hnchakist *Zang* in the early stages of its publication. See H[ayrapet] Panirian, "Hayrapet Paniriani Husherits" [From the memoirs of Hayrapet Panirian], *Hayranik Amsagir* 30, 12 (December 1952): 69.

136. "J. Karakhanian à G. Plekhanov," Tabriz, 15 September 1905, in Chaqueri, *Social-démocratie en Iran*, 33–34. An English translation appears in Chaqueri, *Armenians in Iran*, 311–12.

137. Ibid.

138. "A. Tchilinkirian à G. Plekhanov," Tabriz, 10 December 1908, Chaqueri, *Social-démocratie en Iran*, 50–51. An English translation appears in Chaqueri, *Armenians in Iran*, 335–37.

139. "Khaĉaturian [Khachaturian] à G. Plekhanov," undated, Chaqueri, in *Social-démocratie en Iran*, 39. An English translation, dated 19 November 1908, appears in Chaqueri, *Armenians in Iran*, 324–30.

140. "Lettre de A. Tchilinkirian à K. Kautsky," Tabriz, 16 July 1908, in Chaqueri, *Social-démocratie en Iran*, 19–22. For a Persian translation, see Chaqueri, *Asnad*, 6: 36. For an English translation, see John Riddell, ed., *Lenin's Struggle for a Revolutionary International: Documents: 1907–1916* (New York: Monad Press, 1984), 60–61, and Chaqueri, *Armenians in Iran*, 313–16. Tigran Darvish (Ter-Hakobian), too, in a letter to Plekhanov, asks Plekhanov's advice regarding the two tendencies and what attitude and organizational system the Social Democrats should adopt in the

revolution. See "T. Dervitch à G. Plekhanov," 3 December 1908, in Chaqueri, *Social-démocratie en Iran*, 44–49. An English translation appears in Chaqueri, *Armenians in Iran*, 338–44. Ter Hakobian was a frequent contributor to the constitutionalist paper *Iran-e No.* See Afary, *Iranian Constitutional Revolution*, 268.

141. "K. Kautsky à A. Tchilinkirian," 1 August 1908, trans. from the Russian in *Bor'ba* 2–4 (Tiflis, 1908), in Chaqueri, *Social-démocratie en Iran*, 24. For a Persian translation, see Chaqueri, *Asnad*, 6: 38. For an English translation, see Riddell, *Lenin's Struggle*, 62–63, and Chaqueri, *Armenians in Iran*, 318–21.

142. "A. Tchilinkirian à G. Plekhanov," Tabriz, 10 December 1908, Chaqueri, *Social-démocratie en Iran*, 51. An English translation appears in Chaqueri, *Armenians in Iran*, 335–37. See also "Khaĉaturian [Khachaturian] à G. Plekhanov," undated, in Chaqueri, *Social-démocratie en Iran*, 41.

143. "Khaĉaturian [Khachaturian] à G. Plekhanov," undated, in Chaqueri, *Social-démocratie en Iran*, 41.

144. "Protocole no. 1 de la Conférence des Social-Démocrates de Tabriz, 1908," in Chaqueri, *Social-démocratie en Iran*, 35–36, states that 28 members were present at a meeting and later mentions that 30 voted; therefore in all probability the group had at least 30 members. For a Persian translation, see Chaqueri, *Asnad*, 6: 50. An English translation appears in Chaqueri, *Armenians in Iran*, 331–34.

145. Ibid.

146. Afary, *Iranian Constitutional Revolution*, 246–47.

147. Ibid., 247.

148. "K. Kautsky à A. Tchilinkirian," 1 August 1908, in Chaqueri, *Social-démo cratie en Iran*, 25.

149. "Parskastan: ariunrusht hetadimutiune," *Droshak*, no. 11–12, November–December 1908.

150. "Parskastan: sahmanadrutiune verahastatvats," *Droshak*, no. 5, May 1909.

151. Decisions of the Fourth General Congress: Persian Region (26), in Dasnabedian, *Niuter*, 3: 309.

152. For text of 1907 program, see Dasnabedian, *Niuter*, 3: 315–28; *Droshak*, no. 5, May 1907.

153. Ibid.

154. Ibid.

155. See, for example, Ter Minassian, *Nationalism and Socialism*; Ronald Grigor Suny, "Marxism, Nationalism, and the Armenian Labor Movement in Transcaucasia, 1890–1908," *Armenian Review* 33, 1 (March 1980): 30–47.

156. For Dashnakist response to such critics, see "Rusastan: heghapokhutiun yev kusaktsutiunner" [Russia: revolution and parties], *Droshak*, no. 9–10, September–October 1908.

157. See "VII: Mijazgayin Sotsialistakan Kongrese" [VII: Socialist International Congress], *Droshak*, no. 8, August 1907.

158. For extracts in Armenian translation of the report given to the Second Socialist International, see "Dashnaktsutian gortsuneutenen" [From the Dashnaktsutiun's activity], *Droshak*, no. 9, September 1907.

159. For text of 1907 program, see Dasnabedian, *Niuter*, 3: 315–28; *Droshak*, no. 5, May 1907.

160. Starting in June 1907, *Droshak* began printing a series of articles in order to explain to its readers the party's brand of socialism. See series "Sotsialisti namaknere" [A socialist's letters], starting with no. 6–7, June–July 1907. Briefly, the Social Democrats were more orthodox Marxists, internationalists, who abandoned the national question and perceived industrialization as an essential stage in economic development leading to socialism. The Social Revolutionaries were influenced by the Russian populists, and unlike the Social Democrats, gave a place to the national question and believed industrialization was not an essential stage leading to socialism.

161. See, for example, "Mi kani akamay khosker," *Hnchak*, no. 3, March 1906.

162. "Kay yerkvorakanutiun (dualizm) mer davanats skzbunkneri mej?" [Is there dualism (dualism) in our professed principles?], *Hnchak*, no. 2, February 1907.

163. For discussion of Georgian social democracy and its nationalist sentiments, see Ronald Grigor Suny, "Labor and Socialism Among Armenians in Transcaucasia," in *Looking Toward Ararat: Armenia in Modern History*, ed. Ronald Grigor Suny (Bloomington and Indianapolis: Indiana University Press, 1993), 90.

164. Minutes of Fourth General Congress, Session 86, 16 April 1907, in Dasnabedian, *Niuter*, 3: 234–40.

165. Fourth General Congress: Collaboration with Socialist Parties (16), in Dasnabedian, *Niuter*, 3: 306.

166. Ibid.

167. Fourth General Congress: Communities (25), in Dasnabedian, *Niuter*, 3: 309.

168. Decisions of the Fourth General Congress: Armeno-Turkish Clashes (14), in Dasnabedian, *Niuter*, 3: 305. See also same in *Droshak*, no. 5, May 1907.

169. For the Hnchakist request and Dashnakist response, see "Mijkusaktsakan khndirner" [Interparty problems], *Hnchak*, no. 6, June 1907. For the Dashnakist Congress decision, see Decisions of the Fourth General Congress: The Hnchakian Center's Request (18), in Dasnabedian, *Niuter*, 3: 306–7.

170. Declaration, 21 February 1907, signed by both parties, *Hnchak*, no. 2, February 1907; "Hamerashkhutian hraver" [Summons to solidarity], *Droshak*, no. 3, March 1907. See also Circular signed by both parties in Iran, 15 December 1906, 472/25.

171. For reports of violent conflict between the two parties, see, for example, Suren (Hnchakist representative) to Samson, 5 December 1905, 468/283; Hnchakian Party Mtrak Group Circular, 23 March 1906, 2040/90; Hnchakian Party Azerbaijan Committee Circular, 29 April 1906, 2040/92; Hnchakian Party Rasht Branch Circular, 21 May 1906, 2040/93; Hnchakian Social Democratic Party Shahstan Circular addressed to Tabriz Armenians, undated but found in 1906 correspondence file, 2040/151; Hnchakian Disorders in the Zola Region, undated but found in 1905 file, 469/18; M. S. Piran to Dashnakist Comrades, 15 February 1906, 471/19; Minutes of the Azerbaijan Central Committee, Session 20, 5 May 1907, 540/b; "Mijkusaktsakan khndirner," *Hnchak*, no. 6, June 1906.

172. Negotiations were held from 14 to 16 November 1906 in Tabriz. For minutes and decisions, see *Niuter*, 4: 329–32. See also "Hamerashkhutian hraver," 15

December 1906, signed by both parties, *Droshak*, no. 1, January 1907. For correspondence regarding preliminary plans to negotiate as well as negotiations, see, for example, Azerbaijan Central Committee to Sham Comrades, 30 March 1905, 468/82; Samson to Western Bureau, 7 April 1905, 468/86; Agreement between Salmas Dashnakists and Hnchakists, 4 April 1905, 469/2; Negotiation between Payajuk Dashnakists and Hnchakists, 27 April 1905, 469/5; Garegin to Azerbaijan Central Committee, 4 May 1905, 468/109; Sargis to Vrezh Comrades, 1 September 1905, 468/223; Port Arthur [Anzali] Subcommittee Circular, 23 May 1906, 581/13; Reconciliation Contract, 15 February 1906, 472/4; Azerbaijan Central Committee to Western Bureau, 16 November 1906, 470/237; Azerbaijan Central Committee to Eastern Bureau, 18 November 1906, 470/240; Minaret Committee to Western Bureau, 23 November 1906, 470/249.

173. Report of the Activity of Vrezhstan [Azerbaijan], 1904–1906, in *Niuter H. H. Dashnaktsutian patmutian hamar* [Materials for the history of the A. R. Federation], ed. and comp. Hratch Dasnabedian [Hrach Tasnapetian] (Beirut: Hamazgayin, 1982), 4: 228–37.

174. Samson to Western Bureau, 26 January 1905, file 468/22.

175. Administration des Postes, 3 July 1906, 581/17. See also handwritten copies of order, 49/146 and 49/147. The satirical *Molla Nasr al-Din*, which began publication in Tiflis (Tbilisi) in 1906, was also prohibited, confiscated, and burned. See Customs and Postal Minister J. Naus's Telegram, 1 December 1906, 581/49.

176. "'Droshaki' argilume Parskastanum" ["Droshak's" ban in Persia], *Droshak*, no. 7, July 1907.

177. *Hnchak* was not prohibited from entering Iran. See Gilan Postal and Customs General Director J. Monard to Customs and Postal Minister J. Naus, 1 August 1906, 581/35.

178. *Hayat Gazetesi* was established by Ali Mardan Bey Topçibeşi (Topchibashev), whose involvement in the paper was minor. Ağaev, along with Ali Bey Hüseyinzade, served as the real force behind the paper. Ağaev wrote a great number of articles in the daily, many of which dealt with the demand for "equal rights for Muslims and denouncing Armenian 'intrigues'." See Ada Holland Shissler, "Ahmet Ağaoğlu, 200–2.

179. S. Tseruni [Stepan Stepanian] to Eastern Bureau, 4 July 1906, in Dasnabedian, *Niuter*, 4: 317–19.

180. Statement of Anzali Chief of Postal Service Hasan Khan and Customs Inspector Jule Duhem, July 1906, 581/50; Ministère des Postes to Dr. A. D. Stepanian, 19 July 1906, 581/22. See also Garegin to Vaspurakan (Van) Central Committee, 29 July 1906, 470/101.

181. "'Droshaki' argelman khndire" [The issue of "Droshak's" ban], *Droshak*, no. 8, August 1906.

182. Western Bureau to Vrezh [Azerbaijan] Central Committee, 30 July 1906, 49/3.

183. The measures involved in sending in smaller batches of 20 to 50 papers, changing the color of packaging, sending the batches through another country, and so forth. See Arsen to *Droshak*, 9 August 1906, 581/27; 581/45. In some areas the prohibition continued well into 1907. See, for example, Shavarsh to *Droshak*, 4

January 1907, 582/2; Session 25, 21 May 1907, Minutes of the Azerbaijan Central Committee, 540/b.

184. Western Bureau to Vrezh Central Committee, 18 July 1906, 49/2.

185. Report of Activity in Vrezhstan, 1904–1906, in Dasnabedian, *Niuter*, 4: 228–37. See also Shavarsh to Western Bureau, 8 March 1906. 581/7; Azerbaijan Central Committee to Western Bureau, 5 July 1906, 470/81.

186. Report of Vrezh [Tabriz] Committee, 25 November 1906, in Dasnabedian, *Niuter*, 4: 281–82. See also the report for 1906–1907, 10 September 1907, 473/116.

187. Mikayel Varandian, *H. H. Dashnaktsutian patmutiun* [History of A. R. Federation] (Cairo: Husaber Press, 1950), 2: 61, 63; Afary, *Iranian Constitutional Revolution*, 77–78. See also Minutes from the Sessions of the Azerbaijan Central Committee, Session 3, 20 January 1908, 540/b. This problem continued. According to one report, in 1909, 700 Armenian families were attacked with Russian complicity. See "Parskakan: brnakalutian ankume," *Droshak*, no. 7, July 1909.

188. See, for example, Minutes of the Azerbaijan Central Committee, Session 13, 28 March 1907; Session 17, 22 April 1907; Session 19, 30 April 1907; Session 24, 18 May 1907; Session 39, 3 July 1907, 540/b. Session 39 stated that the "ignorant and fanatic Persian masses" represent a very fertile soil for provocation. See also Proposals by Port Arthur Subcommittee to Fourth General Congress, in Dasnabedian, *Niuter*, 4: 310.

189. For English text of Supplemental Laws, see Edward G. Browne, *The Persian Revolution, 1905–1909* (1910; new edition edited by Abbas Amanat with essays by Abbas Amanat and Mansour Bonakdarian, Mage: Washington, D.C., 1995), 372–84.

190. Mehdi Malekzadeh, *Tarikh-e enqelab-e mashrutiyat-e Iran* [History of Constitutional Revolution of Iran] (Tehran, 1984), 4: 215; Kasravi, *Tarikh-e mashruteh-ye Iran* [History of the constitution of Iran] (1951; Tehran: Amir Kabir, 1984), 1: 324.

191. Browne, *Persian Revolution*, 140–41; Malekzadeh, *Tarikh-e enqelab*, 2: 258–66.

192. For debate, see, for example, Kasravi, *Tarikh-e mashruteh*, 1: 285–96. For Tabriz events, see Kasravi, 1: 296–99, 306–15. For Rahim Khan's son, see 1: 318; Browne, *Persian Revolution*, 141–42; Malekzadeh, *Tarikh-e enqelab*, 2: 255; Azerbaijan Central Committee to Eastern Bureau, Tiflis, 10 May 1907, 473/54.

193. For Persian text of Electoral Laws of 1906, see *Mozakerat-e majles: dowreh-ye avval* [Parliamentary Debates: First Session], vol. 1, *1906–1908*, 6–7; Nazem al-Islam Kermani, *Tarikh-e bidari -ye Iranian* [History of Iranian awakening] (Tehran: 1967), 3: 342–48. For English text of Electoral Laws of 1906, see Browne, *Persian Revolution*, 355–61. For Persian text of Electoral Laws of 1909, see *Mozakerat-e majles*, 1: 589–93. The number of representatives allowed are in the table following the laws, 593. For English text of Electoral Laws of 1909, see Browne, *Persian Revolution*, 385–400. The section that pertains to minorities is under the heading "Districts," no. 36.

194. Kermani, *Tarikh-e bidari*, 3: 322.

195. Ibid., 3: 343–44.

196. For Persian text of Supplementary Fundamental Laws of 1907, see *Mozakerat-e majles*, 1: 582–87. For English text, see Browne, *Persian Revolution*, 372–84.

197. Browne, *Persian Revolution*, 372, 379. Clearly articles one and eight are contradictory, since under Islamic law Christians and Jews as "People of the Book" are not considered equal and therefore do not enjoy the same rights as Muslims.

198. Azerbaijan Central Committee to Eastern Bureau, Tiflis, 10 May 1907, 473/54. The Hnchakists were also concerned about the limitations on ethnic and religious minorities and called for freedom for all Iranians without distinction as to nationality or religion. See "Karavarutiune partvats" [The government defeated], *Hnchak*, no. 2, February 1907.

199. Kasravi, *Tarikh-e mashruteh*, 1: 239–48; Afary, *Iranian Constitutional Revolution*, 96–97.

200. For food riots in Tabriz, see Kasravi, *Tarikh-e mashruteh*, 1: 355.

201. Garmen to Eastern Bureau, Tiflis, 4 July 1907, 473/86.

202. "Kaghakakan tesutiun: Parskastane," *Droshak*, no. 8, August 1907.

203. For the turn of events and change in Tabriz and Azerbaijan in general, see Afary, *Iranian Constitutional Revolution*; Bayat, *Iran's First Revolution*.

204. Report of Vrezhstan, 1904–1906, in Dasnabedian, *Niuter*, 4: 228–37.

205. Aghayan, Ts. P., B. N. Arakelyan, et al., eds. *Hay zhoghovrdi patmutiun* [History of the Armenian people], vol. 6, *Hayastane 1870–1917 tvakannerin* [Armenia in 1870–1917] (Yerevan: Haykakan SSH Gitutiunneri Akademia, 1981), 412.

206. P. A. Stolypin and I. I. Vorontsov-Dashkov, "Borb'a s revoliutsionnym dvizheniem na Kavkaze v epokhu stolypinshchiny (Iz perepiski P. A. Stolypin s gr. I. I. Vorontsovym-Dashkovym), *Krasnyi arkhiv*, no. 3 (1929), 206, cited in Ronald Grigor Suny, *The Baku Commune, 1917–1918: Class and Nationality in the Russian Revolution* (Princeton: Princeton University Press, 1972), 22–23.

207. "Kaszmakerpakan azder" [Organizational notices], *Droshak*, no. 1, January 1909. See also "Rusastan: arian rezhime" [Russia: the regime of blood], *Droshak*, no. 11–12, November–December 1908; "Stolipin-Vorontsovian rezhime yev Dashnaktsutiune" [The Stolypin-Vorontsov regime and the Dashnaktsutiun], *Droshak*, no. 2–3, February–March 1909.

208. "Parskastan: brnakalutian ankume," *Droshak*, no. 7, July 1909.

209. "Kaszmakerpakan azder," *Droshak*, no. 1, January 1909. See also "Rusastan: arian rezhime," *Droshak*, no. 11–12, November–December 1908; "Stolipin-Vorontsovian rezhime yev Dashnaktsutiune," *Droshak*, no. 2–3, February-March 1909.

4

Collaboration, Contribution, and Contention

Armenian participation in the Iranian Constitutional Revolution commenced as early as 1907 but took on greater intensity beginning with the Tabriz resistance (1908–1909). Armenian political parties like the Hnchakian, but especially the Dashnaktsutiun, as well as individual Armenian Social Democrats, collaborated with Iranian and Caucasian constitutionalists and revolutionaries to influence the direction of the movement toward greater democracy and to safeguard gains already achieved. With a few exceptions what has been written on Armenian contribution to the Iranian Constitutional Revolution has concentrated on the military aspect of Armenian participation, particularly Yeprem Khan's battles, subjects that will not be a focal point of this chapter.[1] Furthermore, because of the availability of material on the Dashnaktsutiun and the predominance of the party's activities in the revolution, the bulk of this chapter examines the decision-making process and cooperative and collaborative efforts of the Dashnaktsutiun with Iranian and Caucasian Muslims, men and women alike, and, to a smaller degree, the contributive role of Armenian Social Democrats, including Hnchakists. In addition, this chapter discusses the tense and problematic relations of collaborators on all sides as well as the nature of the conflict between Yeprem Khan and the Dashnaktsutiun.

Dashnakist Dilemmas and Decisions

The decentralized organization of the Dashnaktsutiun made the decision-making process and subsequent action in the Iranian Constitutional Revolution a long and difficult task as Dashnakist Iranian branches attempted to interpret and adapt the general precept of participation to suit their own regional conditions and the differing views of their leadership. Moreover, Dashnakist branches discovered that commitment to

Iran's movement was intertwined with many other issues affecting the lives of Armenians outside Iran and the future of the party, making an already trying task even more arduous.

Fourth General Congress, 1907

The Dashnakist determination to engage actively in the Iranian Constitutional Revolution came at the Fourth General Congress, held in Vienna from February to May 1907. The proceedings on the evening of 26 April 1907 shed light on the actual decision. Stepan Stepanian (Tseruni, Balajan, Vrezhuni, Mefristadam), representative from Iran, as well as Anton Zavarian (Cilicia); Aram Manukian (Van, subsequent interior minister of the Armenian Republic); Hamo Mherian (Hamazasp Ohanjanian, Eastern Bureau, subsequent prime minister of the Armenian Republic); and A. Isahakian (Arshak Jamalian, Europe, subsequently communications minister of the Armenian Republic), attempted to define the Iranian constitutional movement. They described the leaders as belonging to the merchant and religious classes, the former representing the economically threatened and the latter representing the Iranian people's established religious values and laws. In addition, there were others who were being exploited by Russia and/or Britain. The Dashnakist speakers indicated that these leaders, driven by different political and class interests, had become active in the same movement. They considered the movement as one that had political, ideological, and economic components and thus aimed at the establishment of law and order, human rights, and the interests of all working people. Furthermore, they linked the immediate local interests of Iranian Armenians and the long-term interests of Ottoman Armenians with those of Iran's constitutionalist activists, concluding that since the Dashnaktsutiun had taken upon itself the interests of the majority of Armenians—namely, the working class—the party was compelled to join in the Iranian movement. The congress then accepted the following proposal with 25 votes in favor and one abstention.[2]

Considering that the present Persian situation may turn into an immense communal vision, having a popular awakening nature for Persia and the East, and finding its expansion and extension desirable from the humanitarian and Armenian points of view,

The General Congress recommends to the Persian Dashnakist bodies and individuals to aid the progress of that movement by every means, inserting in the Persian movement that emancipatory democratic labor spirit which springs from the program of the Dashnaktsutiun.[3]

While the resolution specifically called for participation in the Iranian Constitutional Revolution, it did not define the kind and extent of that participation, except to state in general terms that the involvement was for the purpose of assisting the "progress" of the constitutional movement "by every means." This left Iranian Dashnakist bodies to settle on the details of the General Congress directive. The resolution reached in Vienna in April 1907 did not automatically translate into action for several reasons. In the first place, there was a certain amount of disagreement between party members regarding the issue of commitment itself, in what opponents of involvement considered a non-Armenian cause. In the second place, there were questions regarding the nature and extent of that participation. For example, was Dashnakist participation to be active and if so, to what extent, and was it to be covert or overt? Among other concerns discussed by Iranian Armenian Dashnakists were the following: (1) How would Armenian activity on the side of Iranian constitutionalists endanger or benefit operations and goals in Ottoman Armenia? (2) Might it provoke harassment and persecution of Iranian Armenians? And (3) what was the nature of the Iranian Constitutional Revolution? Records indicate that these issues were debated among Dashnakists in almost all, if not all, regions in Iran that had Dashnakist groups as well as in regional congresses. They also indicate that in certain areas, as in Tabriz, the champion of constitutionalism and resistance to despotism, Dashnakists took a more active stance much sooner than in other quarters, apparently influenced by events there as well as the influx of Caucasian revolutionaries.

Setting the Groundwork for Collaboration: Azerbaijani Dashnakists at the Forefront

In July 1907, only about two months after the General Congress's conclusion regarding the Iranian Constitutional Revolution and the sit-ins in Tehran against Nuri's revisions to the proposed Supplementary Constitutional Laws, the Azerbaijan Central Committee dealt with the issue of Dashnakist action. In addition to the directive of the congress, the Dashnakists took three factors into consideration: their status as revolutionaries who could not abstain from political movements taking shape in the country, the appeal of Iranian revolutionaries for assistance, and the opportunity to influence the direction of the movement. Having reached agreement on these three issues, they decided to begin preliminary talks with Iranian constitutionalists in Tabriz regarding collaborative efforts in the struggle to maintain the gains made by Iranian constitutionalists.[4] Despite that, they remained concerned about falling victim to provocation by reactionary forces and therefore chose covert participation.[5] The talks took place several months before the agreement reached between the Dashnaktsutiun, represented by party cofounder and member of the Eastern Bureau, Rostom (Stepan Zorian, 1867–1919),[6] and Majles delegates led by the popular Azerbaijani representative Sayyid Hasan Taqizadeh. The discussions of the Azerbaijan Central Committee demonstrated some of the same issues that would continue to concern Armenian constitutionalist participants regarding the character of the Iranian constitutionalists. For example, what were the goals and ideologies of the different Iranian parties, and could collaboration be possible and with whom?

According to the Azerbaijan Central Committee, preliminary talks began in July 1907 exactly a year before the start of the Tabriz resistance at the instigation of a Caucasian Muslim from Qarabagh identified merely as Mirza Hosein "the dentist," who wanted to bring Dashnakists and Iranian revolutionaries closer. Mirza Hosein, who met with Stepan Stepanian, was reported to have said that the decisions of the General Congress regarding pursuing solidarity and cooperation with Turkic peoples after the communal violence in the Caucasus had left a good impression on Azerbaijan's populace. According to Stepanian, Mirza Hosein and his colleagues were interested in the advice the party could offer as one with "revolutionary experience and knowledge."[7] The Central Committee advised discretion and caution in dealings with the Caucasians and Iranians, especially since some of those present at the talks were unfamiliar to the members.[8]

Stepan Stepanian and Vahan Zakarian were also visited by five "Turkish," meaning either Caucasian Muslim or Iranian Azerbaijani, revolutionaries who sought practical advice from the party and promised to keep Armenians away from active participation for fear of Armenians falling victim to provocation if their involvement was publicly known. Evidence suggests that these revolutionaries were aligned with Mirza Hosein and represented an individual named Mir Hashem. According to H. Elmar, which is the pseudonym of leading Iranian Armenian Dashnakist Hovsep Hovhannisian,[9] this may have been the same anticonstitutionalist cleric who had at the beginning of the constitutional movement in Tabriz come out in support of constitutionalism and the revolutionaries, but later allied with the royalists and was hanged for it in 1909.[10] There is also some evidence to suggest that these individuals were connected to or may have represented the Organization of Social Democrats (Ferqeh-ye Ejtima'iyun-e 'Amiyun).[11] The Organization of Social Democrats, founded in Baku in 1905, associated with the Muslim Social Democratic Hemmat (Endeavor) Party and the Baku and Tiflis (Tbilisi) branches of the Russian Social Democratic Workers' Party (RSDWP). In Iran, the organization had, by October 1906, begun forming branches with the help of its Central Committee members. The organization also established branches in other Iranian towns like Rasht and Anzali between 1906 and 1908. The Tabriz body, called the Secret Center Markaz-e ghaibi, worked closely with the Tabriz Anjoman, which seems to have relied heavily on the Secret Center in "its day-to-day activities as well as its general political direction."[12] Soon after the establishment of the Tabriz branch, a volunteer military force, *mojahedin*, was organized, which added to the reputation and power of the organization in Tabriz. They "became the most committed defenders of the Majles."[13] The branches of the Organization of Social Democrats in Iran profited immensely after 1907, but especially during the Tabriz resistance starting in 1908, from Caucasians. This occurred not only because the group's center remained in Baku but because of the return of Iranian workers from the Caucasus as well as the influx of non-Iranian Caucasians, Muslims, and Christian Georgians and Armenians. The party's ideology was a mix of socialism and liberal nationalism, representing the views of its diverse membership, which included, as did the Armenian political parties, some who knew little or nothing about socialism and others who were fervent Social Democrats. Nevertheless, the self-identification of the group as an Organization of Social Democrats points to the positive image of being socialist among Iranian and Caucasian oppositional elements. In addition to the party's main goal of safeguarding the constitution and Majles, the program sought such socialist demands as the eight-hour workday, the right to strike, and redistribution of land.[14]

The Pact Between Dashnakists and Majles Delegates. The Dashnakists set some conditions to the talks. They insisted on knowing the program, organization, and size of the group the five represented and added that a Persian translation of the Dashnakist program would be provided for them. Only after such an exchange could the two groups work together. Moreover, the time had arrived to begin official talks and work out a platform and tactics upon which the two sides could agree.[15]

Even with official talks under way, the Dashnaktsutiun remained concerned and somewhat unclear about the thought and worldview of their Iranian counterparts. While it may not be appropriate to speak of Iranian groups as political parties for the First Constitutional Period (August 1906 to June 1908), that is the term used by Dashnakists, which perhaps underscores their own unfamiliarity with Iranian groups in this early stage of the movement. The Dashnakists wanted to know whether Iranians belonged to organized parties or whether they were part of factions.[16] If they belonged to factions and thus acted in opposition to existing parties, then collaboration with them might be detrimental.[17] Central Committee members decided to inform their Iranian colleagues of their concerns and requested a response to questions regarding their opinion about the causes of the Iranian Constitutional Revolution, its leaders, its supporters, the reasons and expectations behind wanting solidarity with the Dashnakists, and so forth. The Dashnakists hoped to gain a better understanding of their ideological outlook as well as the direction of the constitutional movement.[18]

A major factor binding the Dashnakists and Azerbaijan constitutionalists was their mutual concern regarding Ottoman military incursions into Iranian territory, especially in Urumieh. According to the Dashnakists, they were asked by their Iranian comrades if, in case of war, they would fight with them in Urumieh against Ottoman forces. The Central Committee unanimously concluded that as children of the same country, they would fulfill their obligations.[19] The Iranians had planned to send a few men to Urumieh to place the organization on firm ground and requested the advice of the Dashnakists on how to proceed.[20]

A semiofficial agreement was reached between the Dashnaktsutiun, represented by Rostom, and the Iranian constitutionalists, made up of six Majles members led by Hasan Taqizadeh. According to Rostom, Taqizadeh, an influential Iranian delegate from Tabriz who had close contacts with the Muslim Social Democrats in the Caucasus, was the initiator of the negotiations.[21] However, there are indications that the Dashnaktsutiun may have approached Taqizadeh first, because they considered him "the most influential" delegate.[22] Hovsep Mirzayan (subsequent delegate to the Majles), as the official representative of the Dashnakist Tehran Committee, met with Taqizadeh in September 1907. The Tehran Committee was extremely pleased with the issues discussed at the meeting as well as the resulting amity. Taqizadeh sought the party's assistance in creating a positive image of the Iranian Constitutional Revolution in Europe, in gaining more information regarding Ottoman maneuvers at the Iranian border, and in acquiring Dashnakist fighters in case of war with the Ottoman Empire! All three points, which resurfaced in talks with Rostom, were accepted by Mirzayan and the Tehran Committee with the pending approval of the Central Committee in Azerbaijan.[23]

Mirzayan also joined Rostom in the meetings that took place from 30 December 1907 to 4 January 1908.[24] Although most of the Iranian delegates spoke French with Rostom, a major reason for Mirzayan's presence at the meetings may have been his knowledge of Persian.[25] In addition to Mirzayan, three other Dashnakists, Dr. Harutiun Ter Stepanian, Aleksan Tunian, and Alek Jalalian, led negotiations before Rostom's arrival from Baku. Because of their familiarity with "local conditions and the psychology of Persians" Rostom consulted with them after each meeting.[26]

According to Rostom, several key questions were addressed to the participants of the meeting. First, how safe was the progress of the movement against the shah's incursions? Second, what measures were being taken against the Anglo-Russian convention that in time could threaten the political independence of Iran? Third, what hopes did the Iranian constitutionalists have of pushing back Ottoman troops from Iranian territory? Fourth, what force could they marshal against the Ottomans? Fifth, upon what would the cooperation between the Armenians and Iranians be based? And last, what help could the Iranians give the Dashnaktsutiun? The delegates believed that the constitution had been placed on firm foundations, and the shah's aggression could only slow down the movement but not diminish it. As for the Anglo-Russian agreement, they were concerned about the possibility of Russian troops entering Iran either with the aim or the excuse of removing Ottoman detachments. Britain might then occupy certain territory in order to counterbalance Russia. They deemed the alliance of a neutral third nation like France necessary to offset Britain and Russia. The delegates even considered alliance with Bulgaria and decided to send an envoy to Sophia. When Rostom inquired whether they would be open to help from the Iranian Armenian Malkom Khan (1833–1908), a proponent of reform and constitutionalism and founder of the reformist Qanun (Law, 1890–1896) in London, the delegates responded that they were disappointed with him, because they had tried to correspond with Malkom Khan but to no avail.[27]

The discussions demonstrated a mutual apprehension regarding Ottoman and Russian aggression. The Iranian delegates discussed three scenarios: (1) The Ottoman forces would leave Iranian territory and recognize Iran's sovereignty, and therefore the battle between the two would come to an end; (2) the negotiations over the territories would be postponed; and (3) the Ottoman government would refuse to leave Iranian territory, and a war between Iran and the Ottoman Empire would become unavoidable. After some thought, the meeting found the first scenario unlikely, since there seemed to be no reason to think that Ottoman troops would withdraw. The only incentive for withdrawal would be Russian pressure, which would inevitably result in the replacement of Ottoman detachments with Russian ones—a situation just as threatening to Iran. The third option also seemed improbable as Iran would not declare war on the Ottoman Empire. The second proposal of postponing negotiations seemed not only the most probable but also the most beneficial for Iran, because it would allow time and opportunity to seek diplomatic means by which to resolve the territorial question. In the meantime, the Turkish revolutionary movement would increase in strength and hopefully result in a government that would become the "natural ally" of Iran. The delegates admitted that they could not count on the effectiveness of their own armed forces against the Ottoman military. Ironically, they had instead set hopes on the irregular cavalry of the anti-constitutionalist Shahsevan, Qarahdagh, and Lorestan tribes as well as the chance that they might be able to incite the Shi'is near Baghdad to rebel against the Ottomans. Both the Iranian and Armenian delegates came to the conclusion that any direct action against Ottoman troops would be futile. Rostom suggested the formation of a Committee of National Defense to deal principally with the Ottoman issue.

In the same letter to the Dashnaktsutiun Bureau, Rostom expressed his belief that if the Ottoman stance remained threatening, the Iranian delegates would definitely want to align themselves with the Dashnaktsutiun. If, however, the Ottomans showed signs of weakness, "we have no hope that steps will be taken on their end to associate actively with us."[28]

The agreement reached between the Dashnaktsutiun and the Majles delegates stated:

Whereas the populations of Persia and Turkey are equally interested in that which is established and maintained in both countries, . . . the constitutional regime, . . . the principles of solidarity of nations, and to safeguard the interests of the working classes,

Whereas the government of the sultan aims by its aggressive acts to create international difficulties, to divert popular energy from the interior struggle, and to stop in this way the revolutionary movement gaining ground day by day,

Whereas the normal functioning of the constitution in a neighboring country and in a coreligionist people contributes greatly to the extension of the revolutionary movement in Turkey, and because of this the Ottoman monarchy will see the necessity to discredit and also to overthrow the constitutional regime in Persia,

Whereas consequently the progressive parties in the two countries have an imperative duty to combat the policies of the government of the sultan in all its manifestations, the Dashnaktsutiun pledged:

1. to speak on behalf of Iranian constitutionalists in Europe;
2. to seek French assistance on behalf of Iranian constitutionalists;
3. to pursue an alliance between Iran and Bulgaria;
4. to organize all elements hostile to the Ottoman Empire in active resistance;
5. to propagate against Abdul-Hamid's government and against war between the Ottoman and Iranian governments;
6. to gain the neutrality of Kurdish tribes friendly with the Dashnaktsutiun;

7. to support an alliance of Caucasian Muslim organizations in favor of the Iranian cause;
8. to assist the Majles in its project to engage officers, including Caucasian Muslim ones, into the Iranian army;
9. to establish wireless telegraph capabilities in battle regions;
10. to procure heliographs and specialists to work them;
11. to assist in the organization of medical/sanitary services in the Iranian army.

Moreover, further provisions were accepted by the Dashnaktsutiun to be performed only during military conflict. The party agreed to provide one or two competent officers, specialists in bomb-making, and to organize revolutionary detachments for guerilla warfare. According to Mirzayan, the first three points of agreement were immediately arranged, points four through eight had already been planned to be carried out with or without the pact, and points nine through eleven could be executed when invited to do so by the Iranians. Rostom believed the pact would solidify and reaffirm relations between the party and the Caucasian Muslims from which only good could result.[29]

The Iranian constitutionalists, on their side, promised:

1. to provide the Dashnaktsutiun with free transport of men, arms, munitions, especially in Azerbaijan;[30]
2. to bring into Iran arms, munitions, and literature at the Dashnaktsutiun's expense;
3. to fund in Azerbaijan a cartridge factory and to sell to the Dashnaktsutiun arms, cartridges, cannon powder, and other such material from the arsenals of the Iranian government;
4. to get in contact with Iranians in the Ottoman Empire for the purpose of spreading the message of solidarity between Armenians and Turks;
5. to respect the national rights of Armenians in Iran and to legalize democratic institutions based on said rights;
6. to set aside territory in Salmas or in surrounding regions for Armenian refugees;
7. to insist in all appropriate circumstances, especially in international conferences, on the necessity of the establishment of a constitutional regime in the Ottoman Empire, in general, and the realization of autonomy of Armenian provinces, in particular.

In addition, the Iranians agreed to provide Armenian detachments in Azerbaijan with arms, munitions, horses, and daily necessities.[31]

Neither the Iranian delegates nor the Dashnaktsutiun signed the pact. According to Rostom, because the delegates held "public and political positions, they avoided signing an agreement which is sealed with the representative of a revolutionary party." Rostom expressed that he too did not want to sign the agreement, considering the position held by some Dashnakist members against participation and that both sides were "morally bound" as well as bound by future circumstances to fulfill their promises.[32]

Preliminary talks carried out between July 1907 and January 1908 and resulting agreements demonstrated a willingness by Dashnakist leaders to collaborate with Iranian and Caucasian constitutionalists despite apprehensions and concerns and to carve a place in the Iranian Constitutional Revolution.

Discussions in Azerbaijan Continue. At the same time that Dashnakists and Iranian constitutionalists were carrying out talks, Dashnakists from Gilan, Salmas, Tabriz, and Urumieh were meeting at the Third Regional Congress of Azerbaijan, held from 19 December 1907 to 13 January 1908, to discuss, among other issues, activism in the Iranian Constitutional Revolution. The delegates were involved in long debates on the nature of the revolution and what that could mean for Dashnakist participation. Two figures, Stepan Stepanian (1866–1915) and Yeprem Khan Davitian (1868–1912), stand out in these discussions.

Yeprem Davitian, also known as Hayrik (Father) and Taparakan (Wanderer), was born in 1868 in the village of Barsum in the Ganje (Gandzak, Elisavetpol) province of the Russian Empire. He received his primary education in a village school and then worked in a citrate factory in Tiflis. He took part in the failed Kukunian expedition to cross the Ottoman border from Russia where he was arrested and condemned to five years to the island of Sakhalin, off the Siberian coast. Yeprem escaped with another comrade, Hovsep Movsisian, and with the help of Hovsep's brother, Hnchakist Rafael Movsisian, they reached Iran by convincing authorities that they were merchants. Yeprem arrived in Tabriz in 1896 where he took part in Dashnakist activities, including the Khanasor expedition in July 1897. After spending some time in Salmas and Qarahdagh, Yeprem settled in Rasht where for some time he was a partner in a brick factory.[33]

Stepan Stepanian, a Caucasian Armenian born in Yerevan, had been a comrade-in-arms with Yeprem in the aborted Kukunian expedition of 1890 into Ottoman Armenian provinces. Also like Yeprem, he was exiled to the Sakhalin island off the coast of Siberia and escaped through Japan to Iran. He settled in Tabriz in 1896 where he worked as a photographer and became a member of the Azerbaijan Central Committee and a strong supporter of participation in the Iranian revolution. Stepanian argued that the Dashnakist bodies in Iran were obligated to take part in the revolution because of the directive of the Vienna Congress.[34] Some argued that the movement in Iran was a bourgeois revolution and a consequence of the Russian Revolution of 1905, which had stimulated the beginnings of class struggle. Yeprem Khan, a delegate from Gilan, pointed to the leadership of the movement, which he perceived to be made up of high clergy and elite fighting for their own class interests and exploiting the people's demands against the government. Stepanian disagreed, insisting that the bourgeois had led the demand for a constitution and that the landowning clergy were on the side of the shah's government. In addition to the nature of the revolution, the delegates took into consideration the weakness and lack of development of the movement's leadership, who had been unprepared to prevent or stop harassment of Christians. The delegates then came to the conclusion that Dashnakist bodies should not give "official participation," meaning overt, but instead should assist the movement by providing it with "informal," meaning covert, help in order to give it a democratic labor character. They based this decision on several factors: (1) that the Iranian Constitutional Revolution was the expression of a bourgeois struggle against the country's clerical ranks and their protector, the shah's government; (2) that the movement was unorganized; (3) that the masses were uneducated; and (4) that the movement's "fanatic" and "chauvinist" tendencies might bring about anti-Armenian provocation.[35]

Similar issues were discussed at the Regional Congress of the Eastern Bureau, held between 31 December 1907 and 8 January 1908. In addition, the delegates spoke of ongoing relations between Dashnakists and Iranian constitutionalists, who insisted that Armenians not show active support in the revolution. The delegates were also concerned about how the Ottoman and Iranian border conflict, combined with Armenian participation, would have an impact on Armenians at the border. Some believed that the Dashnaktsutiun's expression of sympathy toward the Iranian constitutionalists was sufficient and expressed fears that any action would endanger the party, its goals, and Ottoman Armenian lives. The debate became heated when one delegate asserted: "We are not going to endanger our party, which is the party for all labor, for 30–40,000 Armenians." Hamo Mherian (Ohanjanian) and other delegates insisted that the border conflict would harm the progress of the constitutional movement and that the Dashnaktsutiun could not remain indifferent as a revolutionary and socialist party. They added that any inaction on the Dashnaktsutiun's part would jeopardize Armenian lives and security and that the party must play an international role. The congress then decided to proceed to act according to the decision of the Fourth General Congress regarding participation and collaboration in the Iranian Constitutional Revolution.[36]

Gilan and Tehran Still Apprehensive

The decisive action taken in Azerbaijan, the directive by its Central Committee to all Dashnakist bodies in Iran to do the same, and the support of the Eastern Bureau for the resolution of the Fourth General Congress were not immediately taken up by the Tehran and Gilan Committees. Both were wary about taking action in the movement.[37] The issue of participation became the topic of some debate in Gilan, causing the resignation of a member of the Gilan Committee and the dissatisfaction of many lower-ranking members who also distanced themselves temporarily from the Gilan branch. The Gilan Committee refrained from participation until December 1907, when it received direct orders from the Azerbaijan Central Committee, although only a few members led by Yeprem Khan were enthusiastic about the idea of participation.[38] The Gilan Committee, like the Anzali branch, pointed to a strong reactionary force in the region as well as a highly nationalist constitutionalist movement.[39] At the end of 1907, the Gilan Committee reported a secret boycott against Christians, especially Armenians, and concluded that the revolution had resulted in nothing positive despite the touting of the Dashnakist press that it was a liberation movement. On the contrary, the report added, the former government was more liberal.[40] At the Regional Congress held by the Gilan Committee in 1908 and attended also by Tabriz representatives, a Gilan Dashnakist identified as Bek gave a report on the Iranian revolutionary movement that he had been asked to prepare by the Gilan Committee. Bek attempted to convince those present that "there are no revolutionaries in Persia and it is not worth it to have anything to do with them," even passively.[41] The Regional Congress, after a lengthy debate, came to the conclusion that the Iranian movement was in fact at the early stages of a revolution and that it was essential to pursue "passive participation" in Gilan.[42] While no specifics were given to explain the meaning of passive participation, it would be safe to assume that it carried the same significance as unofficial, meaning covert and nonproactive, participation.

Azerbaijani Dashnakists Side with Activism

The decision to pursue active participation was first made by the Azerbaijan Central Committee on 19 August 1908, a few months after the coup d'état in Tehran by the Cossack Brigade and the bombing of the Majles during the Tabriz resistance (July 1908–April 1909), and later ac-

cepted by the Fourth Regional Congress in 1909.[43] Until mid-1908, the
Azerbaijan Dashnakists had avoided such activity.[44] Two propositions,
one in favor and the other opposed to active involvement in the Iranian
Constitutional Revolution, were considered for approval. The proposition opposing activism denied that the movement was based on any real
foundation, because resistance had not spread beyond Azerbaijan and
the achievements by Tabriz revolutionaries were incidental. The supporters of this proposition feared that if Iranian revolutionaries were defeated, the Dashnaktsutiun would be left without protection and Iranian
Armenians would become targets of "fanatics." They argued that the
achievement of ambiguous rights would be at the price of annihilation,
since anti-constitutionalists were declaring the constitutional struggle the
war of infidels against Islam. But most importantly, they felt that taking a
strong commitment in Iran would mean the abandonment or at least neglect of Ottoman Armenians merely because the Ottoman constitution
had been restored. Fighting on three fronts, Ottoman, Russian, and Iranian, would weaken Dashnakist strength.

The proposition supporting an active Dashnakist role was approved
by a majority. Supporters drew attention to the party's revolutionary
character as well as the impact of the Iranian Constitutional Revolution
on Iranian Armenians and the whole of the Near East. They rejected the
idea that active involvement would threaten the Ottoman Armenian
cause. Furthermore, they assumed that Dashnakist participation would
drive the movement in a "desirable direction," inspiring the "hopeless"
people of Iran and helping them and their leaders to understand better
the essence and demands of constitutionalism. They concluded that joint
struggle with Iranians against despotism would provide Iranian Armenians with the opportunity to ask for true equality as "children of the
same fatherland."[45]

Azerbaijan's decision was reaffirmed a year later by the Fifth General
Congress held in Varna, Bulgaria, in September 1909, thus finally instructing all Iranian Dashnakist bodies to take on active involvement in the
Iranian Constitutional Revolution, and giving official sanction to activities
that had already been taking place. This decision came only months after
revolutionary forces, including Armenians, from Isfahan and Rasht retook
Tehran, Mohammad Ali Shah was deposed, and Sheikh Fazlollah Nuri
was executed, and at around the same time as the former shah left Iran for
Odessa, Russia. In other words, the situation looked promising.

In reaching its decision, the congress took into consideration five factors: (1) that socialist tendencies existed in the Iranian Constitutional
Revolution; (2) that Iran's rebirth would benefit its neighboring countries; (3) that within the constitutional movement lay the betterment of
the cultural, national, and economic interests of the Iranian Armenian

community; (4) that the Dashnaktsutiun's participation in the movement would reestablish communal ties between Armenians and Muslims; and (5) that the Iranian revolution would bring together Armenians and Muslims in the Caucasus and the Ottoman Empire. It then concluded that active participation was the most appropriate measure to be adopted by Dashnakist bodies in Iran. It would involve maintaining close ties with Iranian democratic elements, working to establish labor parties among Iranians in accordance with the party's worldview, and guaranteeing national/cultural institutions through federal laws.[46]

After long and arduous debate among Dashnakists in Iran and outside and after two years of the original decision in 1907, Iranian Dashnakist bodies began active participation. Some, like the Azerbaijan branch, had already initiated talks with Iranian constitutionalists leading to collaboration.

Dashnakist Collaboration:
From Sweets to Arms

Actual collaboration between Armenians and Iranians did not reach fruition until mid-1908, when Mohammad Ali and the Cossack Brigade carried out a coup (June 1908) and Tabriz became the center of resistance (July 1908), although there were acts symbolizing the solidarity between the two peoples and the support of the Armenian populace in the earlier phases of the Iranian Constitutional Revolution. For example, in July 1906, the Tehran Committee sent five boxes of sugar for tea to those taking sanctuary in the British legation. In August 1906, after the royal decree to allow a Majles and the drafting of the constitution, the Tehran Committee prepared a great welcome to pro-constitutionalist clerics (*mojtaheds*). They raised large tents and served sweets, fruits, lemonade, and tea as Armenian clerics and 100 Armenians greeted the clerics.[47] While sweets were appreciated by the Iranian constitutionalists, arms were even sweeter.

Beginning in July 1908, after Mohammad Ali Shah's successful coup in Tehran, the Tabriz resistance was a significant factor in inspiring and prompting a tangible response from the Dashnakist bodies in Azerbaijan. However, even prior to that, as early as mid-July 1907, the Salmas Anjoman invited the Dashnaktsutiun to extend its gift of wheat to fighters.[48] The Dashnakist Salmas branch was headed by Samson (Stepan Tadeosian, 1870–1945), the nephew of Kristapor Mikayelian, cofounder of the party. Samson, because of his experience as a gunsmith, was placed in charge of Dashnakist armories in Tiflis and later Azerbaijan. Samson left the Caucasus and settled in Iran in 1897, where he forged good relations between Armenians and Iranians of different ethnicities and religions, thus setting the stage for solidarity in the Constitutional Revolution.

Despite warnings by Maku's military commander (*Sardar*) not to participate in the battles for constitutionalism, the Dashnakist Salmas Committee under the leadership of Samson decided in October 1908 to assist
the Iranian fighters and began to prepare Dashnakist fighters as well as
Armenian peasants for battle.[49] This decision may have been influenced
by the temporary victory of the Tabriz resisters in early October, when
they succeeded in pushing back royalist forces from Sattar Khan's and
Baqer Khan's headquarters in Amirkhiz and Khiaban as well as the Russian threat in the same month to send forces into Iran in order to protect
Russian subjects.[50] The Dashnakists agreed to help protect Dilman near
Lake Urumieh and, with the help of the Tabriz *mojahedin* of the Organization of Social Democrats, successfully captured it and other towns and
villages in the area.[51] After the capture of Dilman, two Dashnakists were
elected to the Salmas Anjoman and a mixed Iranian and Armenian committee was established with the participation of two Dashnakists.[52] Similar mixed committees whose members worked together to plan the protection of the city were also established in about the same time in Khoy
and Urumieh.[53]

Sattar Khan

Soon after the beginning of the civil war in Azerbaijan, on 30 July 1908,
the Azerbaijan Central Committee decided to begin talks for collaborative effort with Sattar Khan, one of the leaders of the Tabriz resistance
and a popular figure in the history of the Iranian Constitutional Revolution. The Central Committee authorized its representatives to provide
counsel as well as arms and munitions but to remain extremely cautious
so as not to "provide any opportunity for suspicion or *provocation*"[54]
(emphasis in original).

During the first meeting between Sattar Khan and the Dashnakists,
Sattar Khan, in response to questions by the Dashnakists, explained the
purpose of the movement as one for constitution and against the government and its "official and unofficial protectors." Sattar Khan added that
although the *mojahedin* possessed sufficient fighters and arms for the time
being, they lacked order and discipline and could use support and advice
to remedy this weak aspect.[55] The Dashnakists then provided Sattar
Khan with a list comprising 17 tactical suggestions regarding establishing order and instilling discipline among the troops. They ranged from
division of troops into smaller groups to rules regarding behavior toward
the populace.[56] In addition, the Dashnakists proposed keeping their comrades and the populace abreast of their demands and actions through frequent flyers, maintaining a rebellious mood among the populace through
demonstrations, and making their demands officially known to Euro-

pean representatives and press in the country in order to refute mislead-
ing and misrepresenting explanations. The Dashnakists also warned
against neglect of the rural areas where reactionaries had the most influence.[57]

On 21 August 1908, the Central Committee decided to provide Sattar
Khan with at least 50 fighters, of whom 10 would be grenadiers and can-
noneers in Tabriz, and to expect about 100 *fedayis* from Salmas and Urumieh.[58] On 22 August 1908, the terms of the agreement between the
Dashnakists and *mojahedin* were put into writing and signed, unlike the
agreement between Rostom and Taqizadeh, by both sides, including Sattar Khan and four other *mojahedin* leaders.[59] The pact allowed for the formation of a seven-member committee to spread the constitutional movement to all regions in Iran and restore constitutional law and order and a
three-member committee to coordinate all military activity. The Dashnakists were allowed two or three representatives in the first committee
and one representative in the latter. The Dashnakists would provide 30
soldiers with their own guns and ammunition, who would live in the
same conditions as the Iranian *mojahedin,* as well as for the expense of the
trip to Tabriz, after which the committee would take over the expenses.
In addition, the Dashnakists would carry out strong propaganda in the
press and through other unspecified means. The last point of agreement
obligated the newly formed Tabriz committee to maintain regular contact
with the Dashnaktsutiun's Eastern Bureau.[60]

Sattar Khan recognized the importance of having Caucasian Dashnakist fighters on his side, for they came with a great deal of experience
and knowledge, as did most Caucasian revolutionaries joining the constitutionalist forces. Both Keri and Rostom worked closely with Sattar Khan
and took part in the actual military resistance of Tabriz against Samad
Khan (Shoja al-Dowleh), governor of Maragheh, southeast of Lake Urumieh. The Dashnaktsutiun called on Keri (d. 1916) to bring with him to
Iran Caucasian Armenian fighters, numbering around 25, and to take
their command. Keri, a native of Erzerum, had been a very active Dashnakist *fedayi* who was also involved, like Rostom, in the Caucasian communal violence beginning in 1905.[61] Rostom, like so many of his comrades, was not only an intellectual leader and teacher but also a military
commander who organized *fedayi* missions in the Caucasus and Iran. He
was especially skilled as a bomb-maker and prepared explosives, which
were used by the Tabriz resisters, in the small Dashnakist bomb laboratory in an Armenian quarter of Tabriz.[62] The Caucasian Dashnakists
fought with Sattar Khan's and Baqer Khan's armies in several battles in
Alvar, Sofian, Marand, and Armenian populated Mujumbar, between autumn 1908 and the arrival of Russian troops in April 1909, after which
Rostom left for Van and Keri fled to Salmas, returning later to Tabriz to

join Yeprem Khan in the conquest of Tehran in July 1909.[63] According to Mangol Bayat, Armenian quarters in Tabriz became the primary centers of resistance.[64]

Relations between the Dashnakists and Sattar Khan oscillated between amity and resentment. Publicly, the Dashnaktsutiun praised Sattar Khan as a great hero of the Tabriz resistance.[65] In private correspondence, however, individual Dashnakists differed in their opinion of the commander of the Tabriz forces. For example, at times Sattar Khan was characterized as "ignorant but skillful, self-interested and underhanded," someone who did not fully appreciate or acknowledge the contribution of the Armenian *fedayis,* while others or the same individuals at different times viewed him in a very positive light.[66] In his memoirs, published posthumously, Hovsep Hovhannisian praised Sattar Khan as "honest and openhearted" and "bold and solid," proclaiming that Sattar Khan and Yeprem Khan were the leaders who saved Iran.[67]

Sattar Committee

Despite their reservations, Dashnakists collaborated with the Sattar Committee, named in honor of Sattar Khan, formed in October 1908 in Rasht during the Tabriz resistance. The Central Committee of the Sattar Committee was made up of 13 members, including Mirza Karim Khan, his three brothers, Hosein Kasma'i, and Ali Mohammad Tarbiyat. The War Commission was made up of six members, including Hosein Kasma'i, Valico (Georgian), Yeprem Khan, and others.[68] In his memoirs, Yeprem Khan explained that the seven-member Sattar Committee, formed with three Armenians and four Muslims, called itself social democratic though in actuality it followed the program of the Dashnaktsutiun. Because of the apparent contradiction between the social democratic program, which abandoned the national question altogether, and Dashnakist social revolutionary leanings, which recognized it, Yeprem Khan stated that he went to Anzali where he organized the Barq (Lightning) Committee again with three Armenians and four Muslims who followed the program of the Russian Social Revolutionaries, which was more closely related to the socialist plan of the Dashnaktsutiun.[69] Another source indicates that the Barq Committee was also social democratic and had four Dashnakist members.[70]

According to archival records, it seems likely that the Sattar Committee was in fact social democratic not only in name as its seal indicated but also in ideology. For example, according to the Dashnakist Gilan branch, the Dashnakist members of the Sattar Committee were not allowed by the Sattar Committee itself to be called official representatives of the Dashnaktsutiun, because the committee's social democratic ideals contradicted the social revolutionary tendencies of the Dashnaktsutiun.[71] The Dashnaktsutiun was very much concerned about the Sattar Committee's social democracy and constantly raised the issue of the committee's seal, which included the words "Ejtema'iyun'Amiyun" (Social Democrats). Perhaps in an effort to justify cooperation with the ideologically different Social Democrats, the Dashnakists claimed that when the founders of the Sattar Committee ordered the seal, they had not understood the meaning of "social democracy" and that they really were not Social Democrats. The Dashnakists went so far as to demand the removal of the words, but faced with failure they attributed the continued usage to the necessity of preserving the original name of the committee for the sake of recognition.[72]

During the Third Regional Congress held in Rasht from 29 September to 7 October 1909, which was held after Mohammad Ali left the country to Odessa, some Dashnakists questioned involvement in the social democratic Sattar Committee but were reassured that the Dashnakists, having already begun collaboration prior to the adoption of a social democratic character, did not want to abandon the committee and its work, which would have only complicated matters and hurt the progress of the work being carried out.[73] Therefore, while in theory Dashnakists were opposed to collaboration with Social Democrats, the need to cooperate in the revolutionary movement overrode ideological concerns.

According to the Gilan Committee, the Sattar Committee requested assistance on 1 January 1909. The Gilan Committee could provide only seven volunteer fighters and a small batch of arms. Only a few Dashnakist fighters joined Yeprem Khan in the capture of Rasht in February 1909.[74] According to some sources, 20 Armenians, along with 35 Georgians and three Iranians, were responsible for taking over the arsenal and city of Rasht. Once Rasht had been taken, the Sattar Committee formed a provincial council (Anjoman-e ayalat).[75] In March, the Gilan Committee proposed bringing in 50 Caucasian Armenian fighters. The Sattar Committee agreed to provide the expense of only 20 men and the Gilan Committee made arrangements with Dashnakist bodies in Baku to bring in 20 armed men.[76] The Dashnakists continued to collaborate with the Sattar Committee until its dissolution in August 1909.[77]

Although few Dashnakists were involved in the capture of Rasht with Yeprem Khan, many joined him later, including his second-in-command, Grisha Khan (Grish Ter Danielian). In his memoirs of Yeprem's activities, Grisha describes the participation of Dashnakist fighters in battles from March to June 1909 in the Qazvin province at Yuzbashi-Chay, Kharzan, and Naki (where Yeprem was slightly wounded in the leg), against Shahsevan tribal forces, and at the Karaj bridge, 30 miles from Tehran, against Russian Cossacks who aided the Shahsevans. The figures for Armenian fighters varied in these battles but numbered from as little as 30, at Karaj, to as many as 90, at the government building (*darkhaneh*) in Qazvin. According to Grisha, meetings in Qarahtapa between Yeprem Khan and Sardar As'ad, commander of the Bakhtiari forces, resulted in the decision to march on to Tehran. At the end of June 1909, they arrived in Tehran and after several battles took over the Majles building and the strategically significant Sepahsalar mosque.[78] Yeprem Khan was then appointed chief of Tehran police, a position that led to friction between Yeprem Khan and Iranian Armenian Dashnakists.

Jahangir Committee

In addition to the Sattar Committee, which had played such a significant role in the capture of Rasht, in September 1908 during the Tabriz resistance, the Gilan Committee formed the Jahangir Committee with an equal number of Iranian and Dashnakist members. However, it was dissolved due to inaction and replaced by other similar committees, some of which were as or more successful than the Jahangir Committee. They included among the membership local, Tabrizi, and Caucasian revolutionaries and dealt primarily with the transfer of arms and the preparations for incoming Georgian fighters. There were attempts in 1909 to revive the Jahangir Committee.[79] These attempts may have resulted in the Jahangir Committee that assisted in the reconquest of Tehran in July 1909, which was carried out primarily by revolutionaries from Rasht and Isfahan. According to the Dashnakist Tehran Committee, the Jahangir Committee was recast in 1910 as Union and Progress (Ettefaq va Taraqi), a small party fashioned after the Ottoman Committee of Union and Progress with a few Majles delegates. Mansureh Ettehadieh Nezam Mafi has referred to the Jahangir Committee as a subcommittee of Union and Progress.[80] At the beginning of its formation the Dashnaktsutiun sent two members to take part in the Jahangir Committee's workings; however, when Union and Progress began working with the conservative Social Moderates (Ejtema'iyun E' tedaliyun), the Dashnaktsutiun withdrew its solidarity.[81]

Democrat Party

The Dashnaktsutiun's relations with the left-of-center Democrat Party, founded in 1909 and made up of Social Democrats and liberals, were longer lasting yet still quite problematic. According to Vahan Zakarian, a native of Tabriz and active member of the Azerbaijan Central Committee of the Dashnaktsutiun, meetings had taken place in winter 1909 between Taqizadeh, Rostom, and Zakarian with the goal of forming a party in order to provide a firm foundation for all future collaborative efforts. This information is backed by a letter, dated 11 January 1909, written by the Azerbaijan Central Committee to the Western Bureau informing the bureau of Taqizadeh's invitation to the Dashnaktsutiun to begin talks to form a new organization.[82] Zakarian stated that they had worked together in trying to create a program for the new party and that they had succeeded in producing a platform very similar to that of the Dashnaktsutiun. According to Zakarian, however, Taqizadeh had already secretly devised plans for the Democrat Party in November 1908 with two Armenian Social Democrats, referring to Vram Pilosian and Tigran Ter Hakobian (Darvish). Zakarian expressed some disappointment in Taqizadeh's clandestine action, adding that although the Dashnaktsutiun may have been opposed to joining the party had they been asked, they would have at least been able to assist given their years of experience.[83]

Despite this shaky start, the Dashnaktsutiun continued to be interested in reaching some sort of solidarity and working relationship with the Democrat Party.[84] The two parties began talks sometime in late 1909, definitely after Mohammad Ali Shah's departure to Odessa in September and most probably after the opening of the second Majles where the influential Democrat Party had secured a number of seats in November. The meetings between the two led to an understanding or agreement regarding (1) parliamentarism; (2) reexamination of electoral laws; (3) freedoms of press, speech, assembly, affiliation, as well as individual freedoms and the freedom to strike; (4) peasant ownership of land; (5) elimination of individual and public privileges; (6) government supervision of religious endowments (*vaqf*) and appropriation of its income to education; (7) popular elections; and (8) internal national (ethnic) autonomy. According to the Tehran Committee, it was "only authorized to accept the aforesaid program orally" by the Azerbaijan Central Committee. Therefore, when it refused the Democrat Party's proposal to sign an official agreement, nothing came of the party's efforts.[85]

It is unclear why or whether the Azerbaijan Central Committee decided on such a course. It had no objections to talks between Democrats and Dashnakists in Tehran.[86] In fact, it became quite concerned when it found out about a flyer that had surfaced sometime in summer or autumn 1910, bearing the name of the Tehran Committee and criticizing the Democrat Party. In a letter to Rostom, Zakarian of the Azerbaijan Central Committee expressed surprise since the Dashnakists were collaborating with the Democrats and had even worked out a platform together. He placed the blame, as did the Tehran Committee, on a few Dashnakists led by Arsen Mikayelian who had not received or even asked the Tehran Committee's permission before putting out such a provocative attack.[87] An undated declaration regarding the Democrat Party, bearing the name of the Tehran Committee, exists among the records at the Dashnaktsutiun archives, and it is almost certainly the one described above.[88] The declaration raised the issue of the conflict between the Democrats and the Moderates, which had gone beyond words and turned into a bloody conflict, referring no doubt to the assassinations of Moderate Ayatollah Behbahani and Democrats Tarbiyat and Razzaq (July–August 1910). The declaration also accused the Democrats of acting not for ideological reasons but for government positions and personal gains. Moreover, it concluded that the violence was detrimental to the country and so the Tehran Committee would stay neutral in the conflict, a precept supported by Mirzayan.[89] In an undated rebuttal, the Democrat Party struck back by questioning Dashnakist neutrality and its revolutionary and democratic character. The Democrats refuted the accusations of personal interest and explained the conflict as a consequence of political competition and class struggle, adding that they themselves were the victims of violence. Furthermore, the response charged the Dashnaktsutiun of closing its eyes to the truth and working for its own party interests. The Democrats concluded by cautioning Iranian Armenians that their interests lay not in the Dashnaktsutiun but in a democratic union absent of racial, religious, and national differentiation.[90]

Relations between the Dashnakists and Democrats, especially Taqizadeh, soured after the appearance of the offensive flyer and equally offensive rebuttal. The Azerbaijan Central Committee reported that Taqizadeh had become unfriendly. It was quick to point out, however, that Taqizadeh had always been a strong nationalist as well as "highly cunning and circumspect," directly referring to his dealings with Armenian Social Democrats Pilosian and Ter Hakobian in forming the Democrat Party. Moreover, he stated, Pilosian and Ter Hakobian had influenced the opinion of Taqizadeh and other Iranian leaders against the Dashnaktsutiun by accusing the party of chauvinism.[91] Clearly, Dashnakists felt threatened by the Democrat Party's social democratic elements, including the member of the Social Democratic Hemmat party, Caucasian Muslim Mohammad Amin Rasulzadeh, editor of the party's organ *Iran-e No* and future leader of the Azerbaijani Republic in the Caucasus.[92]

Records indicate that problems existed between Taqizadeh and some Dashnakists even before the appearance of the flyer despite continued collaboration.[93] Part of the cause of strained relations between the two sides may have been to a certain extent personal differences or prejudices, as in the case of Armenian Majles delegate Hovsep Mirzayan and Yeprem Khan. In a letter to Rostom, Mirzayan defended his stance against Dashnakist participation in the Iranian Constitutional Revolution, "because our neighbors are chauvinists," including Young Turks, Social Democrats, and Democrats. Mirzayan feared that if the constitutionalists were defeated, Armenians would be punished for their participation. Moreover, he added that danger would come to Armenians not from reactionary and conservative elements but from "allies" who "with a fraternal kiss drop the fatal poison between your lips."[94] He opposed coming to agreement with Taqizadeh and the Democrats, adding that only Caucasian Armenians who were unaware of the situation in Iran and who did not know Taqizadeh promoted collaboration.[95] Mirzayan was mistaken, however, as Dashnakist Dr. Stepanian was eager to make public the results of talks with the Democrats and complained that the Tehran Committee was procrastinating because of Yeprem Khan and Mirzayan, whose views were based on distrust, suspicion, and some minor unspecified personal issues. Furthermore, he asserted that the majority of Tehran Dashnakist leaders advocated solidarity with the Democrats and that only the aforementioned two were opposed.[96]

It is possible that Yeprem Khan's views regarding the Democrat Party had less to do with the party itself than with its charismatic leader, Taqizadeh. It would be safe to argue that Yeprem was affected by the differences that had surfaced between Taqizadeh and Sattar Khan during May to July 1909 when Yeprem was the commander of the Rasht forces heading to Tehran. Army leaders like Sattar Khan and Yeprem Khan sought the capture of Tehran and the overthrow of Mohammad Ali Shah while Taqizadeh and others were willing to compromise when the shah agreed to reinstitute constitutional rule.[97] This issue, among others, had created a great rift between Taqizadeh on one side and Sattar Khan and Yeprem Khan on the other.

Democrat and Social Democrat Haidar Khan 'Amu Oghlu's letter to Yeprem Khan also provides some clue to Yeprem Khan's concerns, since no record written by Yeprem himself on the subject has been found. Haidar Khan was responding to one Yeprem Khan wrote, expressing his opinions on the Iranian political situation. While in agreement with Yeprem Khan's view regarding the sectarian nature of politics in general, he rejected the idea that the country's problems arose from that and, taking a jab at Yeprem, added that some people did not seem to know Iran well enough to understand that. He also found fault with Yeprem Khan's presumption that the Democrat Party was not a real political party, pointing out that it in fact was a party in the European sense. As for Yeprem Khan's accusation of chauvinism and lack of ideology, if that were the case, then how did the Dashnaktsutiun justify collaboration with such a party? Moreover, Haidar Khan wondered why Yeprem was so keen on discrediting the only democratic party in Iran when it bore no such motives.[98]

Further attempts were made by the Democrat Party to include the Dashnaktsutiun along with the Moderates and Union and Progress in a multiparty conference to unite forces against reactionary elements.[99] The idea for the creation of such a conference and organization, called the National Salvation Committee (Komiteh-ye nejat-e melli), came from the Armenian Social Democrat Tigran Ter Hakobian in a letter to Taqizadeh in November 1910 and may have been influenced by the British ultimatum of October 1910 to set up its own force if Iran's southern trade routes, specifically for British caravans, were not secured by the Iranian government.[100] The interest to create such an organization may have also been influenced by Russian advances into Qazvin, Taqizadeh's dismissal from the Majles, and the violence between the Democrats and Bakhtiaris, all taking place in July and August 1910.

The bylaws of the Committee of National Salvation consisted of 21 points, indicating that the committee would be a multiparty body formed not only of various political parties but also tribal representatives. It would meet twice a week and would refrain from infighting.[101] The primary goals of the party were spelled out in December 1910 and in some instances resembled the Democrat Party's own program[102]:

1. Establishment of constitutional regime and strengthening of Iran's independence;
2. Protection of Majles from attack;
3. Majority vote of Majles and unanimous vote of the Committee of National Salvation necessary for cabinet ministers;
4. Separation of three branches of government and no party intervention on behalf of government employees;
5. Reforms in all government administrations;
6. Organization of military forces;
7. Bringing in foreign advisers;
8. Control over budget;
9. Reform of taxes;
10. Expansion of legal rules;
11. Expulsion of foreign forces by whatever means;
12. Reform of landownership laws, restricting landowner privileges;
13. Resolute effort by all parties and nomadic tribes entering into committee is imperative in increasing the government's influence, surrendering to it their ready forces.

In addition to the above long-term project, the Committee of National Salvation agreed upon immediate plans to recruit representatives of nomadic tribes into the committee, to establish a military tribunal to punish reactionaries in the capital, to bar anti-constitutionalists from ministerial positions, and so forth.[103] In a similar document written a few months later in 1911, the Committee of National Salvation reiterated many of the aforementioned points but added the following: (1) to enlighten the public about the fundamentals of constitution, (2) to attract European support for Iranian independence, (3) to prohibit attempts at exoneration of national traitors, and (4) to punish traitors, and reward those who have served the country.[104]

The Committee of National Salvation was also fraught with difficulties, ranging from minor misunderstandings causing and/or resulting in missed meetings to larger conflicts stemming from distrust and, in some cases, paranoia.[105] This time, however, the Dashnakists blamed the Moderates and Union and Progress for the failure of the Committee of National Salvation. The Tehran Dashnakists felt that the Moderates and Union and Progress, having formed a block in the Majles, no longer needed the Democrats and the Dashnakists and therefore disrupted the meetings of the Committee of National Salvation.[106] Of course, the failure of the Committee of National Salvation and similar efforts had more to do with the course of the Iranian Constitutional Revolution than simply the fault of one party or another.

Other Avenues of Contribution

Armenian Delegates to the Majles

Armenian, specifically Dashnakist, participation in the Iranian Constitutional Revolution also came in the form of an Armenian delegate to the Majles. According to constitutional laws, minorities were allowed one representative each. In the first Majles, Armenians and Jews were represented by Iranian Muslim delegates Tabataba'i and Behbahani respectively. In the second Majles, they could each elect their own delegate. The Armenians, dissatisfied with having only one delegate, campaigned throughout 1909 and part of 1910, at times through Yeprem Khan, to be granted two delegates.[107] Until early 1910, they believed that they would be granted two and postponed elections for that reason.[108] The issue of Armenian delegates to the Majles caused much debate among Dashnakists, who held opposing views regarding the number of delegates to accept. The disagreement occurred primarily between the Azerbaijan and Tehran bodies, although the Tehran branch itself was divided. The majority of the Tehran Committee held out for two delegates while the Azerbaijan Central Committee asserted that no basis existed for demanding more than one deputy.[109] Furthermore, it called for mixed elections to remove the national/religious barrier, which an Armenian or Jewish representative implied. It hoped that mixed elections would result in two or three Armenian delegates, but it suspected that they would more likely result in none. Despite that, it felt Armenians could voice their demands through their Azerbaijani delegates.[110] The dissension not only delayed elections to February 1910, but also resulted in the nonparticipation of central and southern Iranian Armenian communities.[111] The Azerbaijan Armenian community elected Hovsep Mirzayan, who seemed to be the first choice of Dashnakist bodies, although some, like Vahan Zakarian and Yeprem Khan, had doubts about him.[112] Other candidates were considered, for example, Hovhannes Khan Masehian (1894–1931) and Dr. Bazil (Minas Manuk Barsegh).[113]

Masehian, a native of Tehran, was educated in Europe and held diplomatic posts including one as translator to the Qajar court. He was wellknown for his translated works of William Shakespeare, Alexandre Dumas, Charles Dickens, and others. The suggestion for Dr. Bazil's candidacy came from Istanbul.[114] He was a native of New Julfa who had studied in Bengal, Calcutta, and Edinburgh and had begun to teach medicine at Dar al-Fonun, the first higher school in Iran established in 1851. Little information exists on Dr. Bazil, but according to one source, he was opposed to any Armenian participation in Iranian politics, including a delegate in the Majles. The source also suggests that Dr. Bazil wrote in the constitutional paper *Habl al-Matin* (Tehran) in 1907 under the pseudonyms Vazifeh (Duty/Task) and Kabus (Nightmare).[115] Mirzayan was opposed to his candidacy, because he found him insufficiently committed to the Armenian community.[116]

The Majles accepted Mirzayan as the delegate of the Armenian community in December 1910. Mirzayan continued to seek more delegates for Iranian Armenians while at the same time pushing for electoral reforms that would eliminate separate elections for non-Muslims and include them in general elections.[117] Mirzayan also supported the acceptance of Armenians into military service, which caused great debate in the Majles. The conservative religious element opposed such service as it contradicted Islamic law regarding the status of non-Muslims bearing arms.[118] Ironically, armed Armenians had assisted in constitutionalist victories.

Dashnakist Women and the Woman Question

Fully aware of their minority status and special role in the Iranian Constitutional Revolution, Dashnakists explored other avenues as well. They sought solidarity with Assyrians and tried to work among Iranian women of various ethnic and religious backgrounds. Although little information exists on these two undertakings, it is clear that some success was achieved in both cases, especially the latter. In the case of Assyrians, they were bound in some sense by their fear of Ottoman troops making their way into areas like Urumieh, which were highly populated by both groups. There and in Salmas, they formed committees to work together on issues like self-defense. The Dashnakists and Assyrians worked together to organize a force, including 200 Assyrians to ward off Ottoman troops at the border.[119]

Dashnakist women formed two committees called Huys (Hope) and Tsiatsan (Rainbow) with 14 and 19 members, respectively. Both groups tried to educate women on politics, party issues, Ottoman and Iranian constitutionalism, as well as inheritance, hygiene, and the woman's question. Together they formed a Red Cross organization.[120] The activities of Dashnakist women among Iranian women were considered an essential component of the general work being carried out in the Iranian Constitutional Revolution. In language not uncommon to the period's discourse on women's issues, the goal was to "awaken the Persian woman also from her centuries-old sleep and to acquaint her gradually with the woman's question." According to Dashnakist women, they initiated the formation of the Persian Women's Benevolent Society in Tehran despite lack of encouragement and sometimes outright hostility by certain conservative segments of society. While the society began as a charitable organization interested in spreading women's education through opening girls' schools and kindergartens, it planned to gradually change its program and direction to bring the woman's question to the "dark corners" where the concept of equality of women was rejected, where women were "treated as objects," and where they were "subject to man's every whim." The group's income came in large part from its members and fund-raising events like plays and lectures. Among its more successful events was a gathering in April 1910 of 500 Iranian women, Muslims, Jews, Chaldeans, and Armenians, as well as Europeans, in a Tehran park where women gave lectures and recited poems and from which all men were barred. Constitutional historian Janet Afary also mentions such a gathering of 500 women sponsored by the Anjoman of Ladies of the Homeland, also founded in Tehran in 1910.[121] According to the report of the Persian Women's Benevolent Society, it also received permission from the Iranian government to publish a journal on women's issues entitled *Shekufeh* (Blossom).[122] This may have been the same *Shekufeh* that began publication in Tehran in 1913. The scant information on the society allows great room for conjecture, but for the present the relationship between these organizations remains obscure. It may be that these organizations are the same. What remains clear is that solidarity and collaboration with Iranian women indicated another aspect of Armenian cooperation with Iranians during the constitutional movement.

Yeprem Khan's wife, Anahit Davitian, was also involved in women's circles and a member of the Anjoman of Ladies of the Homeland.[123] In addition, she was a great supporter of the constitutionalist troops. To that end, she telegraphed Yeprem informing him of her plans to lead a group of women to tend to wounded fighters. Yeprem rejected the idea, calling it madness, and instructed them to stay where they were.[124]

Conclusion

Dashnakist collaboration took on various forms and involved groups with varying ideologies. Even with continued collaboration and solidarity with different constitutionalist committees and Iranian constitutionalists of different ideologies, the Dashnaktsutiun, somewhat similar to the Hnchakian party, privately persisted in its belief that no Iranian political party or organization satisfied the Dashnaktsutiun's requirements and/or perception of what constituted a political party.[125] In addition, it sought to bring together the different elements under a federation of Iranian revolutionaries reminiscent of the Dashnaktsutiun's own origins.[126] Why it thought the Iranians would be more successful than the Armenians had been is unclear.

Social Democratic Collaboration:
The Pen and the Sword

As Afary's study on the Iranian Constitutional Revolution demonstrates, Caucasian and Iranian Social Democrats took an active and important role in the revolution.[127] Armenian social democratic collaboration, as in the case of Hnchakists, was in some sense similar to Dashnakist collaboration, but in the case of individual Social Democrats not affiliated with Armenian political parties, collaboration was more involved, that is, they were not merely collaborative with Iranian constitutionalists but initiated the formation of a new and subsequently influential Iranian political party.

First Steps

There is yet no evidence that the Hnchakian party took any action in the revolution before autumn 1908 except for a gift of 80 guns to Sattar Khan in July 1908 at the start of the Tabriz resistance.[128] Hnchakists had similar concerns to Dashnakists regarding joining the Iranian Constitutional Revolution. There were some Hnchakists who, despite the social democratic leanings of the party, rejected the prioritization of socialist internationalism over the nationalist aim of Armenian liberation from Ottoman rule. They were concerned about the deleterious effects participation would have on the Armenian liberation movement, especially because the Hnchakist propaganda used in the Iranian Constitutional Revolution was socialist. Others who insisted on involvement objected to socialist propaganda. Both opposing factions were "silenced" by Grigor Yeghikian (subsequently an associate of Kuchek Khan, leader of the Jangali movement, 1914–1921) and Manuel Mozian along with other Hnchakists, one of whom was Srpuhi Davitkhanian, a high-ranking woman within the party organization in Iran who propagated party ideas among Iranian Armenian women.[129]

The Hnchakists, represented by Rafael Movsisian, took part in a "secret military council" in Tabriz with Iranian revolutionary leaders Sattar Khan and Baqer Khan, Sedrak Banvorian (the Armenian representative of the Russian Social Democrats), and Rostom Gharakhanian (Stepan Zorian, representative of the Dashnaktsutiun).[130] The cooperation of these various groups led to the formation of a fighting force of almost 200 men in Gilan to storm Tehran and restore the constitution, which was accomplished in July 1909. This force was divided into seven groups: (1) 23 social democratic Georgians led by Valikov; (2) 21 Hnchakists; (3) 50 Iranian Social Democrats (Ejtema'iyun'Amiyun) with guns provided by the Hnchakists; (4) 17 Dashnakists led by Yeprem Khan; (5) 45 *mojahedin* led by Sattar Khan; (6) 46 *mojahedin* led by Baqer Khan; and (7) an unspecified number of Caucasian Turks. A great number of unaligned fighters also took part under the leadership of Mokhjeh Soltan.[131]

Pact with the Organization of Social Democrats

The Hnchakists, in addition to taking part in military activities with Iranian revolutionaries, attempted to contribute to the revolution ideologically. The Hnchakian party began talks with the Organization of Social Democrats in the latter half of 1908 during the Tabriz resistance at the home of Hnchakist Flora Vardanian and formed an alliance with them in November 1908. The Organization of Social Democrats signed the following statement: "We the Persian mojaheds, the party of Social Democrats [Ejtima'iyun'Amiyun], with the Hnchakian party, by this treaty contracted and swore that from this date forward, we will work with united forces and commit the necessary sacrifices for the establishment of the Iranian constitution and all the steps that we take will be with the agreement of the Hnchakian party and with [its participation]. " Among the nine conditions were that both parties would maintain "Social Democratic principles," would act in Iran only "with the complete agreement of both parties," and the Hnchakian party would provide the "necessary military, material and physical force" for the success of the Iranian Constitutional Revolution, but both parties would assist financially.[132] According to Hnchakist historian Arsen Kitur, the first central committee

of this alliance consisted of Yusef Khalkhali, Sedrak Banvorian, Flora Vardanian, and Rafael Movsisian. The committee saw to the transport of
arms and men from Baku to Anzali.[133] The Hnchakian party, according to
a receipt signed by the Organization of Social Democrats, provided the
first shipment of arms only a few weeks after the signing of the pact.[134]

Relations with the Democrat Party

The Anzali Hnchakists also delivered a number of bombs to the Democrat Party.[135] However, relations between the Hnchakian and Democrat
parties were problematic yet, according to Yeghikian, always close—"to
a certain extent."[136] In fact, at one point relations were cordial enough to
lead to meetings between Majles delegate and Democrat Mirza
Soleiman Eskandari and Hnchakists Yeghikian, Manuel Mozian, and
others. Mirza Soleiman proposed that the Democrats and Hnchakists
take on the assassination of former shah Mohammad Ali, who had left
for Odessa in September 1909, and Salar al-Dowleh, the shah's brother,
in Kermanshah. In return, the assassins would be monetarily compen-
sated. Yeghikian was offended by the offer of money and thus considered the proposition "dishonorable for those making it and for those receiving it." The assignment to kill Salar al-Dowleh was later taken on by
Mozian and another Hnchakist, Tigran Gazanchian, despite Yeghikian's
objections. Both were arrested and hanged in Kermanshah before com-
pletion of the mission.[137]

The occasional friction between the Hnchakists and the democrats may
have been in large part caused by Hnchakist belief that the democratic
ideology had departed from the original views of some of its founders.
The Hnchakists considered the founding members of the Democrat Party
to be former Social Democrats, alluding perhaps to their ties to the Armenian Social Democrats of Tabriz, some of whom were former Hnchakists themselves. Furthermore, the Hnchakists believed that Taqizadeh
and the Democrat Party had begun to espouse more nationalistic ideals
with some "pan-Islamic tendencies."[138] Similarly, the accusation of nationalism was also delivered by the Tabriz Armenian Social Democrats
against the Hnchakists. In a declaration by the Tabriz group on the twen-
tieth-anniversary celebrations of the Hnchakian party, the Armenian Social Democrats asserted that the Hnchakian party "has not been, is not
and is not able to be proletarian and subsequently social democratic."
Also, the party did not defend the rights of workers but rather the rights
of the Armenian people whose interests were contradictory. Therefore,
the Tabriz Social Democrats claimed, the Hnchakian party was a nationalist party, neither socialist nor even democratic.[139]

The difficulty between the Hnchakists and Democrats may have also had a great deal to do with the breakdown of relations between the Democrat Party and the Organization of Social Democrats, an ally of the Hnchakian party. Afary points out that while there were differences between the two former parties early on, relations "deteriorated to the point of open rupture" in early 1910 when the Democrat Party announced the closing down of all social democratic branches and *mojahedin* organizations.[140] She further demonstrates that the rift may have been largely caused by the influence of the minority wing of the Armenian Social Democrats in Tabriz, represented by former Hnchakist Vram Pilosian, who also wrote under the pseudonym Bahr (Sea) and Dehati (Peasant), and Tigran Ter Hakobian (Darvish).

At the end of 1908, the Social Democratic Group of Tabriz, headed by Arshavir Chilinkirian, Vram Pilosian, Vaso Khachaturian, and other Armenian Social Democrats, joined with Caucasian Social Democrats from Baku (30 in number) and Tiflis (no number given) to work together among the workers in Tabriz. Khachaturian referred to the Tabriz social democrat group as a "social-democratic group of Armenian intelligentsia."[141] They formed three circles of workers, ten each to carry out systematic propaganda, and organized a group of young Muslim intellectuals who would form the bulk of "agitators and organizers." Khachaturian indicated that the decision was made to develop a popular militia, but the question remained whether such a militia would be detrimental to the proletariat, since it might later be used by the bourgeoisie as a permanent army.[142] He concluded that although the influence of the Social Democrats was "enormous," the forces were not sufficient to carry on a revolution and that although Muslim workers were needed from Baku, they had not yet arrived despite his written request.[143]

As discussed in the third chapter, the issue of Iran's stage of development and the role of Social Democrats in the Iranian Constitutional Revolution occupied the minds of the Tabriz Armenian Social Democrats. While the majority maintained that Iran had entered the stage of industrial production and possessed the modern working class required for a socialist revolution, the minority position adopted by Pilosian, Sedrak II, and Ter Hakobian viewed Iran as a pre-industrial country without a modern proletariat and therefore lacking the basis for social democratic agitation. Moreover, while the majority rejected a struggle in which they would act merely as Democrats rather than Social Democrats, the minority asserted that it would be necessary to abandon social democratic work as a tactic, not as ideology, and enter the ranks of democratic elements in order to assist in the victory of the Iranian Constitutional Revolution.[144] The contention within the Tabriz group reflects, as Afary shows,

some of the same intellectual debates regarding stages of economic development as were taking place among Russian and German Social Democrats of the same period.[145]

Both Ter Hakobian and Pilosian were organizational and ideological
leaders of the Democrat Party working in Tabriz. It is evident from Pilosian's letter, dated 19 August 1909, that plans to form the party had already taken shape on Taqizadeh's return in November 1908 from London to Tabriz and before his departure to Tehran in July or August
1909.[146] This is further supported by a letter from Dashnakist Vahan Zakarian to Yeprem Khan, wherein Zakarian stated that the foundations of
the party were put into place on Taqizadeh's return to Tabriz.[147] In his
letter, Pilosian informed Taqizadeh that secondary committees had already been formed in Tabriz, that he had already prepared the regulations for the party, and once they were translated into Persian, he would
send them to Tehran for adoption by the central committee of the Democrat Party.[148] In further correspondence with Taqizadeh, Pilosian expressed his great enthusiasm on receiving news from Taqizadeh that the
Democrat Party, which had been formed along European lines, had already attracted 390 members, adding that the party was no longer a
"pipe dream" (*chimère*) but a reality.[149] Pilosian, similar to the Hnchakist-
led Iranian Social Democratic Party, expressed concern regarding the
foreign origin of the term "democrat," suggesting that a Persian equivalent be found since not only did Iranians have a "repugnance" for foreign words, but also the term "democrat" might have been confused
with "social democrat."[150]

Ter Hakobian, like Pilosian, was forming Democrat groups and in addition organizing workers in Tabriz.[151] When he moved to Tehran in
1910, he became a consultant to the Central Committee of the Democrat
Party and became a regular contributor to the Democrat Party organ,
Iran-e No by autumn 1910, writing on such issues as the destructive nature of political terrorism.[152] According to Afary, Ter Hakobian wrote
many of the "more substantial" theoretical essays in the journal, which
he submitted in French for translation to Persian before publication.[153] Interestingly, under attack from the London *Times*, which accused *Iran-e No*
of being run by Armenians and Russians, the paper denied that it had
any Armenians on its staff.[154]

Through Marxist intellectuals like Ter Hakobian, the Democrat Party
began to form a new concept of Iranian nationalism within the constitutional movement, one that was similar in some ways to Hnchakist
Yeghikian's ideas calling for a unified struggle of all Iranians without distinction of nationality or religion, but one that went further by calling for
an Iranian nation based on such principles.

In Persia, we will not recognize neither Armenian nor Jew nor Tartar [Turk] nor Persian. We must create a new nationality that will be Iranian. Whoever speaks a different language, whoever worships different gods—these are all equal for us. For us, there must not be differences among peoples (*nations*). We will recognize one nation—that is the Iranian nation, that is the Persian citizen.[155]

Ter Hakobian believed the Democrat Party should oppose any nationalist tendencies and as a fervent anti-nationalist he believed it to be his duty to "attack" nationalist parties, especially the Dashnaktsutiun, in order to attract more Armenians into the Democrat Party.[156]

Pilosian, too, was very concerned with the Dashnaktsutiun's influence in the Iranian constitutional movement and frequently addressed the issue in his correspondence to Taqizadeh. Pilosian informed Taqizadeh that the Dashnaktsutiun had begun thinking of forming an Iranian party and that the Democrat Party should act in haste to form a majority in the second Majles so that the seats would not be occupied by others.[157] It is apparent from Pilosian's letter that Taqizadeh was attempting to find out more about the Dashnaktsutiun's views by requesting that Pilosian provide him with a copy of the party's program.[158] This is understandable since the Democrat Party was carrying out talks with Dashnakists in Tehran. Pilosian notified Taqizadeh that attempts had been made by the Democrat Party in Tabriz and Qazvin to collaborate with Dashnakists. Without providing any detail, he added that the Qazvin Democrats had been deceived by the Dashnakists and no longer worked with them and that the Dashnakists in Tabriz were not amicable toward the Democrat Party and found it to be an "embryo" of a political party rather than a fully developed one—a charge commonly made by Dashnakists regarding Iranian parties in general. According to Pilosian, three Democrats were assigned to work with the Tabriz Dashnakists but the talks were ended by the Democrats, who felt the Dashnakists to be "insincere." Pilosian added that as long as Vahan Zakarian and Karapet Pionian remained heads of the Tabriz Dashnakist bodies, the Democrats could not work with them.[159] He warned Taqizadeh to be cautious of the Dashnakists and Armenians and Georgians in general, and never to enter into negotiations with them without first asking his advice and the opinion of other democrat Armenians, "because as we do not know Persians well, you do not know Armenians . . . we want you to ask our advice every time the central committee has a need to enter into relations or correspondence with them."[160]

It seems, however, that despite difficulties and negative opinions on both sides, Armenian Social Democrats not affiliated with Armenian political parties, Hnchakists, and Dashnakists succeeded in exchanging ideas and tactics and joining in solidarity in the face of conservative and reactionary elements.

"What Do the Social Democrats Say"

In Anzali, close relations between Hnchakist Simon Simonian and his student in Russian, Hosein Mo'tamed (subsequently Majles delegate Key Ostovan), led to the translation of the Hnchakist program into Persian with the collaborative efforts of Mo'tamed and Grigor Yeghikian who, according to Yeghikian, communicated together in French and Russian. After the translation, meetings were held between Hnchakists Yeghikian, Simonian, Balasan Mkrtchian, Isahak Ter Hovhannesian, and Iranian Social Democrats Mo'tamed, Abu al-Qasem Rezazadeh (subsequently member of the Gilan Republic), and others. The meetings, held in the latter months of 1910, resulted in the creation of a solely Iranian branch of the Hnchakian party whose activities would be limited to Iran. Mo'tamed and Rezazadeh became president and secretary, respectively, of the organization, which was officially named Social-Democratic Hnchakian Party, Anzali Branch, Iran Group (Ferqeh-ye Sosial-Demokrat-e Sho'bah-ye Anzali, Dasteh-ye Iranian) in January 1911.[161] The Socialist International Bureau received information about the organization on 29 October 1910.[162] The group's first order of business became the publication of a pamphlet called "What Do the Social Democrats Say" (*Sosial demokratha cheh miguyand*) written by Yeghikian, which had already appeared in *Gilan*, the organ of the conservative Moderates, which began publication in Rasht in 1910.[163] Yeghikian, in later years, tried to explain the obvious incongruity regarding the Hnchakist and moderate association by pointing to two reasons. First, the Moderates had placed their organ, *Gilan*, and their press under the disposition of Hnchakists, and second, since the moderates and the Dashnakists did not have good relations except in Tehran, the Hnchakists did not want to create further problems, thus "provoking hate among them [Iranians] towards Armenians."[164]

In "What Do the Social Democrats Say," Yeghikian discussed the rise and fall of capitalism, tracing exploitation from the era of slavery through feudalism to capitalism, a stage far worse than the former two because of the lack of protection provided to the working class. In a very rhetorical style, Yeghikian explained that in the capitalist stage, the rich got richer, the poor poorer, and the exploitation and oppression of the proletariat threw "angry arrows at the eyes of humanity." The accumulation of wealth by few individuals led to complete control over the economy as well as government. He criticized representative assemblies, asserting that they merely legitimized the rule of despots and protected the rights of capitalists while attempting to deceive workers with reforms. With the loss of capital by individuals and the predominance of cartels, syndicates, and trusts, however, the end of capitalism and the liberation of the working majority were inevitable.[165]

As the leading theoretician of the party, Yeghikian explained the social democratic view regarding Iran's present circumstances in an essay presented to the regent Naser al-Molk.[166] In this tract, Yeghikian addressed the issue of foreign and domestic politics, stressing the independence of Iran from Britain, Russia, Germany, and the Ottoman Empire. Among other things, he called for the abolition of indirect taxes, the need for modern schools and girls' education, trial by jury, and redistribution of land. He discussed pan-Islamism, which he considered a grave error for Iran and espoused a unified struggle toward freedom, one without distinction of nationality (*meliyyat*), religion (*mazhab*), and race (*nezhad*).[167]

According to Yeghikian, Iranian members of the Social-Democratic Hnchakian Party, Anzali Branch, Iran Group, expressed the desire to drop the "non-Persian" term "Hnchakian." Since no objections were expressed, the group's name was changed on 7 January 1911 to the Iranian Social-Democratic Party.[168] The name change, according to Yeghikian, had a great influence in the increase of membership in the organization, which reached a hundred.[169]

Battles on Different Fronts: "We came, we saw, and we conquered?"[170]

Armenians and Yeprem Khan: The External Struggle

Armenian fighters, especially Dashnakists, under the command of Yeprem Khan and Keri were helpful, and at times critical, in many military operations, including the Tabriz resistance (July 1908–April 1909); the takeover of Rasht, Qazvin, and Tehran (February–July 1909); the battles to defeat the returning Mohammed Ali Shah and his brother, Salar al-Dowleh (June–August 1911 and mid–1912); and other battles against the anti-constitutionalist forces of Rahim Khan and the Shahsevans. In addition to Yeprem Khan and Keri, Dashnakist *fedayis* like Khecho (d. 1915) and Nikol Duman (Nikoghayos Ter Hovhannisian, Gharababa, 1867–1914), who trained *fedayis* in the Caucasus and commanded operations there during the communal conflict (1905–1906), also led Caucasian Armenian *fedayi* groups. Duman, a native of Qarabagh, was a very well-known Dashnakist *fedayi* as well as teacher in Tabriz and Salmas in the early 1890s. He took part along with Yeprem Khan in the Khanasor expedition of 1897, which left from Iran to avenge the killing of *fedayis* by a Kurdish tribe. Duman arrived in Iran in 1911. According to Hovak

Stepanian, who received his information from Nikol Duman's friend, Dashnakist Karapet Pionian, Duman opposed the participation of the Dashnaktsutiun in the Iranian Constitutional Revolution and was convinced that coming to the aid of the Iranian revolutionaries would jeopardize the party by making its activities visible to the Iranian and Ottoman governments. Therefore, if the monarchy was victorious, Armenians would become targets of vengeance. In addition, he felt that involvement did disservice to the national, cultural, and economic interests of the Armenian people. Despite his personal views, he accepted his party's decision and took part in the battle against Mohammad Ali (July–August 1911). According to his friend, however, his motto remained "they at the head, I at the tail," meaning *fedayis* under his command would not be at the forefront of battle, believing that loss of Armenian blood for this revolution would be "needless and in vain."[171] Duman who was suffering from an illness, committed suicide in 1914.

The number of Armenian fighters involved in military struggles in the name of constitutionalism increased after Yeprem Khan's appointment as chief of Tehran police as more Armenians began to join Yeprem's regiment to serve the new constitutional government and its successful Armenian military figure. A large number of Armenian fighters, perhaps as many as 200, led by Yeprem Khan joined an army composed of several hundred Bakhtiaris, *mojahedin,* and Cossacks to stop Rahim Khan's rebellion at Ardabil in eastern Azerbaijan against the constitutional government beginning in autumn 1909. The rebellion spread into Zanjan in northwestern Iran, southeast of Azerbaijan, led by the cleric Qorban Ali and Jahangir Khan Afshar. While the rebellious forces in Zanjan fell somewhat easily to the government's forces, Rahim Khan was a tougher foe.[172] According to Grisha Khan and Yeprem Khan, a force of 200 composed of 50 Bakhtiari, 50 Cossacks, and 100 Armenians met Rahim Khan's army, which included his sons, and Samad Khan in Qarahdagh in northern Azerbaijan in December 1909. Fighting ceased in the month of *moharram* and resumed in mid-January 1910. Qarahdagh became the scene of many battles between the two in such places as Mehravan and Ahar in northeastern Azerbaijan and involved Dashnakists Khecho, who was wounded, and Grisha.[173] According to Grisha Khan, in his attempt to woo the Iranian population and defeat Yeprem Khan's forces, Rahim Khan drew the attention of Ahar's leading clerics (*mojtaheds*) and the provincial governor of Qarahdagh to Yeprem's status as infidel, accusing the governor of aiding Christians against Muslims. When the governor informed Yeprem of Rahim Khan's undertaking to agitate the Muslim population against him, Yeprem Khan told the governor to respond to Rahim Khan: "Yeprem before being a Christian or Armenian is a Persian and fights for the betterment of his fatherland. He enjoys all rights of an

Iranian."[174] Rahim Khan was defeated in January 1910 but was able to flee across the border to Russia. Yeprem Khan's army returned victoriously to Tehran and was greeted most favorably by the general population as well as the Armenian community.[175]

Soon after Yeprem's return to Tehran, he was called to action in Tabriz where Russian troops had remained since their entry in April 1909 and claimed that their continued stay was due to the presence of revolutionaries Sattar Khan and Baqer Khan. While Yeprem Khan was able to convince the two constitutionalist figures to leave Tabriz for Tehran, this did not affect Russian withdrawal.[176] In Tabriz, Yeprem Khan was joined by Keri and an unspecified number of Dashnakists and Bakhtiaris and began the advance to Ardabil against Shahsevan forces at the end of March 1910. The battles lasted until May 1910 when many Shahsevan commanders surrendered.[177] Yeprem Khan's forces returned to Tehran from Ardabil by passing through Astara, Anzali, Rasht, and Qazvin and were enthusiastically greeted throughout by Iranian and Armenian communities, especially women who recited poetry, passed out flowers, and gave speeches in honor of the triumphant heroes.[178]

More than a year passed before the constitutional government was seriously threatened and needed the military skills of Yeprem Khan's men and the Bakhtiaris. In July 1911, news reached Tehran that the former shah Mohammad Ali, having returned from Russia, was making preparations to march on Tehran with his supporters. Command of forces organized against the former shah was given to Sardar Behadur, son of Sardar As'ad, and Yeprem Khan, who had 200 Armenian fighters under his authority.[179] At the same time as government forces defeated Mohammad Ali's supporters, the former shah's brother, Salar al-Dowleh, began his assault in southwestern Iran and captured Hamadan. In addition to several hundred Bakhtiaris and 100 gendarmes, 150 Armenians led by Yeprem Khan and Keri battled Salar al-Dowleh's forces and defeated them in Baq-e Shah in September 1911. They tried unsuccessfully to capture Salar al-Dowleh in Hamadan, but he had already fled to Lorestan, only to return several months later and threaten government control once again.[180]

In these and other battles, Armenian fighters were instrumental despite their small numbers. One can be certain of at least 200 Armenian fighters because of tailor Hovhannes Muratian's written arrangement to provide clothing for Yeprem Khan's group of 200 Armenians against Mohammad Ali Shah's forces in 1911.[181] In addition to this source, there are a variety of other sources from correspondence to memoirs that supplement the 200 by as much as 50 to 100. There were at least 35 more based on a list of 35 killed from 1908 to 1909. Isma'il Ra'in provides a list of 52 names of killed Armenian fighters for the years 1908 to 1912. American financial adviser Morgan Shuster recounts about 300 Armenian fighters in the force organized against the Russians. Therefore, a total of at least 235, mostly Iranian and Caucasian Armenians, fought in the Iranian Constitutional Revolution and perhaps as many as over 300.[182] Despite agreements with Iranian revolutionaries to provide for some of the expense incurred by the Armenian fighters, it is most likely that the majority of the money came from Dashnakist sources, including fund-raisers. According to Dashnakist historian Mikayel Varandian, on several occasions, the Western Bureau in Geneva sent 30,000 Swiss francs to Iran, and in February 1909, a special appeal was made by the bureau to the regional bodies to raise money for the Tabriz fighters. Consequently, money arrived from Egypt, Bulgaria, and the United States.[183] Between 1908 and 1909, fund-raisers took place among Iranian Armenians as well as abroad, resulting in 500 dollars from the United States, 6,000 francs from Istanbul, 10,000 rubles from Baku, and 1,000 *tomans* from Iran.[184]

Dashnakists and Yeprem Khan: The Internal Struggle

Yeprem Khan and his military victories, more than any other aspect of Armenian participation in the Iranian Constitutional Revolution, are particularly discussed in Iranian constitutionalist history and Armenian memoirs for the period. What are often ignored or given less attention are the internal battles, those that have less to do with military operations and more to do with dissension and contention among leading figures and rank-and-file personnel, specifically between Yeprem Khan and Dashnakist members, caused in large part by his position as Tehran police chief and his subsequent role in the disarmament of *mojahedin* led by Sattar Khan and Baqer Khan and the closing of the Majles.

Yeprem Khan is most remembered for his military role in the Iranian Constitutional Revolution and for being an ardent supporter of Dashnakist participation in the movement. The relationship between Yeprem and the party was in general positive but at times very strained and trying. Although there had been disagreements between some Dashnakists and Yeprem regarding different aspects of the workings of the party, for example collaboration with the Democrat Party, serious problems arose only after and because of his appointment as police chief of Tehran in July 1909 and resulted in his request to resign from the ranks of the Dashnaktsutiun in early 1911.[185] While some tried to take advantage of Yeprem's position by requesting posts and money from him, many had other concerns.[186] Yeprem's appointment prompted many debates among party members and the severance of ties between Yeprem and the Tehran Committee. A friend encouraged Yeprem to accept a government position, adding "you finally reached your goal, you wanted to overthrow a king, you did."[187] More than a few, however, wanted Yeprem Khan to resign his post. They felt that, as a Dashnakist, a Socialist, and a revolutionary, he could not occupy such a position.[188] In accepting this position, they added, he had proven that he was more concerned with personal victories than with the Dashnaktsutiun and the party's way of life. His loyalty was questioned.[189] He was even asked by Rostom to resign his post as soon as peace prevailed.[190] The Dashnakist Western Bureau, on the other hand, stated that "it would be good that Yeprem stay in his position as long as it is necessary."[191] There were also concerns regarding his physical safety.[192] In a rare response to his critics, Yeprem defended himself against attempts to discredit him. He accused them of neglecting the party's traditions and philosophy and added: "I don't live the Party life; who is the one who is living the Party life, perhaps they who in times of crisis left everything and found sanctuary in embassies."[193]

Yeprem Khan's unwillingness or inability, due to time constraints, to keep Dashnakist bodies abreast of military operations and events in Tehran also created some tension, prompting Dashnakist commander Nikol Duman to exclaim in a letter to Yeprem Khan: "We know more about Australia and Africa than Iran where we live. If I knew of the comings and goings perhaps I could be more helpful."[194] Yeprem's Dashnakist comrades felt betrayed, in a sense, because he no longer made time for them.[195] Others attributed the problems between Yeprem and some Dashnakists to jealousy.[196] Whatever the real reasons might have been, the feeling of betrayal was very strong as expressed by the following words of a Dashnakist: "You are theirs [Iranians], but perhaps first and foremost you are ours, because we, by the history of blood, conceived and bore you, and your parents have a right to their demands."[197] In a similar vein, the same comrade avowed, "you are *our* Yeprem and we will not let you . . . be only theirs."[198]

Controversy Follows Yeprem Khan: Disarmament and Dissolution

The problem between the party and Yeprem was compounded by his role in two very controversial acts, the disarmament at Atabek Park and the closing of the Majles. On 4 August 1910, the constitutional government gave orders for the disarmament of those *mojahedin* who were not in the service of the government, excluding those under the command of Yeprem Khan, Haidar Khan 'Amu Oghlu, and the forces under Bakhtiari leader Sardar As'ad. The armed *mojahedin* who had played an essential role in the conquest of Tehran were now unemployed and unappreciated by the government. Furthermore, they had joined the Moderates under the leadership of Sattar Khan and Baqer Khan, a situation the new Bakhtiari-Democrat cabinet, which had come to power in July

1910, found threatening. Pressured by the Russian government's threat to send forces into Tehran if the *mojahedin* were not stripped of their weapons and using the recent political violence as further cause, the Bakhtiari-Democrat government ordered disarmament. On 7 August 1910, the government-employed forces under the command of Yeprem Khan, Haidar Khan, and Sardar Bahadur surrounded Sattar Khan's residence and opened fire. Thirty men were killed and 300 wounded. Sattar Khan was shot in the leg and remained disabled until his death a few years later.[199] In November 1909, Sattar Khan himself had committed a similar disarmament. According to British records, Sattar Khan was sent to Ardabil with 1,000 *mojahedin* to fight the Shahsevan tribes. He was invited by the Tabriz governor to limit the power of local *mojahedin* whom Sattar Khan promptly disarmed and ousted from the city.[200]

A few Dashnakists attempted to justify the actions of the new cabinet and Yeprem Khan's role in it.[201] More, however, were concerned about its effect on Iranian Armenian communities, which had become the target of harassment and violence because of Yeprem Khan's role in the wounding of the most popular hero of the Iranian Constitutional Revolution.[202] There is no indication that the Dashnaktsutiun sought or supported disarmament. There is evidence, however, that the Hnchakian party advocated disarmament of *mojahedin* to prevent disorder.[203]

Yeprem seldom responded to his critics, and there is no record of his directly addressing his role in the Atabek Park incident and its consequences. In a letter to his friend and supporter, however, Yeprem gave his reasoning for unspecified actions taken in the past and those to be taken in the future, which one may assume would include the latter shoot-out and the closing of the Majles. "All of government and parliament expect the salvation of the country from me . . . [sic] I must do it." Perhaps in an attempt to spread the blame or express regret, Yeprem Khan also added that the Democrats had destroyed him "morally."[204]

After the Atabek Park incident, Yeprem Khan made a few attempts to resign temporarily or permanently from his post as police chief.[205] According to a letter he wrote to a friend and comrade, he had grown tired of the chaos, party intrigues, political conflicts, and general demoralization in the country. He asserted that he could no longer work with conservatives like Interior Minister 'Ain al-Dowleh. These sincere reasons for resignation were followed, however, by anticipation that he would return to his post, as he wrote down the prophetic phrase, "if various surprises don't come and shake my resolve."[206]

Various surprises did come, one of which brought an end to the second constitutional period—the closing of the Majles in which Yeprem had a role. In mid-1911, the former shah, Mohammad Ali, had attempted a second coup but was defeated by government forces, including as many as 200 Armenians under Yeprem Khan.[207] In November 1911, the Russian government moved its troops into Rasht and with the knowledge and support of the British government gave the Iranian government two ultimatums, the second of which demanded, among other things, American financial adviser Morgan Shuster's dismissal. While the cabinet, led by the Bakhtiari Samsam al-Saltanah and the foreign minister Vosuq al-Dowleh, unanimously accepted the ultimatum, the Majles would not submit. Mass protests and boycotts took place in Tehran and other regions in opposition to the ultimatum and in support of the Majles. In addition, a military coalition of the Dashnaktsutiun, Yeprem Khan, Moderates, Democrats, the Union and Progress, Bakhtiaris, 300 Armenians, and 1,100 of Shuster's treasury gendarmerie was organized to resist Russian incursion. On Shuster's advice, they decided not to openly oppose the Russians, whose force was too strong and who would have crushed the Iranian populace along with the troops.[208]

The Majles continued to hold out against the cabinet's attempts. The cabinet, unable to suspend the Majles itself, requested the assistance of regent Naser al-Molk, who carried out the closing of the assembly with Russian and British support. In the meantime, Sardar As'ad convinced Yeprem Khan to change sides and on 24 December 1911 Yeprem Khan led the troops who closed down the Majles.[209] This move was closely followed by a Russian campaign of terror in Azerbaijan and Gilan. Russian occupying forces disarmed, arrested, and executed Anjoman leaders as well as Caucasian activists. Armenians were also among the victims of Russian excesses, including Petros Melik Andreasian, who was hanged in January 1912, and many others who were persecuted, arrested, exiled, or forced to flee despite their decision not to resist Russian troops.[210]

According to an account by a Dashnakist comrade, published a year after Yeprem's death, Yeprem Khan feared Russian conquest and occupation, which to him meant the loss of Iran's independence. He added that Yeprem Khan regretted the grievous mistake he made in dispersing the Majles. The account was probably not meant to be an exoneration of Yeprem since it admitted that he was after all no longer a revolutionary but a member of the governing body.[211]

Whatever the reasons or justifications for such measures, the incidents were critical enough to cause Dashnakists to sever already damaged ties with Yeprem. Yeprem Khan's friend and fellow Dashnakist, Hambardzum Melik-Sargsian, defended him. Sargsian, writing after Yeprem's death, complained of the stance that had been taken by some members against Yeprem. He expressed his disappointment and stated that he did not want such talk to blemish Yeprem's name and memory.[212] After his

death in battle against Salar al-Dowleh's forces (6 May 1912), for most
Armenians and Dashnakists, Yeprem Khan became an irreproachable
martyr to the constitutional cause.[213]

Conclusion: Still Troubles Ahead

Between 1907 and 1911, Iranian and Caucasian Armenians contributed
through words and deeds to the Iranian Constitutional Revolution, despite their own prejudices and limitations and those of others. Despite
ideological, personal, ethnic, or religious differences, the story remains
one of exchange of ideas and strategies, cooperation, and sincere endeavor to achieve all that constitutionalism implied and to create lasting
bonds. However, disillusionment began to set in early in 1911. While the
Hnchakists had in part withdrawn from Iranian politics after the
reestablishment of the constitution in 1909, Dashnakists continued to attempt to influence the movement. But in 1910 and especially 1911, they
began to express serious doubts about the direction of the movement,
questioned its success, and criticized the Iranian government. The disarmament of the *mojahedin* and the closing of the Majles perhaps would
not have been considered as nefarious had they not involved police
chief Yeprem Khan, an Armenian and a Dashnakist with a long history
of revolutionary activism. Even Yeprem Khan must have grown somewhat disenchanted. His actions certainly did not represent those of a
man who in early 1909 wrote the following acclamation of the movement to his wife: "You wrote that Persia will not be saved by my participation, that the locals must act. Yes, my dear, I too agree with you, but it
is no longer the Persia you have seen, it has changed a lot. All participate, and the work is moving forward miraculously. *In two months,
everything will be in order and Persia will be the freest country* [emphasis
added]."[214] Moreover, perhaps the problems and tension between Dashnakists and other parties had taken their toll as the party began to come
to terms with the reality that the panacea of constitutionalism that they
had sought had failed them.

Notes

1. For a brief discussion of this historiography, see introduction.

2. Minutes of Fourth General Congress, Session 106, 26 April 1907, in *Niuter
H. H. Dashnaktsutian patmutian hamar* [Materials for the history of the A. R. Feder-
ation], ed. and comp. Hratch Dasnabedian [Hrach Tasnapetian] (Beirut: Hamazgayin, 1976), 3: 259–60.

3. Ibid., 260. See also Extracts of the Decisions of Fourth General Congress,
309–10.

4. Minutes of Azerbaijan Central Committee, Session 38, 1 July 1907, Archives of the Armenian Revolutionary Federation [Dashnaktsutiun], Watertown, Massachusetts, file 540, document b.

5. Report of Vrezhstan [Azerbaijan] Central Committee for 1908–1909, 476/141. See also Minutes of Azerbaijan Central Committee, Session 42, 9 July 1907, 540/b.

6. Stepan Zorian's alias was Rostom Gharakhanian but he is most often referred to by contemporaries and party historians simply as Rostom.

7. Minutes of Azerbaijan Central Committee, Session 39, 3 July 1907, 540/b.

8. See Minutes of Azerbaijan Central Committee, Session 61, 4 September 1907, 540/b.

9. Hovsep Hovhannisian by his own account had other pseudonyms, including Farro. See Hovsep Hovhannisian, *Husher* [Memoirs] (Yerevan: Alobon, 1995), 211.

10. Azerbaijan Central Committee to Eastern Bureau, 20 September 1907, 473/20; H. Elmar [Hovsep Hovhannisian], *Yeprem* (Tehran: Modern, 1964), 110–11 n. See also Hovhannisian, *Husher*, 129–30.

11. Ibid.; Azerbaijan Central Committee to Western Bureau, 28 June 1907, 473/82.

12. Janet Afary, *The Iranian Constitutional Revolution, 1906–1911: Grassroots Democracy, Social Democracy, and the Origins of Feminism* (New York: Columbia University Press, 1996), 82.

13. Ibid., 83.

14. For a discussion of the Organization of Social Democrats, see Afary, *Iranian Constitutional Revolution*, 81–87. See also N. K. Belova, "Le 'Parti social-démocrate' d'Iran," in *La Deuxième Internationale et L'Orient*, ed. Georges Haupt and Madeleine Reberioux (Paris: Editions Cujas, 1967), 387–92. For the program of the party, see 395–405. The program also appears in Cosroe Chaqueri, *La Social-démocratie en Iran: articles et documents* (Florence: Mazdak, 1979), 157–60. See also 162.

15. Minutes of Azerbaijan Central Committee, Session 46, 17 July 1907, 540/b; Azerbaijan Central Committee to Western Bureau, 4 July 1907, 473/84.

16. The word used by Dashnakists to express factionalism is the Persian term *tayefeh* (sect).

17. The Dashnakists had concerns about Mir Hashem who, according to them, wanted to form a new party, separate from the Organization of Social Democrats. See Azerbaijan Central Committee to Western Bureau, 20 November 1907, 473/141.

18. Minutes of Azerbaijan Central Committee, Session 53, 30 July 1907, 540/b. Iranian Dashnakist bodies always sought information regarding Iranian organizations and often seemed puzzled or confused as to the "real" ideology of the groups with which they dealt. This concern or preoccupation continued well beyond the early phase of the revolution. See, for example, Azerbaijan Central Committee to Shah Committee, 10 January 1910, 477/3; Azerbaijan Central Committee to Western Bureau, 8 February 1910, 477/9.

19. Minutes of Azerbaijan Central Committee, Session 54, 31 July 1907, 540/b.

20. Ibid., Session 64, 21 September 1907, 540/b.

21. The others present at the meetings were Majles delegates Mostashar al-Dowleh (from Tabriz), Mo'in al-Tujjar and Amin al-Zarb (wealthy merchants),

Mirza Ibrahim (Tabriz, head of the revolutionary anjomans), and Vosuq al-Dowleh, Tehran delegate to the Majles and later foreign minister. See Rostom to Western Bureau, 10 January 1908, 1729/2, also in A[ndre] Amurian, comp. and ed., *Dashnaktsutiun, Yeprem, parskakan sahmanadrutiun, H. H. D. kendronakan arkhiv* [A. R. Federation, Yeprem, Iranian constitution, A. R. F. central archives] (Tehran: Alik, 1976), 1: 2–11, and, in *Rostom: mahvan vatsunamiakin artiv* [Rostom: on the occasion of the sixtieth anniversary of his death], ed. Hratch Dasnabedian [Hrach Tasnapetian], (Beirut: Hamazgayin Vahe Setian, 1979), 164. For a Persian translation, see A. Amurian, *Hamasah-e Yeprem* [The epic of Yeprem] (Tehran: Javid Press, 1976), 31–32.

22. See Minutes of Shah Committee, Session 28, 18 September 1907, 628/2.

23. Minutes of Shah Committee, Session 30, 25 September 1907, 628/2.

24. Mirzayan, whose pseudonym was Arbak Rshtuni, was also known as Yusef Khan Mirzayants.

25. Mirzayan's knowledge of Persian, Armenian, French, and English was sophisticated enough to translate the works of Sa'di, Hafez, Omar Khayyam, Molière, Byron, and others into Armenian.

26. Rostom to Western Bureau, 10 January 1908, 1729/2.

27. Perhaps Malkom Khan considered the movement too radical. No mention was made of Malkom Khan's objectionable promotion of the lottery concession to Britain in 1889. For more on Malkom Khan's activities during Mozaffar al-Din Shah's reign (1896–1907), see, for example, Hamid Algar, *Mirza Malkum Khan: A Study in the History of Iranian Modernism* (Berkeley and Los Angeles: University of California Press, 1973).

28. Rostom to Western Bureau, 10 January 1908, 1729/2.

29. Arbak [Rshtuni/Hovsep Mirzayan] to Comrades, 11 January 1908, 583/2.

30. Rostom considered this item sufficient reason to reach agreement. See Rostom to Western Bureau, 10 January 1908, 1729/2.

31. For the French text of the agreement, see 583/41. This may be the same as the enclosure mentioned in Rostom's letter to the Bureau.

32. Rostom to Western Bureau, 10 January 1908, 1729/2. According to Mirzayan, the Iranians did not sign the agreement, because they did not represent an official body! See Arbak [Rshtuni/Hovsep Mirzayan] to Comrades, 11 January 1908, 583/2.

33. See "Yepremi kensagrutiune" [Yeprem's biography], in Amurian, *Arkhiv*, 1: 14–18; Elmar [Hovsep Hovhannisian], *Yeprem*, 195–216.

34. For an amusing and interesting account about Stepanian and other Dashnakist *fedayis*, see Arthur Moore, "Some Persian Memories," *The Edinburgh Review* 446 (October 1913): 368–82.

35. Third Regional Congress of Vrezhstan, 19 December 1907 to 13 January 1908, 473/156. See especially Session 3, 21 December 1907, and Session 5, 23 December 1907. For a list of concerns, see also Minutes of Azerbaijan Central Committee, Session 51, 25 July 1907, 540/b.

36. Minutes of Eastern Bureau Regional Congress, 31 December 1907 to 8 January 1908, 1587/15; Decisions of the Eastern Bureau Regional Congress, 31 December 1907 to 8 January 1908, 1587/16.

37. For Tehran, see Minutes of Shah [Tehran] Committee, Session 22, 19 July 1907, 628/2.

38. Report of Gilan Committee, 5 April 1908–5 September 1908, 584/34.

39. Report of Port Arthur [Anzali] Subcommittee to Azerbaijan's Third Regional Congress, 584/77.

40. Report of Gilan Committee, 30 November 1907, 582/55. For such "touting" see *Droshak* articles, 1907–1911, which were almost exclusively enthusiastic.

41. Minutes of Gilan Regional Congress, 29 March to 14 April 1908, Session 5, 2 April 1908, 628/4. In an undated letter signed by the Rasht and Azerbaijan branches and presented to the congress, the signatories requested that Iran not be neglected and to take on the struggle on a third front. See 584/61.

42. Minutes of Gilan Regional Congress, 29 March to 14 April 1908, Session 6, 4 April 1908.

43. For decisions of the Fourth Regional Congress, see 475/18. For the debate over the issue of active or passive participation, see Minutes of Fourth Regional Congress, June 1909, Session 7, n.d., 476/66.

44. See Minutes of Azerbaijan Central Committee, Session 26, 10 June 1908, 540/b.

45. Meeting of Azerbaijan Central Committee, 19 August 1908, 475/10. See also Report of Vrezhstan Central Committee, 1908–1909, 476/141; Minutes of Azerbaijan Central Committee, Session 44, 19 August 1908, 540/b. For further material on the issue of harming Ottoman Armenian goals, see, for example, A. Rshtuni [Hovsep Mirzayan] to Rostom, n.d., 584/60. For reasons emphasizing among other things the unpreparedness of constitutionalist leaders to see the revolution through, see Hovhannisian, *Husher*, 156–62.

46. Declaration and Decisions of Fifth General Congress, 1909 (Geneva: H. H. Dashnaktsutiun, 1910), 1539/26.

47. See Shavarsh to Vrezh [Azerbaijan] Central Committee, 9 August 1906, 581/28.

48. Garmen to Eastern Bureau, 4 July 1907, 473/86.

49. Minutes of Minaret [Salmas] Committee, Session 15, 27 October 1908, 533b/1.

50. Afary, *Iranian Constitutional Revolution*, 219–20.

51. Ahmad Kasravi, *Tarikh-e mashruteh-ye Iran* [History of the constitution of Iran] (Tehran: Amir Kabir, 1984), 2: 825, 873–77; Edward G. Browne, *The Persian Revolution, 1905–1909* (1910; new edition edited by 'Abbas Amanat with essays by 'Abbas Amanat and Mansour Bonakdarian, Mage: Washington, D.C., 1995), 265; A[ndre] Amurian, *H. H. Dashnaktsutiune Parskastanum, 1890–1918* [The A. R. Federation in Persia, 1890–1918] (Tehran: Alik, 1950), 88.

52. For details, see Report of Minaret Region, January 1908 to June 1909, 476/68; Salmas Anjoman to Samson, 20 Shaban 1327/1909, 565/46. See also Sadr al-Islam, Salmas Military Commission to Samson, n.d., 565/108; 565/109. See also Salmas Provincial Anjoman to Samson, 13 Rajab 1327/1909, 565/47. According to the note attached to the latter correspondence, Samson went to the celebration of their victories with several merchants and fighters who were welcomed with cries of "Long live [our] Armenian brothers." There are also a few undated

requests for men and arms from Iranians to Salmas Dashnakist leader Samson. See, for example, Mir Alalzadeh to Samson, n.d., 565/120; Nazem Tujjar to Samson, 10 Jamadi Avval [?], 565/136; Abdul Karim to Samson, n.d., 565/149.

53. Regarding committees formed in Khoy and battles, see Report of Khoy Region, 1906–1909, 476/67. For Urumieh, see Paros [Urumieh] Committee to Azerbaijan Central Committee, 16 November 1908, 474/112.

54. Minutes of Azerbaijan Central Committee, Session 35, 30 July 1908, 540/b.

55. Regarding Sattar Khan's concern over discipline, see Isma'il Amirkhizi, *Qeyam-e Azerbaijan va Sattar Khan* [The Azerbaijani revolt and Sattar Khan] (Tehran: Tehran Press, 1960), 218, 240–41.

56. The full text of suggestions made by the Dashnakists to Sattar Khan may be found in Minutes of Azerbaijan Central Committee, Session 36, 31 July 1908, 540/b.

57. Minutes of Azerbaijan Central Committee, Session 36, 31 July 1908, 540/b.

58. Minutes of Azerbaijan Central Committee, Session 45, 21 August 1908, 540/b.

59. The Armenian text of the agreement was signed by a representative of the Eastern Bureau and members of the Azerbaijan Central Committee, Vahan Zakarian and Stepan Stepanian. The Persian text was signed by Sattar Khan and four others whose names are semilegible. They may be Haji Agha, Mirza Sayyid Hosein Khan, Mirza Alakbar, and Mirza Mohammad Bagh. A draft of the Armenian version of the agreement includes the name of the Azerbaijani leader of the Secret Center of the Organization of Social Democrats, 'Ali Monsieur.

60. For Armenian and Persian texts of the agreement signed in Tabriz on 22 August 1908, see 475/11. For a draft of the Armenian version of the agreement, 21 August 1908, see 528b/4.

61. According to Hovhannisian who witnessed the close collaboration of Sattar Khan with Keri and Rostom, Sattar Khan respected their expertise and followed their advice and recommendations. See Hovhannisian, *Husher*, 176, 196–97.

62. For an interesting sketch of Rostom, see Moore, "Some Persian Memories," 377.

63. See, for example, Elmar [Hovsep Hovhannisian], *Yeprem*, 140–44, 151–164; Amurian, *Dashnaktsutiune Parskastanum*, 57–59, 60–63, 66–73; Kasravi, *Tarikh-e mashruteh*, 2: 838, 842. See also "Parskastan: mi ej parskakan heghap[okhakan] patmutiunits" [Persia: a page from Persia's revolutionary history], *Droshak*, no. 1, January 1911.

64. Mangol Bayat, *Iran's First Revolution: Shi'ism and the Constitutional Revolution of 1905–1909* (Oxford: Oxford University Press, 1991), 237.

65. See, for example, "Parskastan: heghapokhutiune anenkcheli" [Persia: The invincible revolution], *Droshak*, no. 9–10, September–October 1908; "Parskastan: ariunrusht hetadimutiun" [Persia: bloodthirsty regression], *Droshak*, no. 11–12, November–December 1908.

66. For negative depictions, see, for example, Azerbaijan Central Committee to Western Bureau, 14 August 1908, 474/75. For similar sentiments regarding both Sattar Khan and Baqer Khan, see Stepan [Stepanian] to Honan [Davitian], 20 November 1908, 474/116. For more positive depictions, see Azerbaijan Central Com-

mittee to American Central Committee, Boston, 22 September 1908, 474/79; 12 November 1908, 474/103.

67. Hovhannisian, *Husher*, 151, 154.

68. For a list of members, see Ibrahim Fakhra'i, *Gilan dar jonbesh-e mashrutiyat* [Gilan in the constitutional movement] (Tehran: Ketabha-ye Jibi, 1974), 113–14. For another version, see Ali Furuhi, "Aramanha-ye Gilan va nehzat-e mashrutiyat" [Armenians of Gilan and the constitutional movement], *Ayandeh* 19, 7–9 (Fall 1993): 699–700. See also Ahmad Kasravi, *Tarikh-e hijdah saleh-ye Azerbaijan* [The eighteen-year history of Azerbaijan] (Tehran, 1967), 1: 8; Mehdi Malekzadeh, *Tarikh-e enqelab-e mashrutiyat-e Iran* [History of the constitutional revolution of Iran] (Tehran: Soqrat, 1949–1953), 5: 147–148. Dashnakist historian Varandian inaccurately states that Sattar Khan was involved in the formation of this committee. See Mikayel Varandian, *H. H. Dashnaktsutian patmutiun* [History of A. R. Federation] (Cairo: Husaber Press, 1950), 2: 70.

69. Yeprem Khan, *Az Anzali ta Tehran: yaddashtha-ye khususi-ye Yeprem Khan mojahed-e Iran* [From Anzali to Tehran: the private memoirs of Yeprem Khan mojahed of Iran: from Anzali to Tehran], trans. Narus (Tehran: Babak, 1977), 23–25. Yeprem is also cited in Elmar [Hovsep Hovhannisian], *Yeprem*, 222. The original Armenian of Yeprem's memoirs appears in Elmar [Hovsep Hovhannisian], *Yeprem*, 238–75. See also editor's article entitled "Yepreme Rashtum" [Yeprem in Rasht], Amurian, *Arkhiv*, 1: 21, who writes that the Barq Committee worked closely with both the Sattar and Jahangir Committees.

70. Port Arthur Subcommittee to Western Bureau, 11 April 1909, 584/12; Minutes of Gilan Committee Third Regional Congress, 29 September to 7 October 1909, Session 3, 1 October 1909, 584/39.

71. Report of Gilan Committee, 5 April 1908 to 5 September 1909, 584/34. See also Third Regional Congress, 29 September 1909 to 7 October 1909, Rasht, Session 3, 1 October 1909, 584/39.

72. Port Arthur Subcommittee to Western Bureau, 11 April 1909, 584/12; Gilan to Azerbaijan Central Committee, 19 June 1909, 584/18. See also Isahak Ter Zakarian to Yeprem, 23 April 1909, 1728g/90, also in Amurian, *Arkhiv*, 1: 356–58; Isahak Ter Zakarian to Yeprem, 25 April 1909, 1728g/91; Aleksandr Khachatrian to Yeprem, 22 April 1909, 1728g/158; Aleksandr Khachatrian to Yeprem, 7 May 1909, 1728g/159; Azerbaijan Central Committee to Western Bureau, 8 February 1910, 477/9.

73. Third Regional Congress, 29 September 1909 to 7 October 1909, Rasht, Session 5, 2 October 1909, 584/39.

74. Report of Gilan Committee, 5 April 1908 to 5 September 1909, 584/34. See also Port Arthur Subcommittee to Western Bureau, 11 April 1909, 584/12; "Yepreme Rashtum," in Amurian, *Arkhiv*, 1: 25.

75. Elmar [Hovsep Hovhannisian], *Yeprem*, 240, 241; Hayrik, comp., "Heghapokhakan banaki arshave Tehrani vray yev Yepremi gndi dere (khmbapeti hushere)" [March of the revolutionary army on Tehran and the role of Yeprem's regiment (memoirs of the commander)], *Hayrenik Amsagir*, 3, 7 (May 1925): 27, 28; Amurian, *Dashnaktsutiune Parskastanum*, 110; "Yepreme Rashtum," Amurian, *Arkhiv*, 1: 27.

76. Report of Gilan Committee, 5 April 1908 to 5 September 1909, 584/34. See also Port Arthur Subcommittee to Western Bureau, 11 April 1909, 584/12. For more correspondence by the Sattar Committee to the Dashnaktsutiun regarding meetings and transfer of arms and men, see 584/65–73; 1728d/24.

77. Report of Gilan Committee, 5 April 1908 to 5 September 1909, 584/34. According to the Gilan Committee, Sattar Committee members had become untrustworthy, seeking only personal gain. See Gilan Committee to Azerbaijan Central Committee, 22 September 1909, 584/33.

78. For a description of events by Yeprem Khan, see the Armenian original in Elmar [Hovsep Hovhannisian], *Yeprem*, 242–64. For a Persian translation, see Yeprem Khan, *Yaddashtha*. See also Elmar [Hovsep Hovhannisian], *Yeprem*, 276–82; "Tarikhcheh az Yeprem Khan" [Short history from Yeprem Khan], in *Chand tarikhcheh* [A few short histories], ed. Ahmad Kasravi, trans. from the original Armenian (Tehran: Zendegi, 1960) 83–124; Farro [Hovsep Hovhannisian], comp., "Yepremi gortsuneutiune Parskastanum (Grishayi hushere)" [Yeprem's activity in Persia (Grisha's memoirs)], *Hayrenik Amsagir* 2, 1 (November 1924): 64–72; Hayrik, "Heghapokhakan banaki arshave," 28–35; Amurian, *Dashnaktsutiune Parskastanum*, 112–14, 116–22; "Yepreme Rashtum," in Amurian, *Arkhiv*, 1: 22–42; Varandian, *Dashnaktsutian patmutiun*, 2: 81–89; Browne, *Persian Revolution*, 300; Kasravi, *Tarikh-e hijdah saleh*, 1: 8, 12, 23, 27, 31, 34, 52; Isma'il Ra'in, *Yeprem Khan-e Sardar* [Commander Yeprem Khan] (Tehran: Zarin, 1971), see chapters four and five. Russian general Liakhov bombarded the Haykazian school in Tehran, which drove some Armenian families who had taken refuge there to move to the Ottoman and British legations as other Armenians already had. Some also took up residence at the Park Hotel until Liakhov surrendered. See, 266–68, 271.

79. Report of Gilan Committee, 5 April 1908 to 5 September 1909, 584/34.

80. For the program of Union and Progress, see Mansureh Ettehadieh Nezam Mafi, ed., *Majmu'eh-ye motun va asnad-e tarikhi* [Collection of historical texts and documents] (Tehran: Naqsh-e Jahan, 1982), 4: 131–44. See also Mansureh Ettehadieh Nezam Mafi, *Paydayesh va tahavvol-e ahzab-e siyasi-ye mashrutiyat: dowrah-ye avval va dovvom-e majles-e showra-ye melli* [Appearance and evolution of political parties of constitutionalism: the first and second period of the National Consultative Assembly] (Tehran: Gostardeh, 1982), 235, 237. One of the party's papers, *Sharq* (East), was financially assisted by a Dashnakist. See Report of Shah City, September 1909 to 6 July 1911, 587/30; Minutes of Shah Committee, 15 September 1909 to 7 October 1911, Session 11, n.d., 628/2. Another source mentions Dashnakists on the editorial staff. See Azerbaijan Central Committee to Western Bureau, 12 November 1909, 476/110. Although *Esteqlal-e Iran* is considered the party's official organ, *Sharq* too represented the party's ideas for a time. See Edward G. Browne, *The Press and Poetry of Modern Persia* (1914; Los Angeles: Kalimat Press, 1983), 40, 110. For a brief mention of the connection between the Dashnaktsutiun and Union and Progress, see British vice-consul at Rasht, Hyacinth L. Rabino's memoirs in Mohammad Roshan, ed., *Mashruteh-ye Gilan az yaddashtha-ye Rabino* [Gilan's constitution according to Rabino's memoirs] (Gilan: Haidari, 1973), 129.

81. Report of Shah City, September 1909 to 6 July 1911, 587/30; Kayts to Yeprem, 1909, 1728d/23; Hovsep Mirzayan to Rostom, 23 February 1910, 585/10.

For discussion of the Jahangir Committee, see also Minutes of Gilan Regional Congress, 9 October 1909 to 16 November 1910, 628/8; Jumshut Ghazarian to Yeprem, 1 October 1909, 1728g/31; Azerbaijan Central Committee to Western Bureau, 12 November 1909, 476/110.

82. Azerbaijan Central Committee to Western Bureau, 11 January 1909, 476/3.

83. Zakarian to Yeprem, 18 July 1909, Dashnaktsutiun Archives, 1728a/21. The same letter appears in Amurian, *Arkhiv*, 1: 254–63, bearing an incorrect date of 18 July 1910.

84. For a discussion of the Democrat Party, see Afary, *Iranian Constitutional Revolution*.

85. Report of Shah City Committee, September 1909 to 6 July 1911, 587/30; Azerbaijan Central Committee to Western Bureau, 7 June 1910, 477/43. For a draft of the platform, see also 588/94.

86. Azerbaijan to Central Committee, 13 May 1910, 477/37.

87. See Vahan Zakarian to Rostom, 26 November 1910, 477/70; Report of Shah City Committee, September 1909 to 6 July 1911, 587/30. The Tehran Committee's report also considered the unlikely possibility that the problem may have been caused by mistranslation from Armenian to Persian. Arsen Mikayelian was appointed by Yeprem Khan to organize the police in different provinces. For his letters to Yeprem, see Amurian, *Arkhiv*, 1: 422–37.

88. Records of the Tehran Committee provide further evidence that these flyers are the same. See Minutes of Shah Committee, Session 44, 10 October 1910, 628/2.

89. See Mirzayan to Sixth General Congress, August 1911, 1543/18a.

90. For Tehran Committee declaration, see 587/67. For Democrat Party rebuttal, see 587/68.

91. Azerbaijan Central Committee to Western Bureau, 30 December 1910, 477/75. See also Azerbaijan Central Committee to Shah Committee, 13 December 1910, 477/73.

92. The organ's financial backer was an Armenian named Bazil who is referred to by Mirzayan as anti-Dashnakist. See Rshtuni [Mirzayan] to Tehran Committee, 28 August 1910, 586/58. Mirzayan even went so far as to state, inaccurately, that Calcutta's *Habl al-Matin* was more sympathetic to Armenians and Dashnakists than *Iran-e No*. Interestingly, according to Elmar [Hovsep Hovhannisian], the financier of *Iran-e No* is the same Hambartsum Bazil who later financed the Dashnakist paper, *Aravot* (Morning, 1909–1912). See, Elmar [Hovsep Hovhannisian], *Yeprem*, 398; Hovhannisian, *Husher*, 303. Sadr-e Hashemi refers to the financier as Yusef (the equivalent of the English Joseph and Armenian Hovsep) or Monsieur Bazil. See Mohammad Sadr-e Hashemi, *Tarikh-e jara'ed va majallat-e Iran* [The history of newspapers and magazines of Iran] (Isfahan: Kemal, 1984), 1: 110–11. Browne does not provide a first name. See Browne, *Press and Poetry*, 52–53.

93. See, for example, Minutes of Shah Committee, 15 September 1909 to 7 October 1911, Session 26, 26 May 1910; Session 29, 28 July 1910, 628/2. Problems between Dashnakists and Taqizadeh existed throughout the period of the constitutional movement; see, for example, Azerbaijan Central Committee to Shah Committee, 14 July 1911, 478/58; Azerbaijan Central Committee to Eastern Bu-

reau, 15 August 1911, 478/68; Azerbaijan Central Committee to Western Bureau, 31 October 1911, 478/116.

94. Mirzayan to Rostom, 23 February 1910, 585/10; Mirzayan to Rostom, 17 March 1910, 585/14. In the latter, Mirzayan even finds Taqizadeh responsible for Yeprem Khan's resignation. See also Mirzayan Report to Sixth General Congress, August 1911, 1543/18a; Mirzayan to Rostom, 9 November 1910, 585/60. For Yeprem Khan's views, see Yeprem to V. [Vahan Zakarian?], 20 October 1910, 585/54.

95. Mirzayan to Rostom, 12 July 1910, 585/37. In this letter, Mirzayan accuses Taqizadeh of Azerbaijani, not merely Iranian, chauvinism. For views regarding Caucasian and Iranian Dashnakists and the Democrats, see also Mirzayan Report to Sixth General Congress, August 1911, 1543/18a.

96. Dr. A. D. Stepanian to Rostom, 4 August 1910, 585/40. The letter was written on Qajar royal stationery, indicating Dr. Stepanian's position as dentist to the shah.

97. Afary, *Iranian Constitutional Revolution*, 248–52.

98. Haidar Khan ['Amu Oghlu] to Yeprem, 28 November 1910, 1729/7, also in Amurian, *Arkhiv*, 1: 149–53.

99. See, for example, Democrat Party to Dashnaktsutiun, 22 Zihajjah 1328/1910, 586/89, wherein the Democrat Party confirms the Dashnaktsutiun's affirmative response to the formation of the Committee of National Salvation.

100. Ter Hacobian [Hakobian] to Taqizadeh, 1 November 1910, in Iraj Afshar, ed., *Awraq-e tazehyab-e mashrutiyat va naqsh-e Taqizadeh* [Newlyfound constitutional papers and the role of Taqizadeh] (Tehran: Bahman, 1980), 320.

101. For full text, see document dated 22 Zihajjah 1328/1910, 1728d/40.

102. For the Democrat Party Program, see Ettehadieh Nezam Mafi, *Majmu'eh*, 1–19.

103. For full text, see document dated 22 Zihajjah 1328/1910, 1728d/39. See also Democrat Party to Dashnaktsutiun, 11 Zihajjah 1328/1910, 585/67.

104. For full text of new terms, see document dated 1329/1911, 1728d/68.

105. See, for example, correspondence between the Democrat Party and the Dashnaktsutiun, 585/66; 587/60; 1728d/63; 1728d/65.

106. Report of Shah City Committee, September 1909 to 6 July 1911, 587/30.

107. Azerbaijan Central Committee to Constantinople Responsible Body, 6 July 1909, 476/72; Azerbaijan Central Committee to Minaret Committee, 6 August 1909, 476/81.

108. See, for example, Vahan [Zakarian] to Shah Committee, 14 May 1909, 476/47.

109. Mirzayan Report to Sixth General Congress, August 1911, 1543/18a.

110. Azerbaijan Central Committee to Shah Committee, 13 May 1910, 477/37; Azerbaijan Central Committee to Shah Committee, 23 September 1910, 477/61; Azerbaijan Central Committee to Shah Committee, 30 September 1910, 477/62. The Gilan Regional Congress sided with Azerbaijan, agreeing to one delegate. See Minutes of Gilan Regional Congress, 9 October 1909 to 16 November 1910, Session 40, 18 June 1910, 628/8.

111. Azerbaijan Central Committee to Western Bureau, 5 April 1910, 477/28.

112. See, for example, Zakarian to Yeprem, 18 July 1909, 1728a/21; Yeprem to Rostom, 20 May 1910, 585/29.

113. Minutes of Shah Committee, Session 45, 24 October 1910, 682/2; Report of Shah City Committee, September 1909 to 6 July 1911, 587/30.

114. Azerbaijan Central Committee to Shah, 4 February 1910, 477/8; Minutes of Shah Committee, Session 21, 24 March 1910, 682/2.

115. Hrant Der Sarkisian, Dr. Bazil's grandson provided me with the following article. "Prof. Tokt. Pazil Khan" [Prof. Doct. Basil Khan], *Taretsuyts bzhshkakan yev aroghjapahakan* [Medical and hygienic yearbook], ed. Vardan Ghazarian (Istanbul, 1914), 1: 25–28. See also *Habl al-matin*, no. 68, 15 July 1907; no. 87, 11 August 1907; no. 133, 6 October 1907; no. 142, 15 October 1907; no. 144, 17 October 1907; no. 168, 23 November 1907; no. 212, 21 January 1908.

116. Mirzayan to Rostom, 23 February 1910, 585/10.

117. See, for example, *Mozakerat-e majles* [Parliamentary debates], Session 208, 23 Shaval 1329/1911; Session 218, 5 Safar 1329/1911; Session 288, 2 Ramazan 1329/1911. See also Mirzayan Report to Sixth General Congress, August 1911, 1543/18a.

118. See, *Mozakerat-e majles*, Session 209, 11 Safar 1329/1911; Session 210, 14 Safar 1329/1911. See also Mirzayan Report to Sixth General Congress, August 1911, 1543/18a.

119. Minutes of Fourth Regional Congress, June 1909, Session 7, n.d., 476/66; Report of Minaret Region, June 1909 to June 1909, 476/68; Paros Committee to Azerbaijan Central Committee, November 16, 1908, 474/112. Regarding the military group, see Mohammad Mukhlis to Samson, 1324/1906, 565/1/2.

120. The number of members may be 13 (Huys) and 17 (Tsiatsan). There is a discrepancy in the Report of Vrezh Central Committee, 14 March 1910, 477/17. See also Minutes of Gilan Committee Third Regional Congress, 29 September 1909 to 7 October 1909, Session 5, 2 October 1909, 584/39.

121. Afary, *Iranian Constitutional Revolution*, 186, 196; Badr al-Moluk Bamdad, *From Darkness into Light: Women's Emancipation in Iran*, trans. and ed. F. R. C. Bagley (Smithtown, NY: Exposition Press, 1977), 34.

122. See Report of Shah City Committee, September 1909 to 6 July 1911, 587/30; Report of Persian Women's Benevolent Society, 15 December 1910, 586/78.

123. Bamdad, *From Darkness into Light*: 34; Afary, *Iranian Constitutional Revolution*, 186–87; Ettehadieh Nezam Mafi, *Paydayesh*, 253; Mirzayan to Rostom, 23 February 1910, 585/10.

124. See, Yeprem Khan to Comrades, 6 January 1910, 1728e/12.

125. See, for example, Third Regional Congress, 29 September 1909 to 7 October 1909, Rasht, Session 10, 5 October 1909, 584/39. For similar Hnchakist views, see G. Astghuni, [Grigor Yeghikian], "Chshmartutiunner Parskastani heghapokhakan sharzhumneri masin (akanatesi hishoghutiunnerits)" [Truths about the Persian revolutionary movements (from the memoirs of an eyewitness)] *Yeritasard Hayastan* 9, 49 (2 September 1913); 9, 50 (9 September 1913).

126. Third Regional Congress, 29 September 1909 to 7 October 1909, Rasht, Session 11, 5 October 1909, 584/39.

127. For discussion of Caucasian and Iranian Social Democrats, see Afary, *Iranian Constitutional Revolution*; Bayat, *Iran's First Revolution*. Tria's pamphlet presented at the Socialist International Congress at Copenhagen also sheds some light on the social democratic element. Tria (Vlass Mgeladze) was a Georgian Social Democrat who had taken part in the Russian Revolution of 1905 and the Tabriz resistance. Tria, "La Caucase et la Révolution persane," *Revue du monde musulman*, 13, 2 (February 1911). For discussions of Armenian Social Democrats in Iran, see Afary, *Iranian Constitutional Revolution*, 241–48, 267–69, 293–98; Cosroe Chaqueri, "The Role and Impact of Armenian Intellectuals in Iranian Politics, 1905–1911," *Armenian Review* 41, 2 (Summer 1988): 1–51; Ettehadieh Nezam Mafi, *Paydayesh*, 212–14, 220–21.

128. Arsen Kitur, *Patmutiun S. D. Hnchakian Kusaktsutian* [History of the S. D. Hnchakian Party] (Beirut: Shirak Press, 1962), 1: 400.

129. G. Astghuni [Grigor Yeghikian], "Inchpes kazmvets Parskastani S. D. Kusaktsutiune" [How Persia's S. D. Party was organized] in S[otsial]-D[emokrat] Hnchakian Kusaktsutian Fransayi Shrjan, *Hushardzan nvirvats Sotsial Demokrat Hnchakian Kusaktsutian karasunamiakin* [Commemorative volume dedicated to the fortieth anniversary of the Hnchakian Party] (Paris: H. B. Tiurapian, 1930), 196. For a brief biography of Yeghikian, see Sots[ial] Dem[okrat] Hnch[akian] Kus[aktsutian] Amer[ikayi] Shrjan, *Hnchakian taregirk (Amerikayi shrjani)* [Hnchakian yearbook (American region)] (Providence, 1931), 185–93; Aram Arkun, "Elikean (Yaqikiyan), Grigor E.," in *Encylopædia Iranica*, ed. Ehsan Yarshater (Costa Mesa, CA: Mazda Pulishers, 1998), 3: 364–65. For a study of Yeghikian, see Aram Arkun, "Grigor Yaghikian: Writer and Journalist," in *Armenians in Iran, The Paradoxical Role of a Minority in a Dominant Culture: Articles and Documents*, ed. Cosroe Chaqueri (Cambridge: Center for Middle Eastern Studies of Harvard University, 1998), 162–89. For a study of Armenians and the Jangali movement, see Aram Arkun, "Armenians and the Jangalis," *Iranian Studies* 30, 1–2 (Winter/Spring 1997): 25–52.

130. Kitur, *Patmutiun*, 1: 399.

131. Ibid., 1: 399–400. For a French translation, see Chaqueri, *Social-démocratie en Iran*, 238. See also Sokrat Khan Gelofiants, *Kayts: S. D. Hnch. Kusaktsutian gortsuneutiunits togh pastere khosin* [Spark: let the evidence from the S. D. Hnch. Party activity speak] (Providence: Yeritasard Hayastan, 1915), 13–15, 24–27; Hrand Gangruni, *Hay heghapokhutiune Osmanian brnatirutian dem (1890–1910)* [The Armenian revolution against Ottoman despotism] (Beirut: n.p., 1973), 195–96. See also Afary, *Iranian Constitutional Revolution*, 239.

132. For complete text of agreement, see Gelofiants, *Kayts*, 4–6. For partial text, see Kitur, *Patmutiun*, 1: 399; Gangruni, *Hay heghapokhutiune*, 195.

133. Kitur, *Patmutiun*, 1: 399–400.

134. For text, see Gelofiants, *Kayts*, 6–7.

135. For partial text, see ibid., 8.

136. Astghuni [Yeghikian], "Chshmartutiunner," 9, 44 (29 July 1913); 46 (12 August 1913); 49 (2 September 1913). Yeghikian completed writing the articles on 26 September 1911, which is the date on the last segment of the series.

137. Astghuni [Yeghikian], "Inchpes kazmvets," 196–97. See also Kitur, *Patmutiun*, 1: 403.

138. Astghuni [Yeghikian], "Chshmartutiunner," 9, 44 (29 July 1913); 46 (12 August 1913); 49 (2 September 1913).

139. Declaration of Tabriz Social Democrats, 8 December 1907, 473/151.

140. Afary, *Iranian Constitutional Revolution*, 266–67.

141. "Khachaturian à G. Plekhanov," Chaqueri, *Social-démocratie en Iran*, 39. An English translation, dated 19 November 1908, appears in Chaqueri, *Armenians in Iran*, 324–30.

142. Ibid., 42.

143. Ibid., 43.

144. "Protocole no. 1 de la Conférence des Social-Démocrates de Tabriz, 1908," in Chaqueri, *Social-démocratie en Iran*, 35–37. For a Persian translation, see Chaqueri, *Asnad*, 6: 50. An English translation appears in Chaqueri, *Armenians in Iran*, 331–34. See also Tigran Darvish to George Plekhanov, 3 December 1908, in Chaqueri, *Social-démocratie en Iran*, 44–49. An English translation appears in Chaqueri, *Armenians in Iran*, 338–44.

145. Afary, *Iranian Constitutional Revolution*, 247–48.

146. Ettehadieh Nezam Mafi gives the date of Taqizadeh's return to Tabriz as Rajab 1327 (*qamri*), which may be July or August 1909. See Ettehadieh Nezam Mafi, *Paydayesh*, 199.

147. For Zakarian's letter, see Amurian, *Arkhiv*, 1: 254–262. For Pilosian's letter, see Afshar, *Awraq*, 238–40. See also Astghuni [Yeghikian], "Chshmartutiunner," 9, 46 (12 August 1913).

148. Pilosian to Taqizadeh, 19 August 1909, in Afshar, *Awraq*, 238–40. For program and regulations of the Democrat Party, see Ettehadieh Nezam Mafi, *Majmu'eh*, 4: 3–19.

149. Pilosian to Taqizadeh, 26 January 1910, in Afshar, *Awraq*, 247–48.

150. Ibid., 259.

151. Ter Hacobian [Hakobian] to Taqizadeh, 1 November 1910, in Afshar, *Awraq*, 315.

152. Afary, *Iranian Constitutional Revolution*, 269. For a discussion of Ter Hakobian's series of articles entitled "Terror," which appeared in *Iran-e No* from 18 December 1910 to 4 January 1911, see 293–98.

153. Ibid., 275, 388 n. 81.

154. See Browne, *Persian Revolution*, 443.

155. Ter Hacobian [Hakobian] to Taqizadeh, 21 January 1910, in Afshar, *Awraq*, 303–4.

156. Ibid., 302.

157. Pilosian to Taqizadeh, 19 August 1909, in Afshar, *Awraq*, 240. See also Pilosian to Taqizadeh, 19 September 1909, in Afshar, *Awraq*, 245, wherein Pilosian denied that the Dashnaktsutiun would be successful, because according to Dashnakist regulations a Dashnakist could not be a member of another party.

158. Pilosian to Taqizadeh, 26 January 1910; 10 February 1910, in Afshar, *Awraq*, 255, 263.

159. Pilosian to Taqizadeh, 9 October 1911, in Afshar, *Awraq*, 283, 290–91.

160. Pilosian to Taqizadeh, 26 January 1910, in Afshar, *Awraq*, 254–55.

161. Astghuni [Yeghikian], "Inchpes kazmvets,"192–93; Arkun, "Elikean."

162. See "Bulletin Périodique du B[ureau] S[ocialiste] I[nternationale]," no. 7, 1911, p. 37 in Chaqueri, *Social démocraties en Iran*, 229.

163. Two papers called *Gilan* appeared in Rasht; one was connected with the Provincial Anjoman of Gilan (1908–1909) and the other connected with the Moderates. Yeghikian specifically points out that his series of articles appeared in the latter. See Astghuni [Yeghikian], "Inchpes Kazmvets," 193. See also Browne, *Press and Poetry in Modern Persia*, 130–31. For Persian text of "What Do the Social Democrats Say," see Ettehadieh Nezam Mafi, *Majmu'eh*, 4: 235–41; Cosroe Chaqueri [Khosrow Shakeri], *Asnad-e tarikh-e jonbesh-e kargari/sosial demokrasi va komunistiye Iran* [Documents of the history of the worker/social democratic and communist movement in Iran] (Tehran: Padzahr, 1985), 19: 100–4.

164. Astghuni [Yeghikian], "Inchpes kazmvets," 194.

165. Ettehadieh Nezam Mafi, *Majmu'eh*, 4: 235–41.

166. Astghuni [Yeghikian], "Inchpes kazmvets," 193. A meeting between Naser al-Molk and Yeghikian may have taken place in January or February 1911 when the regent was in Anzali. See Chaqueri, "Role and Impact of Armenian Intellectuals," 23.

167. For the original Persian text of Yeghikian's essay, see Chaqueri, *Asnad*, 6: 5–9. French text in Chaqueri, *Social-démocratie en Iran*, 141–47. Persian text also in Ettehadieh Nezam Mafi, *Majmu'eh*, IV: 225–32.

168. The Persian name is not given by Astghuni. The Armenian appears in two versions: *Parskastani Sotsial-Demokrat Kusatsutiun* (Iran's Social-Democratic Party) and *Parsik Sotsial-Demokrat Kusatsutiun* (Iranian Social-Democratic Party). See Astghuni [Yeghikian], "Inchpes kazmvets," 193. According to Kitur, the date of the change is 11 January 1911 and the reason for the name change was the opposition in the Iranian reactionary circles who wished to portray the group as "anti-Islamic." See Kitur, *Patmutiun*, 1: 401–2.

169. Astghuni [Yeghikian], "Inchpes kazmvets," 193.

170. Yeprem to Stepan [Stepanian], 12 January 1910, in Amurian, *Arkhiv*, I: 65.

171. See Hovak Stepanian, "Nikol Duman (mahvan 15-amiaki artiv)" [Nikol Duman (on the occasion of the 15th anniversary of his death)], *Hayrenik Amsagir* 8, 12 (October 1930): 158. For Duman's limited role during Mohammad Ali Shah's assault in 1911, see Amurian, *Dashnaktsutiune Parskastanum*, 81–85.

172. Farro [Hovsep Hovhannisian], "Grishayi hushere," 3, 2 (December 1924): 68–69; Kasravi, *Tarikh-e hijdah saleh*, 1: 102–5; Ra'in, *Yeprem Khan Sardar*, 299–317; "Yeprem yev ir gortse" [Yeprem and his activity], in Amurian, *Arkhiv*, 1: 87–90.

173. Farro [Hovsep Hovhannisian], "Grishayi hushere," 3, 2 (December 1924): 70–74; Kasravi, *Tarikh-e hijdah saleh*, 1: 106–08; "Yepreme yev ir gortse," in Amurian, *Arkhiv*, 1: 90–97; Amurian, *Dashnaktsutiune Parskastanum*, 92–94. For Armenian text of Yeprem's description of battles, see Farro [Hovsep Hovhannisian], "Grishayi hushere," 3, 3 (January 1925): 131–37. For a shorter version of same, see Elmar [Hovsep Hovhannisian], *Yeprem*, 321–32 . For Persian text, see Ra'in, *Yeprem Khan Sardar*, 326–39.

174. Farro [Hovsep Hovhannisian], "Grishayi hushere," 3, 2 (December 1924): 75.

175. Ibid., 75–77.

176. Kasravi, *Tarikh-e hijdah saleh*, 1: 112; Farro [Hovsep Hovhannisian], "Grishayi Hushere," 3, 4 (February 1925): 89; Elmar [Hovsep Hovhannisian], *Yeprem*, 336–38.

177. Kasravi, *Tarikh-e hijdah saleh*, 1: 115–17; Farro [Hovsep Hovhannisian], "Grishayi hushere," 3, 4 (February 1925): 90–92; Elmar [Hovsep Hovhannisian], *Yeprem*, 338–46; Ra'in, *Yeprem Khan Sardar*, 321–25; "Yepremi arshave Atrpatakan" [Yeprem's march to Azerbaijan], in Amurian, *Arkhiv*, 1: 43–44; "Yeprem yev ir gortse," in Amurian, *Arkhiv*, 1: 97–102, 105–10.

178. See, for example, Farro [Hovsep Hovhannisian], "Grishayi hushere," 3, 4 (February 1925): 94–95; "Yeprem yev ir gortse," in Amurian, *Arkhiv*, 1: 102–4.

179. Kasravi, *Tarikh-e hijdah saleh*, 1: 182–84; Ibrahim Fakhra'i, *Gilan dar jonbesh-e mashrutiyat* [Gilan in the constitutional movement] (Tehran: Ketabha-ye Jibi, 1974), 215–16; Farro [Hovsep Hovhannisian], "Grishayi hushere," 3, 5 (March 1925): 110–12; Amurian, *Dashnaktsutiune Parskastanum*, 160–62; "Yepremi arshave Arshad Dovlei dem" [Yeprem's march against Arshad al-Dowleh], in Amurian, *Arkhiv*, 1: 44–46; W. Morgan Shuster, *The Strangling of Persia* (New York: Century, 1912), 127, 135; Elmar [Hovsep Hovhannisian], *Yeprem*, 457–75, includes extracts from Grisha's memoirs and Shuster. See also "Parskastan: verjin tarvay chakatamartnere yev 'Dashnaktsutian' masnaktsutiune" [Persia: the battles of the last years and the participation of the Dashnaktsutiun], *Droshak*, no 2, February 1912.

180. Farro [Hovsep Hovhannisian], "Grishayi hushere," 3, 5 (March 1925): 112–15; Fakhra'i, *Gilan*, 216–18. See also "Yepremi arshave Salar Dovlei dem," in Amurian, *Arkhiv*, I: 46–48; Amurian, *Dashnaktsutiune Parskastanum*, 162–66; "Parskastan: verjin tarvay chakatamartnere yev 'Dashnaktsutian' masnaktsutiune," *Droshak*, no. 4, April 1912; Elmar [Hovsep Hovhannisian], *Yeprem*, 483, 489–93, which includes extracts from Grisha's memoirs.

181. The agreement is dated 18 July 1911, 1728b/47. See also 1728b/297, undated. The agreement also appears in Amurian, *Arkhiv*, 1: 418. This was in preparation for the battle against Mohammad Ali Shah's return in July 1911. See Farro [Hovsep Hovhannisian], "Grishayi hushere," 3, 5 (March 1925): 110.

182. For a list of Armenians killed, see 476/137; Elmar [Hovsep Hovhannisian], *Yeprem*, 665–66; Ra'in, *Yeprem Khan-e Sardar*, 515–17. The following sources were also consulted to reach a total: Yeprem Khan, *Yaddashtha*, 26, 32, 41; Shuster, *Strangling of Persia*, 190; "Tarikhcheh az Yeprem Khan," in Kasravi, *Chand Tarikhcheh*, 94–95, 99, 101, 102, 105, 107, 110, 111; Ivan Alexovich Zinoviev, *Enqelab-e mashrutiyat-e Iran: nazaret-e yek diplomat-e rus* [The constitutional revolution of Iran: the views of a Russian diplomat], trans. Abu al-Qasem E'tesami (Tehran: Eqbal, 1983), 88, 122, 123; Report of Vrezhstan Central Committee, 1908–1909, 476/141; Getap [New Julfa] Report to Vrezh Regional Congress, 12 June 1909, 476/61; Report of Vrezhstan Central Committee, 1908–1909, 476/141; Azerbaijan Central Committee to American Central Committee, 12 November 1908, 474/103; Report of Azerbaijan Central Committee to Western Bureau, 27 April 1909, 476/24; Arshaluys to Vrezh Central Committee, 12 June 1911, 587/24; Yeprem to Comrades, 9 January 1910, 1728e/13; Isahak Ter Zakarian to Yeprem, 17 July 1911, 1728g/97, also in Amurian, *Arkhiv*, 1: 363–64; Keri to Hayrik [Yeprem], 23 October 1911, 1728b/128; Declaration, unsigned, undated, 565/213; "Yepremi mghats krivnere

est Grish Khani (Ter Danielian)" [Yeprem Khan's waged battles according to Grish Khan (Ter Danielian)], in Amurian, *Arkhiv*, 1: 77–81; L[evon] G. Minasian, *Patmutiun Periayi Hayeri (1606–1956)* [History of Fereydan's Armenians, 1606–1956] (Antilias, Lebanon: Tparan Katoghikosutian Hayots Metsi Tann Kilikio, 1971), 149–50; "Heghapokhakan banaki arshave," 28–37; Nikol Odabashian, "Im kianki patmutiune" [My life story], *Hayrenik Amsagir* 19, 10 (August 1941): 72; H. Panirian, "H. H. Dashnaktsutiune yev parskakan sharzhume" [A. R. Federation and the Persian movement], *Droshak*, no. 3, March 1927; *Raffi taregirk* [Raffi yearbook] (Tehran: Modern, 1969), 404–6; Farro [Hovsep Hovhannisian], "Grishayi hushere," 3, 1 (November 1924): 67–72; 3, 2 (December 1924): 71–76; 3, 5 (March 1925): 109–16; "Krivner Parskastanum" [Battles in Persia], *Droshak* no. 5–6 (May–June 1910); "Parskastan: mi ej parskakan heghapokhutian patmutiunits" [Persia: A page from the history of the Persian revolution], *Droshak*, no. 1 (January 1911); "Parskastan: verjin tarvay chakatamartnere yev Dashnaktsutian masnaktsutiune," *Droshak* no. 2 (February 1912); "Kensakrakan: Zulumat" [Biography: Zulumat], *Droshak* no. 3 (March 1912); "Yeprem," *Droshak* no. 4 (April 1912).

183. Varandian, *Dashnaktsutian patmutiun*, 2: 75. Elmar [Hovsep Hovhannisian] also asserts that all costs were paid by the Dashnaktsutiun, the money being sent through the Bureau. See Elmar [Hovsep Hovhannisian], *Yeprem*, 138–139, reprint in Dasnabedian, *Rostom*, 266.

184. Report of Vrezhstan Central Committee, 1908–1909, 476/141.

185. The Tehran Committee received a letter in March 1911 from Yeprem requesting that he be allowed to resign from the party. See Minutes of Shah Committee, Session 54, 15 March 1911, 682/2. See also Alek Aghayan to Yeprem, 6 July 1911, 1728b/42.

186. For requests, see, for example, Russian correspondence to Yeprem, 1728g/45/46/48/50/53/55/58/69/214.

187. Hambardzum [Melik-Sargsian] to Yeprem, 6 July 1909, 1729/4.

188. Aleksandr Khachatrian to Yeprem, 14 July 1909, 1728g/162; Isahak Ter Zakarian to Yeprem, 29 July 1909, 1728g/93, also in Amurian, *Arkhiv*, 1: 359–60; Azerbaijan Central Committee to Western Bureaus, 5 April 1910, 477/28. Tria, expressing the Social Democratic view, relates that when Tehran was taken, it was suggested that the revolutionaries occupy official positions, but except for the Dashnakists, the revolutionaries refused this offer. He refers to this decision as a "mistake," because after the convening of the second Majles, the clergy profited by their action accusing Dashnakists of monopolizing important and secondary government positions. Tria, "La Caucase et la révolution persane," 332.

189. Stepanian to Yeprem, 30 January 1911, 1728a/89.

190. Rostom to Yeprem, 26 July 1909, in Amurian, *Arkhiv*, 1: 180. Also in Dasnabedian, *Rostom*, 169–70.

191. Western Bureau, 22 February 1910, in Amurian, *Arkhiv*, 2: 74.

192. Hovsep Movsisian to Yeprem, 30 March 1911, 1728b/72; Zakarian to Yeprem, 11 October 1910, 1728a/23, also in Amurian, *Arkhiv*, 1: 252–54; Stepanian to Yeprem, 8 July 1910, 1728a/83.

193. Yeprem to Hambardzum [Melik-Sargsian], 20 July 1911, 1728e/19/20, also in Amurian, *Arkhiv*, 1: 168–71.

194. The archives are full of telegrams demonstrating a correspondence regarding military operations between commanders of forces like Keri, Yeprem, and others. See, for example, telegrams in files 1728b, 1728g, and 1728d. It seems, however, that they were not sufficient. Duman complained of not being informed of the simplest but most important details regarding military tactics and strategy. See Nikol Duman to Yeprem, 15 August 1911, 1728a/41, also in Amurian, *Arkhiv*, 1: 182.

195. Stepanian to Yeprem, 26 February 1911, 1728a/90; Petros Melik Andreasian to Yeprem, 31 January 1911, 1728a/60, also in Amurian, *Arkhiv*, 1: 299–300; Stepanian to Yeprem, 15 August 1911, 1728a/101; Misak Ghazarian to Yeprem, 5 August 1911, 1728g/149; 15 August 1911, 1728g/150.

196. Samson to Stepan [Stepanian], 7 March 1911, 478/20; Western Bureau, 22 February 1910, in Amurian, *Arkhiv*, 2: 74. For similar sentiments, see Samson to Stepan [Stepanian], 21 February 1911, also in Amurian, *Arkhiv*, 1: 190–91; Hovhannisian, *Husher*, 254–55; H. Elmar [Hovsep Hovhannisian], *H. H. Dashnaktsutiune yev Parsits sahmanadrakan sharzhume* [A. R. Federation and the Persian constitutional movement]. *Hayrenik Amsagir* 30, 1 (January 1952)–30, 3 (March 1952).

197. Khecho [Grigor Mirzabekian] to Yeprem, 10 May 1911, 1728g/179, also in Amurian, *Arkhiv*, 1: 322–24.

198. Khecho [Grigor Mirzabekian] to Yeprem, 26 July 1911, 1728g/180. See also Stepanian to Yeprem, 30 June 1911, 1728a/98. For a brief discussion of Khecho's sentiments as expressed to Hovhannisian, see Hovhannisian, *Husher*, 255–57.

199. *Iranian Constitutional Revolution*, 299–302; Kasravi, *Tarikh-e hijdah saleh*, 1: 137–146; Malekzadeh, *Tarikh-e enqelab*, 6: 232–36. According to Grisha Khan, a participant in the disarming of the *mojahedin*, when Yeprem's men found Sattar Khan they asked him how he was wounded, and he replied that it was one of his own people who shot him. See Farro [Hovsep Hovhannisian], "Grishayi hushere," 3, 5 (March 1925): 109.

200. Great Britain, *Further Correspondence Regarding the Affairs of Persia*, no. 261, 3 November 1909, cited in Janet Afary, "Grassroots Democracy and Social Democracy in the Iranian Constitutional Revolution, 1906–1911," Ph.D. dissertation, (University of Michigan, 1991), 447 n. 118.

201. Hovsep [Mirzayan] to Rostom, 1 November 1910, 585/56. For later accounts, see Farro [Hovsep Hovhannisian], "Grishayi hushere," 3, 5 (March 1925): 108–10; Panirian, "H. H. Dashnaktsutiune yev parskakan sharzhume," 85.

202. Gilan Committee to *Droshak*, 7 September 1910, 585/45; Khecho [Grigor Mirzabekian] to Yeprem, 18 October [1910], 1728g/185, also in Amurian, *Arkhiv*, 1: 310–13; Potorik, 10 December 1911, 587/57. See also Chargé d'affaires Charles Marling's report cited in Afary, *Iranian Constitutional Revolution*, 302.

203. Kitur, *Patmutiun*, 1: 400–401. See also Astghuni [Yeghikian], "Chshmartutiunner," 9, 48 (26 August 1913).

204. Yeprem to Hambardzum [Melik-Sargsian], 20 July 1911, 1728e/19/20, also in Amurian, *Arkhiv*, 1: 168–71.

205. According to Grisha Khan, Yeprem requested a leave of absence, which was denied. See Farro [Hovsep Hovhannisian], "Grishayi hushere," 3, 5 (March 1925): 110. According to a report from Tehran, Yeprem planned to leave his post as early as August 1909. See "Parskastani shurje" [About Persia], *Mshak*, no. 174,

11 August 1909. According to Shuster, Yeprem also resigned in December 1911 after the Russian ultimatum because of a disagreement with the Bakhtiaris but later resumed his post when their dispute was "patched up." See Shuster, *Strangling of Persia*, 209.

206. Yeprem to Hambardzum [Melik-Sargsian], n.d, 1728e/21. Yeprem also claimed that 'Ain al-Dowleh had offered him 10,000 tomans to return. See Yeprem to Hambardzum [Melik-Sargsian], 25 December 1910, 1728e/18. His resignation was welcomed by Dashnakist comrades for various reasons. See Vahan Zakarian to Yeprem, 28 October 1910, 1728a/24, also in Amurian, *Arkhiv*, 1: 249–51; Samson to Yeprem, 24 November 1910, in Amurian, *Arkhiv*, 1: 187–88.

207. Kasravi, *Tarikh-e hijdah saleh*, 2: 496; Farro [Hovsep Hovhannisian], "Grishayi hushere," 3, 6 (April 1925): 88–90; Elmar [Hovsep Hovhannisian], *Yeprem*, 517–26; Stepanian, "Nikol Duman," 159.

208. Shuster, *Strangling of Persia*, 190–91.

209. Afary, *Iranian Constitutional Revolution*, 330–36; Kasravi, *Tarikh-e hijdah saleh*, 1: 255–60.

210. See, for example, P. [?] to *Droshak*, 9 January 1912, 1728e/40; Shah Committee, n.d., 1728e/120; Stepan Stepanian to Karo, 6 January 1912, 479/1. See also Bonnard [?] to *Droshak*, 9 January 1912, in Amurian, *Arkhiv*, 2: 153–56; Tigran Devoyiants, "Kiankis drvagnerits" [Episodes from my life], *Hayrenik Amsagir* 22, 1 (January-February, 1944): 84–85. Melik Andreasian, a native of Azerbaijan, had taken part in battles in Rasht and in the takeover of Tehran with Yeprem Khan. See Elmar [Hovsep Hovhannisian], *Yeprem*, 192–93 n. *; Kasravi, *Tarikh-e hijdah saleh*, 1: 356–67.

211. Cited by Kasravi, *Tarikh-e hijdah saleh*, 1: 257–58.

212. Hambardzum Melik-Sargisian to Comrades, 22 July 1912, 1728e/44, 479/29, 589/32, also in Amurian, *Arkhiv*, 1: 163–165. Iranian Dashnakist bodies attempted to discover the origins and development of the conflict with Yeprem Khan after his death. See Minutes of Shahstan Central Committee First Regional Congress, Session 3, 28 May 1913, 592/8.

213. See, for example, a booklet of compilations by Armenian poets and activists, published right after his death. It had at least three printings in 1912 alone. *Sgapsak Yepremin* [Wreath for Yeprem] (Constantinople/Istanbul, 1912), 1728e/45. See also text in Elmar [Hovsep Hovhannisian], *Yeprem*, 637–60; Amurian, *Arkhiv*, 1: 132–59.

214. Yeprem to Anahit, 22 February 1909, in Amurian, *Arkhiv*, 1: 67.

5

Retreat and Shift of Focus

By 1911, the last year of the Iranian Constitutional Revolution, the political situation in Iran had deteriorated. American adviser Morgan Shuster's attempts to reform the country's finances had met with constant opposition not only from the British and Russians but also from Prime Minister Sepahdar and later Samsam al-Saltanah and conservatives in the Majles. The British-backed Russian ultimatum to oust Shuster and the Russian occupation of northern Iranian regions, specifically Azerbaijan and Gilan, ended the second constitutional period (July 1909 to December 1911) and began a harsh reactionary period. The Potsdam meeting of Russia and Germany in August 1911 on the one hand undermined the position Britain had hoped for in the Anglo-Russian convention and on the other hand obliged Russia to recognize Germany's right to engage in commerce in the northern sphere of Iran.[1] By 1911, perhaps in an attempt to counter British and Russian influence and to gain additional territorial and political ground in Iran, the Ottoman Empire had also made further inroads into Iranian territory. In the summer of 1910, Ottoman troops entered Maku and established supervision over all roads leading into Tabriz, Kermanshah, and Urumieh, and in 1911 surrounded Salmas from three sides, leaving only the road to Tabriz open.[2] Most importantly, after Shuster's dismissal, Iran came under almost complete British and Russian military and political control.

In this political environment, the Dashnaktsutiun began at the end of 1911 and early 1912 to reexamine seriously its role in Iran, to question its continued relationship with the government, and to consider retreat. The party's decision to withdraw fully from Iranian politics came in autumn 1912 and was greatly influenced by Russian occupation in northern Iran, which among other consequences resulted in the devastation of the Dashnakist organizations in Azerbaijan and Gilan. Continued government disregard toward constitutional laws and freedoms, government determination to rule without a Majles, and its weakness in the face of

mounting foreign encroachment served as impetus in the final Dashnakist decision to terminate active involvement in the political affairs of
Iran. The uncertain political future of the country and its effect on the
populace, especially Iranian Armenian communities, was doubly felt after Yeprem Khan's death in the already controversial struggle against the
incursions of Salar al-Dowleh, the former shah's brother.

It is possible that the Dashnaktsutiun was also picking up on the general discontent and at times direct hostility of the Iranian populace toward the government and its representatives. Armenian Social Democrat
Arshavir Chilinkirian reported in 1911 that the public was so angry that it
would attack provincial and departmental *anjomans* (not popular *anjomans*) and new political institutions. Chilinkirian pointed to three factors
undermining the constitutional order: Russia's support for the return to
throne of Mohammad Ali Shah and its attempt to turn back the reform
measures of the Democrats, the support given by the tribes to reactionary
elements in destroying the constitution and the taxes burdening the
lower classes.[3]

Russian Terror and the Threat of
Dissolution: "Finito Persia"[4]

The British-backed Russian ultimatum to remove Shuster and military
occupation of northern Iran ended the Iranian Constitutional Revolution
in an abrupt and cruel way as Russian troops dissolved *anjomans*, disarmed *mojahedin*, and carried out an all-out assault on constitutionalist
leaders and the populace of Azerbaijan and Gilan.[5] Harrassment, arrests,
exiles, searches, and hangings became commonplace. Russian authorities
especially targeted Caucasian revolutionaries, including Dashnakists, despite their policy of neutrality toward Russian occupation. Contradictory
evidence exists regarding the role the Dashnaktsutiun desired to play in
the resistance to Russian incursion into Tabriz. Tigran Devoyiants, an
eyewitness to the "anarchy" in Tabriz and the "terrorism" of Russian
troops, states that the Azerbaijan Central Committee of the Dashnaktsutiun after two days of meetings decided not to raise arms against the Russian forces, because its struggle was against the Iranian monarchy, and
ordered all Armenian fighters to withdraw to Van.[6] Hovak Stepanian,
Nikol Duman's biographer, in contrast, states that the Central Committee
sought to actively resist Russian troops while Duman opposed such action against the Russians and departed for Van.[7] The chaotic and fierce
situation devastated Dashnakist branches in Russian-occupied Azerbaijan and Gilan. Many of the leaders were persecuted, exiled, or escaped,
thus leaving Dashnakist branches leaderless and in disarray.[8] Many

lower-ranking members also left the party out of fear or despair.[9] Dashnakists in Gilan tried to safeguard their arsenal by transferring arms to the Tehran branch or to the Ottoman embassy.[10] Some Azerbaijani Dashnakist leaders even took sanctuary in the Ottoman embassy.[11] Others, like Vahan Zakarian of the Azerbaijan Central Committee who fled immediately after the Russians entered Tabriz, crossed the Ottoman border.[12]

Dashnakist bodies in Tabriz, Rasht, Anzali, and other areas were almost completely devastated and in great disorder; they no longer held meetings because of Russian surveillance, increased activity of reactionary, "dark elements," both Iranian and Armenian, and a lack of members.[13] The Azerbaijan Central Committee even proposed dissolution of all Dashnakist groups in the region and offered its resignation to the Western Bureau. While the Western Bureau remained silent on the issue, the Tehran Central Committee at first opposed such drastic action.[14] By the end of 1913, the organizational situation had deteriorated to such a level that the region's existing Dashnakist groups were dissolved officially in order to effect changes and restructure regional bodies, whose main concern remained self-defense of the Iranian Armenian communities, especially after the outbreak of World War I and the arrival of Ottoman troops in Azerbaijan.[15]

Partial Retreat: Doubts and Demands

The internal conflict between the constitutionalists, resulting in the Iranian government's disarmament of the *mojahedin* and the cabinet's closing of the Majles after it resisted the ultimatum, and the external pressures of Britain, Russia, the Ottoman Empire, and to some extent Germany had caused the Dashnaktsutiun to question its continued activism in Iranian politics. Concerns about Armenian participation had always existed, especially during times of crisis or constitutionalist defeat.[16] Dashnakists continued, however, to remain positive and optimistic about the future of constitutional rule in Iran even when Mohammad Ali Shah tried to overthrow the constitutional regime with Russian support. They called on Armenian *fedayis* to fight to save the threatened constitution and come to the aid of their Iranian brethren. By continued sacrifices they hoped to become free and equal citizens.[17]

Therefore, despite second thoughts about supporting the constitutional government, the Dashnaktsutiun had continued its activities. In the Sixth General Congress (17 August–17 September 1911), held in the Black Sea coastal town of Varna, Bulgaria, the party took into consideration the strength of Iranian constitutional elements, the party's own active involvement that had assisted the constitutional movement, and the possibility that events in Iran would encourage revolutionary elements in the Ottoman and Russian Empires. It then instructed its Caucasian and Ottoman bodies to bring even greater military help to the Iranian Constitutional Revolution. In order to strengthen its bodies in Iran and in recognition of the importance of the capital, it gave the Tehran Committee the powers and title of a Central Committee. In addition, it recommended that relations with democratic elements be maintained to protect the constitutional ranks, to guarantee Armenian "national-cultural self-determination," to gain the right to collect a tax for an Iranian Armenian National Congress, which would represent the Iranian Armenian community, and to eliminate all limitations in the Fundamental Laws that went against the spirit of constitutionalism and that were based on national or religious distinctions. Last, the General Congress decided to propose to the constitutional government the confiscation of the properties of anti-constitutionalists and distribution of such properties to the peasants.[18]

A factor that contributed to continued Dashnakist participation was the all-important issue of self-defense of the Iranian Armenian community. It remained a constant concern throughout the Iranian Constitutional Revolution and was the only point of agreement even among those who shunned active participation in Iranian politics. The reasons for apprehension and fear varied at different periods between 1906 and 1911 from concerns about Ottoman, Russian, and royalist instigation and troop movements, to conservative anti-Armenian as well as Armenian anti-constitutionalists' agitation and backlash, to general political crisis and civil war.[19]

Serious doubts set in early 1912 after Shuster's removal and the closing of the Majles in December 1911 and began the long process of Dashnakist retreat, which came in two stages, partial and complete pullout. Two currents of thought arose regarding Dashnakist withdrawal from the Iranian political scene. The assault by the former shah's brother, Salar al-Dowleh, on the government in early and mid-1912 in an effort to win the Qajar throne for himself and the question of Dashnakist participation in the battles against his forces generated debates among Dashnakist leaders. Debates centered around whether the present government was constitutional and whether the Iranian Constitutional Revolution had come to an end. In addition, these discussions brought forth once again tension and disagreements between leading Dashnakists on one side and Yeprem Khan and Majles delegate Hovsep Mirzayan on the other.

The newly authorized Tehran Central Committee took the first step to express publicly its doubts about the Iranian government and its view regarding new battles against Salar al-Dowleh. With the following declaration began the first stage of retreat.

For what is this new battle, for the country's independence? No! Persia's independence has already been sold by the men who today rule the country
. . .

Is it perhaps for the constitution that they rearm themselves? Never. The constitution has already been buried by the hands of today's rulers of Persia. The Majles is closed, free speech and press are persecuted, assembly is banned, and only the fist rules in place of law.

Is it the good of the people that perhaps drives them to the battlefront? Not at all. Two armies are fighting against each other, but both pillage and plunder with the same appetite and savagery the same people whose bread they eat every day . . .

But what do you have to do with this dishonorable battle, fellow countrymen?

You came of your own free will to protect Persia's independence and constitution. That same government, which today conducts you to a new battle, itself has sold independence and betrayed freedom. What link could there be between traitors and the Armenian soldier?!

Not one soldier to this battle and not one bullet; that must be our motto.

There is only one battle, for which every Armenian must be ready—the sacred battle of self-defense against oppression.[20]

The Tehran Central Committee's concerns regarding the Russian- and British-backed Iranian cabinet and its battles were influenced to some extent by the Dashnaktsutiun's fear that it too would become the target of persecution as had other parties, such as the Democrat Party. In addition, Dashnakists seemed worried about the state of affairs in the country, which they found to be oppressive. In such a political atmosphere, they felt they could no longer work openly and actively.

Iran's independence has already been sold and the constitution abrogated by the hands of this country's unworthy children. The Majles is closed and there is no hope that the present government will reopen it. On the contrary, today's government is very happy that it can act without supervision.

Press and speech are not free, as assemblies are not. Thieves love the dark night and Iran's present government has corked every free mouth and veiled the light of the press in order to cover its theft.

A group of traitors who complyingly and obediently carry out the decisions of the Russo-British agreement govern the country.

Martial law, which was declared temporarily in Iran, supposedly for the country's protection has now become perpetual. That situation was as necessary to the traitors as Judas's kiss in order to pull off their dark deeds and it is still necessary so that they can flee from just indignation and evenhanded revenge.

> The atmosphere is completely polluted. . .
> In such circumstances our role is extremely difficult and our responsibility grown heavier . . .
> Men who did not desist from selling their fatherland . . . persecute us also
> . . . prudence demands that we spare our strengths . . .
> . . . we declare the Dashnaktsutiun in our area a secret organization.[21]

Yeprem Khan and Hovsep Mirzayan and their supporters disagreed strongly with the Central Committee's views on the government and opposed such measures. They sought the help of the Western Bureau in Geneva to compel the Tehran and Azerbaijan Central Committees to join the struggle against Salar al-Dowleh.[22] The Bureau instructed all sides to hold meetings and to settle the issue appropriately. Yeprem Khan and Dashnakist representatives made two attempts to meet. The first failed miserably as it deteriorated into a match of insults. In the meantime, the Central Committee circular caused fourteen Dashnakist soldiers to leave Yeprem Khan's Armenian regiment, and Mirzayan warned the Tehran Central Committee that Yeprem Khan planned to arrest them.[23]

The Armenian regiment of the Iranian army was Yeprem's creation. At first it was recognized also as a Dashnakist division, but according to the Tehran Central Committee, after some of the soldiers took part in pillaging, the party no longer recognized the detachment as Dashnakist but merely Armenian. The Central Committee made some attempts to stop such offenses through circulars and lectures.[24] In early 1912, in an unrelated matter, the Iranian government had tried to disarm these Armenian soldiers as it had done almost two years earlier to the Iranian and Caucasian *mojahedin* with the help of Yeprem Khan and his Armenian men. The Dashnakists believed the directive came from Russia and Britain despite assertions by the Iranian government that it no longer had a use for them. Some of the targeted Armenian soldiers objected to being dismissed without reimbursement for their weapons and thus opposed government attempts by holding their arms ransom for two months' salary. According to a report by the Tehran Central Committee, Yeprem Khan killed the protest "harshly." The report does not mention what measures Yeprem utilized.[25] Full disarmament, however, must not have taken place, as the Armenian regiment led by Yeprem Khan fought against Salar al-Dowleh's forces. The Armenian division published its own statement at about the same time as the Tehran Central Committee announcement, perhaps in response to it. The proclamation called Armenians to battle against Salar al-Dowleh, declaring that the struggle was for the sake of neighbors and workers and that it would be fought without regard to race, religion, or ethnicity.[26]

The debate over support of the Iranian government and participation in its new battles took center stage in the Dashnakist Bureau's proposed meetings, chaired by Dr. Stepanian, to settle the many problems between the Tehran and Azerbaijan Central Committees on the one side and Yeprem Khan and Mirzayan on the other. Contrary to the bureau's request, however, the three Armenian commanders, Yeprem, Keri, and Khecho, could not attend, because they were not in Tehran. Their views, or at least Yeprem Khan's views, were represented by Mirzayan.[27]

It would be an exaggeration to say that there were two factions at the meetings. Rather, there were two currents of thought, one represented by Mirzayan, the other by everyone else. Mirzayan rationalized the government's actions by trying to redefine Iran's independence. He asserted that there were two kinds of independence, juridical and practical. In the juridical sense, one could assume that Iran was by no means independent, but after all, he asked, which country has "absolute independence?" Although Mirzayan did not pursue the matter of what he called practical independence, one may speculate that he thought Iran's independence fit that category. Mirzayan also tried to distinguish between regime and government. He insisted that the Iranian regime was constitutional although the existing government, which had resorted to harsh measures only to benefit constitutionalism in the long run, was not. He then deduced that the only solution would be to protect the regime by participation in government actions and then topple the unconstitutional government once its enemies had been defeated.

The representatives of the Azerbaijan and Tehran Central Committees saw the new military conflict between the government and Salar al-Dowleh as a consequence of British and Russian intrigues. They believed that Iran was neither independent nor constitutional, since it was under foreign control and lacked basic freedoms like those of the press, assembly, speech, and so forth. A state of martial law in the country had killed any semblance of constitutionalism. The government had become oppressive and reactionary. The Majles had not been reopened nor had plans been made for elections. Furthermore, even if they were to transpire, how could people have been expected to come out and take part in elections after such persecution and oppression? They demanded that constitutional laws and freedoms be reestablished. To that end, the participants decided to send two representatives, Mirzayan and Stepanian, to present their demands to regent Naser al-Molk and the cabinet. Dashnakist participation would depend on the government's unconditional written promise to quickly announce individual rights and freedoms of speech, assembly, and press.[28]

Mirzayan reported in the next session that he met with Regent Naser al-Molk, who expressed his support in approaching the cabinet. Then he met Foreign Minister Vosuq al-Dowleh who approved of reopening the Majles and claimed that the cabinet had not yet declared elections because of foreign intervention and events in Tabriz, referring perhaps to Russian excesses there. He then informed Mirzayan that the Dashnaktsutiun should make its demands in writing and the cabinet would respond in kind.[29] Mirzayan also spoke to Vosuq al-Dowleh about reinstituting freedom of press, to which Vosuq al-Dowleh replied that there would be no restrictions on newspapers as long as, of course, they steered away from certain subjects such as foreign affairs, politics in general, and anything that might agitate the populace.[30]

In response to the cabinet's wishes, the Dashnakists demanded in writing that the present government reopen the Majles and prepare ground for elections by reinstituting freedoms of press and assembly, by guaranteeing the inalienable rights of individuals, and by lifting martial law.[31] In its written reply to the Dashnaktsutiun, the cabinet expressed its pleasure that the party supported Iranian independence and constitutionalism. It reassured the party that the government's only purpose was to protect both of those ideals. It added that if some freedoms had been limited in the past, that was done only to benefit the country and to protect it. Moreover, the government's primary goal and action would be to declare Majles elections "at the first possible moment, meaning at a time when the country's state is such that it would be possible to elect a sufficient number of delegates in Tehran and the provinces." Second, once elections began, the government would allow the demanded freedoms "to such a degree that is necessary for the regular progress of elections," and it would "ban such steps that may limit the freedom of those voting."[32]

Although doubts remained as to the sincerity of the cabinet's written promises, once the Dashnaktsutiun received them, it agreed to participate in the government's struggle against Salar al-Dowleh.[33] Of course, the cabinet's assurances were not carried out and elections for the third Majles were not held until the latter half of 1914.[34] Despite the decision to fight, however, Dashnakists continued to express some apprehensions regarding Yeprem Khan and his men. Not only were Yeprem's men no longer regarded by Dashnakists as comrades but neither was Yeprem, although their actions were interpreted by most Armenians and Iranians as such, which was an element that caused great anxiety for Dashnakists.[35]

Salar al-Dowleh had successfully organized an army in order to overthrow the current regime and claim the Qajar throne. After his occupation of Kermanshah, the government sent 500 troops led by Farman Farma, which included an unspecified number of Armenian soldiers under Keri's command. They were later joined by Yeprem Khan and 10 to 14 Armenian soldiers, including Yeprem's comrade-in-arms, Grisha Khan (Ter Danielian), all of whom arrived on 5 May 1912 in Hamadan where Salar al-Dowleh's army had moved. The next day, Yeprem's army faced that of Salar al-Dowleh in the village of Surjeh, where Yeprem Khan was killed instantly while attempting to reach his wounded friend, Dr. Zohrab Khan. Keri immediately took command of the Armenian forces and Salar al-Dowleh was ultimately defeated.[36]

Yeprem Khan's sudden death came as a great blow to Armenian constitutionalist elements and helped drive Dashnakists toward complete retreat of all Armenian troops and termination of relations with the government.

Complete Retreat: Disillusion and Resignation

After Yeprem Khan's death on 6 May 1912, the Dashnaktsutiun took steps to withdraw completely from Iranian politics. Despite the internal conflict between Yeprem Khan and the party, and that Yeprem Khan did not always fully protect Dashnakists and at times punished them if they crossed him, Dashnakists had enjoyed at least a certain amount of safety. After his death, however, they felt completely vulnerable.[37]

Iranian Armenian Dashnakist bodies convened from September to December 1912 at the First Regional Congress in Tehran to decide on present and future actions in Iran. They came to the conclusion that Iran had lost its independence, especially after the latest Russian ultimatum. With growing foreign political and economic encroachment, government leaders had become mere tools in Russian hands. Having buried the constitution, the Iranian government was leaning more and more toward reaction, free from the control and supervision of popular representatives in the Majles. Demands and protests of the Dashnaktsutiun and other parties had been completely ignored. Moreover, Dashnakist participation in government-sponsored battles, which previously had a liberal character, now had a factional, even reactionary, nature and was waged against the government's enemies, even liberal elements. The Regional Congress then declared that since all of the above were against Dashnakist ideals, the party decided to end all ties with the present Iranian government and recall its soldiers from the battlefront.

> To break off relations and stop every kind of military and moral alliance to the present reactionary government, . . . by giving strength and allying with the country's liberal-constitutional elements and in that way . . . to rebuild the country's Constitutional ranks, at the same time utilizing means that are worthy of a revolutionary-socialist party as is our organization.
>
> To recall from the army Keri and all Dashnakist comrades, . . . considering those soldiers who stay in the army and do not submit to the organization as independent individuals having no ties to the organization.
>
> To execute in haste the final liquidation of government activities . . .

In addition, the party no longer allowed Dashnakists to serve in the Iranian army in any capacity, because the Dashnakist soldier possessed "no moral right to sell himself as a combatant." In addition, the Dashnaktsutiun considered the revolutionary period over and the government reactionary. Drawing from its past experience, it prohibited any Dashnakist from occupying a governmental administrative post, especially in the police or gendarmes. Employment in all other government positions would be decided by the Azerbaijan and Tehran Central Committees.

The party's stance regarding a future Dashnakist role in Iran significantly curtailed activity by instructing all bodies to go underground but to continue to exert every effort on reinstituting constitutional laws and freedoms, reopening the Majles, collaborating with democratic elements, continuing the self-defense of the Iranian Armenian community, and propagating socialist principle among workers and the peasantry.[38]

The Tehran and Azerbaijan Central Committees twice published the decisions of the Regional Congress in the form of a circular. Since the first printing had not reached Armenian soldiers, who had not yet returned to Tehran, the flyer was reprinted on 4 November 1912. It stated that because Iran had lost its self-determination, if not de jure at least de facto, and the government had become reactionary, the party had "decided to break off its relationship and stop all sorts of military and moral alliance with the present reactionary government . . . [while] allying with the country's liberal-constitutional elements and . . . utilizing means that are worthy of a revolutionary socialist party." The statement concluded by recalling all Armenian troops and "liquidating in haste" all ties with the government.[39] The Seventh General Congress of the Dashnaktsutiun, held in August 1913 at Erzerum, verified the decisions of both Central Committees.[40]

While some may have been saddened by the turn of events that had resulted in the Dashnaktsutiun's pullout, others found even covert action problematic, calling it "Don Quixotism," and were happy that the party "finally came to the realization that our efforts and martyrs were almost in vain," adding that one did not need to be a prophet to have suspected that.[41] Still others, for example Mirzayan, knowingly or unknowingly tested the decisions made at the Regional Congress, especially that which dealt with military service. After Yeprem's death, Keri had been assigned commander of the Armenian forces. When the Iranian Dashnakist bodies declared complete retreat from all government and military service in November 1912, the Armenian regiment had just arrived in Tehran. By the first week of December, Keri had resigned from his post, thus complying with the party's final decree. According to the

Tehran Central Committee, the government did not want to relinquish the service of the Armenian regiment and Mirzayan considered becoming commander.[42] Mirzayan, on the other hand, denied that he had been assigned commander, attributing the news to mere rumors.[43] The issue of Mirzayan's "insubordination" became hotly debated in the Dashnakist First Regional Congress of Tehran in mid-1913. According to the Central Committee, Mirzayan's activities indicated that he had taken on the post of commander of the Armenian regiment in the Iranian army and after unsuccessful attempts to convince him to distance himself, the Central Committee had found it necessary to expel him from party ranks on 1 January 1913. Mirzayan, in his defense, insisted that his role had not been official, that he had not been paid, and that he acted merely as a consultant, a link (*"trait d'union"*) between the government and regiment. Moreover, he added, his resignation was on 20 or 21 December 1912, ten days after Keri's resignation. As the Tehran Central Committee's letter indicates, Keri's resignation came prior to 6 December 1912. In a sweeping majority, the Regional Congress resolved that Mirzayan, with his actions on behalf of the government and army, had challenged the party's decisions and thus was guilty of insubordination. On that basis, the congress found the Central Committee's decision to dismiss Mirzayan appropriate, but taking into consideration its slow and wavering action that provided him with the opportunity to continue in his post, reduced the period of his suspension to one year until June 1914.[44]

Mirzayan, in his protest against the decision of the Regional Congress, clearly expressed his dissatisfaction not only with his disciplinary sentence, but also with the party's "absurd logic" in liquidating all ties with the government and military. He maintained that an Armenian regiment was a necessary stage for future participation in Iran's general military service, a position he had pursued on the Dashnaktsutiun's behalf in the Majles. As for his disciplinary action, he reasserted his innocence and felt that a one-year dismissal sentence was too harsh. After all, he pointed out in flawed reasoning, he had not served in the military and therefore did not go against the "spirit of the decision."[45]

Despite objections by Mirzayan, who now stood alone without Yeprem as an ally, the Dashnakists took further steps to retire from the Iranian political scene by boycotting Majles elections.

Majles Boycott

News of the much demanded and anticipated elections for the Majles came in 1913, but the Dashnaktsutiun did not have the expected enthusiastic reaction. On the contrary, Dashnakists spent many months debating participation in elections. At issue were many of the concerns expressed earlier in the debates over withdrawal from the Iranian political scene and ending relations with the government. Those who opposed Armenian and Dashnakist participation in Majles elections pointed to the lack of democracy, the absence of "pure" constitutional elements in the country, and the control of foreign powers, especially Britain and Russia. They warned that a representative assembly would merely be used to legitimize the policies of the two foreign powers. They also feared that a socialist party in the new Majles would not be able to function according to its conscience. Those who favored taking part in the electoral process considered several factors. They believed that regardless of the weakness of a new Majles, it might still have the capacity to limit the actions of cabinet. They hoped that a new Majles would reinstitute constitutional freedoms and allow for their voices to be heard through representatives. They advised against cynicism and distrust; instead they preferred to concentrate only on the gains that could be achieved through a new assembly. Moreover, they pointed to the development of democratic elements, on the one hand, and the growing reactionary activism, on the other, both of which necessitated taking part.[46]

At first, both sides had an almost equal number of advocates, with a small majority supporting the optimists.[47] The cabinet's postponement of elections to December 1913 and then again until after the outbreak of war in summer 1914, however, did much to bolster the arguments of the cynics or realists.[48] They expressed a sense of great disappointment in having sacrificed so much and gained so little. Seeing no hope in a new Majles that they considered the "illegitimate child of the revolution" and a "gathering of traitors," they resolved to boycott elections.[49] In June 1914, having taken into consideration (1) the inequality of all peoples inherent in the fundamental and electoral laws, (2) the reactionary nature of cabinet rule, (3) the improbability of making any constructive gains in such a political situation, (4) the government's obvious attempts to disrupt free elections by placing obstacles that ensure the election of its candidates who merely sanction its policies and those of foreign interests, and (5) the implausibility of the Majles serving the interests of the people, the Second Regional Congress in Tehran determined "to boycott the third Majles and instruct all bodies to abstain from elections."[50]

Conclusion: The End of the End

Iran remained neutral during World War I but still became a battlefield for Allied and Central powers, and by 1917 the whole of the country was occupied by Britain and Russia. In 1914, Ottoman troops moved into Azerbaijan, replacing Russian troops physically and tactically, victimizing Assyrian and Armenian communities, of which thousands fled to the other side of the Araxes River.[51] The deteriorating situation in Iran and its effect on Iranian Armenians further motivated concentration on self-defense and withdrawal from overt and public activity.

Having pulled out all its forces from the battlefront and having withdrawn support from the only existing government in Iran, the Dashnaktsutiun withdrew from active participation in Iranian politics. Its focus shifted away from international involvements and toward nationalist politics.[52] For instance, in 1912, the Armenian National Bureau was established to pursue the issue of Ottoman reforms. In February 1914, the European powers reached a promising plan of reforms for Ottoman Armenian provinces. Moreover, in the same year, the bureau asked Catholicos Gevorg to solicit the protection of Tsar Nicholas to protect Ottoman Armenian lives and property and to guarantee reforms. In exchange for Russian protection, viceroy for the Caucasus Count Vorontsov-Dashkov asked that "the Catholicos keep his flock prepared to act in case of armed conflict." In the years before and during World War I, the viceroy attempted to gain the loyalty of the Dashnaktsutiun as he convinced Tsar Nicholas to free Dashnakist prisoners or pardon and allow the return of exiles of the Stolypin years. After the German declaration of war, Vorontsov-Dashkov suggested the creation of an Armenian volunteer corps that would be provided with arms, matériel, and money. Despite objection from national leaders who warned that the Young Turks might use the existence of volunteer units as an excuse for violence against its Armenian subjects, the National Bureau agreed to the proposal and Armenian revolutionaries active in the Iranian Constitutional Revolution commanded (as in the case of Keri) or joined the volunteer units.[53] Having reached some sort of rapprochement with Russia, the Dashnaktsutiun no longer perceived the tsarist regime as the great danger it had seemed just a few years earlier. More importantly, beginning in 1915, under the guise of the world war, the Armenians in the Ottoman Empire became victims of mass deportations and massacres.[54] Those who survived ended up as refugees dispersed throughout the Caucasus, Arab lands, and Iran. After the war, the focus of the Dashnaktsutiun and that of Armenians in general changed at least partially from Ottoman Armenian provinces and almost completely from Iran to the Armenian Republic in the Caucasus as it had only a few years before turned from the Caucasus to Iran and the Ottoman Armenian provinces. The tragedy of war, the promise of independence, growing Armenian nationalism, and the Iranian policy of centralization, homogenization, and nationalism created obstacles in the way of Armenian activity in Iranian or internationalist politics. In rare cases, individual Armenians continued to participate in Iranian political movements, including Hnchakist Grigor Yeghikian, who was an associate of Kuchek Khan and the Jangalis, and Avetis Sultan-

zadeh (Mikayelian), a native of Iranian Azerbaijan who was the first secretary of the Communist Party of Iran.

The Iranian Constitutional Revolution was unique in bringing together
peoples from different economic and social backgrounds, ethnicities, religious convictions, ideologies, and even countries in a struggle for parliament and constitution. The movement advanced even beyond this, taking on different meaning for different groups. For Armenians, the Iranian
revolution had wide ramifications affecting their self-perception, their
ideological development, and the fate of the Armenian people. They participated in the constitutional struggle, because they perceived the
present and future condition of the Armenian people in Iran, the Caucasus, and the Ottoman Empire to be directly tied to the unfolding events
in Iran. The prerevolutionary position and activities of Armenian political parties in Iran and their effort to come closer to the ideals of socialism
permitted active involvement in the revolution and made feasible their
collaboration with Iranian and Caucasian constitutionalists.

The Dashnakists, like the Hnchakists and other Social Democrats,
made a significant contribution to the course of the constitutional movement. Their service in every capacity—intellectual, military, or other-
wise—in the later stages of the movement gave way, however, to disillusion and frustration because of internal and external elements. In a short
span of time, hope and inspiration had overcome to a great extent communal prejudice and conflict and had encouraged struggle for a common
cause. At the end of that same time, a sense of defeat and disenchantment
with the lack of progress and even regression had also set in, forcing
many to question the wisdom behind such sacrifice.[55] The Hnchakists
withdrew from the Iranian Constitutional Revolution before 1910, and
disappointment befell the Dashnaktsutiun in 1912, at the same time as
the party began to concentrate on developments in Ottoman and Russian
Armenian provinces, which by the end of the second decade of the century completely absorbed the Armenian people and nearly threatened
their existence in the region. That is not to say that individual Armenians
made no contributions to Iranian politics, nor was this the end of Armenian involvement in Iranian progressive movements. Participation, even if
not to the extent of that in the Iranian Constitutional Revolution, was dis-
proportionately high relative to the Iranian Armenian population. The
examples are numerous. In the 1920s, Armenians rose to the occasion
once again in support of the Soviet Socialist Republic in Rasht by even
taking part in a fighting force that was to march onto Tehran.[56] An Iranian Armenian Communist, Avetis Mikayelian, better known as Sultanzadeh, was the "leading theoretician" of the Communist Party of Iran
(Ferqeh-e Komunist-e Iran) formed in 1920. Contribution and support of

radical movements continued and reached their height in the 1940s. Armenians played an important role in the Tudeh party and participated in the 1945 movement for Azerbaijani autonomy.[57]

It is often assumed that the majority of Iranian Armenians began to identify more closely with an exclusive Armenian nationalism rather than a more inclusive Iranian nationalism, influenced by World War I refugees swelling the ranks of the community, the establishment of an independent republic from 1918 to 1920, and the continued existence of a republic in the Soviet Union.[58] The majority of Iranian Armenians of the mid-twentieth century, however, had no direct link to Armenia. It is very probable that while Armenia may have been the ideal homeland and while Iranian Armenians may have desired a Soviet-free Armenia, the first priority of most was not the liberation of the ideal homeland but the preservation and prosperity of their own community. Iran was the real home and in daily life identity was linked intimately with the Iranian reality. Although diaspora is generally seen as a transitory place of existence until the inevitable return to the homeland, for average Iranian Armenians, Iran bore a sense of permanence. This was not the case perhaps with the more politicized smaller segment of the Iranian Armenian population—those who participated in Armenian political parties whose main goal remained liberation, to different degrees, of the Armenian homeland. For these parties, a different situation and reality may have existed, one in which they were more closely linked to a national Armenian identity. For most, including the political parties, it became more important to maintain the Iranian Armenian community rather than to sacrifice it for interests elsewhere. Identification with an Armenian dream and an Iranian reality demonstrates that the compound identity that Iranian Armenians experienced and forged for themselves continued to develop well into the twentieth century, although it may not have been as fluid and was bound by more limitations. Moreover, the Iranian policy of centralization, homogenization, and nationalism had a double effect on Iranian Armenian identity as both Pahlavi shahs attempted to integrate the community into the larger Iranian sphere by taking away some rights and privileges. The Pahlavi language and school policy or even integration of Armenian boy scouts into a newly created broader Iranian scouting system resulted in a dual effect. While Iranian Armenians may have resented and objected to forced Iranicization, forced integration may have reduced feelings or the reality of marginalization and elicited inclusion in the wider Iranian society. Moreover, for Iranian nationalists seeking to forge a direct link to the pre-Islamic ancient past and a modern uniform national identity, "Armenians provided an unbroken cultural bond to their Aryan past."[59] The Iranian Constitutional Revolution, however, was

the first and last time any Armenian political party would commit its re-
sources and its members with such vigor and sacrifice to a cause other
than the one encompassing the ideal or real Armenian homeland.

Notes

1. W. Morgan Shuster, *The Strangling of Persia* (New York: Century, 1912), 254,
259, 267; V. A. Bayburdyan, *Turk-Iranakan haraberutiunnere, 1900–1914 tt.* [Turko-
Iranian relations, 1900–1914] (Yerevan: Haykakan SSH Gitutiunneri Akademia,
1974), 279.

2. Ibid., 206, 212, 269. Evacuation of Ottoman forces did not take place until
November 1912. See 329.

3. Cosroe Chaqueri [Khosrow Shakeri], *Asnad-e tarikh-e jonbesh-e kargari/sosial
demokrasi va komunisti-ye Iran* [Documents of the history of the labor/social democratic and communist movement in Iran] (Tehran: Padzahr, 1985), 19: 67–68,
72–73.

4. Alek [Galstian], 9 December 1911, in A[ndre] Amurian, *Dashnaktsutiun,
Yeprem, parskakan sahmanadrutiun, H. H. D. kendronakan arkhiv* [A. R. Federation,
Yeprem, Iranian constitution, A. R. F. central archives] (Tehran: Alik, 1976), 1:
391–92. Dashnakists referred to the ultimatum as not merely Russian but "Rus-
sian-British." See, for example, idem; Shahstan [Tehran] Central Committee to
Azerbaijan Central Committee, 22 September 1912, Archives of the Armenian
Revolutionary Federation [Dashnaktsutiun], Watertown, Massachusetts, file 589,
document 38.

5. See, for example, Azerbaijan Central Committee to Western Bureau, 1 December 1911, 478/125; Azerbaijan Central Committee to Shah [Tehran] Committee, 17 December 1911, 478/127; Azerbaijan Committee to Western Bureau, 21 December 1911, 478/128.

6. See Tigran Devoyiants, "Kiankis drvagnerits" [Episodes from my life],
Hayrenik Amsagir 22, 1 (January–February 1944): 84. See also note 8. For a similar
view, see H[ayrapet] Panirian, "Hayrapet Paniriani usherits" [From the memoirs
of Hayrapet Panirian], *Hayranik Amsagir* 31, 2 (February 1953): 79.

7. See Hovak Stepanian, "Nikol Duman (mahvan 15-amiaki artiv)" [Nikol Duman (on the occasion of the 15th anniversary of his death)], *Hayrenik Amsagir* 8, 12
(October 1930): 160.

8. See, for example, Report of Azerbaijan Central Committee, 1911–1913,
480/23; Azerbaijan Committee to Western Bureau, 21 December 1911, 478/128;
Alek [Galstian?] to *Azatamart* [Battle for Freedom, Istanbul], 14 December 1911, in
Amurian, *Arkhiv*, 1: 388–90; Stepan Stepanian to Karo, 6 January 1912, 479/1;
Minutes of Azerbaijan Central Committee, 1910–1913, 540g/1.

9. Report of Shahstan Central Committee, 16 October 1911 to 20 April 1913,
592/2.

10. Report of Gilan Committee, 3 December 1910 to December 1913, 592/5.

11. Report of Azerbaijan Central Committee, 1911–1913, 480/23.

12. Zakarian then went to Germany, where in 1921 he served as translator to
Soghomon Tehlirian who was on trial in Berlin for Talat Paşa's assassination.

13. Gaghazan [?] General Situation, n.d., 592/16; Minutes of Shahstan Central Committee First Regional Congress, Session 6, 1 June 1913, 592/8; Shahstan Central Committee to Eastern Bureau, 14 March 1912, 589/7; Report of Gilan Committee, 3 December 1910 to December 1913, 592/5; Shahstan Central Committee to Azerbaijan Central Committee, 22 September 1912, 589/38.

14. Report of Azerbaijan Central Committee, 1911–1913, 480/23; Azerbaijan Central Committee to Western Bureau, 2 September 1912, 479/33; Azerbaijan Central Committee to Western Bureau, 24 May 1912, 479/21.

15. Report of Shah City [Tehran] Committee, 1 May 1913 to 31 May 1914, 594/12; Shahstan Region Self-Defense Body, 17 October 1914, 593/77; Azerbaijan Central Committee to Vrezh [Tabriz] Committee, 28 October 1914, 481/11; Gilan Committee Fifth Regional Congress, 20 March 1914, 592/5; Report of Shah City Committee, 1 May 1913 to 31 May 1914, 594/12.

16. See, for example, Isahak Ter Zakarian to Yeprem, 29 May 1909, 1728g/92, also in Amurian, *Arkhiv*, 1: 351–55; Isahak Ter Zakarian to Yeprem, n.d., 1728g/97, also 365–67. Ter Zakarian was mostly concerned about the sacrifices made by Armenian soldiers who, he felt, were not sufficiently appreciated by Iranian constitutionalists.

17. Tehran Committee Circular, 26 July 1911, 587/35. See also Tehran Committee Circular to Dashnakist Soldiers, 4 August 1911, 587/37; Tehran Committee Circular to Iranian Nation, n.d., 588/95. The latter, although undated, specifically addresses the threat of Mohammad Ali Shah's return and the need to fight.

18. Sixth General Congress, 17 August to 17 September 1911, 1542/37.

19. For self-defense issue, see, for example, 584/39; 540b/2/3; 638/8; 533b/3; 1728g/70/165; Report of Khoy, 1906–1909, 476/67; 587/21; 587/43; 1728d/18; 586/36/39; 1728a/30; 1728b/36; 1728g/29/103/169/170/183; 478/58. For conservative anti-Armenian elements specifically, see 584/15/24; 1728g/28/29/ 103/183/185; 1728d/18. For Armenian anti-constitutionalist elements, see 628/8 session 37, 21 May 1910.

20. Tehran Central Committee Circular, 22 March 1912, in Amurian, *Arkhiv*, 1: 119–20.

21. Shahstan Central Committee Circular, 30 March 1912, 589/10.

22. Yeprem [Khan] and Hovsep [Mirzayan] to Western Bureau, 21 March 1912, 589/8.

23. Shahstan Central Committee to Western Bureau, 28 April 1912, 589/18. Hovhannisan also refers to unsuccessful meetings of reconciliation called by the bureau to put a stop to the dissension, although he refers to it in the context of the general tensions regarding Yeprem's role as police chief. See Hovsep Hovhannisian, *Husher* [Memoirs] (Yerevan: Alobon, 1995), 260–61.

24. Report of Shahstan Central Committee, 16 October 1911 to 20 April 1913, 592/2; Shahstan Central Committee to Eastern Bureau, 14 March 1912, 589/7.

25. Mehdi Malekzadeh, *Tarikh-e enqelab-e mashrutiyat-e Iran* [History of the constitutional revolution of Iran] (Tehran: Soqrat, 1949–1953), 6: 239; Report of Shahstan Central Committee, 16 October 1911 to 20 April 1913, 592/2; Shahstan Central Committee to Eastern Bureau, 14 March 1912, 589/7. See also Shahstan Central Committee to Eastern Bureau, 14 March 1912, 589/7, where the Tehran Central Committee accuses Yeprem Khan of breaking up meetings in schools and

being the first in the Iranian government to subject Armenian "cultural" elements to the government.

26. Tehran Army Dashnakist Organization of Soldiers, March 1912, 590/5, also published in *Droshak*, no. 5, May 1912.

27. It is not clear how Keri and Khecho stood on these issues, except for a note by Tehran Central Committee member N. Hanguyts [Nikol Aghbalian] stating that Yeprem and Keri were fighting for the government and had declared the revolutionary struggle over. See Shahstan Central Committee to Vrezhstan [Azerbaijan] Central Committee, 6 April 1912, 589/14.

28. Minutes of Responsible Meeting, Session 1, 26 April 1912, 589/23.

29. Ibid., Session 2, 27 April 1912. See also Shahstan Central Committee to Western Bureau, 28 April 1912, 589/18.

30. Minutes of Responsible Meeting, Session 3, 1 May 1912.

31. Report of Shahstan Central Committee, 16 October 1911 to 20 April 1913, 592/2; Shahstan Central Committee to Western Bureau, 28 April 1912, 589/18.

32. Only an Armenian text of the cabinet's letter could be found, dated Jamadi-ye avval 1330/1912, signed by President Samsan al-Saltaneh, Foreign Minister Vosuq al-Dowleh, Interior Minister Qavam al-Saltaneh, War Minister Sardar Mohtashem, Finance Minister Mohtashem al-Saltaneh, and Education Minister Hakim al-Molk see Minutes of Responsible Meeting, Session 3, 1 May 1912.

33. Azerbaijan Central Committee to Shahstan Central Committee, 10 May 1912, 479/18; Report of Shahstan Central Committee, 16 October 1911 to 20 April 1913, 592/2.

34. Ervand Abrahamian, *Iran Between Two Revolutions* (Princeton: Princeton University Press, 1982), 111.

35. Shahstan Central Committee to Western Bureau, 28 April 1912, 589/18; Azerbaijan Central Committee to Shah Central Committee, 9 April 1912, 479/16. Dashnakists had expressed concern over the use of the Dashnakist name even earlier in the battles against Mohammad Ali Shah's coup. They wanted Mirzayan and Dr. Stepanian to find out under what flag Armenian soldiers would be fighting. See, for example, Minutes of Shah Committee, 15 September 1909–7 October 1911, Session 57, 16 July 1911, 628/2; Shah Committee Report, 7 July–10 October 1911, 587/47. The Democrat Party must have been aware of the conflict between Yeprem, his men, and Dashnakist leaders as they requested to know whether Yeprem acted with the approval and consent of the party. See Minutes of Shah Committee, 15 September 1909–7 October 1911, Session 54, 15 March 1911, 628/2. The Dashnaktsutiun, however, wanted to keep the existing conflict internal and therefore did not publicize the great rift between Yeprem and the party. See Minutes of Shahstan Central Committee First Regional Congress, Session 5, 29 May 1913, 592/8.

36. Farro [Hovsep Hovhannisian], comp., "Yepremi gortsuneutiune Parskastanum (Grishayi hushere)" [Yeprem's activity in Persia (Grisha's memoirs)], *Hayrenik Amsagir* 3, 6 (April 1925): 90–93; H. Elmar [Hovsep Hovhannisian], *Yeprem* (Tehran: Modern, 1964), 529–36; Ahmad Kasravi, *Tarikh-e hijdah saleh-ye Azerbaijan* [The eighteen-year history of Azerbaijan] (Tehran: Amir Kabir, 1967), 2: 510–22. Grisha Khan's memoirs also appeared in *Arshaluys* (Twilight, Tehran, 1912). Extracts of it may be found in Isma'il Ra'in, *Yeprem Khan-e Sardar* [Com-

mander Yeprem Khan] (Tehran: Zarin, 1971), 439–42, and Kasravi, *Tarikh-e hijdah saleh*, 2: 518–22.

37. See, for example, Azerbaijan Central Committee to *Droshak*, 24 May 1912, 1728e/43.

38. Decisions of First Regional Congress, Tehran, 9 September to 6 December 1912, 479/46 and 1728d/72. See also Azerbaijan Central Committee to Western Bureau, 2 September 1912, 479/33; Minutes of Shahstan Central Committee First Regional Congress, Session 7, 4 June 1913, 592/8.

39. Shahstan Central Committee Circular to Comrades, November 1912, 479/42 and 1729/15, also in Amurian, *Arkhiv*, 1: 120–22. For a draft of the text, see 589/45. For the Persian text, see Zihajjah 1330/November 1912, 478/135.

40. For the text of the decision, see Elmar [Hovsep Hovhannisian], *Yeprem*, 123–24, and *Droshak*, 9–10, September–October 1913.

41. Getap [Julfa] Subcommittee to Shahstan Central Committee, 10 January 1913, 591/5.

42. Shahstan Central Committee to Comrades, 6 December 1912, 589/53.

43. Mirzayan to Shahstan Central Committee, 9 December 1912, 590/60.

44. Minutes of Shahstan Central Committee Regional Congress, Session 9, 8 June 1913, 592/8. See also Shahstan Central Committee to Mirzayan, 12 August 1913, 627a/10; Mirzayan to *Droshak*, 15 September 1913, 627a/15; Report of Shahstan Central Committee, 16 October 1911 to 20 April 1913, 592/2. According to Hovhannisian, Mirzayan was not able to regain his good standing with the Dashnakists after this incident. See Hovhannisian, *Husher*, 312.

45. Mirzayan to *Droshak*, 15 September 1913, 627a/15. According to Panirian, Mirzayan continued to stay away until 1918/1919 even after the Dashnaktsutiun called him back into the party. Later, when Mirzayan requested to come back, the party refused. In addition, Panirian accuses Mirzayan of working against the party. See Panirian, "Hayrapet Paniriani Husherits," *Hayranik Amsagir* 31, 3 (March 1953). According to Hovhannisian, years later, two months before his death, Mirzayan requested to meet with his former comrades Hovhannisian and Aleksan Hovhannisian. Hovhannisian reports that the conversation revolved around Mirzayan's problems with the party. Mirzayan described the problems as emotionally devastating; he felt he had been betrayed by comrades and that the actions of certain comrades were reprehensible and that he was undeserving of them. He also added that he was always a Dashnakist, had remained one, and would die one. See Hovhannisian, *Husher*, 390–92. Hovhannisian also accused Mirzayan of questionable tactics during Majles elections in which Mirzayan, although not the candidate of the Dashnaktsusiun, won a seat. See 312.

46. Shahstan Central Committee to Eastern Bureau, 24 October 1913, 591/92; Azerbaijan Central Committee to Shahstan Central Committee, 25 September 1913, 480/18. See also Azerbaijan Central Committee to Shahstan Central Committee, 5 September 1913, 480/15; Azerbaijan Central Committee to Shahstan Central Committee, 15 September 1913, 480/15.

47. Minutes of Shahstan Central Committee First Regional Congress, Session 11, 12 June 1913, 592/8; Shahstan Central Committee to Eastern Bureau, 24 October 1913, 591/92; Azerbaijan Central Committee to Shahstan Central Committee,

25 September 1913, 480/18. See also Report of Shah City Committee, 1 May 1913 to 31 May 1914, 594/12.

48. Shahstan Central Committee to Eastern Bureau, 17 November 1913, 592/99.

49. Shahstan Central Committee Circular, 19 June 1914, 593/57. See also Shahstan Central Committee Circular, n.d., 593/121; Political Report of Shahstan to Eastern Bureau, 29 January 1914, 503/15.

50. Minutes of Shahstan Second Regional Congress, 6 June 1914, 594/13.

51. For a study on this subject, see Magdalena Golnazarian, "Les Arméniens d'azerbaïdjan iranien pendant la première guerre mondiale," presented at the International Round Table "La Perse et la Grande Guerre", Tehran, 2–3 March 1997. See also Panirian, "Hayrapet Paniriani husherits," *Hayranik Amsagir* 31, 4 (April 1953): 85–94 and 31, 5 (May 1953): 73–79; Hovhannisian, *Husher*, 343–49.

52. For the beginning of such considerations by Dashnakist bodies in Iran, see Azerbaijan Central Committee to Western Bureau, 2 September 1912, 479/33.

53. Richard G. Hovannisian, Armenia on the Road to Independence, 1918 (Berkley and Los Angeles: University of California Press, 1967), 43–44.

54. See, for example, Richard G. Hovannisian, ed., *The Armenian Genocide in Perspective* (New Brunswick and London: Transaction Publishers, 1986); Richard G. Hovannisian, ed., *The Armenian Genocide: History, Politics, Ethics* (New York: St. Martin's Press, 1992); Vahakn Dadrian, *The History of the Armenian Genocide: Ethnic Conflict from the Balkans to Anatolia to the Caucasus* (Providence: Berghahn Books, 1995).

55. Some Dashnakists became rather bitter about the whole experience, regretting their participation. Giulkhandanian recounts the words of a Dashnakist facing the loss of a comrade in the revolution. "The whole of the revolutionary movement of the Persian people is not worth one Martiros." See, for example, A[braham] Giulkhandanian, *Hay-Tatarakan endharumnere* [Armeno-Tatar Clashes], vol. 1, *Bakui arajin endharumnere* [Baku's first clashes] (Paris: Typographie Franco-Caucasienne, 1933), 71.

56. Abrahamian, *Iran Between Two Revolutions*, 116.

57. Ibid., 386–88. For a biography of Sultanzadeh, see Cosroe Chaqueri, "Sultanzade: The Forgotten Revolutionary Theoretician of Iran: A Biographical Sketch." *Iranian Studies*, 17, 2–3 (Spring–Summer 1984): 215–35.

58. There is a lack of research and study on the process by which nationalism spread to the country's many linguistic and religious minorities in the twentieth century. According to David Yaghoubian, a Ph.D. candidate in history at UC Berkeley whose research and study focus on bringing together broad theories of nationalism with the everyday reality of Iranian Armenians who held diverse allegiances and layered identities that included, in addition to an Armenian identity, a strong sense of Iranian identity "Armenians are categorized as an ancient people with links to an historic homeland and a religio-linguistic heritage too strong to allow for another or even a mixed national identity." Yaghoubian demonstrates that the contrary is true, that "many Armenians developed a strong sense of Iranian identity and in fact played and continue to play an important role in the development of Iranian nationalism. " See David N. Yaghoubian, Draft

Introduction of "Ethnicity, Identity and the Development of Nationalism in Iran," Ph.D. Dissertation, University of California, Berkeley, forthcoming.

59. R. Hrair Dekmejian, "The Armenian Diaspora," in *The Armenian People from Ancient Times to Modern Times*, vol. 2: *Foreign Dominion to Statehood: The Fifteenth Century to the Twentieth Century*, ed. Richard G. Hovannisian (New York: St. Martin's Press, 1997), 422.

Bibliography

Primary Sources

Archives of the Armenian Revolutionary Federation [Dashnaktsutiun], Watertown, Massachusetts.

Mozakerat-e Majles [Parliamentary debates]. 4 vols. 1906–1911.

Collected Primary Documents

Afshar, Iraj, ed. *Awraq-e tazehyab-e mashrutiyat va naqsh-e Taqizadeh* [Newly found constitutional papers and the role of Taqizadeh]. Tehran: Bahman, 1980.

Amurian [Ter Ohanian], A[ndre]. *Dashnaktsutiun, Yeprem, parskakan sahmanadrutiun, H. H. D. kendronakan arkhiv* [A. R. Federation, Yeprem, Persian constitution, A. R .F. central archives]. 2 vols. Tehran: Alik, 1976–1979.

Chaqueri, Cosroe [Shakeri, Khosrow], comp. and ed. *Asnad-e tarikh-e jonbesh-e kargari/sosial demokrasi va komunisti-ye Iran* [Documents of the history of the labor/social democratic and communist movement in Iran]. 22 vols. Tehran: Padzahr Publ., 1983–1993.

———. comp. and ed. *La Social-démocratie en Iran: articles et documents*. Florence: Mazdak, 1979.

Dasnabedian, Hratch [Tasnapetian, Hrach], comp. and ed., *Niuter H. H. Dashnaktsutian patmutian hamar* [Materials for the history of the A. R. Federation]. 4 vols. Beirut: Hamazgayin, 1972–1982.

Revolyutsion kocher yev trutsikner, 1902–1921 [Revolutionary proclamations and flyers]. Yerevan: Hayastani Petakan Hratarakchutyun, 1960.

Vratsian, S[imon], ed. *Divan H. H. Dashnaktsutian* [Records of the A. R. Federation]. 2 vols. Boston: H. H. D. Amerikian Komite, 1934–1938.

Newspapers

Droshak [Banner] (Geneva)
Hnchak [Bell] (London)
Mshak [Cultivator] (Tiflis)
Murch [Hammer] (Tiflis)
Yeritasard Hayastan [Young Armenia] (New York)

Other Primary and Secondary Sources

Armenian

Abgariants, Tigran T. *Nor Jughayi angir grakanutiun* [New Julfa's oral literature]. Tehran: Modern, 1966.

_____. *Nor-Jughayi azg[ayin] tatrone, 1888–1913* [New Julfa's national theater]. New Julfa: S. Amenabrkichian Vank, 1913.

_____. *Nor-Jughayi dprotsnere* [New Julfa's schools]. New Julfa: S. Amenabrkichian Vank, 1914.

Abrahamyan, A. G. *Hamarot urvagits hay gaghtavaireri patmutian* [Brief outline of the history of Armenian colonies]. 2 vols. Yerevan: Hayastan, 1964–1967.

Acharyan, Hr[achia]. *Kyankis husherits* [Memoirs of my life]. Yerevan: Mitk, 1967.

Achemian, Hayk. *Patmutiun Aramian azgayin dprotsi: hariuramiay hobeliani artiv, 1835–1935* [History of the Aramian national school: on the 100th anniversary jubilee, 1835–1935]. Tabriz: Atrpatakani Hayots Temakan Tparan, 1936.

Aghayan, Ts. P. *Revolyutsion sharzhumnere Hayastanum, 1905–1907 t.t.* [Revolutionary movements in Armenia, 1905–1907]. Yerevan: Haykakan SSR Gitutyunneri Akademia, 1955.

Aghayan, Ts. P., B. N. Arakelyan, et al. *Hay zhoghovrdi patmutyun* [History of the Armenian people]. 8 vols. Yerevan: Haykakan SSH Gitutyunneri Akademia, 1967–1984.

Aknuni, E. [Khachatur Malumian]. *Boghoki dzayn: kovkasahay kaghakakan bantarkialnere (tsarakan halatsanki mi ej)* [The voice of protest: Caucasian Armenian political prisoners (a page from tsarist persecution)]. Beirut: Ghukas Karapetian, 1978.

Alpoyachian, Arshak. *Patmutiun hay gaghtakanutian: Hayeru tsrvume ashkharhi zanazan masere* [History of Armenian migration: the dispersion of Armenians to various parts of the world]. 3 vols. Cairo: Nor Astgh, 1941–1961.

Amurian [Ter Ohanian], A[ndre], ed. *Heghapokhakan Yepremi vodisakane* [Revolutionary Yeprem's odyssey]. Tehran: Alik, 1972.

_____. *H. H. Dashnaktsutiune Parskastanum, 1890–1918* [The A. R. Federation in Persia, 1890–1918]. Tehran: Alik, 1950.

Ananun, D. "Hnchakyanneri harume Rusastani heghapokhutyan u Sotsialismin" [The Hnchakists' blow to Russia's revolution and socialism]. *Nork* 2 (Jan.–March 1923): 274–315.

_____. *Rusahayeri hasarakakan zarkatsume* [The social development of Russian Armenians]. 3 vols. Venice: S. Ghazaru, 1926.

Arakelian, H. *Parskastani Hayere: nrants antsiale, nerkan yev apagan* [Persia's Armenians: their past, present and future]. Vienna: Mkhitarian, 1911.

Astghuni, G. [Yeghikian, Grigor]. "Chshmartutiunner Parskastani heghapokhakan sharzhumneri masin (akanatesi hishoghutiunnerits)" [Truths about the Persian revolutionary movements (from the memoirs of an eyewitness)]. *Yeritasard Hayastan* 9, 33 (13 May 1913)–9, 50 (9 September 1913).

_____. "Inchpes kazmvets Parskastani S. D. Kusaktsutiune" [How Persia's S. D. Party was organized]. In *Hushardzan nvirvats Sotsial Demokrat Hnchakian Kusaktsutian karasunamiakin* [Commemorative volume dedicated to the fortieth anniversary of the Hnchakian Party], ed. S. D. Hnchakian Kusaktsutian Fransayi Shrjan. Paris: H. B. Tiurapian, 1930.

Avagyan, Nazik. *Haykakan zhoghovrdakan taraze (XIV d.–XX d. skizb)* [Armenian popular dress (from the 14th century to the beginning of the 20th century)]. Yerevan: Haykakan SSH Gitutyunneri Akademia, 1983.

Balian Ter-Hakobian, Babken and Seta. *Patmutiun Iranahayeri* [History of Iranian Armenians]. Glendale: Alco, 1985.

Barkhudaryan, V. B., and D. A. Muradyan. *Hayastani ashkhatavorner tsarizmi dem mghats hamazhoghovrdakan paykarum (1905–1907)* [Armenia's workers in the popular struggle against tsarism]. Yerevan: Haykakan SSH Gitutyunneri Akademia, 1988.

Bayburdyan, V. A. *Turk-Iranakan haraberutiunnere, 1900–1914 tt.* [Turko-Iranian relations, 1900–1914]. Yerevan: Haykakan SSH Gitutyunneri Akademia, 1974.

Darbinian, Artak. *Hay azatakrakan sharzhman oreren (husher 1890–1940)* [From the days of the Armenian liberation movement (memoirs 1890–1940)]. Paris: Araks Topalian Brothers, 1947.

Dasnabedian, Hratch [Tasnapetian, Hrach]. *H. H. Dashnaktsutiune ir kazmutenen minjev Zh. endhanur zhoghov (1890–1924)* [A. R. Federation from its formation to the Tenth General Congress (1890–1924)]. Athens: Droshak, 1988.

_____, ed. *Rostom: mahvan vatsunamiakin artiv* [Rostom: On the occasion of the sixtieth anniversary of his death]. Beirut: Hamazgayin Vahe Setian, 1979.

Davrizhetsi, Arakel. *Hayots patmutiun* [Armenian history]. Vagharshapat, 1896.

_____. *Girk patmutiants* [Book of history]. Yerevan: Matenadaran, 1990.

Demirchian, Vardan. *Divan Atrpatakani Hayots patmutian* [Records of the history of Azerbaijani Armenians]. Tabriz, Tehran: Nurbakhsh, 1966.

Devoyiants, Tigran. "Kiankis drvagnerits" [Episodes from my life]. *Hayrenik Amsagir* 22, 1 (January–February 1944): 77–90.

Elmar, H [Hovhannisian, Hovsep]. *H. H. Dashnaktsutiune yev Parsits sahmanadrakan sharzhume* [A. R. Federation and the Persian constitutional movement]. *Hayrenik Amsagir* 30, 1 (January 1952)–30, 3 (March 1952).

_____. *Yeprem.* Tehran: Modern, 1964.

Farro [Hovhannisian, Hovsep], comp. "Yepremi gortsuneutiune Parskastanum (Grishayi hushere)" [Yeprem's activity in Persia (Grisha's memoirs)]. *Hayrenik Amsagir* 3, 1 (November 1924)–3, 7 (May 1925).

Frangian, E. [Yervand]. *Atrpatakan* [Azerbaijan]. Tiflis: Hermes, 1905.

Galstyan, S. A. *Aknarkner ashkharhabari patmutyan* [Glances at the history of the vernacular Armenian]. Yerevan: Haykakan SSR Gitutyunneri Akademia, 1963.

Galust. "Chanaparhordutian Parskastanum (Tavrizits depi Urmia)" [Travel in Persia (from Tabriz to Urmieh)]. *Murch* 18, 11–12 (November–December 1906): 11–42.

Gandzaketsi, Kirakos. *Patmutiun Hayots* [History of the Armenians]. Yerevan: Haykakan SS HA Hrat., 1961.

Gangruni, Hrand. *Hay heghapokhutiune Osmanian brnatirutian dem (1890–1910)* [The Armenian revolution against Ottoman despotism (1890–1910)]. Beirut: n.p., 1973.

Giulkhandanian, A[braham]. *Hay-Tatarakan endharumnere* [The Armeno-Tatar clashes]. 2 vols. Paris: Typographie Franco-Caucasienne, 1933.

_____. *Heghapokhakan Hayhuyiner* [Revolutionary Armenian women]. Paris: Araks, 1939.

Goroyiants, Nazar H. *Parskastani Hayere: patmakan, teghagrakan yev vijakagrakan hamarot teghekutiunner Parskastani Hayeri masin amenahin zhamanaknere minjev 1898 t.* [Persia's Armenians: Brief historical, demographic and statistical information about Persia's Armenians from the most ancient times to the year 1898]. Tehran: Modern, 1968.

Hachian, H. [Kahana]. *Hay yev Parsik barekamutiune* [Armenian and Persian friendship]. Tehran: Modern, 1945.

Hakobyan, Hovhannes. *Aghbyurner Hayastani yev Andrkovkasi patmutyan: ughegrutiunner* [Sources for the history of Armenia and the Caucasus: travel writings]. Yerevan: Melkonyan, 1932.

Hakovbiants, Iskuhi. "Tavrizi Hay gaghuti antsialits" [From the past of the Tabriz Armenian community]. *Hayrenik Amsagir* 35, 11 (November 1957): 90–100.

_____. "Tumaniantsneri entanike" [The Tumanian family]. *Hayrenik Amsagir* 44, 1 (January 1966)–44, 4 (April 1966).

_____. "Yeghbayrk Tumaniantsnere." [The Tumanian brothers]. *Hayrenik Amsagir* 43, 9 (September 1965): 1–11.

Hambaryan, A. S. *Yeritturkeri azgayin u hoghayin kaghakakanutyune yev azatagrakan sharzhumnern arevmtyan Hayastanum (1908–1914)* [The national and territorial policy of the Young Turks and the liberation movements in Western Armenia (1908–1914)]. Yerevan: Haykakan SSH Gitutyunneri Akademia, 1979.

Hanguyts, N. [Nikol Aghbalian], comp. "Samsoni jushere" [Samson's memoirs]. *Hayrenik Amsagir* 1, 10 (August 1923)–2, 10 (August 1924).

Harutyunyan, G. *Revolyutsyon sharzhumnere Hayastanum 1905–1907 tt.* [Revolutionary movements in Armenia, 1905–1907]. Yerevan: Hayastani Petakan Hratarakchutyun, 1956.

Hay hegh[apokhakan] kusaktsutiunnere [Armenian revolutionary parties]. Trans. from the Turkish. n.p., 1916.

Hayrik, comp. "Heghapokhakan banaki arshave Tehrani vray yev Yepremi gndi dere (khmbapeti hushere)" [March of the revolutionary army on Tehran and the role of Yeprem's regiment (memoirs of the commander)], *Hayrenik Amsagir* 3, 7 (May 1925): 26–38.

Herardian, M. *Azgayin sahmanadrutiun* [National Constitution]. Antilias: Tparan Katoghikosutian Hayots Metsi Tann Kilikioy, 1959.

H. H. Dashnaktsutiun. *Heghapokhakan dashn: mijkusaktsayin khorhrdazhoghovneri voroshumnere* [Revolutionary pact: decisions of the interparty conference]. Geneva: Droshak Tparan, 1905.

Hovhannisian, Hovsep. *Husher* [Memoirs]. Yerevan: Abolon, 1995.

Injikyan, H. G., ed. *Merdzavor yev Mijin Arevelki yerkrner yev zhoghovurdner* [Countries and peoples of the Near and Middle East], vol. 8, *Iran*. Yerevan: Haykakan SSH Gitutyunneri Akademia, 1975.

Jughayetsi, Khachatur. *Patmutiun Parsits* [History of the Persians]. Vagharshapat: Tparan Mayr Atoroy Srpoy Ejmiatsni, 1905.

Khachikyan, Sh. L. *Nor Jughayi hay vajarakanutyune yev nra arevtratntesakan kapere Rusastani het XVII–XVIII darerum* [New Julfa Armenian trade and its commercial economic ties with Russia in the 17th–18th centuries]. Yerevan: Haykakan SSH Gitutyunneri Akademia, 1988.

Khan-Azat, Ruben. "Hay heghapokhakani husherits" [From the memoirs of an Armenian revolutionary], *Hayrenik Amsagir* 5, 9 (July 1927)–7, 7 (May 1929).

Kitur, Arsen. *Patmutiun S. D. Hnchakian Kusaktsutian* [History of the S. D. Hnchakian Party]. 2 vols. Beirut: Shirak Press, 1962.

Kretatsi, Abraham [Catholicos of Armenia]. *Patmutiun hamarhot harhaji zhamanakn Nadr Shahin* [Brief history of the first period of Nadr Shah]. Yerevan, 1973.

Lastiverttsi, Aristakes. *Patmutiun Aristakes Lastiverttsvo* [Aristakes Lastiverttsi's History]. Venice, 1901.

Lazian, G[abriel], ed. *Hayastan yev hay date est dashnagreru* [Armenia and the Armenian cause according to treaties]. Cairo: Tparan Husaber, 1942.

_____. *Hayastan yev hay date: Hayevrus haraberutiunneru luysin tak* [Armenia and the Armenian cause: under the light of Armeno-Russian relations]. Cairo: Tparan Husaber, 1957.

_____, ed. *Hayastan yev hay date (vaveragrer)* [Armenia and the Armenian question (documents)]. Cairo: Husaber, 1946.

_____. *Hayhuyin yev hay heghapokhutiune* [The Armenian woman and the Armenian revolution]. Cairo: Tparan Husaber, 1959.

_____. *Heghapokhakan demker (mtavorakanner, haydukner)* [Revolutionary figures (intellectuals, hayduks)]. Cairo: Tbaran Nupar, 1945.

Leo [A. Babakhanian]. *Tiurkahay heghapokhutian gaghaparabanutiune* [The ideology of the Turkish Armenian revolution]. 2 vols. Paris: Pahri Yeghbarts, 1934–1935.

Levonyan, Garegin, comp. *Hayots parberakan mamule: liakatar tsutsak hay Iragrutyan skzbits minjev mer orere (1794–1934)* [The Armenian periodical press: complete list from the beginning of Armenian journalism to our days (1794–1934)]. Yerevan: Hratarakutyun Melkonyan Fondi, 1934.

Lima, Gregory. *Hayuhin yev ir taraznere* [The Armenian woman and her costumes]. Tehran: International Communicators, 1974[?].

Malkhas [Artashes Hovsepian]. *Aprumner* [Life experiences]. Boston: Hayrenik, 1931.

Mamikonian, K. A. *Hay Sotsial-Demokratneri miutyune (1902–1903)* [The union of Armenian Social Democrats (1902–1903)]. Yerevan: Hayastan, 1969.

Manikian, Hakob. *Hushamatian Hay Heghapokhakan Dashnaktsutian: Albom-Atlas* [Memory Book of the Armenian Revolutionary Federation: Album-Atlas]. Vol. 1, Dutsaznamart, 1890–1914 [The Heroic Battle]. Los Angeles: Hay Heghapokhakan Dashnaktsutian Arermtian Amerikayi: Kendronakan Komite, 1992.

Martuni, Al [A. Measnikian]. *Kusaktsutiunnere gaghutahayutian mej* [Parties in the Armenia diaspora]. Berlin, 1925.

Metsobetsi, Tovma. *Patmutiun Lank-Temuray yev hajordats iurots* [History of Timur Leng and his successors]. Paris: I Gortsatan K. V. Shahnazarian, 1860.

Mikayelian, K. "Bekorner im husherits" [Fragments from my memories], *Hayrenik Amsagir* 2, 10 (August 1924): 54–62.

Minasian, L[evon] G. *Nor Jughayi tparann u ir tpagrats grkere (1636–1972)* [New Julfa's library and its published books (1636–1972)]. New Julfa: S. Amenaprkchian Vank, 1972.

_____. *Patmutiun Periayi Hayeri (1606–1956)* [History of Fereydan's Armenians, 1606–1956]. Antilias, Lebanon: Tparan Katoghikosutian Hayots Metsi Tann Kilikio, 1971.

Muradyan, D. A. *Hayastane rusakan arajin revolutsutsiayi tarinerin (1905–1907)* [Armenia in the years of the first Russian revolution (1905–1907)]. Yerevan: Haykakan SSR Gitutyunneri Akademia, 1964.

Najaryan, H. Kh. *Turk-Iranakan haraberutiunnere XVI darum u XVII dari arajin kesin yev hayastane* [Turko-Iranian relations in the 16th and the first half of the 17th century and Armenia]. Yerevan: Yerevani Hamalsaran, 1961.

Odabashian, Nikol. "Im kianki patmutiune" [My life story]. *Hayrenik Amsagir* 19, 9 (July 1941)–19, 11–12 (September–October 1941).

Pahlevanyan, H. L. *Iranahay hamaynke (1941–1979)* [The Iranian Armenian community]. Yerevan: Haykakan KhSH Gitutyunneri Akademia, 1989.

Panirian, H[ayrapet]. "Hayrapet Paniriani Husherits" [From the memoirs of Hayrapet Panirian]. *Hayrenik Amsagir* 30, 6 (June 1952)–31, 7 (July 1953).

_____. *Heghapokhakan sharzhumnere Parskastanum* [Revolutionary movements in Persia]. Tabriz: Paros, 1917.

Parsamyan, V[ardan] A[ram]. *Hay zhoghovrdi patmutyun (1801–1917 tt.)* [History of the Armenian people (1801–1917)]. 4 vols. Yerevan: Luys, 1963–1970.

_____. *Hay azatagrakan sharzhumneri patmutyunits: usumnasirutyun yev pastatghter* [From the history of the Armenian movements: study and documents]. Yerevan: Haypetdrat, 1958.

_____. *Revolyutsion sharzhumnere hayastanum, 1905–1907 t.t.* [Revolutionary movements in Armenia, 1905–1907]. Yerevan: Petakan Hamalsaran, 1955.

Patrik, Arakel. *Haykakan taraz: hnaguyn zhamanaknerits minjev mer orere* [Armenian costume: from ancient times to our days]. Yerevan: Sovetakan Grogh, 1983.

"Prof. Tokt. Pazil Khan" [Prof. Doct. Basil Khan]. In *Taretsuyts bzhshkakan yev aroghjapahakan* [Medical and hygienic yearbook], ed. Vardan Ghazarian, 25–28. Vol. 1. Istanbul, 1914.

Raffi. *Parskakan patkerner* [Persian images]. Vienna: Mkhitarian Tparan, 1913.

Raffi taregirk [Raffi yearbook]. Tehran: Modern, 1969.

Raffi taregirk [Raffi yearbook]. Tehran: Modern, 1970.

Samson [Stepan Tadeosian]. "Atrpatakani hay kanants gortsuneutiune" [The activity of the Armenian women of Azerbaijan]. *Hayrenik Amsagir* 18, 1 (November 1939): 80–103.

Sarukhan. *Haykakan khndiren yev azgayin sahmanadrutiune Turkiayum. 1860–1910* [The Armenian question and the national constitution in Turkey, 1860–1910]. Tiflis, 1912.

Sots[ial] Dem[okrat] Hnch[akian] Kus[aktsutian] Amer[ikayi] Shrjan. *Hnchakian taregirk (Amerikayi shrjan)* [Hnchakian yearbook (American region)]. Providence, 1931.

S[otsial]-D[emokrat] Hnchakian Kusaktsutian Fransayi Shrjan. *Hushardzan nvirvats Sotsial Demokrat Hnchakian Kusaktsutian karasunamiakin* [Commemorative volume dedicated to the fortieth anniversary of the Hnchakian Party]. Paris: H. B. Tiurapian, 1930.

Stepanian, Hovak. "Nikol Duman (mahvan 15-amiaki artiv)" [Nikol Duman (on the occasion of the 15th anniversary of his death)], *Hayrenik Amsagir* 8, 4 (February 1930)–9, 1 (November 1930).

Teotik. *Amenun taretsuytse* [Everyone's yearbook]. Istanbul: M. Hovakimian, 1922.

Ter Hovhaniants, Harutiun. *Patmutiun Nor Jughayu vor Haspahan* [History of New Julfa and Isfahan]. 2 vols. New Julfa, 1880–1881.

Ter Vardanian, A[leksan], comp. *Hamarot patmutiun Tavrizi Aramian dprotsi vatsunamiaki goyutian* [Brief history of the sixty-year existence of the Tabriz Aramian school]. Tabriz: Paros, 1913.

Urhayetsi, Matteos [Matthew of Edessa]. *Zhamanakagrutiun* [Chronology]. 1898. Yerevan: Petakan Hamalsaran, 1991.

Varandian, Mikayel. *H. H. Dashnaktsutian patmutiun* [History of A. R. Federation]. 2 vols. Cairo: Husaber, 1932–1950.

Vratsian, Simon. "Bagrat Vrd. Tavakaliani namaknere" [Letters of Bagrat Vrd. Tavakalian], *Hayrenik Amsagir*, 12, 1 (November 1933): 103–10.

_____, ed. *Hushapatum H. H. Dashnaktsutian, 1890–1950* [Memorial to the A. R. Federation]. Boston: Hayrenik, 1950.

_____. ed. *Vatsunamiak (1890–1950)* [Sixtieth Year (1890–1950)]. Boston: Hayrenik 1950.

_____. *Nor Jugha* [New Julfa]. New Julfa: S. Amenaprkchian Vank, 1919.

Yedgarian, A[vedis] V. Kah[ana]. *Irani Chaharmahal gavare* [Iran's Chaharmahal province]. Tehran: Ani, 1963.

Yeremian, Aram. *Spahani Peria gavare* [Isfahan's Fereydan province]. New Julfa: S. Amenaprkchian Vank, 1919.

Zeytlian, Sona. *Hay knoj dere hay heghapokhakan sharzhman mej* [The role of the Armenian woman in the Armenian revolutionary movement]. Antilias, Lebanon: Tparan Katoghikosutian Hayots, 1968.

Zhirair, Nayiri. *Hnchakian Kusaktsutiune yev haykakan hoghayin date* [The Hnchakian Party and the Armenian territorial cause]. Beirut: Ararat, 1968.

Persian

Adamiyat, Feridun. *Fekr-e demokrasi ejtema' i dar nehzat-e mashrutiyyat-e Iran* [Social demoratic thought in the constitutional movement of Iran]. Tehran: Payam, 1976.

_____. *Idiolozhi-ye nehzat-e mashrutiyyat-e Iran* [Ideology of the constitutional movement of Iran]. 2 vols. Tehran: Payam, 1976–1991.

Amirkhizi, Isma'il. *Qeyam-e Azerbaijan va Sattar Khan* [The Azerbaijani revolt and Sattar Khan]. Tehran: Tehran Press, 1960.

Amurian [Ter Ohanian], A[ndre]. *Hamasah-e Yeprem* [The epic of Yeprem]. Tehran: Javid Press, 1976.

Bamdad, Badr al-Muluk. *Zanan-e Irani az enqelab-e mashrutiyat ta enqelab-e Sefid* [Women of Iran from the constitutional revolution to the white revolution]. Tehran: Ibn Sina, 1968.

Ettehadieh Nezam Mafi, Mansureh, ed. *Majmu' eh-ye motun va asnad-e tarikhi* [Collection of historical texts and documents]. Vol. 4. Tehran: Naqsh-e Jahan, 1982.

_____. *Paidayesh va tahavvol-e ahzab-e siyasi-ye mashrutiyat: dowreh-ye avval va dovvom-e majles-e showra-ye melli* [Appearance and evolution of political parties of constitutionalism: the first and second period of the National Consultative Assembly]. Tehran: Gostardeh Press, 1982.

Fakhra'i, Ibrahim. *Gilan dar jonbesh-e mashrutiyat* [Gilan in the constitutional movement]. Tehran: Ketabha-ye Jibi, 1974.

Falsafi, Nasr Allah. *Zandegani-ye Shah Abbas Avval* [The life of Shah Abbas the First]. 5 vols. Tehran: Ilmi, 1985.

Kasravi, Ahmad, ed. *Chand tarikhcheh* [A few short histories]. Tehran: Zendegi, 1960.

_____. *Tarikh-e hijdah saleh-ye Azerbaijan* [The eighteen-year history of Azerbaijan]. 2 vols. Tehran: Amir Kabir, 1978.

_____. *Tarikh-e mashruteh-ye Iran* [History of the constitution of Iran]. 2 vols. Tehran: Amir Kabir, 1984.

Kermani, Nazem al-Islam. *Tarikh-e bidari-ye Iran* [History of the awakening of Iran]. 3 vols. Tehran: Khusheh va Sobh-e Emruz, 1967.

Malekzadeh, Mehdi. *Tarikh-e enqelab-e mashrutiyat-e Iran* [History of the constitutional revolution of Iran]. 7 vols. Tehran: Soqrat, 1949–1953.

Maraghah'i, Zein al- 'Abidin. *Siyahatnameh-ye Ibrahim Beik* [Travel account of Ibrahim Bey]. Tehran: Sipideh Press, 1983.

Omid, Hosein. *Tarikh-e farhang-e Azerbaijan* [History of the culture of Azerbaijan]. Vol. 1. Tabriz: Farhang, 1953.

Ra'in, Isma' il. *Anjomanha-ye sirri* [Secret councils]. Tehran: Mosavvar Press, 1966.

_____. *Iranian-e Armani* [Iranian Armenians]. Tehran, 1970.

_____. *Mirza Malkum Khan: zendagi va kusheshha-ye u* [Mirza Malkom Khan: his life and efforts]. Tehran: Safi Ali Shah Press, 1971.

_____. *Yeprem Khan-e Sardar* [Commander Yeprem Khan]. Tehran: Zarin, 1971.

Rafi'i, Mansureh. *Anjoman* [Council]. Tehran: Nashr-e Tarikh-e Iran, 1983.

Roshan, Mohammed, ed. *Mashruteh-ye Gilan az yaddashtha-ye Rabino* [Gilan constitution according to Rabino's memoirs]. Gilan: Haidari, 1973.

Sadr-e Hashemi, Mohammad. *Tarikh-e jara'ed va majallat-e Iran* [The history of newspapers and magazines of Iran]. 4 vols. Isfahan: Kemal, 1984.

Safa'i, Ibrahim. *Rahbaran-e mashruteh* [Leaders of constitution]. 2 vols. Tehran: Javidan Press, 1967.

Sepehr, Abd al-Hosein Khan. *Mer'at al-vaqaye' -e Mozaffari va yaddashtha-ye Malek al-Movarrekhin* [Mirror of events of the Mozaffar period and the memoirs of Malek al-Movarrekhin], ed. Abd al-Hosein Nava'i. Tehran: Zarin, 1989.

Taherzadeh-Behzad, Karim. *Qeyam-e Azerbaijan dar enqelab-e mashrutiyat-e Iran* [The revolt of Azerbaijan in the constitutional revolution of Iran]. Tehran: Eqbal Press, n.d.

Taqizadeh, Hasan. *Khatabeh-ye Aqa-ye Sayyid Hasan-e Taqizadeh* [The lecture of Sir Sayyid Hasan Taqizadeh]. Tehran: Bashgah-e Mehregan Press, 1959.

_____. "Tarikh-e enqelab-e Iran" [The History of the revolution of Iran]. *Yaghma* 14, 2–8 (1961).

Vijuyeh, Mohammad Baqer. *Tarikh-e enqelab-e Azerbaijan va balva-ye Tabriz* [The history of the revolution of Azerbaijan and the riot of Tabriz]. Tehran: Amir Kabir, 1969.

Yeprem Khan, *Az Anzali ta Tehran: Yaddashtha-ye khususi-ye Yeprem Khan mojahed-e armani* [From Anzali to Tehran: Personal Memoirs of Yeprem Khan, Armenian mojahed]. Trans. Narus. Tehran: Babak, 1977.

Ziya'pur, Jalil. *Zivarha-yi zanan-e Iran az dirbaz ta kanun* [The ornaments of the women of Iran from ancient times to the present]. Tehran: Jashn-e Farhang va Honar, 1969.

Zinoviev, Ivan Alexovich. *Enqelab-e mashrutiyat-e Iran: Nazarat-e yek diplomat-e rus, havades-e Iran dar salha-ye 1905 ta 1911* [The Iranian constitutional revolution of Iran: the views of a Russian diplomat, the events of Iran in the years 1905 to 1911]. Trans. Abu al-Qasem E' tesami. Tehran: Eqbal, 1983.

English

Abrahamian, Ervand, "The Causes of the Constitutional Revolution in Iran." *International Journal of Middle East Studies* 10 (1979): 381–414.

_____. "The Crowd in the Persian Revolution." *Iranian Studies* 2 (Autumn 1969): 128- 50.

_____. *Iran Between Two Revolutions*. Princeton: Princeton University Press, 1982.

Afary, Janet. "Grassroots Democracy and Social Democracy in the Iranian Constitutional Revolution, 1906–1911." Ph. D. dissertation. University of Michigan, 1991.

_____. *The Iranian Constitutional Revolution, 1906–1911: Grassroots Democracy, Social Democracy, and the Origins of Feminism*. New York: Columbia University Press, 1996.

_____. "On the Origins of Feminism in Early Twentieth-Century Iran." *Journal of Women's History* 1, 2 (Fall 1989): 65–87.

_____. "Social Democracy and the Iranian Constitutional Revolution of 1906–11." In *A Century of Revolution: Social Movements in Iran*, ed. John Foran. Minneapolis: University of Minnesota, 1994.

Afshari, Mohammad Reza. "The Historians of the Constitutional Movement and the Making of the Iranian Populist Tradition." *International Journal of Middle East Studies* 25, 3 (August 1993): 477–94.

_____. "The Pishirvan and Merchants in Precapitalist Iranian Society: An Essay on the Background and Causes of the Constitutional Revolution." *International Journal of Middle East Studies* 15 (1983): 133–55.

Ahmad, Feroz. "Unionist Relation with the Greek, Armenian, and Jewish Communities of the Ottoman Empire, 1908–1914." In *Christians and Jews in the Ottoman Empire: The Functioning of a Plural Society*. Vol. 1, *The Central Lands*, ed.

Benjamin Braude and Bernard Lewis, 401–34. New York: Holmes and Meier Publishers, 1982.

Ahmad, Ishtiaq. *Anglo-Iranian Relations, 1905–1919.* Bombay: Asia Publishing House, 1975.

Aknouni, E. [Khachatur Malumian]. *Political Persecution: Armenian Prisoners of the Caucasus (A Page of the Tzar's Persecution.* Trans. A. M. and H. W. New York: n.p., 1911.

Algar, Hamid. *Mirza Malkum Khan: A Study in the History of Iranian Modernism.* Berkeley and Los Angeles: University of California Press, 1973.

_____. "The Oppositional Role of the Ulama in Twentieth Century Iran." In *Scholars, Saints and Sufis,* ed. Nikki R. Keddie. Berkeley and Los Angeles: University of California Press, 1972.

_____. *Religion and State in Iran, 1785–1906: The Role of the Ulama in the Qajar Period.* Berkeley and Los Angeles: University of California Press, 1969.

Altstadt, Audrey L. *The Azerbaijani Turks: Power and Identity Under Russian Rule.* Stanford: Hoover Institution Press, 1992.

Amurian [Ter Ohanian], A[ndre], and M. Kasheff, "Armenians of Modern Iran." In *Encyclopædia Iranica,* ed. Ehsan Yarshater. London & New York: Routledge & Kegan Paul, 1987.

Anthias, Floya, and Nira Yuval-Davis, eds. *Woman, Nation, State.* London: MacMillan, 1989.

Arasteh, Reza A. *Education and Social Awakening in Iran, 1850–1968.* 1962. 2d rev. ed. Leiden: E. J. Brill, 1969.

Arjomand, Said Amir. "The Ulama's Traditionalist Opposition to Parliamentarianism: 1907–1909." *Middle Eastern Studies* 17, 2 (1981): 174–87.

Arkun, Aram. "Armenians and the Jangalis." *Iranian Studies.* 30, 1–2 (Winter/Spring 1997): 25–52.

_____. "Dašnak." In *Encyclopædia Iranica,* ed. Ehsan Yarshater. 7, 1 (1994).

_____. "E'likean (Yaqikiyan), Grigor E." In *Encyclopædia Iranica* ed. Ehsan Yarshater. (Costa Mesa, CA: Mazda Pulishers, 1998), 3: 364–65.

_____. "Grigor Yaghikian: Writer and Journalist." In *Armenians in Iran, The Paradoxical Role of a Minority in a Dominant Culture: Articles and Documents,* ed. Cosroe Chaqueri. Cambridge: Center for Middle Eastern Studies of Harvard University, 1998.

Artinian, Vartan. "A Study of the Historical Development of the Armenian Constitutional System in the Ottoman Empire." Ph.D. dissertation. Brandeis University, 1970.

Ascher, Abraham. *The Revolution of 1905.* 2 vols. Stanford: Stanford University Press, 1988–1992.

Astourian, Stephan. Review of *Ottoman Population, 1830–1914: Demographic and Social Characteristics* by Kemal H. Karpat. Madison: University of Wisconsin Press, 1985. *Jusūr* 2 (1986): 123–26.

Atamian, Sarkis. *The Armenian Community: The Historical Development of a Social and Ideological Conflict.* New York: Philosophical Library, 1955.

Avery, Peter. *Modern Iran.* London: Ernest Benn, Ltd., 1965.

Baggs, Shokram. "The Armenian Woman in History." *Armenian Review* 9, 4 (Winter 1956): 64–71.

Baghdiantz McCabe, Ina. "The Armenian Merchants of New Julfa: Some Aspects of Their International Trade in the Seventeenth Century." Ph.D. dissertation. Columbia University, 1993.

_____. *The Shah's Silk for Europe's Silver: The Eurasian Trade of the Julfa Armenians in Safavid Iran and India (1530–1750)*. Atlanta: Scholars Press, 1999.

Bakhash, Shaul. *Iran: Monarchy, Bureaucracy, and Reform Under the Qajars, 1858–1896*. London: Ithaca Press, 1978.

Bamdad, Badr al-Molk. *From Darkness into Light: Women's Emancipation in Iran*. Trans. and ed. F. R. C. Bagley. Smithtown, NY: Exposition Press, 1977.

Bardakjian, Kevork B. "The Rise of the Armenian Patriarchate of Constantinople." In *Christians and Jews in the Ottoman Empire: The Functioning of a Plural Society*. Vol. 1, *The Central Lands*, ed. Benjamin Braude and Bernard Lewis, 89–100. New York: Holmes and Meier Publishers, 1982.

Baron, Beth. "Mothers, Morality, and Nationalism in Pre–1919 Egypt." In *The Origins of Arab Nationalism*, ed. Rashid Khalidi et al. Chicago: University of Chicago Press, 1991.

Barsoumian, Hagop. "The Dual Role of the Armenian *Amira* Class with the Ottoman Government and the Armenian *Millet* (1750–1850)." In *Christians and Jews in the Ottoman Empire: The Functioning of a Plural Society*. Vol. 1, *The Central Lands*, ed. Benjamin Braude and Bernard Lewis, 171–84. New York: Holmes and Meier Publishers, 1982.

_____. "Economic Role of the Armenian Amira Class in the Ottoman Empire." *Armenian Review* 31, 3 (March 1979): 310–16.

Bayat, Mangol. *Iran's First Revolution: Shi'ism and the Constitutional Revolution of 1905–1909*. Oxford: Oxford University Press, 1991.

_____. *Mysticism and Dissent: Socioreligious Thought in Qajar Iran*. New York: Syracuse University Press, 1982.

_____. "Women and Revolution in Iran, 1905–1911." In *Women in the Muslim World*, ed. Nikki R. Keddie and Lois Beck, 295–308. Cambridge: Harvard University Press, 1978.

Berberian, Houri. "Armenian Women in Turn-of-the-Century Iran: Education and Activism." In *Iran and Beyond: Essays in Middle Eastern History in Honor of Nikki R. Keddie*, ed. Rudi Matthee and Beth Baron. Costa Mesa, CA: Mazda, 2000.

_____. "The Dashnaktsutiun and the Iranian Constitutional Revolution, 1905–1911." *Iranian Studies* 29, 1–2 (Winter/Spring 1996): 7–33.

Bharier, Julien. *Economic Development in Iran 1900–1970*. London: Oxford University Press, 1971.

Bonakdarian, Mansour. "Edward G. Browne and the Iranian Constitutional Struggle: From Academic Orientalism to Political Activism." *Iranian Studies* 26, 1, 2 (Winter–Spring 1993): 7–31.

"The Borderlands of Soviet Central Asia: Persia: Part I." *Central Asian Review* 4, 3 (1956): 287–331.

Bosworth, Edmund, and Carole Hillenbrand, eds. *Qajar Iran: Political, Social and Cultural Changes, 1800–1925*. Edinburgh: Edinburgh University Press, 1983.

Bournoutian, George. "The Armenian Community of Isfahan in the Seventeenth Century." *Armenian Review* 24, 4–96 (Winter 1971): 27–45; 25, 1–97 (Spring 1972): 33–50.

Browne, Edward G. *The Persian Revolution, 1905–1909*. 1910. New edition edited by Abbas Amanat with essays by Abbas Amanat and Mansour Bonakdarian. Washington, D.C.: Mage, 1995.

_____. *The Press and Poetry of Modern Persia*. 1914. Reprint, Los Angeles: Kalimat Press, 1983.

Calhoun, Craig. "Social Theory and the Politics of Identity." In *Social Theory and the Politics of Identity*, ed. Craig Calhoun. Cambridge, MA: Blackwell, 1994.

Chaqueri, Cosroe, "The Role and Impact of Armenian Intellectuals in Iranian Politics 1905–1911." *Armenian Review* 41, 2 (Summer 1988): 1–51.

_____. *The Soviet Socialist Republic of Iran, 1920–1921: Birth of the Trauma*. Pittsburgh and London: University of Pittsburgh Press, 1995.

_____. "Sultanzade: The Forgotten Revolutionary Theoretician of Iran: A Biographical Sketch." *Iranian Studies*, 17, 2–3 (Spring–Summer 1984): 215–35.

_____, ed. *Armenians in Iran, The Paradoxical Role of a Minority in a Dominant Culture: Articles and Documents*. Cambridge: Center for Middle Eastern Studies of Harvard University, 1998.

Cottam, Richard W. *Nationalism in Iran*. Pittsburgh: University of Pittsburgh Press, 1979.

Curzon, George N. *Persia and the Persian Question*. 2 vols. 1892. London: Frank Cass, 1966.

Dadrian, Vahakn. *The History of the Armenian Genocide: Ethnic Conflict from the Balkans to Anatolia to the Caucasus*. Providence: Berghahn Books, 1995.

Dasnabedian, Hratch. "The A. R. F. Record: The Balance Sheet of Ninety Years." *Armenian Review* 34, 2 (June 1981): 115–26.

_____. *The History of the Armenian Revolutionary Federation Dashnaktsutiun (1890–1924)*. Milan: Grafiche Editoriali Ambrosiane, 1990.

_____. "The Hnchakian Party." *Armenian Review* 41, 4 (Winter 1988): 18–39.

Davison, Roderic. "The *Millet* as Agents of Change in the Nineteenth-Century Ottoman Empire." In *Christians and Jews in the Ottoman Empire: The Functioning of a Plural Society*. Vol. 1, *The Central Lands*, ed. Benjamin Braude and Bernard Lewis, 319–37. New York: Holmes and Meier Publishers, 1982.

_____. *Reform in the Ottoman Empire, 1856–1876*. Princeton: Princeton University Press, 1963.

DuBois, W. E. B., *The Souls of Black Folk*. New York: Vintage Books Library of America, 1990.

Dussen, van der W. J, "The Question of Armenian Reforms in 1913–1914." *Armenian Review* 39 (Spring 1986): 11–28.

Entner, Marvin L. *Russo-Persian Commercial Relations, 1828–1914*. Gainesville: University of Florida Monographs, 1965.

Epstein, A. L. *Ethos and Identity: Three Studies in Ethnicity*. London: Tavistock, 1978.

Etmekjian, James. *The French Influence on the Western Armenian Renaissance, 1843–1915*. New York: Twayne, 1964.

Fathi, Asghar. "The Role of the 'Rebels' in the Constitutional Movement in Iran." *International Journal of Middle East Studies* 10 (1979): 55–66.

Feroz, Ahmad. "Some Thoughts on the Role of Ethnic and Religious Minorities in the Genesis and Development of the Socialist Movement in Turkey, 1876–1923." In *Socialism and Nationalism in the Ottoman Empire, 1876–1923*, ed. Mete Tunçay and Erik Jan Zürcher, 13–25. London: British Academic Press, 1994.

Findley, Carter. "The Acid Test of Ottomanism: The Acceptance of the Non-Muslims in the Late Ottoman Bureacracy." In *Christians and Jews in the Ottoman Empire: The Functioning of a Plural Society*. Vol. 1, *The Central Lands*, ed. Benjamin Braude and Bernard Lewis, 339–68. New York: Holmes and Meier Publishers, 1982.

Floor, Willem M. "The First Printing-Press in Iran," *Zeitschrift der Deutschen Morgenländischen Gesellschaft* 130, 2 (1980): 369–71.

_____. "The Merchants in Qajar Iran," *Zeitschrift der Deutsche Morgenländischen Geselschaft* 126, 1 (1976):101–35.

Foran, John, ed. *A Century of Revolution: Social Movements in Iran*. Minneapolis: University of Minnesota Press, 1994.

_____. "The Strengths and Weaknesses of Iran's Populist Alliance: A Class Analysis of the Constitutional Revolution of 1905–1911." *Theory and Society* 20, 6 (December 1991): 795–823.

Forand, Paul G. "Accounts of Western Travellers Concerning the Role of Armenians and Georgians in 16th Century Iran." *The Muslim World* 65, 4 (October 1975): 264–76.

Fraser, David. *Persia and Turkey in Revolt*. London: William Blackwood and Sons, 1910.

Garthwaite, Gene. "The Bakhtiyari Khans, The Government of Iran, and the British, 1846–1915." *International Journal of Middle East Studies* 3 (1972): 24–44.

Gellner, Ernest. *Nations and Nationalism*. Ithaca: Cornell University Press, 1983.

Ghougassian, Vazken. *The Emergence of the Armenian Diocese of New Julfa in the Seventeenth Century*. Atlanta: Scholars Press, 1998.

Gilbar, Gad G. "The Big Merchants and the Persian Constitutional Revolution of 1906." *Asian and African Studies* 11, 3 (1977): 275–303.

Gilroy, Paul. *The Black Atlantic: Modernity and Double Conciousness*. London, New York: Verso, 1993.

Glazer, Nathan, and Daniel A. Moynihan, eds. *Ethnicity: Theory and Experience*. Cambridge: Harvard University Press, 1975.

Greaves, Rose Louise. "British Policy in Persia, 1892–1903." *Bulletin of the School of Oriental and African Studies* 28 (1965): 34–60 (I), 284–307 (II).

Gregorian, Vartan. "Minorities of Isfahan: The Armenian Community of Isfahan, 1587- 1722." *Armenian Studies* 7, 3–4 (Summer–Autumn 1974): 652–80.

Haag-Higuchi, Roxane. "A Topos and Its Dissolution: Japan in Some 20th-Century Iranian Texts." *Iranian Studies* 29, 1–2 (Winter/Spring 1996): 71–83.

Hakimian, Hasan. "Wage Labor and Migration: Persian Workers in Southern Russia, 1880–1914." *International Journal of Middle Eastern Studies* 17 (1985): 443–62.

Herzig, Edmund. "The Armenian Merchants of New Julfa, Isfahan: A Study in Pre-Modern Asian Trade." Ph.D. dissertation, University of Manchester, 1991.

_____. "The Deportation of the Armenians in 1604–1605 and Europe's Myth of Shah 'Abbas I." In *Persian and Islamic Studies in Honour of P.W. Avery*, ed.

Charles Melville. Cambridge: University of Cambridge Centre of Middle East Studies, 1990.

Higgins, Patricia J. "Minority-State Relations in Contemporary Iran." In *The State, Religion, and Ethnic Politics: Afghanistan, Iran, and Pakistan*, ed. Ali Banuazizi and Myron Weiner. Syracuse: Syracuse University Press, 1986.

Hone, J. M., and Page L. Dickinson. *Persia in Revolution with Notes of Travel in the Caucasus*. London: T. Fisher Unwin, 1910.

Hovannisian, Richard G. *Armenia on the Road to Independence, 1918*. Berkeley and Los Angeles: University of California Press, 1967.

_____. ed. *The Armenian Genocide: History, Politics, Ethics*. New York: St. Martin's Press, 1992.

_____., ed. *The Armenian Genocide in Perspective*. New Brunswick and London: Transaction Publishers, 1986.

_____., ed. *The Armenian People from Ancient Times to Modern Times*. Vol. 2: *Foreign Dominion to Statehood: The Fifteenth Century to the Twentieth Century*. New York: St. Martin's Press, 1997.

Issawi, Charles. *Economic History of Iran 1800–1914*. Chicago: University of Chicago Press, 1971.

_____. "Iranian Trade, 1800–1914." *Iranian Studies* 16, 3–4 (1983): 229–41.

_____. "The Transformation of the Economic Position of the *Millet* in the Nineteenth Century." In *Christians and Jews in the Ottoman Empire: The Functioning of a Plural Society*. Vol. 1, *The Central Lands*, ed. Benjamin Braude and Bernard Lewis, 261–85. New York: Holmes and Meier Publishers, 1982.

Kandiyoti, Deniz. "Identity and Its Discontents: Women and the Nation." In *Colonial Discourse and Post-Colonial Theory: A Reader*, ed. Patrick Williams and Laura Chrisman. New York: Columbia University Press, 1994.

_____. "Islam, Nationalism, and Women in Turkey." In *Women, Islam, and the State*, ed. Deniz Kandiyoti. Philadelphia: Temple University Press, 1991.

Karal, Enver Ziya. "Non-Muslim Representatives in the First Constitutional Assembly, 1876–1877." In *Christians and Jews in the Ottoman Empire: The Functioning of a Plural Society*. Vol. 1, *The Central Lands*, ed. Benjamin Braude and Bernard Lewis, 369–85. New York: Holmes and Meier Publishers, 1982.

Karpat, Kemal H. *Ottoman Population, 1830–1914: Demographic and Social Characteristics*. Wisconsin: University of Wisconsin Press, 1985.

_____. "Ottoman Population Records and the Census of 1881/82–1893." *International Journal of Middle East Studies* 9, 2 (May 1978): 237–74.

Kazemzadeh, Firuz. *Russia and Britain in Persia, 1864–1914*. New Haven: Yale University Press, 1968.

Keddie, Nikki R. "The Assassination of the Amin as-Sultan (Atabak-i A' zam), 31 August 1907." In *Iran and Islam: In Memory of the Late Vladimir Minorsky*, ed. C. E. Bosworth, 315–30. Edinburgh: Edinburgh University Press, 1971.

_____. "British Policy and the Iranian Opposition, 1901–1907," *Journal of Modern History* 39, 3 (1967): 266–82.

_____. "The Economic History of Iran 1800–1914 and Its Political Impact." *Iranian Studies* 7, 2–3 (1972): 58–78. Reprinted in *Iran: Religion, Politics and Society*, ed. Nikki R. Keddie. London: Frank Cass, 1980.

_____. "Iran 1979–1941." In *Commoners, Climbers, and Notables,* ed. C. A. O. van Nieuwenhujse. London: Brill, 1977. Reprinted in *Iran: Religion, Politics and Society,* ed. Nikki R. Keddie. London: Frank Cass, 1980.

_____. "Iranian Politics 1900–1905: Background to Revolution." *Middle Eastern Studies* 1 (1969): 3–31; 2 (1969): 151–67; 3 (1969): 234–50.

_____. "Iranian Revolutions in Comparative Perspective." *American Historical Review* 88, 3 (June 1983): 579–98.

_____. "The Origins of the Religious-Radical Alliance in Iran." *Past and Present* 34 (July 1966): 70–80. Reprinted in *Iran: Religion, Politics and Society,* ed. Nikki R. Keddie. London: Frank Cass, 1980.

_____. "Popular Participation in the Persian Revolution of 1905–1911." In *Iran: Religion, Politics and Society,* ed. Nikki R. Keddie, 66–79. London: Frank Cass, 1980.

_____. "Religion and Irreligion in Early Iranian Nationalism." In *Iran: Religion, Politics and Society,* ed. Nikki R. Keddie, 13–52. London: Frank Cass, 1980.

_____. *Religion and Rebellion in Iran: The Tobacco Protest, 1891–1892.* London: Frank Cass, 1966.

_____. *Roots of Revolution: An Interpretive History of Iran.* New Haven: Yale University Press, 1981.

Khatanassian, Yervant. "Two Glossaries for the Assistance of Researchers in the History of the Armenian Revolutionary Federation." *Armenian Review* 32, 3 (September 1979): 267–79.

Krikorian, Mesrob K. *Armenians in the Service of the Ottoman Empire, 1860–1908.* London: Routledge and Kegan Paul Ltd., 1977.

Lambton, Ann K. S. "The Persian Constitutional Revolution of 1905–1906." In *Revolution in the Middle East and Other Case Studies,* ed. P. J. Vatikiotis, 173–82. Totowa: Rowman and Littlefield, 1972.

_____. "Persian Political Societies, 1906–1911." In St. Anthony's Papers, no. 16. *Middle Eastern Affairs,* no. 3. London: Chatto and Windus, 1963.

_____. "The Persian 'Ulama' and Constitutional Reform." In *Le Shi' isme imamite,* ed. T. Fahd. Paris, 1968.

_____. ed. *Qajar Persia: Eleven Studies.* Austin: University of Texas Press, 1987.

_____. "The Tobacco Regie: Prelude to Revolution," *Studia Islamica* 23 (1965): 71–90.

Lewis, Bernard. *The Emergence of Modern Turkey.* 1961. 2d ed. Oxford: Oxford Unviersity Press, 1968.

Lima, Gregory. *The Costumes of Armenian Women.* Tehran: International Communications, 1974[?].

Lockhart, Laurence. "The Constitional Laws of Persia: An Outline of Their Origin and Development." *Middle East Journal* 13 (Autumn 1959): 372–88.

_____. *The Fall of the Safavi Dynasty and the Afghan Occupation of Persia.* Cambridge: Cambridge University Press, 1958.

Lyashchenko, Peter I. *History of the National Economy of Russia to the 1917 Revolution.* Trans. L. M. Herman. New York: Macmillan Co., 1949.

Lynch, H. F. B. *Armenia: Travels and Studies.* Vol. 1, *The Russian Provinces.* 1901. Reprint, New York: Armenian Prelacy, 1990.

_____. *Armenia: Travels and Studies*. Vol. 2, *The Turkish Provinces*. 1901. Reprint, New York: Armenian Prelacy, 1990.

Mahdavi, Asghar. "The Significance of Private Archives for the Study of the Economic and Social History of Iran in the Late Qajar Period." *Iranian Studies* 16, 3–4 (Summer/Fall 1983): 243–78.

Malcolm, Sir John. *The History of Persia from the Most Early Period to the Present Time*. 2 vols. London: John Murray, 1829.

Marashlian, Levon. *Politics and Demography: Armenians, Turks, and Kurds in the Ottoman Empire*. Cambridge, MA: The Zoryan Institute, 1991.

Martin, Vanessa. *Islam and Modernism: The Iranian Revolution of 1906*. Syracuse: Syracuse University Press, 1989.

Matthee, Rudolph P. *The Politics of Trade in Safavid Iran: Silk for Silver 1600–1730*. Cambridge: Cambridge University Press, 1999.

McCarthy, Justin. *Muslims and Minorities: The Population of Ottoman Anatolia and the End of the Empire*. New York: New York University Press, 1983.

McDaniel, Robert A. *The Shuster Mission and the Constitutional Revolution*. Minneapolis: Bibliotheca Islamica, 1974.

Menashri, David. *Education and the Making of Modern Iran*. Ithaca: Cornell University Press, 1992.

Merguerian, Barbara J. "The Beginnings of Secondary Education for Armenian Women: The Armenian Female Seminary in Constantinople." *Journal of the Society for Armenian Studies* 5 (1990–1991): 103–24.

Minorsky, V. *Studies in Caucasian History*. London: Taylor's Foreign Press, 1953.

Momeni, Jamshid A., ed. *The Population of Iran: A Selection of Readings*. Honolulu: East-West Population Institute, 1977.

Mooradian, Karlen. "Armenian Journalism: A History and Interpretation." Ph.D. Dissertation. Northwestern University, 1963.

Moore, Arthur. "Some Persian Memories." *The Edinburgh Review* 446 (October 1913): 368–82.

Moreen, Vera B. "The State of Religious Minorities in Safavid Iran, 1617–61." *Journal of Near Eastern Studies* 40, 2 (April 1981): 119–34.

Morier, James. *A Journey Through Persia, Armenia, and Asia Minor, to Constantinople in the Year 1808 and 1809*. London: J. G. Barnard, 1812.

Najmabadi, Afsaneh. *The Story of the Daughters of Quchan: Gender and National Memory in Iranian History*. New York: Syracuse University Press, 1998

_____. "'Is Our Name Remembered?': Writing the History of Iranian Constitutionalism as if Women and Gender Mattered." *Iranian Studies* 28, 1–2 (Winter/Spring 1996): 85–109.

_____. "Zanha-ye Millat: Women or Wives of the Nation." *Iranian Studies* 26, 1–2 (Spring 1994): 51–72.

Nalbandian, Louise. *The Armenian Revolutionary Movement: The Development of Armenian Political Parties Through the Nineteenth Century*. Berkeley and Los Angeles: University of California Press, 1963.

Oberling, Pierre. "The Role of Religious Minorities in the Persian Revolution, 1906–1912." *Journal of Asian History* 12 (1978): 1–29.

Ormanian, Malachia. *The Church of Armenia: Her History, Doctrine, Rule, Discipline, Liturgy, Literature, and Existing Condition.* Trans. G. Marcar Gregory. London: A. R. Mowbray & Co., 1955.

Paidar, Parvin. *Women and the Political Process in Twentieth-Century Iran.* New York: Cambridge University Press, 1995.

Papazian, K. S. *Merchants from Ararat: A Brief Survey of Armenian Trade Through the Ages.* New York: Ararat Press, 1979.

Perry, John R. "Forced Migration in Iran During the Seventeenth and Eighteenth Centuries." *Iranian Studies* 8, 4 (Autumn 1975): 199–215.

Peteet, Julie. *Gender in Crisis: Women and the Palestine Resistance Movement.* New York: Columbia University Press, 1991.

Polo, Marco. *The Travels.* Trans. Ronald Latham. New York: Penguin Books, 1958.

Reysner, I. M. "The Russian Revolution of 1905–1907 and the Awakening of Asia." *Central Asian Review* 4, 3 (1956): 218–25. Abridged translation from the Russian.

Riddell, John. *Lenin's Struggle for a Revolutionary International: Documents 1907–1916.* New York: Monad Press, 1984.

Rosenthal, Steven. "Minorities and Municipal Reform in Istanbul, 1850–1870." In *Christians and Jews in the Ottoman Empire: The Functioning of a Plural Society.* Vol. 1, *The Central Lands,* ed. Benjamin Braude and Bernard Lewis, 369–85. New York: Holmes and Meier Publishers, 1982.

Ruysbroeck, Willem van. *The Mission of Friar William of Rubruck: His Journey to the Court of the Great Khan Moengke, 1253–55.* 1900. London: Hakluyt Society, 1990.

Sanasarian, Eliz. *The Women's Rights Movement in Iran: Mutiny, Appeasement, and Repression from 1900 to Khomeini.* New York: Praeger, 1982.

Sarafian, Kevork A. *History of Education in Armenia.* Laverne, CA: Press of the Laverne Leader, 1930.

Sarafian, Vahe A. "The Problem of Caucasian Population Statistics Under Tsarist and Soviet Rule." *Armenian Review* 23 (September 1953): 107–24.

_____. "Turkish Armenia and Expatriate Population Statistics." *Armenian Review* 9, 3 (Autumn 1956): 118–28.

Sarkissian, A. O. *History of the Armenian Question to 1885.* Urbana: University of Illinois Press, 1938.

Savory, Roger. *Iran Under the Safavids.* Cambridge: Cambridge University Press, 1980.

Shaw, Stanford J. "The Ottoman Census System and Population, 1831–1914." *International Journal of Middle East Studies* 9, 3 (August 1978): 325–38.

Shaw, Stanford J., and Ezel Kural Shaw. *History of the Ottoman Empire and Modern Turkey.* 2 vols. 1977. Reprint, Cambridge: Cambridge University Press, 1978.

Sheikholeslami, Reza, and Dunning Wilson. "The Memoirs of Haydary Khan Amu Ughlu." *Iranian Studies* 6 (Winter 1973): 21–51.

Shissler, Ada Holland. "Ahmet Ağaoğlu (Aghaev), Turkish Identity between Two Empires 1869–1919." Ph.D. dissertation. University of California, Los Angeles, 1995.

Shuster, William Morgan. *The Strangling of Persia.* New York: The Century Co., 1912.

Smith, Eli. *Researches of the Rev. E. Smith and Rev. H. G. O. Dwight in Armenia: Including a Journey Through Asia Minor, and into Georgia and Persia, with a Visit to the Nestorian and Chaldean Christians of Oormiah and Salmas.* 2 vols. Boston: Crocker and Brewster, 1833.

Soleimani, Mansour. "The Educational Impact of American Church Missionaries on the Educational Programs of Iran (1834–1925 C.E.)." Ed.D. dissertation. University of the Pacific, 1980.

Somakian, Manoug. *Empires in Conflict: Armenian and the Great Powers, 1895–1920.* London: Tauris, 1995.

Spector, Ivar. *The First Russian Revolution: Its Impact on Asia.* Englewood Cliffs, NJ: Prentice-Hall, 1962.

Suny, Ronald Grigor. *Armenia in the Twentieth Century.* Chico, CA: Scholars Press, 1983.

_____. *The Baku Commune, 1917–1918: Class and Nationality in the Russian Revolution.* Princeton: Princeton University Press, 1972.

_____. *Looking Toward Ararat: Armenia in Modern History.* Bloomington and Indianapolis: Indiana University Press, 1993.

_____. *The Making of the Georgian Nation.* 1988. 2d ed. Bloomington and Indianapolis: Indiana University Press, 1994.

_____. "Marxism, Nationalism, and the Armenian Labor Movement in Transcaucasia, 1890–1903." *Armenian Review* 33, 1 (March 1980): 30–47.

_____. ed. *Transcaucasia, Nationalism and Social Change: Essays in the History of Armenia, Azerbaijan, and Georgia.* 1983. Reprint, Ann Arbor: University of Michigan Press, 1996.

Swietochowski, Tadeusz. "National Conciouness and Political Orientation in Azerbaijan, 1905–1920." In *Transcaucasia, Nationalism and Social Change: Essays in the History of Armenia, Azerbaijan, and Georgia,* ed. Ronald Grigor Suny. 1983. Reprint, Ann Arbor: University of Michigan Press, 1996.

_____. *Russian Azerbaijan, 1905–1920: The Shaping of National Identity in a Muslim Community.* Cambridge: Cambridge University Press, 1985.

Taqizadeh, Seyyed Hassan. "Document: The Background of the Constitutional Movement in Azerbaijan." Trans. Nikki R. Keddie. *Middle East Journal* 14, 4 (1960): 456–65.

Tavakoli-Targhi, Mohamad. "Refashioning Iran: Language and Culture During the Constitutional Revolution." *Iranian Studies* 23, 1–4 (1990): 77–101.

Ter Minassian, Anahide. "The Revolution of 1905 in Transcaucasia." *Armenian Review* 42, 2 (Summer 1989): 1–23.

_____. "The Role of the Armenian Community in the Foundation and Development of the Socialist Movement in the Ottoman Empire and Turkey: 1876–1923." In *Socialism and Nationalism in the Ottoman Empire, 1876–1923,* ed. Mete Tunçay and Erik Jan Zürcher, 109–56. London: British Academic Press, 1994.

Tunçay, Mete. "In Lieu of a Conclusion." In *Socialism and Nationalism in the Ottoman Empire, 1876–1923,* ed. Mete Tunçay and Erik Jan Zürcher, 157–68. London: British Academic Press, 1994.

Vassilian, Hamo B., ed. *Armenians and Iran: A Comprehensive Bibliographic Guide to Books Published in the Armenian, Persian, English and Russian Languages*. 1991. 2d ed. Glendale: Armenian Reference Books Co., 1994.

Villari, Luigi. *Fire and Sword in the Caucasus*. London: T. Fisher Unwin, 1906.

Vucinich, Wayne S. ed. *Russia and Asia: Essays on the Influence of Russia on the Asian Peoples*. Stanford: Hoover Institution Press, 1972.

Waterfield, Robin E. *Christians in Persia*. London, 1973.

Wilson, Sir Charles, ed. *Handbook for Travellers in Asia Minor, Transcaucasia, Persia*. London: John Murray, 1895.

Yaghoubian, David N. "Ethnicity, Identity and the Development of Nationalism in Iran." Ph.D. dissertation. University of California, Berkeley, forthcoming.

Zeno, Caterino. *A Narrative of Italian Travels in Persia in the Fifteenth and Sixteenth Centuries*. Trans. Charles Grey. London: Hakluyt Society, 1873.

French

Berard, Victor. *Révolutions de la Perse*. Paris: Librairie Armand Colin, 1910.

Chardin, Jean. *Voyages de Paris à Ispahan*. 2 vols. 1686. Reprint, Paris: La Découverte/Maspero, 1983.

Golnazarian, Magdalena. "Les Arméniens d'azerbaïdjan iranien pendant la première guerre mondiale." Presented at the International Round Table "La Perse et la Grande Guerre" [Persia and the Great War), Tehran, 2–3 March 1997.

Haupt, Georges, and Madeleine Reberioux, eds. *La Deuxième Internationale et l'Orient*. Paris: Editions Cujas, 1967.

Mans, du P. Raphael, *Estat de la Perse en 1660*. Paris, 1890.

Minassian, Gaïz. *Le Parti Dachnagtsoutioun*. n.p., 1993.

Ormanian, Malachia. *L'Eglise arménienne: son histoire, sa doctrine, son régime, sa discipline, sa liturgy, sa littérature, son présent*. Paris: Ernest Leroux, 1910.

Orsolle, Ernest. *Le Caucase et la Perse*. Paris: E. Plon, 1885.

Patriarchat Arménienne de Constantinople. *Population arménienne de la Turquie avant la guerre*. Paris: Imprimerie H. Turabian, 1920.

Tavernier, Jean-Baptiste. *Les Six voyages de Turquie et de Perse*. 2 vols. 1676–1679. Reprint, Paris: Librairie François Maspero, 1981.

Tchobanian, Archag. *Victor Hugo, Chateaubriand et Lamartine dans la litterature Arménienne*. Paris: Librairie Ernest Leroux, 1935.

Ter Minassian, Anahide. "Le Cas Armenian: Socialistes et marxistes arméniens et la question nationale." In *Colloque sur l'experience sovietique et le probléme national dans le monde (1920–1939), Paris, 6, 7, 8 Decembre 1978*. Vol. 1: 105–57. Paris: Publications Langues'O, 1981.

_____. "Le Mouvement révolutionnaire arménien, 1890–1903." *Cahiers du monde russe et soviétique* 14, 4 (October–December 1973): 536–607.

_____. *La Question arménienne*. Roquevaire: Éditions Parenthèses, 1983.

Ternon Yves, and J.-C. Kebabdjian. *Armenie 1900*. Paris: Editions Astrid, 1980.

Tria. "Le Caucase et la révolution persane." *Revue du monde musulman* 13, 2 (February 1911): 324–33.

Zarcone, Th[ierry], and F[ariba] Zarinebaf, eds. *Les Iraniens d'Istanbul*. Paris, Tehran, Istanbul: Institut Française de Recherches en Iran, 1993.

Russian

Arutyunyan, G. S. *Iranskaya revolyutsiya 1905–1911 gg. i bolsheviki Zakavkazya* [The Iranian revolution of 1905–1911 and the Bolsheviks of the Caucasus]. Yerevan: Armyanskoi Gosudarstvennoi Uzdatelstvo, 1956.

Ivanov, M. S. *Iranskaya revoliutsiya, 1905–1911 godov* [Iranian Revolution, 1905–1911]. Moscow: Izdatel'stvo Imo, 1957.

Lisitsian, Srbui. *Starinnye pliaski i teatral'nye predstavleniia Armianskovo Naroda* [The ancient dances and theatrical presentations of the Armenian people]. 2 vols. Yerevan: Izdatelstvo Akademii Nauk Armianskoi SSR, 1958–1972.

Index

Abbas I, Shah, 34, 36
Abdul-Hamid II, Sultan, 24, 47, 68(ff),
    75, 77, 95, 123
    opposition to, 92
    pogroms of, 38
    policy of, 73
    Tanzimat period and, 19
Abdulmejid, Sultan, 17
Abovian, Khachatur, 21
Acharian, Hrachia, 43
Afary, Janet, 141, 146, 154
    on Iranian Constitutional Revolution,
      4, 142, 145–46
    on Tabriz Social Democrats, 88
Afshar, Iraj, 12(n11)
    on Armenian contribution, 4
Ağaev, Ahmet, 83, 84, 95, 113(n178)
Ağaoğlu. *See* Ağaev, Ahmet
Aghbalian, Nikol, 43, 165(n120),
    190(n27)
Ahmet R'za, Bey, 71
Ain, Al-Dowleh, 154
Ahmad Shah, 3
Aknuni, E.: on Armenian deaths, 13(n19)
Alexander II, Russification by, 24
Alexander III, 24
Alexandropol
    Catholicos and, 77
    demonstrations in, 76
All Saviour's Monastery, 40
Aloyan, Galust, 49
Amatuni, Srpuhi, 46
Amira class, 18, 30(n12)
Amu Oghlu, Haidar Khan, 137, 153, 154
Amurian, Andre: on Armenian
    contribution, 4
Andreasian, Petros Melik, 155

Anglo-Russian Agreement (1907), 74
Anjoman-e ayalat, 133
Anjoman-e makhfi, 97
Anjoman of Gilan, 168(n164)
Anjoman of Ladies of the Homeland,
    141–42
Anjomans, 2, 69, 97, 133, 168(n164), 174
Annayian school, 45
Anti-Armenian sentiments, 26, 93
Anti-constitutionalists, 128, 138, 176
Anzali, 73, 97
    anti-revolutionary forces and, 96
Ararat, publication of, 21
Aravot, publication of, 49
Arkomed, S. T.: Hnchakian party and, 25
Armenakan party, 49
    arms/ammunition and, 21
    formation of, 20–21
Armenia, 20
Armenian Church, 23, 42–43, 53,
    60(n46)
    education and, 18
    missionaries and, 41
    Naser al-Din Shah and, 41
    property confiscation for, 76, 80
Armenian Girls' School, 46
Armenian National Bureau, 185
Armenian National Constitution, 17, 18
Armenian Patriarch
    Armenian population and, 16
    control by, 15–16
Armenian Question, 20, 26
    internationalization of, 16, 17, 18–19
    resolution of, 24
Armenian Revolutionary Federation. *See*
    Dashnaktsutiun Party
Armenian vernacular, 18, 21, 23